Also by Charles Wright

POETRY

The Grave of the Right Hand
Hard Freight
Bloodlines
China Trace
The Southern Cross
Country Music: Selected Early Poems
The Other Side of the River
Zone Journals
Xionia
The World of the Ten Thousand Things: Poems 1980–1990
Chickamauga
Black Zodiac
Appalachia
North American Bear
Negative Blue: Selected Later Poems
A Short History of the Shadow
Buffalo Yoga
Scar Tissue
Littlefoot
Sestets
Bye-and-Bye: Selected Late Poems
Caribou

TRANSLATIONS

The Storm and Other Things (Eugenio Montale)
Orphic Songs (Dino Campana)

NONFICTION

Halflife: Improvisations and Interviews, 1977–87
Quarter Notes: Improvisations and Interviews

OBLIVION BANJO

OBLIVION BANJO

THE POETRY OF

CHARLES WRIGHT

FARRAR STRAUS GIROUX ■ NEW YORK

Farrar, Straus and Giroux
120 Broadway, New York 10271

First edition, 2019

Grateful acknowledgment is made for permission to reprint the following poems: "Homage to Ezra Pound," "Homage to Arthur Rimbaud," "Homage to Baron Corvo," "Homage to X," "The New Poem," "Portrait of the Poet in Abraham von Werdt's Dream," "Chinoiserie," "One Two Three," "Slides of Verona," "Grace," "Negatives," "Dog Creek Mainline," "Blackwater Mountain," "Sky Valley Rider," "Northanger Ridge," "Primogeniture," "Nightdream," "Congenital," "Clinchfield Station," "Virgo Descending," "Easter, 1974," "Cancer Rising," "Tattoos," "Notes to Tattoos," "Hardin County," "Delta Traveller," "Skins," "Notes to Skins," "Link Chain," "Bays Mountain Covenant," "Rural Route," "Childhood," "Snow," "Self-Portrait in 2035," "Morandi," "Dog," "Snapshot," "Indian Summer," "Wishes," "Quotidiana," "At Zero," "Sentences," "Death," "Next," "January," "1975," "Nerval's Mirror," "Edvard Munch," "Bygones," "Equation," "California Twilight," "Anniversary," "12 Lines at Midnight," "Dino Campana," "Invisible Landscape," "Remembering San Zeno," "Born Again," "Captain Dog," "Depression Before the Solstice," "Stone Canyon Nocturne," "Reply to Chi K'ang," "Reunion," "'Where Moth and Rust Doth Corrupt,'" "April," "Signature," "Noon," "Going Home," "Cloud River," "Reply to Lapo Gianni," "Thinking of Georg Trakl," "Spider Crystal Ascension," "Moving On," "Clear Night," "Autumn," "Sitting at Night on the Front Porch," "Saturday 6 a.m.," and "Him," from Country Music, *copyright © 1982 Charles Wright. Published by Wesleyan University Press and reprinted with permission.*

Library of Congress Cataloging-in-Publication Data
Names: Wright, Charles, 1935- author.
Title: Oblivion banjo : the poetry of Charles Wright.
Description: First edition. | New York : Farrar, Straus and Giroux, 2019. | Includes index.
Identifiers: LCCN 2018060810 | ISBN 9780374539085
Classification: LCC PS3573.R52 A6 2019 | DDC 811/.54—dc23
LC record available at https://lccn.loc.gov/2018060810

Designed by Crisis

www.fsgbooks.com
www.twitter.com/fsgbooks
www.facebook.com/fsgbooks

P1

The country was always better than the people.

—ERNEST HEMINGWAY

Mingliaotse: "*I would like to house my spirit within my body, to nourish my virtue by mildness, and to travel in ether by becoming a void. But I cannot do it yet... And so, being unable to find peace within myself, I made use of the external surroundings to calm my spirit, and being unable to find delight within my heart, I borrowed a landscape to please it. Therefore, strange were my travels.*"

—T'U LUNG (T'U CH'IHSHUI),
TRANSLATED BY LIN YUTANG

CONTENTS

FROM *Hard Freight* (1973)

FROM *Bloodlines* (1975)

FROM *China Trace* (1977)

FROM *The Southern Cross* (1981)

FROM *The Other Side of the River* (1984)

FROM *Zone Journals* (1988)

FROM *Xionia* (1990)

FROM *Chickamauga* (1995)

FROM *Black Zodiac* (1997)

FROM *Appalachia* (1998)

FROM North American Bear (1999)

FROM A Short History of the Shadow (2002)

FROM *Buffalo Yoga* (2004)

FROM *Scar Tissue* (2006)

FROM *Caribou* (2014)

FROM

HARD FREIGHT

(1973)

Homage to Ezra Pound

Past San Sebastiano, past
The Ogni Santi and San Trovaso, down
The Zattere and left
Across the tiered bridge to where
—Off to the right, half-hidden—
The Old Dogana burns in the spring sun:
This is how you arrive.

This is the street where Pound lives,
A cul-de-sac
Of rheumy corners and cracked stone,
At whose approach the waters
Assemble, the gulls cry out;
In here—unspeaking, unturned—he waits,
Sifting the cold affections of the blood.

Others have led the way,
Vanishing in their sleep, their beds
Unmade, the sheets still damp
From what has set them apart—
Cancer or bad lungs, the wrack
Of advancing age, the dull
Incense of suicide . . .

And he has survived,
Or refused to follow, and now

Walks in the slow strobe of the sunlight,
Or sits in his muffled rooms,
Wondering where it went bad,
And leans to the signal, the low
Rustle of wings, the splash of an oar.

Today is one of those days
One swears is a prophesy:
The air explicit and moist,
As though filled with unanswered prayers;
The twilight, starting to slide
Its sooty fingers along the trees;
And you, Pound,

Awash in the wrong life,
Cut loose upon the lagoon (the wind
Off-shore, and gaining), the tide going out . . .
Here is your caul and caustic,
Here is your garment,
Cold-blooded father of light—
Rise and be whole again.

VENICE

Homage to Arthur Rimbaud

Laying our eggs like moths
In the cold cracks of your eyes,
Brushing your hands with our dark wings

—Desperate to attempt
An entrance, to touch that light
Which buoys you like a flame,
That it might warm our own lives—,

We cluster about your death
As though it were reachable.

For almost a hundred years
We've gathered outside your legend (and been afraid
Of what such brilliance affords;

And knew the while you were risen, your flight
Pneumatic and pure, invisible as a fever;
And knew the flight was forever,
Leaving us what we deserve:

Syllables, flowers, black ice;
The exit, the split cocoon . . .

CHARLEVILLE

Homage to Baron Corvo

Of all the poses, of all the roles,
This is the one I keep: you pass
On the canal, your pope's robes
Aflame in a secret light, the four
Oars of your gondola white
As moth wings in the broken dark,
The quail-eyed fisher-boys

Sliding the craft like a coffin out to sea;
The air grows hard; the boat's wake
Settles behind you like a wasted breath.

(For months, Corvo, you floated through my sleep
As I tried to track you down:
That winter you lived in a doorway;
The days and nights on these back canals
You spent in a musty blanket,
Your boat both bed and refuge—
And writing always
The book, the indescribable letters . . .
Was it the vengeance only
That kept you alive, the ripe corkscrew
Twisted and deep in the bottle's throat?

One afternoon—in the late spring—I went
To San Michele, to see
The sealed drawer that holds your name,
To take you flowers, as one
Is moved to do for the dead, and found
Not even a vase to put them in.
Leaving, I spread them on the lagoon,
Ungraftable shoots of blood. There is, you said,
A collusion of things in this world . . .)

And so you escape. What books there are,
Old hustler, will never exhume you,

Nor places you stayed.
Hadrian, Nicholas Crabbe, you hide
Where the dust hides now,
Your con with its last trick turned,
Stone nightmare come round again—
Fadeout: your boat, Baron, edges
Toward the horizon, a sky where toads,
Their eyes new fire,
Alone at the landings blink and blink.

VENICE

Homage to X

The red earth, the light diffuse
In the flat-leaved limbs of the trees;
A cold, perpetual rain
As though from a heaving breast;
O loved ones, O angels . . .

The thing, as always, begins
In transit, the water infusion
Oily and phosphorescent—
The vine is a blue light,
The cup is a star.

In the dream you will see a city,
Foreign and repetitious,
The plants unspeakably green;
That is of no concern; your job
Is the dust, the belly-relinquishing dust.

It's the day before yesterday,
It's the other side of the sky:
The body that bears your number
Will not be new, will not be your own
And will not remember your name.

PRAGUE / PRAGUE-STRASHNITZ

The New Poem

It will not resemble the sea.
It will not have dirt on its thick hands.
It will not be part of the weather.

It will not reveal its name.
It will not have dreams you can count on.
It will not be photogenic.

It will not attend our sorrow.
It will not console our children.
It will not be able to help us.

Portrait of the Poet in Abraham von Werdt's Dream

Outside, the Venice skyline, and stars
Half-seen through an opened window;
Inside, it's the Renaissance,
The men in hose,
The furnishings elegant, but spare;
A griffin rears in the archway;
An eagle dives from the ceiling;
And over the far wall—like Dürer's—
Two cherubs support the three
Disordered initials of my signature.

Paper is stacked in neat piles, as I
First drew them; square blocks of type, their beds
Tilted and raised, their letters reversed,
Glisten among the shadows;
Two men in the foreground work
A press, inking and setting; a third
Is washing his hands, kneeling
In front of a tub; a fourth, his right arm
Extended, adjusts the unused type;
A fifth is correcting proof.

Alone in an alcove, a sixth man, unnoticed
And unfamiliar, his strange clothes
Centuries out of date, is writing, his back turned
To what I tried to record.
The lines, a spidery darkness, move
Across the page. Now
He looks this way. And now he rises
—XYZ, his mouth says, XYZ—,
Thrusting the paper into my hands.
These words are the words he has written.

Chinoiserie

Why not? The mouths of the ginger blooms slide open,
The willows drag their knuckles across the earth;
Each year has its fields that no one tends.

Our days, unlike the long gasps of the wind,
Stay half in love with the rushes, and half with the water reeds.
Outside the body, all things are encumbrances.

One Two Three

A shift in the wind the darkness
Beading about your eyelids
The sour pull of the blood
Everything works against you
The way the evening comes down
Its trellises one rose at a time
The watery knots of light
That lap at your memory
The way you thought of your life once
An endless falling of seeds

Already places exist
Which cannot reshelter you
Hands you have clasped for the last time
Familiar mirrors remain
That will not contain your face

Words you have uttered
That will not remember your tongue
The sofas that held your sleep
Gradually rise to assume
Their untouched shapes and their dreams

The wave will deliver you
Your arms thrown out like driftwood the shore
Eroding away at your touch
Your fingers ingrained in its loose skin
The idea of absence
Sprouting like grass from your side
Your autobiography
Completed no less than what
Always you claimed it would be the stone
That no one will roll away

Slides of Verona

1. Here where Catullus sat like snow
   Over the Adige the blooms drift
   West on the west-drifting wind

2. Cangrande mellifluous ghost sails
   His stone boat above the yard

3. St George and Trebizond each
   Elsewhere still hold their poses still burn

4. Death with its long tongue licks
Mastino's hand affection he thinks
Such sweetness such loyalty

5. Here comes Whatever Will Come
His shoulders hunched under lost baggage

6. Two men their necks broken hang
Opposite where the hill once was
And that's where the rainbow ends

7. The star of the jasmine plant
Who follows you now who leads

8. The great gates like wings unfold
The angel gives him a push
The rosaries click like locks

9. White glove immaculate touch
How cold you are how quiet

Grace

Its hair is a fine weed,
Matted, where something has lain,
Or fallen repeatedly:

Its arms are rivers that sink
Suddenly under the earth,
Elbow and wristbone: cold sleeve:

Its face is a long soliloquy,
A language of numerals,
Impossible to erase.

Negatives

This is the light we dream in,
The milk light of midnight, the full moon
Reversing the balance like shapes on a negative:
The chalk hills, the spectral sky,
The black rose in flame,
Its odors and glittery hooks
Waiting for something to snag.

The mulberries wink like dimes;
Fat sheep, the mesquite and chaparral
Graze at their own sweet speed,
The earth white sugar;
Two miles below, and out,
The surf has nothing to add.

—Is this what awaits us, amorphous
Cobalt and zinc, a wide tide
Of brilliance we cannot define
Or use, and leafless, without guilt;
No guidelines or flutter, no
Cadence to pinpoint, no no?

Silence. As though the doorway behind
Us were liquid, were black water;
As though we might enter; as though

The ferry were there,
Ready to take us across,
—Remembering now, unwatermarked—
The blackout like scarves in our new hair.

Dog Creek Mainline

Dog Creek: cat track and bird splay,
Spindrift and windfall; woodrot;
Odor of muscadine, the blue creep
Of kingsnake and copperhead;
Nightweed; frog spit and floating heart,
Backwash and snag pool: Dog Creek

Starts in the leaf reach and shoal run of the blood;
Starts in the falling light just back
Of the fingertips; starts
Forever in the black throat
You ask redemption of, in wants
You waken to, the odd door:

Its sky, old empty valise,
Stands open, departure in mind; its three streets,
Y-shaped and brown,
Go up the hills like a fever;
Its houses link and deploy
—This ointment, false flesh in another color.

Five cutouts, five silhouettes
Against the American twilight; the year
Is 1941; remembered names
—Rosendale, Perry and Smith—
Rise like dust in the deaf air;
The tops spin, the poison swells in the arm:

The trees in their jade death-suits,
The birds with their opal feet,
Shimmer and weave on the shoreline;
The moths, like forget-me-nots, blow
Up from the earth, their wet teeth
Breaking the dark, the raw grain;

The lake in its cradle hums
The old songs: out of its ooze, their heads
Like tomahawks, the turtles ascend
And settle back, leaving their chill breath
In blisters along the bank;
Locked in their wide drawer, the pike lie still as knives.

Hard freight. It's hard freight
From Ducktown to Copper Hill, from Six
To Piled High: Dog Creek is on this line,
Indigent spur; cross-tie by cross-tie it takes
You back, the red wind
Caught at your neck like a prize:

(The heart is a hieroglyph;
The fingers, like praying mantises, poise
Over what they have once loved;

The ear, cold cave, is an absence,
Tapping its own thin wires;
The eye turns in on itself.

The tongue is a white water.
In its slick ceremonies the light
Gathers, and is refracted, and moves
Outward, over the lips,
Over the dry skin of the world.
The tongue is a white water.)

Blackwater Mountain

That time of evening, weightless and disparate,
When the loon cries, when the small bass
Jostle the lake's reflections, when
The green of the oak begins
To open its robes to the dark, the green
Of water to offer itself to the flames,
When lily and lily pad
Husband the last light
Which flares like a white disease, then disappears:
This is what I remember. And this:

The slap of the jacklight on the cove;
The freeze-frame of ducks
Below us; your shots; the wounded flop
And skid of one bird to the thick brush;
The moon of your face in the fire's glow;
The cold; the darkness. Young,

Wanting approval, what else could I do?
And did, for two hours, waist-deep in the lake,
The thicket as black as death,
Without success or reprieve, try.

The stars over Blackwater Mountain
Still dangle and flash like hooks, and ducks
Coast on the evening water;
The foliage is like applause.
I stand where we stood before and aim
My flashlight down to the lake. A black duck
Explodes to my right, hangs, and is gone.
He shows me the way to you;
He shows me the way to a different fire
Where you, black moon, warm your hands.

Sky Valley Rider

Same place, same auto-da-fé:
Late August, the air replete, the leaves
Grotesque in their limp splendor,
The dust like guilt on the window sills,
On the pressed pants of suits
Hung like meat on their black hooks:

I walked these roads once, two steps
Behind my own life, my pockets stuffed with receipts
For goods I'd never asked for:
Complacency, blind regret; belief;
Compassion I recognized in the left palm;
Respect, slick stick, in the right:

One I have squandered, one
I have sloughed like a cracked skin; the others,
Small charms against an eventual present,
I keep in the camphor box
Beside my handkerchiefs, the slow roll
Of how I'll unravel, signatures.

The tinkly hymns, the wrong songs:
This one's for you, 15, lost
On the wide waters that circle beneath the earth;
You touched me once, but not now,
Your fingers like blue streamers, the stump
Of your hand, perhaps, in time to that music still:

Down by the haying shed, the white pines
Commence with their broomy sounds;
The orchard, the skeletal trunks on Anne's Ridge
—Stone and stone-colored cloud—
Gather the light and hold fast;
Two thousand acres of loneliness:

Leaf over leaf, the green sky:
Sycamore, black gum, oak, ash;
Wind-scythe at work in the far fields;
In the near, plum-flame of larkspur:
Whatever has been, remains—
Fox fire, pale semaphore in the skull's night.

The past, wrecked accordion, plays on, its one tune
My song, its one breath my breath,
The square root, the indivisible cipher . . .

Northanger Ridge

Half-bridge over nothingness,
White sky of the palette knife; blot orange,
Vertical blacks; blue, birdlike,
Drifting up from the next life,
The heat-waves, like consolation, wince—
One cloud, like a trunk, stays shut
Above the horizon; off to the left, dream-wires,
Hill-snout like a crocodile's.

Or so I remember it,
Their clenched teeth in their clenched mouths,
Their voices like shards of light,
Brittle, unnecessary.
Ruined shoes, roots, the cabinet of lost things:
This is the same story,
Its lips in flame, its throat a dark water,
The page stripped of its meaning.

Sunday, and Father Dog is turned loose:
Up the long road the children's feet
Snick in the dust like raindrops; the wind
Excuses itself and backs off; inside, heat
Lies like a hand on each head;

Slither and cough. Now Father Dog
Addles our misconceptions, points, preens,
His finger a white flag, run up, run down.

Bow-wow and arf, the Great Light;
O, and the Great Yes, and the Great No;
Redemption, the cold kiss of release,
&c.; sentences, sentences.
(Meanwhile, docile as shadows, they stare
From their four corners, looks set:
No glitter escapes
This evangelical masonry.)

Candleflame; vigil and waterflow:
Like dust in the night the prayers rise:
From 6 to 6, under the sick Christ,
The children talk to the nothingness,
Crossrack and wound; the dark room
Burns like a coal, goes
Ash to the touch, ash to the tongue's tip;
Blood turns in the wheel:

Something drops from the leaves; the drugged moon
Twists and turns in its sheets; sweet breath
In a dry corner, the black widow reknits her dream.
Salvation again declines,
And sleeps like a skull in the hard ground,
Nothing for ears, nothing for eyes;
It sleeps as it's always slept, without
Shadow, waiting for nothing.

BIBLE CAMP, 1949

Primogeniture

The door to the book is closed;
The window which gives on the turned earth is closed;
The highway is closed;
Closed, too, are the waters, their lips sealed;
The door to the grass is closed.

Only the chute stays open,
The ruined chute, entering heaven—
Toehold and handhold, the wind like an accident,
The rain like mosquitoes inside your hair,
You stall still, you suffer it not.

—Rose of the afterlife, black mulch we breathe,
Devolve and restore, raise up:
Fireblight and dead bud; rust; spot;
Sore skin and shot hole:
Rechannel these tissues, hold these hands.

Nightdream

Each day is an iceberg,
Dragging its chill paunch underfoot;
Each night is a tree to hang from,
The wooden knife, the mud rope
You scratch your initials on—
Panoply, panoply.

Up and up from his green grave, your father
Wheels in the wind, split scrap of smoke;

Under him stretch, in one file, Bob's Valley, Bald Knob,
The infinite rectitude
Of all that is past: Ouachita,
Ocoee, the slow slide of the Arkansas.

Listen, the old roads are taking flight;
Like bits of string, they, too,
Rise in the pendulous sky,
Whispering, whispering:
Echo has turned a deaf ear,
The wayside is full of leaves.

Your mother floats from her bed
In slow-motion, her loose gown like a fog
Approaching, offering
Meat; across the room, a hand
Again and again
Rises and falls back, clenching, unclenching.

The chambers you've reached, the stones touched,
All stall and worm to a dot;
Sirens drain through the night; lights
Flick and release; the fields, the wet stumps,
Shed their hair and retire;
The bedroom becomes a rose:

(In Kingsport, beneath the trees,
A Captain is singing Dixie; sons
Dance in their gold suits, clapping their hands;
And mothers and fathers, each
In a soft hat, fill
With dust-dolls their long boxes.)

Congenital

Here is where it begins here
In the hawk-light in the quiet
The blue of the shag spruce
Lumescent
                    night-rinsed and grand

It ends in the afterdamp the rails
Shinned the saltlamps unworkable
It ends in anatomy
In limp wheels in a wisp of skin

—These hands are my father's hands these eyes
Excessively veined his eyes
Unstill ever-turning
The water the same song and the touch

Clinchfield Station

The road unwinds like a bandage.
These are the benchmarks:
A letter from Yucatan, a ball,
The chairs of the underlife.

Descent is a fact of speech,
A question of need—lampblack, cold-drill,
A glint in the residue:
Dante explained it, how

It bottoms out, becoming a threshold,
The light like a damp confetti,
The wind an apostrophe, the birds
Stone bone in the smooth-limbed trees.

Mums in a vase, flakes in a hope chest:
Father advise us, sift our sins—
Ferry us back and step down;
Dock at the Clinchfield Station:

Our Lady of Knoxville reclines there
On her hard bed; a golf club
Hums in the grass. The days, dry cat tracks, come round,
A silence beneath the leaves:

The way back is always into the earth.
Hornbeam or oak root, the ditch, the glass:
It all comes to the same thing:
A length of chain, a white hand.

FROM

BLOODLINES

(1975)

Virgo Descending

Through the viridian (and black of the burnt match),
Through ox-blood and ochre, the ham-colored clay,
Through plate after plate, down
Where the worm and the mole will not go,
Through ore-seam and fire-seam,
My grandmother, senile and 89, crimpbacked, stands
Like a door ajar on her soft bed,
The open beams and bare studs of the hall
Pink as an infant's skin in the floating dark;
Shavings and curls swing down like snowflakes across her face.

My aunt and I walk past. As always, my father
Is planning rooms, dragging his lame leg,
Stroke-straightened and foreign, behind him,
An aberrant 2-by-4 he can't fit snug.
I lay my head on my aunt's shoulder, feeling
At home, and walk on.
Through arches and door jambs, the spidery wires
And coiled cables, the blueprint takes shape:
My mother's room to the left, the door closed;
My father's room to the left, the door closed—

Ahead, my brother's room, unfinished;
Behind, my sister's room, also unfinished.
Buttresses, winches, block-and-tackle: the scale of everything
Is enormous. We keep on walking. And pass
My aunt's room, almost complete, the curtains up,

The lamp and the medicine arranged
In their proper places, in arm's reach of where the bed will go . . .
The next one is mine, now more than half done,
Cloyed by the scent of jasmine,
White-gummed and anxious, their mouths sucking the air dry.

Home is what you lie in, or hang above, the house
Your father made, or keeps on making,
The dirt you moisten, the sap you push up and nourish . . .
I enter the living room, it, too, unfinished, its far wall
Not there, opening on to a radiance
I can't begin to imagine, a light
My father walks from, approaching me,
Dragging his right leg, rolling his plans into a perfect curl.
That light, he mutters, that damned light.
We can't keep it out. It keeps on filling your room.

Easter, 1974

Against the tin roof of the back porch, the twilight
Backdrops the climbing rose, three
Blood stars, redemptive past pain.

Trust in the fingernail, the eyelash,
The bark that channels the bone.
What opens will close, what hungers is what goes half-full.

Cancer Rising

It starts with a bump, a tiny bump, deep in the throat.
The mockingbird knows: she spreads it around
Like music, like something she's heard, a gossip to be
Repeated, but not believed.
And the bump grows, and the song grows, the song
Ascendant and self-reflective, its notes
Obscuring the quarter-tone, the slick flesh and the burning.
And the bump drops off and disappears, but
Its roots do not disappear—they dig on through the moist meat.

The roots are worms, worms in a cheese.
And what they leave, in their blind passage,
Filtered, reorganized, is a new cheese, a cheese
For one palate and one tongue.
But this takes time, and comes later,
The small mounds, heaps of a requisite sorrow,
Choked and grown in the beds,
The channels no longer channels, but flesh of a kind
Themselves, the same flesh and the song . . .

Midnight again, the mockingbird, high
In the liquidambar, runs through her scales. What burdens
Down-shift and fall, their weights sprung:
The start, the rise, the notes
Oil for the ear of death, oil for the wind, the corpse
Sailing into the universe, the geranium . . .
The music, like high water, rises inexorably . . .
Toward heaven, that intergalactic queasiness
Where all fall to the same riff.

Tallow, tallow and ash. The fire winds
Like a breath through the bone, a common tune,
Hummable, hard to extrapolate:
That song again, the song of burnt notes.
The blue it rises into, the cobalt,
Proves an enduring flame: Persian death bowl,
The bead, crystal
And drowned delta, Ephesian reed.
Blue of the twice-bitten rose, blue of the dove . . .

Tattoos

1.

Necklace of flame, little dropped hearts,
Camellias: I crunch you under my foot.
And here comes the wind again, bad breath
Of thirty-odd years, and catching up. Still,
I crunch you under my foot.

Your white stalks sequester me,
Their roots a remembered solitude.
Their mouths of snow keep forming my name.
Programmed incendiaries,
Fused flesh, so light your flowering,

So light the light that fires you
—Petals of horn, scales of blood—,
Where would you have me return?
What songs would I sing,
And the hymns . . . What garden of wax statues . . .

1973

2.

The pin oak has found new meat,
The linkworm a bone to pick.
Lolling its head, slicking its blue tongue,
The nightflower blooms on its one stem;
The crabgrass hones down its knives:

Between us again there is nothing. And since
The darkness is only light
That has not yet reached us,
You slip it on like a glove.
Duck soup, you say. *This is duck soup.*

And so it is.
                    Along the far bank
Of Blood Creek, I watch you turn
In that light, and turn, and turn,
Feeling it change on your changing hands,
Feeling it take. Feeling it.

1972

3.

Body fat as my forearm, blunt-arrowed head
And motionless, eyes
Sequin and hammer and nail
In the torchlight, he hangs there,
Color of dead leaves, color of dust,

Dumbbell and hourglass—copperhead.
Color of bread dough, color of pain, the hand
That takes it, that handles it
—The snake now limp as a cat—
Is halfway to heaven, and in time.

Then Yellow Shirt, twitching and dancing,
Gathers it home, handclap and heartstring,
His habit in ecstasy.
Current and godhead, hot coil,
Grains through the hourglass glint and spring.

1951

4.

Silt fingers, silt stump and bone.
And twice now, in the drugged sky,
White moons, black moons.
And twice now, in the gardens,
The great seed of affection.

Liplap of Zuan's canal, blear
Footfalls of Tintoretto; the rest
Is brilliance: Turner at 3 a.m.; moth lamps
Along the casements. O blue
Feathers, this clear cathedral . . .

And now these stanchions of joy,
Radiant underpinning:
Old scaffolding, old arrangements,
All fall in a rain of light.
I have seen what I have seen.

1968

5.

Hungering acolyte, pale body,
The sunlight—through St Paul of the 12 Sorrows—
Falls like Damascus on me:

I feel the gold hair of Paradise rise through my skin
Needle and thread, needle and thread;

I feel the worm in the rose root.
I hear the river of heaven
Fall from the air, I hear it enter the wafer
And sink me, the whirlpool stars
Spinning me down, and down. O . . .

Now I am something else, smooth,
Unrooted, with no veins and no hair, washed
In the waters of nothingness;
Anticoronal, released . . .
And then I am risen, the cup, new sun, at my lips.

1948

6.

Skyhooked above the floor, sucked
And mummied by salt towels, my left arm
Hangs in the darkness, bloodwood, black gauze,
The slow circle of poison
Coming and going through the same hole . . .

Sprinkle of rain through the pine needles,
Shoosh pump shoosh pump of the heart;
Bad blood, bad blood . . .
                                        Chalk skin like a light,
Eyes thin dimes, whose face
Comes and goes at the window?

Whose face . . .
                        For I would join it,

And climb through the nine-and-a-half footholds of fever
Into the high air,
And shed these clothes and renounce,
Burned over, repurified.

1941

7.

This one's not like the other, pale, gingerly—
Like nothing, in fact, to rise, as he does,
In three days, his blood clotted,
His deathsheet a feather across his chest,
His eyes twin lenses, and ready to unroll.

Arm and a leg, nail hole and knucklebone,
He stands up. In his right hand,
The flagstaff of victory;
In his left, the folds of what altered him.
And the hills spell V, and the trees V . . .

Nameless, invisible, what spins out
From this wall comes breath by breath,
And pulls the vine, and the ringing tide,
The scorched syllable from the moon's mouth.
And what pulls them pulls me.

1963

8.

A tongue hangs in the dawn wind, a wind
That trails the tongue's voice like a banner, star
And whitewash, the voice
Sailing across the 14 mountains, snap and drift,
To settle, a last sigh, here.

That tongue is his tongue, the voice his voice:
Lifting out of the sea
Where the tongue licks, the voice starts,
Monotonous, out of sync,
Yarmulke, tfillin, tallis.

His nude body waist deep in the waves,
The book a fire in his hands, his movements
Reedflow and counter flow, the chant light
From his lips, the prayer rising to heaven,
And everything brilliance, brilliance, brilliance.

1959

9.

In the fixed crosshairs of evening,
In the dust-wallow of certitude,
Where the drop drops and the scalding starts,
Where the train pulls out and the light winks,
The tracks go on, and go on:

The flesh pulls back and snaps,
The fingers are ground and scraped clean,
Reed whistles in a green fire.
The bones blow on, singing their bald song.
It stops. And it starts again.

Theologians, Interpreters:
Song, the tracks, crosshairs, the light;
The drop that is always falling.
Over again I feel the palm print,
The map that will take me there.

1952

10.

It starts here, in a chair, sunflowers
Inclined from an iron pot, a soiled dishcloth
Draped on the backrest. A throat with a red choker
Throbs in the mirror. High on the wall,
Flower-like, disembodied,

A wren-colored evil eye stares out
At the white blooms of the oleander, at the white
Gobbets of shadow and shade,
At the white lady and white parasol, at this
Dichogamous landscape, this found chord

(And in the hibiscus and moonflowers,
In the smoke trees and spider ferns,
The unicorn crosses his thin legs,
The leopard sips at her dish of blood,
And the vines strike and the vines recoil).

1973

11.

So that was it, the rush and the take-off,
The oily glide of the cells
Bringing it up—ripsurge, refraction,
The inner spin
Trailing into the cracked lights of oblivion . . .

Re-entry is something else, blank, hard:
Black stretcher straps; the peck, peck
And click of a scalpel; glass shards
Eased one by one from the flesh;
Recisions; the long bite of the veins . . .

And what do we do with this,
Rechuted, reworked into our same lives, no one
To answer to, no one to glimpse and sing,
The cracked light flashing our names?
We stand fast, friend, we stand fast.

1958

12.

Oval oval oval oval push pull push pull . . .
Words unroll from our fingers.
A splash of leaves through the windowpanes,
A smell of tar from the streets:
Apple, arrival, the railroad, shoe.

The words, like bees in a sweet ink, cluster and drone,
Indifferent, indelible,
A hum and a hum:
Back stairsteps to God, ropes to the glass eye:
Vineyard, informer, the chair, the throne.

Mojo and numberless, breaths
From the wet mountains and green mouths; rustlings,
Sure sleights of hand,
The news that arrives from nowhere:
Angel, omega, silence, silence . . .

1945

13.

What I remember is fire, orange fire,
And his huge cock in his hand,
Touching my tiny one; the smell

Of coal dust, the smell of heat,
Banked flames through the furnace door.

Of him I remember little, if anything:
Black, overalls splotched with soot,
His voice, *honey, O honey*...
And then he came, his left hand
On my back, holding me close.

Nothing was said, of course—one
Terrible admonition, and that was all...
And if that hand, like loosed lumber, fell
From grace, and stayed there? We give,
And we take it back. We give again...

1940

14.

Now there is one, and still masked;
White death's face, sheeted and shoeless, eyes shut
Behind the skull holes.
She stands in a field, her shadow no shadow,
The clouds no clouds. Call her Untitled.

And now there are four, white shoes, white socks;
They stand in the same field, the same clouds
Vanishing down the sky. Cat masks and mop hair
Cover their faces. Advancing, they hold hands.

Nine. Now there are nine, their true shadows
The judgments beneath their feet.
Black masks, white nightgowns. A wind
Is what calls them, that field, those same clouds
Lisping one syllable *I, I, I.*

1970

15.

And the saw keeps cutting,
Its flashy teeth shredding the mattress, the bedclothes,
The pillow and pillow case.
Plugged in to a socket in your bones,
It coughs, and keeps on cutting.

It eats the lamp and the bedpost.
It licks the clock with its oiled tongue,
And keeps on cutting.
It leaves the bedroom, and keeps on cutting.
It leaves the house, and keeps on cutting . . .

—Dogwood, old feathery petals,
Your black notches burn in my blood;
You flutter like bandages across my childhood.
Your sound is a sound of good-bye.
Your poem is a poem of pain.

1964

16.

All gloss, gothic and garrulous, staked
To her own tree, she takes it off,

Half-dollar an article. With each
Hike of the price, the gawkers
Diminish, spitting, rubbing their necks.

Fifteen, and staked to *my* tree,
Sap-handled, hand in my pocket, head
Hot as the carnival tent, I see it out—as does
The sheriff of Cherokee County,
Who fondles the payoff, finger and shaft.

Outside, in the gathering dark, all
Is fly buzz and gnat hum and whine of the wires;
Quick scratch of the match, cicadas,
Jackhammer insects; drone, drone
Of the blood-suckers, sweet dust, last sounds . . .

1950

17.

I dream that I dream I wake
The room is throat-deep and brown with dead moths
I throw them back like a quilt
I peel them down from the wall
I kick them like leaves I shake them I kick them again

The bride on the couch and the bridegroom
Under their gauze dust-sheet
And cover up turn to each other
Top hat and tails white veil and say as I pass
It's mother again just mother the window open

On the 10th floor going up
Is Faceless and under steam his mask

Hot-wired my breath at his heels in sharp clumps
Darkness and light darkness and light
Faceless come back O come back

1955 FF.

18.

Flash click tick, flash click tick, light
Through the wavefall—electrodes, intolerable curlicues;
Splinters along the skin, eyes
Flicked by the sealash, spun, pricked;
Terrible vowels from the sun.

And everything dry, wrung, the land flaked
By the wind, bone dust and shale;
And hills without names or numbers,
Bald coves where the sky harbors.
The dead grass whistles a tune, strangely familiar.

And all in a row, seated, their mouths biting the empty air,
Their front legs straight, and their backs straight,
Their bodies pitted, eyes wide,
The rubble quick glint beneath their feet,
The lions stare, explaining it one more time.

1959

19.

The hemlocks wedge in the wind.
Their webs are forming something—questions:
Which shoe is the alter ego?
Which glove inures the fallible hand?
Why are the apple trees in draped black?

And I answer them. In words
They will understand, I answer them:
The left shoe.
The left glove.
Someone is dead; someone who loved them is dead.

Regret is what anchors me;
I wash in a water of odd names.
White flakes from next year sift down, sift down.
I lie still, and dig in,
Snow-rooted, ooze-rooted, cold blossom.

1972

20.

You stand in your shoes, two shiny graves
Dogging your footsteps;
You spread your fingers, ten stalks
Enclosing your right of way;
You yip with pain in your little mouth.

And this is where the ash falls.
And this is the time it took to get here—
And yours, too, is the stall, the wet wings
Arriving, and the beak.
And yours the thump, and the soft voice:

The octopus on the reef's edge, who slides
His fat fingers among the cracks,
Can use you. You've prayed to him,
In fact, and don't know it.
You *are* him, and think yourself yourself.

1973

Notes to Tattoos

1. Camellias; Mother's Day; St Paul's Episcopal Church, Kingsport, Tennessee.
2. Death of my father.
3. Snake-handling religious service; East Tennessee.
4. Venice, Italy.
5. Acolyte; fainting at the altar; Kingsport, Tennessee.
6. Blood-poisoning; hallucination; Hiwassee, North Carolina.
7. *The Resurrection*, Piero della Francesca, Borgo San Sepolcro, Italy.
8. Harold Schimmel's morning prayers; Positano, Italy.
9. Temporary evangelical certitude; Christ School, Arden, North Carolina.
10. Visions of heaven.
11. Automobile wreck; hospital; Baltimore, Maryland.
12. Handwriting class; Palmer Method; words as 'things'; Kingsport, Tennessee.
13. The janitor; kindergarten; Corinth, Mississippi.
14. Dream.
15. The day of my mother's funeral, in Tennessee; Rome, Italy.
16. Sideshow stripper; Cherokee County Fair, Cherokee, North Carolina.
17. Recurrent dream.
18. The Naxian lions; Delos, Greece.
19. Death of my father.
20. The last stanza is an adaptation of lines from Eugenio Montale's *Serenata Indiana.*

Hardin County

—CPW, 1904–1972

There are birds that are parts of speech, bones
That are suns in the quick earth.
There are ice floes that die of cold.
There are rivers with many doors, and names
That pull their thread from their own skins.
Your grief was something like this.

Or self-pity, I might add, as you did
When you were afraid to sleep,
And not sleep, afraid to touch your bare palm,
Afraid of the wooden dog, the rose
Bleating beside your nightstand; afraid
Of the slur in the May wind.

It wasn't always like that, not in those first years
When the moon went on without its waters,
When the cores blew out of their graves in Hardin County.
How useless it is to cry out, to try
And track that light, now
Reduced to a grain of salt in the salt snow.

I want the dirt to go loose, the east wind
To pivot and fold like a string.
I want the pencil to eat its words,
The star to be sucked through its black hole.
And everything stays the same,
Locks unpicked, shavings unswept on the stone floor.

The grass reissues its green music; the leaves
Of the sassafras tree take it and pass it on;
The sunlight scatters its small change.
The dew falls, the birds smudge on their limbs.
And, over Oak Hill, the clouds, those mansions of nothingness,
Keep to their own appointments, and hurry by.

Delta Traveller

—MWW, 1910–1964

Born in the quarter-night, brash
Tongue on the tongueless ward, the moon down,
The lake rising on schedule and Dr Hurt
Already across the water, and headed home—
And so I came sailing out, first child,
A stream with no bed to lie in,
A root with no branch to leaf,
The black balloon of promise tied to your wrist,
One inch of pain and an inch of light.

No wonder the children stand by those moist graves.
And produce is spread on the cobbled streets,
And portraits are carried out, and horns play.
And women, in single file, untangle
Corn from the storage bins, and soft cheese.
I shield my eyes against the sunlight,
Holding, in one hand, a death's-head,
Spun sugar and marzipan. I call it Love,
And shield my eyes against the sunlight.

I lie down with you, I rise up with you.
If a grain turns in my eye,
I know it is you, entering, leaving,
Your name like a lozenge upon my tongue.
You drift through the antilife,
Scrim and snow-scud, fluff stem, hair
And tendril. You bloom in your own throat,
Frost flame in the frost dust,
One scratch on the slipstream, a closed mouth.

High-necked and high-collared, slumped and creased,
A dress sits in a chair. Your dress,
Or your mother's dress, a dress
On a wooden chair, in a cold room, a room
With no windows and no doors, full of the east wind.
The dress gets up, windbone and windskin,
To open the window. It is not there.
It goes to the door. It is not there.
The dress goes back and sits down. The dress gets up . . .

Three teeth and a thumbnail, white, white; four
Fingers that cradle a black chin;
Outline of eye-hole and nose-hole. This skull
And its one hand float up from the tar
And lime pit of dreams, night after slick night,
To lodge in the fork of the gum tree,

Its three teeth in the leaflight,
Its thumbnail in flash and foil,
Its mouth-hole a nothing I need to know.

Cat's-eye and cloud, you survive.
The porcelain corridors
That glide forever beneath your feet,
The armed lawn chair you sit in,
Your bones like paint, your skin the wrong color—
All this you survive, and hold on,
A way of remembering, a pulse
That comes and goes in the night,
Match flare and wink, that comes and goes in the night.

If the wafer of light offends me,
If the split tongue in the snake's mouth offends me,
I am not listening. They make the sound,
Which is the same sound, of the ant hill,
The hollow trunk, the fruit of the tree.
It is the Echo, the one transmitter of things:
Transcendent and inescapable,
It is the cloud, the mosquito's buzz,
The trickle of water across the leaf's vein.

And so with the dead, the rock dead and the dust:
Worm and worm-fill, pearl, milk-eye

And light in the earth, the dead are brought
Back to us, piece by piece—
Under the sponged log, inside the stump,
They shine with their secret lives, and grow
Big with their messages, wings
Beginning to stir, paths fixed and hearts clocked,
Rising and falling back and rising.

Skins

1.

Whatever furrow you dig in the red earth,
Whatever the tree you hang your lights on,
There comes that moment
When what you are is what you will be
Until the end, no matter
What prayer you answer to—a life
Of margins, white of the apple, white of the eye,
No matter how long you hold your hands out.
You glance back and you glance back. Ahead, in the distance, a cry
Skreeks like chalk on a blackboard.
Through riprap or backfill, sandstone or tidedrift,
You go where the landshed takes you,
One word at a time, still
Counting your money, wearing impermanent clothes.

2.

In the brushstroke that holds the angel's wing
Back from perfection; in
The synapse of word to word; in the one note
That would strike the infinite ear

And save you; and in
That last leap, the sure and redeeming edge . . .
In all beauty there lies
Something inhuman, something you can't know:
In the pith and marrow of every root
Of every bloom; in the blood-seam
Of every rock; in the black lung of every cloud
The seed, the infinitesimal seed
That dooms you, that makes you nothing,
Feeds on its self-containment and grows big.

3.

And here is the ledge,
A white ledge on a blue scarp, blue sky
Inseparable in the definition; a lens
Is tracking inexorably toward you.
Your shadow trails like a train
For miles down the glacierside, your face into view
Obliquely, then not at all,
Eyes thumbed, lips like pieces of cut glass:
This is the fair print:
Take it, eat it, it is your body and blood,
Your pose and your sacrifice; it is
Your greed and your sustenance . . .
The lens retracks, the shot unmistakable.
Take it, and be glad.

4.

First came geometry, and its dish of sparks,
Then the indifferent blue.
Then God, Original Dread, Old Voodoo Wool,
Lock-step and shadow-sprung,
Immense in the oily wind . . .

Later, the gatherings: ice, dust and its fiery hair,
The seeds in their endless scattering . . .
This linkage is nondescript
But continuing, the stars drifting into the cold
Like the corpses of Borneo
Set forth on their own rafts, washing into oblivion;
Like the reliquary tears
Of prophets, falling and falling away,
Back to geometry, back to its dish of ash.

5.

Nevertheless, the wheel arcs; nevertheless,
The mud slides and the arms yearn;
Nevertheless, you turn your face
Toward the black stone, the hard breath on the lip of God,
And find cloud, the clot you can't swallow,
The wishbone you can't spit out.
And move on, to the great fall of water;
And the light that moves there, and the click:
In the shallows, the insects,
Quick kernels of darkness, pale and explain themselves; newts
Shuttle their lanterns through the glassy leaves;
The crayfish open their doors;
The drenched wings of sunclusters rise
Like thousands of tiny cathedrals into their new language . . .

6.

Under the rock, in the sand and the gravel run;
In muck bank and weed, at the heart of the river's edge:
Instar, and again, instar,
The wing cases visible. Then
Emergence: leaf drift and detritus; skin split,
The image forced from the self.

And rests, wings drying, eyes compressed,
Legs compressed, constricted
Beneath the dun and the watershine—
Incipient spinner, set for the take-off . . .
And does, in clean tear: imago rising out of herself
For the last time, slate-winged and many-eyed.
And joins, and drops to her destiny,
Flesh to the surface, wings flush on the slate film.

7.

Sucked in and sucked out, tidewash
Hustles its razzmatazz across the cut lips
Of coral, the thousands of tiny punctures
Spewing and disappearing . . .
Where is that grain of sand that Blake saw,
The starfish that lights the way?
Pools and anemones open and close . . .
And now, on the sea's black floor,
A hand is turning your card,
One card, one turn: two dogs bark at the moon;
The crab resets her glass clock.
The weight of the sea
Is killing: you pack it forever. Shift it, sluff it;
You pack it, blue mother, forever.

8.

Something has grazed your cheek, your foot and your fingertips:
The tedious scarf of sleep, adrift
Through the afternoon. At one end, a lizard
Darts from a red rock into shade;
At the other, birds rise in the rank, inveterate blue.
July, and the olive is silhouette. The lake
Shrugs its shoulders, and goes on

Slapping its palms on the wet shale, goes on
Washing its laundry. Under
The fish-silver flash of the olive leaves, poppies
Crane up with their one good eye, and do
Nothing; the bees drag their yellow slumber.
Small pleasures: the poor man's pickpurse, the rich man's cutthroat.
Grainout... And so what? You're only passing through.

9.

The earth is what salivates, what sticks like a new glue.
It is to walk on, it is to lie down in,
A sure sheet for the resurrection.
The earth is what follows you,
Tracing your footsteps, counting your teeth, father
And son, father and grandson,
A knife, a seed, each planted just deep enough.
You start there. The birds from your sleeve burst into flame;
Your shoes catch fire, your good shoes;
Your socks sink in the dirt, all pain gone;
Your ankles sink in the dirt, your shinbones, your legs...
Necessity's after-breeder,
Inflamed like asparagus in the night field,
You try for the get-away by the light of yourself.

10.

Androgynous tincture, *prima materia*;
The quintessential reprieve
And coupling; sod-lifting, folly and light
In the crucible, and in the air;
And in the crosswinds, the details of diffidence...
This is the stung condition, and silencer:
To have come this far, to have got the jump,
The radiant archipelagos

From fog into fog beneath your body streaming—
And abstract from this
Fabric, this silkscreen that patterns you
(The chancelled dawn, vast
Surplice and undershine), one glint of the golden stitch,
The thread that will lead you home:

11.

Upriver, then, past landfall and watertrace,
Past wheels, past time and its bufferings . . .
A clearing appears; reed huts
Extend from the jungle face, its vinelap and overbite;
Out of them step, in cadence—a slip skip slip—,
Two men with their six-foot flutes, two women behind them,
Their dance, their song ascending like smoke and light
Back to the sky, back to the place it came from . . .
Of course, it's unworkable.
Better to dig a round hole in the earth, be lowered
And fixed in the clay in a stranger's arms;
Be covered with thick feathers,
Your stiff arms stiff at your sides, knees flexed,
Marked for the tilt and the blind slide.

12.

Exurgent mortui et ad me veniunt . . .
Midnight, the Christmas Mass; and the host raised, and the summoned
Summoned. And then to the boneyard, eyes eastward,
Two bones in the right hand, St Andrew's cross
Pathetic against the dawn's skull.
Then north, four thousand and nineteen hundred paces,
To lie down, outstretched, hands on the legs,
Eyes heavenward, unlocked to the quarter moon:
Ego sum, te peto et videre queo . . .

And will they step from their dust?
Will they sit in their rocking chairs, decayed hands
Explaining the maps you must follow?
Will circles be explicated, the signs shriven?
The land of the chosen has one door, there is no knob . . .

13.

Naked, spindled, the hand on the chimney mantel,
Length-fingered, bud-sprouted bone:
The Hand of Glory, spread toward its one address:
The right hand, or the left hand,
Lopped at the new moon, and fresh from the gibbet;
Wrapped in a funeral pall, squeezed, palmed;
Then brought, in the dog-days, from its pot,
Pumiced by zimat, nitre and long peppers;
Then to the oven; vervain
And fern imbue its grainlessness; the candle
—Man-fat, wax, ponie and sesame—
Forks from its wonder; lighted,
It freezes the looker's reach, and locks both
The mark and beholder, ghost forms on the negative . . .

14.

They talk of a city, whose moon-colored battlements
Kneel to the traveller, whose
Windows, like after-burners, stream
Out their chemistry, applying their anodyne.
They talk of a river, its waters
A balm, an unguent unscrubbable. They talk. And they talk
Of the light that lights the stars
Through the five organs, like a wind spread by the rain.
They talk of a medicine, a speck
—Omnipotent, omnipresent, clogged

With the heavy earth and the mind's intractable screen—
To be shaken loose, dissolved, and blown
Through the veins, becoming celestial.
They talk, and nothing appears. They talk and it does not appear.

15.

And so downriver, yourself, and yourself's shadow,
All that you bring back.
Still, it's enough: sounding board, handhold,
Ear-rig and in-seeing eye . . .
Back from the seven-caved mountain, its cross
Where the serpent is nailed; back
From the oak-stock and rose, their rivulet
Sought by the blind with their dry touch; back
From the Innocents, that vat where the sun and the moon
Dip to their red bath . . .
The Echo is arbitrary: flame, wind, rainwrack
And soil, each a survivor, each one
An heir to the fingerprint, the slip of a tongue.
Each is where you begin; each one an end in itself . . .

16.

Procedure and process, the one
Inalterable circulation. First, cleared ground, swept
And unhindered; next, bark moss, pine pitch,
Their angles of termination
Exact, the boughs that are added exact; then loblolly, split
From the fall felling; then ball bats, blue shoes,
All the paraphernalia of past lives:
The headrests, the backrests, all the poor furniture . . .
As the fire builds, you enter and lie down:
You feed the flames; you feed them with all you've got:
Finger and forearm, torso,

Shoulders and hair . . . And the sparks
That rise, the cinders,
Rework you and make you new, burned to an ash.

17.

The wind hauls out its valued baggage in three steps
Tonight, and drops it with some relief
In the full dark, in the leaves of an avocado tree.
The grass rises to meet it.
As always, you, too, rise, and meet them halfway,
And nod your head, and accept
Their leavings, and give thanks, crumbs
For the tablecloth, crumbs for the plate, and wolf them down . . .
The rivers of air you've filtered and rearranged
Since birth, and paid no heed to,
Surprise you now, and start to take on
The acid and eye of what's clear,
That milky message of breath on cold mornings—
That what you take in is seldom what you let out.

18.

There is a shine you move towards, the shine
Of water; you want it to step from,
And out of, wearing its strings and slick confetti.
You come to the sea, but turn back, its surgy retractions
Too slippery, and out of place,
Wrecked looking-glass, bundles of grief.
And inland, the necklace of lakes—High Lonesome
And pendant, the 40s its throat,
Its glint like icicles against the skin . . . ?
There's no one to wear it now, or hand it down.
The river will have it, shine

Of the underlight, shine of the lost quarter;
The river, rope of remembering, unbroken shoe,
The flushed and unwavering mirror . . .

19.

You thought you climbed, and all the while you descended.
Go up and go down; what other work is there
For you to do, what other work in this world?
The seasons back off. The hills
Debase themselves, and keep on growing. Over the land,
Your feet touch down like feathers,
A brushstroke here, a gouge there, lacking a print
Always, and always without direction.
Or so it seems. But what, for one meandering man,
Is all that, who looks for the willow's change,
The drift and slip of smoke through the poplar leaves,
The cliff's dance and wind's shift,
Alone with the owl and the night crawler
Where all is a true turning, and all is growth.

20.

You've talked to the sun and moon,
Those idols of stitched skin, bunch grass and twigs
Stuck on their poles in the fall rain;
You've prayed to Sweet Medicine;
You've looked at the Hanging Road, its stars
The stepstones and river bed where you hope to cross;
You've followed the cricket's horn
To sidestep the Lake of Pain . . .
And what does it come to, Pilgrim,
This walking to and fro on the earth, knowing
That nothing changes, or everything;

And only, to tell it, these sad marks,
Phrases half-parsed, ellipses and scratches across the dirt?
It comes to a point. It comes and it goes.

Notes to Skins

1—Situation, Point A
2—Beauty
3—Truth
4—Destruction of the universe
5—Organized religion
6—Metamorphosis
7—Water
8—Water/Earth
9—Earth/Fire
10—Aether
11—Primitive Magic
12—Necromancy
13—Black Magic
14—Alchemy
15—Allegory
16—Fire
17—Air
18—Water
19—Earth
20—Situation, Point A

Link Chain

Palm Sunday. Banana leaves
Loll in the breaklight. Back home, on Ravine Street
25 years ago, Philbeck and I
Would count the crosses, arrange
The pins on their silver plate, and bank
On a full house. The palm crosses, tiny
And off-green against their purple cloth,
Are stacked like ricks for the match flame. 11 o'clock.
I take a cross and two pins—
One for the cross, and one again for the heart.

On the front seat of a Yellow Coach,
Pistol Red at the wheel, 10 miles this side of Surgoinsville
On US 11-W, I'd lay my body down, in Tennessee,
For the 1st time. The 2nd time
I'd pick a tree, black cherry,
That grows on the north side of Chestnut Ridge, and looks out
Over the Cumberlands;
I'd build a floor and face west.
For number 3, I'd float in a boat downriver,
Whatever river, and be a leaf.

Circle by circle, link chain
And hair breadth, I'm bound to the oak mulch, those leaves
Stuffed in their croker sacks
My brother and I were sent for each week-end
In autumn, in Moody's Woods, to drag back

Up Hog Hill and feed the shredder with.
Later, confettied and packed tight in their little mounds,
They warmed the milk root and the slip stalk.
Later still, and less coarse, they'll warm me,
Bone stock and finger peg, the cold room.

From this pocket to that pocket, bright coin
Whose slot in the crossed box was cut
38 years ago, and cut well,
I roll through the world, Peter's pence
For the red clay, defrocked and worn smooth,
The payment in someone's hand.
Lord of the Anchorite, wind-blown bird,
Dangle your strings and hook me.
I am the gleam in your good eye, I am your ticket;
Take me up, and drop me where I belong.

Each tree I look at contains my coffin,
Each train brings it closer home.
Each flower I cut, I cut for a plastic vase
Askew on the red dirt, the oak trees
Whisking their wash in the May wind.
Each root I uncover uncovers me.
Below, 19 By-pass swings straight to the state line
5 miles north, Virginia across the bridge—
Each car is the car that brings
That tree to earth, the earth to the earth again.

Big Sister, hair heaped like a fresh grave,
Turns in my arms as my arms turn,
Her fingers cool tubers against my skin
As we slide slide to the music, humming
An old tune, knee touching knee,
Step-two-three, step-two-three
Under a hard hatful of leaves,
The grass with its one good limb holding
The beat, a hint of impending form.
It gathers, it reaches back, it is caught up.

Bays Mountain Covenant

For my own speech and that which I leave unspoken
For my own death and the deaths that will follow me
For the three thrones for the sticks for the wires
For the whole hog and the half-truth
For my knot of life and its one string
That goes from this man's rumor to that one's promise
For the songs I hear and the hush I should imitate
For the sky my eye sees and the one that it cannot find
For the raising up and the setting down
For the light for the light for the light

He praised for 10 years and was suckered by
A foot in the wrong shoe a hat in the wind
Sir you will pardon him you will wave if he now turns
To the leaf to the fire in the swamp log to the rain
The acorn of crystal at the creek's edge which prove
Nothing expect nothing and offer nothing
Desire no entrance and harbor no hope of change

Foxglove that seeks no answer nightshade that seeks no answer
Not to arrive at and be part of but to take
As the water accepts the whirlpool the earth the storm

Rural Route

The stars come out to graze, wild-eyed in the new dark.
The dead squeeze close together,
Strung out like a seam of coal through the raw earth.
I smell its fragrance, I touch its velvet walls.

The willow lets down her hooks.
On the holly leaves, the smears of light
Retrench and repeat their alphabet,
That slow code. The boxwood leans out to take it on,

Quicker, but still unbroken.
Inside the house, in one room, a twelve-year-old
Looks at his face on the windowpane, a face
Once mine, the same twitch to the eye.

The willow flashes her hooks.
I step closer. Azalea branches and box snags
Drag at my pants leg, twenty-six years gone by.
I enter the wedge of light.

And the face stays on the window, the eyes unchanged.
It still looks in, still unaware of the willow, the boxwood
Or any light on any leaf. Or me.
Somewhere a tire squeals, somewhere a door is shut twice.

And what it sees is what it has always seen:
Stuffed birds on a desk top, a deer head
On the wall, and all the small things we used once
To push the twelve rings of the night back.

How silly! And still they call us
Across the decades, fog horns,
Not destinations, outposts of things to avoid, reefs
To steer clear of, pockets of great abandon.

I back off, and the face stays.
I leave the back yard, and the front yard, and the face stays.
I am back on the West Coast, in my studio,
My wife and my son asleep, and the face stays.

FROM

CHINA TRACE

(1977)

Childhood

Shrunken and drained dry, turning transparent,
You've followed me like a dog
I see through at last, a window into Away-From-Here, a place
I'm headed for, my tongue loosened, tracks
Apparent, your beggar's-lice
Bleaching to crystal along my britches leg:

I'm going away now, goodbye.
Goodbye to the locust husk and the chairs;
Goodbye to the genuflections. Goodbye to the clothes
That circle beneath the earth, the names
Falling into the darkness, face
After face, like beads from a broken rosary...

Snow

If we, as we are, are dust, and dust, as it will, rises,
Then we will rise, and recongregate
In the wind, in the cloud, and be their issue,

Things in a fall in a world of fall, and slip
Through the spiked branches and snapped joints of the evergreens,
White ants, white ants and the little ribs.

Self-Portrait in 2035

The root becomes him, the road ruts
That are sift and grain in the powderlight
Recast him, sink bone in him,
Blanket and creep up, fine, fine:

Worm-waste and pillow tick; hair
Prickly and dust-dangled, his arms and black shoes
Unlinked and laceless, his face false
In the wood-rot, and past pause . . .

Darkness, erase these lines, forget these words.
Spider recite his one sin.

Morandi

I'm talking about stillness, the hush
Of a porcelain center bowl, a tear vase, a jug.

I'm talking about space, which is one-sided,
Unanswered, and left to dry.

I'm talking about paint, about shape, about the void
These objects sentry for, and rise from.

I'm talking about sin, red drop, white drop,
Its warp and curve, which is blue.

I'm talking about bottles, and ruin,
And what we flash at the darkness, and what for . . .

Dog

The fantailed dog of the end, the lights out,
Lopes in his sleep,
The moon's moan in the glassy fields.
Everything comes to him, stone
Pad prints extending like stars, tongue black
As a flag, saliva and thread, the needle's tooth,
Everything comes to him.

If I were a wind, which I am, if I
Were smoke, which I am, if I
Were the colorless leaves, the invisible grief,
Which I am, which I am,
He'd whistle me down, and down, but not yet.

Snapshot

Under the great lens of heaven, caught
In the flash and gun of the full moon,
Improbable target in the lunar click,

My own ghost, a lock-shot lanyard of blue flame,
Slips from the deadeyes in nothing's rig,
Raiment and sustenance, and hangs

Like a noose in the night wind. Or like a mouth,
O-fire in the scaffolding. You are wine
In a glass, it says, you are sack, you are silt.

Indian Summer

The plains drift on through the deep daylight.

I watch the snow bees sent mad by the sun.

The limbs of the hickory trees swing loose in the noontide,
Feathery, stretching their necks.

The wind blows through its own hair forever.

If something is due me still
—Firedogs, ashes, the soap of another life—
I give it back. And this hive

Of shelved combs, my wax in its little box.

Wishes

I wish I were unencumbered, in Venice or South Bay.
I wish I were thrust down by enormous weights
Anywhere, anywhere.
I wish that the blood fly would crawl from its hiding place.

The sun slides up through the heat, and has no dreams.
The days drop, each nosed by the same dog.
In some other language
I walk by this same river, these same vowels in my throat.

I wish I could say them now, returned
Through the dry thread of the leaf, the acorn's root.
It's somewhere I can't remember, but saw once.
It's late in the afternoon there, the lights coming on.

Quotidiana

The moss retracts its skin from the laced grass.
This mist is a cold address,
This late light a street that others have moved from too.
The river stays shut, and writes my biography.

Midwinter, midwinter,
Your necktie of ice, your salt shoes,
Trees in a numb nudge, you
Come through the sand sieve, you bear me up.

At Zero

In the cold kitchen of heaven,
Daylight spoons out its cream-of-wheat.

Beside the sidewalk, the shrubs
Hunch down, deep in their bibs.

The wind harps its same song
Through the steel tines of the trees.

The river lies still, the jeweled drill in its teeth.

I am glint on its fingernails.
I am ground grains on its wheel.

Sentences

The ash fish has been away for a long time now,
The snow transparent; a white cane rakes back and forth
In the hush, no sweet sound from the leaves.

Whatever is dead stays dead: the lighted and cold
Blue blank pavilions of the sky,
The sand, the crystal's ring in the bushy ear—
Voices logy with sleep, their knapsacks
The color of nothing, full of the great spaces they still must cross.

The trees take care of their own salvation, and rocks
Swell with their business: and there, on the clean cloth
Of the river, a Host is floating without end.

Heaven, that stray dog, eats on the run and keeps moving.

Death

I take you as I take the moon rising,
Darkness, black moth the light burns up in.

Next

I am weary of daily things,
How the limbs of the sycamore
Dip to the snow surge and disaffect;
How the ice moans and the salt swells.
Where is that country I signed for, the one with the lamp,
The one with the penny in each shoe?

I want to lie down, I am so tired, and let
The crab grass seep through my heart,
Side by side with the inchworm and the fallen psalm,
Close to the river bank,
In autumn, the red leaves in the sky
Like lost flags, sidle and drift . . .

January

In some other life
I'll stand where I'm standing now, and will look down, and will see
My own face, and not know what I'm looking at.

These are the nights
When the oyster begins her pearl, when the spider slips
Through his wired rooms, and the barns cough, and the grass quails.

1975

Year of the Half-Hinged Mouth and the Hollow Bones,
Year of the Thorn,
Year of the Rope and the Dead Coal,
Year of the Hammering Mountain, Year of the Sponge . . .

I open the book of What I Can Never Know
To page 1, and start to read:
"The snow falls from the hills to the sea, from the cloud
To the cloud's body, water to water . . ."

At 40, the apricot
Seems raised to a higher power, the fire ant and the weed.
And I turn in the wind,
Not knowing what sign to make, or where I should kneel.

Nerval's Mirror

I'll never know what the clouds promised,
Or what the stars intended to say;
I'll never return the call of What's-To-Come.

I'm safe now, and well fed.
Don't look for me in the white night of the Arctic;
I'm floating here, my side iced to its side.

Edvard Munch

We live in houses of ample weight,
Their windows a skin-colored light, pale and unfixable.
Our yards are large and windraked, their trees bent to the storm.
People we don't know are all around us.

Or else there is no one, and all day
We stand on a bridge, or a cliff's edge, looking down.
Our mothers stare at our shoes.

Hands to our ears, our mouths open, we're pulled on
By the flash black, flash black flash of the lighthouse
We can't see on the rock coast,
Notes in a bottle, our lines the ink from the full moon.

Bygones

The rain has stopped falling asleep on its crystal stems

Equation

I open the phone book, and look for my adolescence.
How easy the past is—
Alphabetized, its picture taken,
It leans in the doorway, it fits in the back pocket.

The crime is invisible,
But it's there. Why else would I feel so guilty?

Why else would that one sorrow still walk through my sleep,
Looking away, dressed in its best suit?

I touch my palm. I touch it again and again.
I leave no fingerprint. I find no white scar.
It must have been something else,
Something enormous, something too big to see.

California Twilight

Late evening, July, and no one at home.
In the green lungs of the willow, fly-worms and lightning bugs
Blood-spot the whips and wings. Blue

Asters become electric against the hedge.
What was it I had in mind?
The last whirr of a skateboard dwindles down Oak Street hill.

Slowly a leaf unlocks itself from a branch.
Slowly the furred hands of the dead flutter up from their caves.
A little pinkish flame is snuffed in my mouth.

Anniversary

At dawn, in the great meadow, a solitude
As easy as white paint comes down from the mountains
To daydream, bending the grass.

I take my body, familiar bundle of sorrows, to be
Touched by its hem, and smoothed over . . .

There's only one secret in this life that's worth knowing,
And you found it.
I'll find it too.

12 Lines at Midnight

Sleep, in its burning garden, sets out the small plants.
Behind me an animal breaks down,
One ear to the moon's brass sigh.

The earth ticks open like a ripe fruit.
The mist, with its sleeves of bone, slides out of the reeds,
Everything hushed, the emptiness everywhere.

The breath inside my breath is the breath of the dream.
I lick its charred heart, a piece of the same flaked sky
The badger drags to his hole.

The bread bleeds in the cupboard,
The mildew tightens. The clocks, with their tiny hands, reach out,
Inarticulate monitors of the wind.

Dino Campana

After the sad tunes on the dog's tooth,
The twistwort and starbane
—Blood lilies the heart breeds—,
Your mouth is the blue door I walk through,
The lamp lit, the table laid.

Invisible Landscape

This is the way it must have been in the first dusk:
Smokeclouds sculling into their slips in the Claw Mountains,
Bats jerked through the plumlight by strings of white sound;
The wind clicks through its turnstiles
Over the high country, the hush of a steady pulse . . .

I bring to this landscape a bare hand, these knuckles
Slick as a cake of soap,
The black snag of a tamarack,
The oddments and brown jewelry of early September evenings
In wet weather, a Colt-colored sky . . .

God is the sleight-of-hand in the fireweed, the lost
Moment that stopped to grieve and moved on . . .

Remembering San Zeno

After the end, they'll bring you
To someplace like this, columns of light propped through a west-facing
  door,
People standing about, echo of shoe-taps,
The gloom, like a grease-soaked rag, like a slipped skin
Left in a corner, puddled
In back of the votive stick stands, matter-of-factly—

Under the lisp and cold glow of the flames
Everything stares and moves closer, faces and blank hands,

October the 1st, 1975.
The banked candles the color of fresh bone,
Smoke rising from chimneys beyond the beyond,
Nightfires, your next address . . .

Born Again

Sunday night and a full moon,
October the 19th, moon glyphs on the grass and leaves.
In the endless expanse of heaven,
3 stars break out through the cover-up, and hang free.
Behind the veneer of light and the scorched lungs
Are walks I will take.

Nothingness, tilt your cup.
I am the wafer just placed on your tongue,
The transubstantiation of bone and regret
To air and a photograph;
I am the diamond and bad heart,
Breath's waste, the slip-back and failure of What's Past.

Captain Dog

Another December, another year
Gone to the bleached Pacific, a little castle of snow
Falling across the sky
I wanted to linger in for a while.

And so I lose touch, the walls, in their iced dismemberings,
Shrinking like aches, a slide and a by-your-leave.

The nights, with their starred palms, press down,
Black moths on the screen door,
Slow breaths to stop the body's bleeding, deep breaths.

I'm jump-cut and Captain Dog, staked
In the shadow of nothing's hand.
I bend like a finger joint, I gather, I burn.

1975

Depression Before the Solstice

4 days till the solstice, the moon
Like an onion thin in the afternoon sky, the few leaves
In the liquidambar arthritic and holding on.
The weightless, unclarified light from the setting sun
Lies like despair on the ginger root. Windows
Go up in flame. Now

The watchers and holy ones set out, divining
The seal, eclipses
Taped to their sleeves with black felt,
Their footprints filling with sparks
In the bitter loam behind them, ahead of them stobbed with sand,
And walk hard, and regret nothing.

Stone Canyon Nocturne

Ancient of Days, old friend, no one believes you'll come back.
No one believes in his own life anymore.

The moon, like a dead heart, cold and unstartable, hangs by a thread
At the earth's edge,
Unfaithful at last, splotching the ferns and the pink shrubs.

In the other world, children undo the knots in their tally strings.
They sing songs, and their fingers blear.

And here, where the swan hums in his socket, where bloodroot
And belladonna insist on our comforting,
Where the fox in the canyon wall empties our hands, ecstatic for more,

Like a bead of clear oil the Healer revolves through the night wind,
Part eye, part tear, unwilling to recognize us.

Reply to Chi Kang

There is no light for us at the end of the light.
No one redeems the grass our shadows lie on.

Each night, in its handful of sleep, the mimosa blooms.
Each night the future forgives.
Inside us, albino roots are starting to take hold.

Reunion

Already one day has detached itself from all the rest up ahead.
It has my photograph in its soft pocket.
It wants to carry my breath into the past in its bag of wind.

I write poems to untie myself, to do penance and disappear
Through the upper right-hand corner of things, to say grace.

"Where Moth and Rust Doth Corrupt"

No moon in the eastern sky, the Big Dipper
Spilling its nothingness from Baja to Prudhomme Bay,
Ashes strewn through my life like old clothes.
The outline of 10 crosses still dampens and stains my childhood,
Oppressive forehead, infinite hymn . . .

Lie back and regenerate,
                                        family of dust,
Invisible groom, father and son I step through.
Spread for the fly's fall,
Its body released and sucked clean and full of the air.
I whisper into a different ear.

I mimic the tongues of green flame in the grass.
I live in the one world, the moth and rust in my arms.

April

The plum tree breaks out in bees.
A gull is locked like a ghost in the blue attic of heaven.
The wind goes nattering on,
Gossipy, ill at ease, in the damp rooms it will air.
I count off the grace and stays
My life has come to, and know I want less—

Divested of everything,
A downfall of light in the pine woods, motes in the rush,
Gold leaf through the undergrowth, and come back

As another name, water
Pooled in the black leaves and holding me there, to be
Released as a glint, as a flash, as a spark . . .

Signature

Don't wait for the snowfall from the dogwood tree.
Live like a huge rock covered with moss,
Rooted half under the earth
                                        and anxious for no one.

Noon

I look up at the black bulge of the sky and its belt of stars,
And know I can answer to nothing in all that shine,
Desire being ash, and not remembered or brought back by the breath,
Scattered beneath the willow's fall, a figure of speech . . .

And know that what I have asked for cannot be granted, that what
Is waiting for me is laced in my 2 shoes,
Wind that will alter me, extension that one day will ease me on
In my slow rise through the dark toward the sweet wrists of the rose.

The dirt is a comforting, and the night drafts from the sucker vines.
The grass is a warm thing, and the hollyhocks, and the bright bursts from
    the weeds.
But best of all is the noon, and its tiny horns,
When shadows imprint, and start
                                        their gradual exhalation of the past.

Going Home

The ides of a hangdog month.
Dirt roads and small towns come forth
And fall from the pepper tree,
                                        evening flashing their panes
And stray flakes through a thin drizzle of darkness,
Strikes in the dry fields of the past,
                                              bonesparks
From the nailed feet that walk there.

I ask for a second breath,
Great Wind, where everything's necessary
And everything rises,
                              unburdened and borne away, where
The flash from the setting sun
Is more than a trick of light, where halflife
Is more than just a watery glow,
                                          and everything's fire . . .

Cloud River

The unborn children are rowing out to the far edge of the sky,
Looking for warm beds to appear in. How lucky they are, dressed
In their lake-colored gowns, the oars in their oily locks
Taking them stroke by stroke to circumference and artery . . .

I'd like to be with them still, pulling my weight,
Blisters like small white hearts in the waxed palms of my hands.
I'd like to remember my old name, and keep the watch,
Waiting for something immense and unspeakable to uncover its face.

Reply to Lapo Gianni

Lapo, we're all slow orphans under the cruel sleep of heaven.
We're all either creased and sealed or somebody's cough.

Outside the window, twilight slips on its suede glove.
The river is fine balsam, fragrant and nicked by cold feathers.
Under the grass, the lights go on in their marled rooms.

Lapo, the dreams of the dog rose are nothing to you and me.

Thinking of Georg Trakl

August, the bones of summer, the chamber and last lunch
Before the fall. All day the creatures and small wings
Have hung back or held their tongues.
All day they have known what we will know when the time comes.

Sister of Mercies, a body is laid out, look,
Under the ghost light of the stars. 11:15. With different breaths,
Silently, up from the river, its wet-sheet of mist
Is drawn forth and arranged.

Lips part in the bleached willows.
Finger by finger, above Orion, God's blue hand unfolds.

Spider Crystal Ascension

The spider, juiced crystal and Milky Way, drifts on his web through the night sky
And looks down, waiting for us to ascend . . .

At dawn he is still there, invisible, short of breath, mending his net.

All morning we look for the white face to rise from the lake like a tiny star.
And when it does, we lie back in our watery hair and rock.

Moving On

Once it was lamb's fleece and the fall.
Once it was wedge of the eyelid and eyelid down to poison and sheer slumber,
The flesh made flesh and the word.

Now it's the crack in the porcelain stick,
And midnight splashed on the 1st rocks and gone,
The wafer of blood in its chalk robes,

The bright nail of the east I usher my body toward.

Clear Night

Clear night, thumb-top of a moon, a back-lit sky.
Moon-fingers lay down their same routine

On the side deck and the threshold, the white keys and the black keys.
Bird hush and bird song. A cassia flower falls.

I want to be bruised by God.
I want to be strung up in a strong light and singled out.
I want to be stretched, like music wrung from a dropped seed.
I want to be entered and picked clean.

And the wind says "What?" to me.
And the castor beans, with their little earrings of death, say "What?" to me.
And the stars start out on their cold slide through the dark.
And the gears notch and the engines wheel.

Autumn

November the 1st. Gold leaves
Whisper their sentences through the blue chains of the wind.
I open a saint-john's-bread.

Green apples, a stained quilt,
The black clock of the heavens reset in the future tense.
Salvation's a simple thing.

Sitting at Night on the Front Porch

I'm here, on the dark porch, restyled in my mother's chair.
10:45 and no moon.
Below the house, car lights
Swing down, on the canyon floor, to the sea.

In this they resemble us,
Dropping like match flames through the great void
Under our feet.
In this they resemble her, burning and disappearing.

Everyone's gone
And I'm here, sizing the dark, saving my mother's seat.

Saturday 6 a.m.

The month gone and the day coming up like a bad cold
Insistent behind the eyes, a fine sweat on the mustard stalks.
There's something I want to say,

But not here, stepped out and at large on the blurred hillside.
Over my shoulder, the great pane of the sunlight tilts toward the sea.
I don't move. I let the wind speak.

Him

His sorrow hangs like a heart in the star-flowered boundary tree.
It mirrors the endless wind.

He feeds on the lunar differences and flies up at the dawn.

When he lies down, the waters will lie down with him,
And all that walks and all that stands still, and sleep through the thunder.

It's for him that the willow bleeds.

Look for him high in the flat black of the northern Pacific sky,
Released in his suit of lights,
                                        lifted and laid clear.

FROM

THE SOUTHERN CROSS

(1981)

Homage to Paul Cézanne

At night, in the fish-light of the moon, the dead wear our white shirts
To stay warm, and litter the fields.
We pick them up in the mornings, dewy pieces of paper and scraps of cloth.
Like us, they refract themselves. Like us,
They keep on saying the same thing, trying to get it right.
Like us, the water unsettles their names.

Sometimes they lie like leaves in their little arks, and curl up at the edges.
Sometimes they come inside, wearing our shoes, and walk
From mirror to mirror.
Or lie in our beds with their gloves off
And touch our bodies. Or talk
In a corner. Or wait like envelopes on a desk.

They reach up from the ice plant.
They shuttle their messengers through the oat grass.
Their answers rise like rust on the stalks and the spidery leaves.

We rub them off our hands.

Each year the dead grow less dead, and nudge
Close to the surface of all things.
They start to remember the silence that brought them there.
They start to recount the gain in their soiled hands.

Their glasses let loose, and grain by grain return to the riverbank.
They point to their favorite words

Growing around them, revealed as themselves for the first time:
They stand close to the meanings and take them in.

They stand there, vague and without pain,
Under their fingernails an unreturnable dirt.
They stand there and it comes back,
The music of everything, syllable after syllable

Out of the burning chair, out of the beings of light.
It all comes back.
And what they repeat to themselves, and what they repeat to themselves,
Is the song that our fathers sing.

In steeps and sighs,
The ocean explains itself, backing and filling
What spaces it can't avoid, spaces
In black shoes, their hands clasped, their eyes teared at the edges:
We watch from the high hillside,
The ocean swelling and flattening, the spaces
Filling and emptying, horizon blade
Flashing the early afternoon sun.

The dead are constant in
The white lips of the sea.
Over and over, through clenched teeth, they tell
Their story, the story each knows by heart:
Remember me, speak my name.
When the moon tugs at my sleeve,
When the body of water is raised and becomes the body of light,
Remember me, speak my name.

The dead are a cadmium blue.
We spread them with palette knives in broad blocks and planes.

We layer them stroke by stroke
In steps and ascending mass, in verticals raised from the earth.

We choose, and layer them in,
Blue and a blue and a breath,

Circle and smudge, cross-beak and buttonhook,
We layer them in. We squint hard and terrace them line by line.

And so we are come between, and cry out,
And stare up at the sky and its cloudy panes,

And finger the cypress twists.
The dead understand all this, and keep in touch,

Rustle of hand to hand in the lemon trees,
Flags, and the great sifts of anger

To powder and nothingness.
The dead are a cadmium blue, and they understand.

The dead are with us to stay.
Their shadows rock in the back yard, so pure, so black,
Between the oak tree and the porch.

Over our heads they're huge in the night sky.
In the tall grass they turn with the zodiac.
Under our feet they're white with the snows of a thousand years.

They carry their colored threads and baskets of silk
To mend our clothes, making us look right,
Altering, stitching, replacing a button, closing a tear.
They lie like tucks in our loose sleeves, they hold us together.

They blow the last leaves away.
They slide like an overflow into the river of heaven.
Everywhere they are flying.

The dead are a sleight and a fade
We fall for, like flowering plums, like white coins from the rain.
Their sighs are gaps in the wind.

The dead are waiting for us in our rooms,
Little globules of light
In one of the far corners, and close to the ceiling, hovering, thinking our
    thoughts.

Often they'll reach a hand down,
Or offer a word, and ease us out of our bodies to join them in theirs.
We look back at our other selves on the bed.

We look back and we don't care and we go.

And thus we become what we've longed for,
                                        past tense and otherwise,
A BB, a disc of light,
                    song without words.
And refer to ourselves
In the third person, seeing that other arm
Still raised from the bed, fingers like licks and flames in the boned air.

Only to hear that it's not time.
Only to hear that we must re-enter and lie still, our arms at rest at our sides,
The voices rising around us like mist

And dew, *it's all right, it's all right, it's all right . . .*

The dead fall around us like rain.
They come down from the last clouds in the late light for the last time
And slip through the sod.

They lean uphill and face north.
                                        Like grass,
They bend toward the sea, they break toward the setting sun.

We filigree and we baste.
But what do the dead care for the fringe of words,
Safe in their suits of milk?
What do they care for the honk and flash of a new style?

And who is to say if the inch of snow in our hearts
Is rectitude enough?

Spring picks the locks of the wind.
High in the night sky the mirror is hauled up and unsheeted.
In it we twist like stars.

Ahead of us, through the dark, the dead
Are beating their drums and stirring the yellow leaves.

We're out here, our feet in the soil, our heads craned up at the sky,
The stars streaming and bursting behind the trees.

At dawn, as the clouds gather, we watch
The mountain glide from the east on the valley floor,
Coming together in starts and jumps.
Behind their curtain, the bears
Amble across the heavens, serene as black coffee . . .

Whose unction can intercede for the dead?
Whose tongue is toothless enough to speak their piece?

What we are given in dreams we write as blue paint,
Or messages to the clouds.
At evening we wait for the rain to fall and the sky to clear.
Our words are words for the clay, uttered in undertones,
Our gestures salve for the wind.

We sit out on the earth and stretch our limbs,
Hoarding the little mounds of sorrow laid up in our hearts.

Mount Caribou at Night

Just north of the Yaak River, one man sits bolt upright,
A little bonnet of dirt and bunch grass above his head:
Northwestern Montana is hard relief,
And harder still the lying down and the rising up . . .

I speak to the others there, lodged in their stone wedges, the blocks
And slashes that vein the ground, and tell them that Walter Smoot,
Starched and at ease in his bony duds
Under the tamaracks, still holds the nightfall between his knees.

Work stars, drop by inveterate drop, begin
Cassiopeia's sails and electric paste
Across the sky. And down
Toward the cadmium waters that carry them back to the dawn,

They squeeze out Andromeda and the Whale,
Everything on the move, everything flowing and folding back
And starting again,
Star-slick, the flaking and crusting duff at my feet,

Smoot and Runyan and August Binder
Still in the black pulse of the earth, cloud-gouache
Over the tree line, Mount Caribou
Massive and on the rise and taking it in. And taking it back

To the future we occupied, and will wake to again, ourselves
And our children's children snug in our monk's robes,
Pushing the cauly hoods back, ready to walk out
Into the same night and the meadow grass, in step and on time.

Self-Portrait

Charles on the Trevisan, night bridge
To the crystal, infinite alphabet of his past.
Charles on the San Trovaso, earmarked,
Holding the pages of a thrown-away book, dinghy the color of honey
Under the pine boughs, the water east-flowing.

The wind will edit him soon enough,
And squander his broken chords
in tiny striations above the air,
No slatch in the undertow.
The sunlight will bear him out,
Giving him breathing room, and a place to lie.

And why not? The reindeer still file through the bronchial trees,
Holding their heads high.
The mosses still turn, the broomstraws flash on and off.
Inside, in the crosslight, and St. Jerome
And his creatures . . . St. Augustine, striking the words out.

Holy Thursday

Begins with the *ooo ooo* of a mourning dove
In the pepper tree, crack
Of blue and a flayed light on the hills,
Myself past the pumpkin blooms and out in the disced field,
Blake's children still hunched in sleep, dollops
Of bad dreams and an afterlife.
Canticles rise in spate from the bleeding heart.
Cathedrals assemble and disappear in the water beads.
I scuff at the slick adobe, one eye
On the stalk and one on the aftermath.

There's always a time for rust,
For looking down at the earth and its lateral chains.
There's always a time for the grass, teeming
Its little four-cornered purple flowers,
                                                  tricked out in an oozy shine.
There's always a time for the dirt.
Reprieve, reprieve, the flies drone, their wings
Increasingly incandescent above the corn silk.
No answer from anything, four crows
On a eucalyptus limb, speaking in tongues.
No answer for them, either.

It's noon in the medlar tree, the sun
Sifting its glitter across the powdery stems.
It doesn't believe in God
And still is absolved.
It doesn't believe in God
And seems to get by, going from here to there.

Butterflies blow like pieces of half-burned construction paper over the
sweet weeds,
And take what is given them.
Some hummer is luckier
Downwind, and smells blood, and seeks me out.

The afternoon hangs by a leaf.
The vines are a green complaint
From the slaking adobe dust. I settle and stand back.
The hawk realigns herself.
Splatter of mockingbird notes, a brief trill from the jay.
The fog starts in, breaking its various tufts loose.
Everything smudges and glows,
Cactus, the mustard plants and the corn,
Through the white reaches of four o'clock . . .
There's always a time for words.

Surf sounds in the palm tree,
Susurrations, the wind
making a big move from the west,
The children asleep again, their second selves
Beginning to stir, the moon
Lopsided, sliding their ladder down.
From under the billowing dead, from their wet hands and a saving grace,
The children begin to move, an angle of phosphorescence
Along the ridgeline.
Angels
Are counting cadence, their skeletal songs
What the hymns say, the first page and the last.

Virginia Reel

In Clarke County, the story goes, the family name
Was saved by a single crop of wheat,
The houses and land kept in a clear receipt for the subsequent suicides,
The hard times and non-believers to qualify and disperse:
Woodburn and Cedar Hall, Smithfield, Auburn and North Hill:
Names like white moths kicked up from the tall grass,
Spreading across the countryside
From the Shenandoah to Charles Town and the Blue Ridge.

And so it happened. But none of us lives here now, in any of them,
Though Aunt Roberta is still in town,
Close to the place my great-great-grandfather taught Nelly Custis's
    children once
Answers to Luther. And Cardinal Newman too.
Who cares? Well, I do. It's worth my sighs
To walk here, on the wrong road, tracking a picture back
To its bricks and its point of view.
It's worth my while to be here, crumbling this dirt through my bare hands.

I've come back for the first time in twenty years,
Sand in my shoes, my pockets full of the same wind
That brought me before, my flesh
Remiss in the promises it made then, the absolutes it's heir to.
This is the road they drove on. And this is the rise
Their blood repaired to, removing its gloves.
And this is the dirt their lives were made of, the dirt the world is,
Immeasurable emptiness of all things.

I stand on the porch of Wickliffe Church,
My kinfolk out back in the bee-stitched vines and weeds,

The night coming on, my flat shirt drawing the light in,
Bright bud on the branch of nothing's tree.
In the new shadows, memory starts to shake out its dark cloth.
Everyone settles down, transparent and animate,
Under the oak trees.
Hampton passes the wine around, Jaq toasts to our health.

And when, from the blear and glittering air,
A hand touches my shoulder,
I want to fall to my knees, and keep on falling, here,
Laid down by the articles that bear my names,
The limestone and marble and locust wood.
But that's for another life. Just down the road, at Smithfield, the last of
    the apple blossoms
Fishtails to earth through the shot twilight,
A little vowel for the future, a signal from us to them.

Self-Portrait

Marostica, Val di Ser. Bassano del Grappa.
Madonna del Ortolo. San Giorgio, arc and stone.
The foothills above the Piave.

Places and things that caught my eye, Walt,
In Italy. On foot, Great Cataloguer, some twenty-odd years ago.

San Zeno and Caffè Dante. Catullus' seat.
Lake Garda. The Adige at Ponte Pietra
—I still walk there, a shimmer across the bridge on hot days,
The dust, for a little while, lying lightly along my sleeve—
Piazza Erbe, the twelve Apostles . . .

Over the grave of John Keats
The winter night comes down, her black habit starless and edged with ice,
Pure breaths of those who are rising from the dead.

Dino Campana, Arthur Rimbaud.
Hart Crane and Emily Dickinson. The Black Château.

Called Back

Friday arrives with all its attendant ecstasies.
Mirrors bloom in the hushed beds.

The ocotillo starts to extend
                        its orange tongues
Down in Sonora, the cactus puts on its beads.
Juan Quesada's Angel of Death, socket and marrow bone,
Stares from its cage and scorched eyes.

I've made my overtures to the Black Dog, and backed off.
I've touched the links in its gold chain.
I've called out and bent down and even acknowledged my own face.

Darkness, O Father of Charity, lay on your hands.

For over an hour the joy of the mockingbird has altered the leaves.
Stealthily, blossoms have settled along the bougainvillaea like purple
  moths
Catching their breaths, the sky still warm to the touch.
Nothing descends like snow or stiff wings
Out of the night.
                Only the dew falls, soft as the footsteps of the dead.

Language can do just so much,
                                                            a flurry of prayers,
A chatter of glass beside the road's edge,
Flash and a half-glint as the headlights pass . . .

When the oak tree and the Easter grass have taken my body,
I'll start to count out my days, beginning at one.

Self-Portrait

In Murray, Kentucky, I lay once
On my side, the ghost-weight of a past life in my arms,
A life not mine. I know she was there,
Asking for nothing, heavy as bad luck, still waiting to rise.
I know now and I lift her.

Evening becomes us.
I see myself in a tight dissolve, and answer to no one.
Self-traitor, I smuggle in
The spider love, undoer and rearranger of all things.
Angel of Mercy, strip me down.

This world is a little place,
Just red in the sky before the sun rises.
Hold hands, hold hands
That when the birds start, none of us is missing.
Hold hands, hold hands.

Composition in Grey and Pink

The souls of the day's dead fly up like birds, big sister,
The sky shutters and casts loose.
And faster than stars the body goes to the earth.

Heat hangs like a mist from the trees.
Butterflies pump through the banked fires of late afternoon.
The rose continues its sure rise to the self.

Ashes, trampled garlands . . .

I dream of an incandescent space
                                        where nothing distinct exists,
And where nothing ends, the days sliding like warm milk through the
    clouds,
Everyone's name in chalk letters once and for all,

The dogstar descending with its pestilent breath . . .

Fatherless, stiller than still water,
I want to complete my flesh
                                    and sit in a quiet corner
Untied from God, where the dead don't sing in their sleep.

Laguna Blues

It's Saturday afternoon at the edge of the world.
White pages lift in the wind and fall.
Dust threads, cut loose from the heart, float up and fall.

Something's off-key in my mind.
Whatever it is, it bothers me all the time.

It's hot, and the wind blows on what I have had to say.
I'm dancing a little dance.
The crows pick up a thermal that angles away from the sea.
I'm singing a little song.
Whatever it is, it bothers me all the time.

It's Saturday afternoon and the crows glide down,
Black pages that lift and fall.
The castor beans and the pepper plant trundle their weary heads.
Something's off-key and unkind.
Whatever it is, it bothers me all the time.

Driving Through Tennessee

It's strange what the past brings back.
Our parents, for instance, how ardently they still loom
In the brief and flushed
Fleshtones of memory, one foot in front of the next
Even in retrospect, and so unimpeachable.

And towns that we lived in once,
And who we were then, the roads we went back and forth on
Returning ahead of us like rime
In the moonlight's fall, and Jesus returning, and Stephen Martyr
And St. Paul of the Sword . . .

—I am their music,
Mothers and fathers and places we hurried through in the night:

I put my mouth to the dust and sing their song.
Remember us, Galeoto, and whistle our tune, when the time comes,
For charity's sake.

Landscape with Seated Figure and Olive Trees

Orange blossoms have dropped their threads
On the stone floor of the heart
                                        more often than once
Between last night's stars and last night's stars.
And the Preludes have left their rings
On the chalk white of the walls.
                                        And the slide-harp has played and played.

And now, under the fruit trees,
                                        the olives silver then not silver, the wind
In them then not, the old man
Sits in the sunfall,
Slouched and at ease in the sunfall, the leaves tipped in the wind.

The world is nothing to him.
And the music is nothing to him, and the noon sun.
Only the wind matters.
Only the wind as it moves through the tin shine of the leaves.
And the orange blossoms,
                                        scattered like poems on the smooth stones.

Dog Yoga

A spring day in the weeds.
A thread of spittle across the sky, and a thread of ash.
Mournful cadences from the clouds.

Through the drives and the cypress beds,
                                        twenty-five years of sad news.

Mother of Thrushes, Our Lady of Crows,
Brief as a handkerchief,
                        twenty-five years of sad news.

Later, stars and sea winds in and out of the open window.

Later, and lonesome among the sleepers,
                                    the day's thunder in hidden places,
One lissome cheek a notch in the noontide's leash,

A ghostly rain of sunlight among the ferns.

Year in, year out, the same loom from the dark.
Year in, year out, the same sound in the wind.

Near dawn, the void in the heart,
The last coat of lacquer along the leaves,
                                        the quench in the west.

California Spring

At dawn the dove croons.
A hawk hangs over the field.
The liquidambar rinses its hundred hands.

And the light comes on in the pepper trees.
Under its flat surfaces horns and noises are starting up.
The dewdrops begin to shrink.

How sad the morning is.
There is a tree which rains down in the field.
There is a spider that swings back and forth on his thin strings in the heart.

How cold the wind is.
And the sun is, caught like a kite in the drooped limbs of the tree.
The apricot blossoms scatter across the ice plant.

One angel dangles his wing.
The grass edges creak and the tide pools begin to shine.
Nothing forgives.

Laguna Dantesca

I want, like a little boat, to be isolate,
slipping across one element
Toward the horizon, whose lips know something but stay sealed
under the heaven of the moon.

There's something I want to look on, face to face.

Like a rock, or some other heavy thing, I want to descend through clear water
Endlessly,
disappearing as she did,
Line after leached line, into the lunar deeps.

I want, like these lavender bells from the jacaranda tree,
To flare with the fixed stars,
used up and self-satisfied.

Tree frogs drum in the dark. The small brass of the natural world
Is drumming and what I want
                                        is nothing to them.

Above me, the big dog lies low in the southern sky and bides its time.

Like a scrap of charred paper, I want to return.
There's something I want to look on whose face
                                                            rises and falls like a flame.

I want to sit down there, the dog asleep at my feet.

Dog Day Vespers

Sun like an orange mousse through the trees,
A snowfall of trumpet bells on the oleander;
                                                        mantis paws
Craning out of the new wisteria; fruit smears in the west . . .
DeStael knifes a sail on the bay;
A mother's summons hangs like a towel on the dusk's hook.

Everything drips and spins
In the pepper trees, the pastel glide of the evening
Slowing to mother-of-pearl and the night sky.
Venus breaks clear in the third heaven.
Quickly the world is capped, and the seal turned.

I drag my chair to the deck's edge and the blue ferns.
I'm writing you now by flashlight,
The same news and the same story I've told you often before.

As the stag-stars begin to shine,
A wing brushes my left hand,
                                        but it's not my wing.

Portrait of the Artist with Hart Crane

It's Venice, late August, outside after lunch, and Hart
Is stubbing his cigarette butt in a wineglass,
The look on his face pre-moistened and antiseptic,
A little like death or a smooth cloud.
The watery light of his future still clings in the pergola.

The subject of all poems is the clock,
I think, those tiny, untouchable hands that fold across our chests
Each night and unfold each morning, finger by finger,
Under the new weight of the sun.
One day more is one day less.

I've been writing this poem for weeks now
With a pencil made of rain, smudging my face
And my friend's face, making a language where nothing stays.
The sunlight has no such desire.
In the small pools of our words, its business is radiance.

Portrait of the Artist with Li Po

The "high heavenly priest of the White Lake" is now
A small mound in an endless plain of grass,
His pendants clicking and pearls shading his eyes.

He never said anything about the life after death,
Whose body is clothed in a blue rust and the smoke of dew.

He liked flowers and water most.
Everyone knows the true story of how he would write his verses and float them,
Like paper boats, downstream
just to watch them drift away.
Death never entered his poems, but rowed, with its hair down, far out on the lake,
Laughing and looking up at the sky.

Over a thousand years later, I write out one of his lines in a notebook,
The peach blossom follows the moving water,
And watch the October darkness gather against the hills.
All night long the river of heaven will move westward while no one notices.
The distance between the dead and the living
is more than a heartbeat and a breath.

The Monastery at Vršac

We've walked the grounds,
inspected the vaults and the old church,
Looked at the icons and carved stalls,

And followed the path to the bishop's grave.

Now we sit in the brandy-colored light of late afternoon
Under the locust trees,
attended and small

From the monastery. Two nuns hop back and forth like grackles
Along the path. The light drips from the leaves.

Little signals of dust rise uninterpreted from the road.
The grass drones in its puddle of solitude.

The stillness is awful, as though from the inside of a root . . .

—Time's sluice and the summer rains erode our hearts
                                        and carry our lives away.
We hold what we can in our two hands,
Sinking, each year, another inch in the earth . . .

Mercy upon us,
                    we who have learned to preach but not to pray.

Hawaii Dantesca

White-sided flowers are thrusting up on the hillside,
                                        blank love letters from the dead.
It's autumn, and nobody seems to mind.

Or the broken shadows of those missing for hundreds of years
Moving over the sugar cane
                            like storks, which nobody marks or mends.

This is the story line.

And the viridescent shirtwaists of light the trees wear.
And the sutra-circles of cattle egrets wheeling out past the rain showers.
And the spiked marimbas of dawn rattling their amulets . . .

Soon it will be time for the long walk under the earth toward the sea.

And time to retrieve the yellow sunsuit and little shoes
                                                            they took my picture in
In Knoxville, in 1938.

Time to gather the fire in its quartz bowl.

I hope the one with the white wings will come.
I hope the island of reeds is as far away as I think it is.

When I get there, I hope they forgive me if the knot I tie is the wrong
   knot.

Ars Poetica

I like it back here

Under the green swatch of the pepper tree and the aloe vera.
I like it because the wind strips down the leaves without a word.
I like it because the wind repeats itself,
                                                  and the leaves do.

I like it because I'm better here than I am there,

Surrounded by fetishes and figures of speech:
Dog's tooth and whale's tooth, my father's shoe, the dead weight
Of winter, the inarticulation of joy . . .

The spirits are everywhere.

And once I have them called down from the sky, and spinning and
    dancing in the palm of my hand,
What will it satisfy?
                                        I'll still have

The voices rising out of the ground,
The fallen star my blood feeds,
                                        this business I waste my heart on.

And nothing stops that.

Bar Giamaica, 1959–60

Grace is the focal point,
                                        the tip ends of her loosed hair
Like match fire in the back light,
Her hands in a "Here's the church . . ."
                                        She's looking at Ugo Mulas,
Who's looking at us.

Ingrid is writing this all down, and glances up, and stares hard.

This still isn't clear.

I'm looking at Grace, and Goldstein and Borsuk and Dick Venezia
Are looking at me.
                                        Yola keeps reading her book.

And that leaves the rest of them: Susan and Elena and Carl Glass.
And Thorp and Schimmel and Jim Gates,
                                        and Hobart and Schneeman

One afternoon in Milan in the late spring.

Then Ugo finishes, drinks a coffee, and everyone goes away.
Summer arrives, and winter;
                                        the snow falls and no one comes back
Ever again,
                all of them gone through the star filter of memory,
With its small gravel and metal tables and passers-by . . .

Gate City Breakdown

Like a vein of hard coal, it was the strike
We fantasized, the pocket of sure reward we sidestepped the roadblocks
  for
In southwest Virginia, seamed in its hillside
Above the North Fork of the Holston River.

One afternoon before Christmas
In 1953, we crossed the bridge from Tennessee on a whiskey run,
Churchill and Bevo Hammond and Philbeck and I,
All home for the holidays.
On the back road where they chased us, we left the Sheriff's Patrol in
  their own dust,
And washed ours down with Schlitz on the way home.

Jesus, it's so ridiculous, and full of self-love,
The way we remember ourselves,
                                                and the dust we leave . . .
Remember me as you will, but remember me once
Slide-wheeling around the curves,
                                            letting it out on the other side of the line.

New Year's Eve, 1979

After the picture show, the explanation is usually found in
The moralistic overtones of our lives:
We are what we've always been,
Everybody uses somebody,
In the slow rise to the self, we're drawn up by many hands.

And so it is here.
                    Will Charles look on happiness in this life?
Will the past be the present ever again?
Will the dead abandon their burdens and walk to the riverbank?

In this place, at year's end, under a fitful moon, tide pools
Spindle the light.
Across their floors, like spiders,
Hermit crabs quarter and spin.
                              Their sky is a glaze and a day . . .

What matters to them is what comes up from below, and from out there
In the deep water,
                    and where the deep water comes from.

LAGUNA BEACH

The Southern Cross

Things that divine us we never touch:

The black sounds of the night music,
The Southern Cross, like a kite at the end of its string,

And now this sunrise, and empty sleeve of a day,
The rain just starting to fall, and then not fall,

No trace of a story line.

All day I've remembered a lake and a sudsy shoreline,
Gauze curtains blowing in and out of open windows all over the South.

It's 1936, in Tennessee. I'm one
And spraying the dead grass with a hose.
The curtains blow in and out.

And then it's not. And I'm not and they're not.

Or it's 1941 in a brown suit, or '53 in its white shoes,
Overlay after overlay tumbled and brought back,
As meaningless as the sea would be
                    if the sea could remember its waves . . .

Nothing had told me my days were marked for a doom
                    under the cold stars of the Virgin.
Nothing had told me that woe would buzz at my side like a fly.

The morning is dark with spring.
The early blooms on the honeysuckle shine like maggots after the rain.
The purple mouths of the passion blossoms
                    open their white gums to the wind.

How sweet the past is, no matter how wrong, or how sad.
How sweet is yesterday's noise.

All day the ocean was like regret,
clearing its throat, brooding and self-absorbed.

Now the wisteria tendrils extend themselves like swans' necks under Orion.

Now the small stars in the orange trees.

At Garda, on Punto San Vigilio, the lake,
In springtime, is like the sea,
Wind fishtailing the olive leaves like slash minnows beneath the vineyards,
Ebb and flow of the sunset past Sirmio,
flat voice of the waters
Retelling their story, again and again, as though to unburden itself

Of an unforgotten guilt,
and not relieved
Under the soothing hand of the dark,

The clouds over Bardolino dragging the sky for the dead
Bodies of those who refuse to rise,
Their orange robes and flaming bodices trolling across the hills,

Nightwind by now in the olive trees,
No sound but the wind from anything
under the tired Italian stars . . .
And the voice of the waters, starting its ghostly litany.

River of sighs and forgetfulness
                                        (and the secret light Campana saw),
River of bloom-bursts from the moon,
                                        of slivers and broken blades from the moon
In an always-going-away of glints . . .

Dante and Can Grande once stood here,
Next to the cool breath of S. Anastasia,
                                        watching the cypress candles
Flare in their deep green across the Adige
In the Giusti Gardens.
                                        Before that, in his marble tier,
Catullus once sat through the afternoons.
Before that, God spoke in the rocks . . .

And now it's my turn to stand
Watching a different light do the same things on a different water,
The Adige bearing its gifts
                                        through the April twilight of 1961.

When my father went soldiering, apes dropped from the trees.
When my mother wrote home from bed, the stars asked for a pardon.

They're both ghosts now, haunting the chairs and the sugar chest.

From time to time I hear their voices drifting like smoke through the
    living room,
Touching the various things they owned once.
Now they own nothing
                                        and drift like smoke through the living room.

Thinking of Dante, I start to feel
What I think are wings beginning to push out from my shoulder blades,
And the firm pull of water under my feet.

Thinking of Dante, I think of La Pia,
                                        and Charles Martel
And Cacciaguida inside the great flower of Paradise,
And the thin stem of Purgatory
                                    rooted in Hell.

Thinking of Dante is thinking about the other side,
And the other side of the other side.
It's thinking about the noon noise and the daily light.

Here is the truth. The wind rose, the sea
Shuffled its blue deck and dealt you a hand:
Blank, blank, blank, blank, blank.
Pelicans rode on the flat back of the waves through the green afternoon.
Gulls malingered along its breezes.
The huge cross of an airplane's shadow hurried across the sand,
                                                  but no one stayed on it
For long, and nobody said a word.
You could see the island out past the orange gauze of the smog.

The Big Dipper has followed me all the days of my life.
Under its tin stars my past has come and gone.

Tonight, in the April glaze
                                        and scrimshaw of the sky,
It blesses me once again
With its black water, and sends me on.

After twelve years it's hard to recall
That defining sound the canal made at sundown, slap
Of tide swill on the church steps,
Little runnels of boat wash slipping back from the granite slabs
In front of Toio's, undulant ripples
Flattening out in small hisses, the oily rainbows regaining their loose shapes
Silently, mewling and quick yelps of the gulls
Wheeling from shadow into the pink and grey light over the Zattere,
Lapping and rocking of water endlessly,
At last like a low drone in the dark shell of the ear
As the night lifted like mist from the Ogni Santi
And San Sebastiano
                                into the cold pearl of the sky . . .

All that year it lullabied just outside my window
As Venice rode through my sleep like a great spider,
Flawless and Byzantine,
                                        webbed like glass in its clear zinc.
In winter the rain fell
                                    and the locust fell.
In summer the sun rose
Like a whetstone over the steel prows of the gondolas,
Their silver beak-blades rising and falling,
                                                            the water whiter than stone.
In autumn the floods came, and oil as thick as leaves in the entry way.

In spring, at evening, under the still-warm umbrellas,
We watched the lights blaze and extend
                                        along the rio,
And watched the black boats approaching, almost without sound.
And still the waters sang lullaby.

I remember myself as a figure among the colonnades,
Leaning from left to right,
                              one hand in my pocket,
The way the light fell,
                              the other one holding me up.
I remember myself as a slick on the slick canals,
Going the way the tide went,
The city sunk to her knees in her own reflection.
I remember the way that Pound walked
                                        across San Marco
At *passeggiata*, as though with no one,
                                        his eyes on the long ago.
I remember the time that Tate came.
                                        And Palazzo Guggenheim
When the floods rose
                              and the boat took us all the way
Through the front doors and down to the back half
Of *da Montin*, where everyone was, clapping their hands.

What's hard to remember is how the wind moved and the reeds clicked
Behind Torcello,
                         little bundles of wind in the marsh grass
Chasing their own tails, and skidding across the water.
What's hard to remember is how the electric lights
Were played back, and rose and fell on the black canal
Like swamp flowers,
                              shrinking and stretching,

Yellow and pale and iron-blue from the oil.
It's hard to remember the way the snow looked
on San Gregorio,
And melting inside the pitch tubs and the smoke of San Trovaso,
The gondolas beached and stripped,
The huge snowflakes planing down through the sea-heavy air
Like dead moths,
drifting and turning . . .

As always, silence will have the last word,
And Venice will lie like silk
at the edge of the sea and the night sky,
Albescent under the moon.
Everyone's life is the same life
if you live long enough.

Orioles shuttle like gold thread
through the grey cloth of daylight.
The fog is so low and weighted down
Crows fall through like black notes from the sky.
The orioles stitch and weave.
Somewhere below, the ocean nervously grinds its teeth
As the morning begins to take hold
and the palm trees gleam.

There is an otherness inside us
We never touch,
no matter how far down our hands reach.

It is the past,
                    with its good looks and *Anytime, Anywhere* . . .
Our prayers go out to it, our arms go out to it
Year after year,
But who can ever remember enough?

Friday again, with its sack of bad dreams
And long-legged birds,
                              a handful of ashes for this and that
In the streets, and some for the squat piano.

Friday beneath the sky, its little postcards of melancholy
Outside each window,
                              the engines inside the roses at half speed,
The huge page of the sea with its one word *despair*,

Fuchsia blossoms littered across the deck,
Unblotted tide pools of darkness beneath the ferns . . .
And still I go on looking,
                                match after match in the black air.

The lime, electric green of the April sea
                                              off Ischia
Is just a thumb-rub on the window glass between here and there:
And the cloud cap above the volcano
That didn't move when the sea wind moved;
And the morning the doves came, low from the mountain's shadow,
                                                       under the sunlight,
Over the damp tops of the vine rows,

Eye-high in a scythe slip that dipped and rose and cut down toward the sea;
And the houses like candy wrappers blown up against the hillside
Above Sant'Angelo,
                    fuchsia and mauve and cyclamen;
And the story Nicola told,
How the turtle doves come up from Africa
On the desert winds,
                    how the hunters take the fresh seeds
From their crops and plant them,
The town windows all summer streaked with the nameless blooms.

The landscape was always the best part.

Places swim up and sink back, and days do,
The edges around what really happened
                                        we'll never remember
No matter how hard we stare back at the past:

One April, in downtown Seville,
                                alone on an Easter morning
Wasted in emerald light from the lemon trees,
I watched a small frog go back and forth on the lily pads
For hours, and still don't know
                                just what I was staying away from . . .

(And who could forget Milano in '59,
                                    all winter under the rain?
Cathedrals for sure,
And dry stops in the Brera,
                            all of her boulevards ending in vacant lots.

And Hydra and Mykonos,
Barely breaking the calm with their white backs
As they roll over
                    and flash back down to the dark . . .)

Places swim up and sink back, and days do,
Larger and less distinct each year,
As we are,
                and lolling about in the same redress,
Leaves and insects drifting by on their windows.

Rome was never like that,
                              and the Tiber was never like that,
Nosing down from the Apennines,
                              color of *café-au-lait* as it went through town . . .

Still, I can't remember the name of one street
                                                  near Regina Coeli,
Or one block of the Lungotevere on either side,
Or one name of one shop on Campo dei Fiori.
Only Giordano Bruno,
                            with his razed look and black caul,
Rises unbidden out of the blank
Unruffled waters of memory,
                                his martyred bronze
Gleaming and still wet in the single electric light.

I can't remember the colors I said I'd never forget
On Via Giulia at sundown,
The ochers and glazes and bright hennas of each house,
Or a single day from November of 1964.

I can't remember the way the stairs smelled
or the hallway smelled
At Piazza del Biscione.
Or just how the light fell
Through the east-facing window over the wicker chairs there.

I do remember the way the boar hung
in the butcher shop at Christmas
Two streets from the Trevi fountain, a crown of holly and mistletoe
Jauntily over his left ear.
I do remember the flower paintings
Nodding throughout the May afternoons
on the dining-room walls
At Zajac's place.
And the reliquary mornings,
And Easter, and both Days of the Dead . . .

At noon in the English Cemetery no one's around.
Keats is off to the left, in an open view.
Shelley and Someone's son are straight up ahead.

With their marble breath and their marble names,
the sun in a quick squint through the trees,
They lie at the edge of everywhere,
Rome like a stone cloud at the back of their eyes.

Time is the villain in most tales,
and here, too,
Lowering its stiff body into the water.
Its landscape is the resurrection of the word,
No end of it,
the petals of wreckage in everything.

I've been sitting here tracking the floor plan
of a tiny, mottled log spider
Across the front porch of the cabin,
And now she's under my chair,
off to her own devices,
Leaving me mine, and I start watching the two creeks

Come down through the great meadow
Under the lodgepole pine and the willow run,
The end of June beginning to come clear in the clouds,
Shadows like drowned men where the creeks go under the hill.

Last night, in the flood run of the moon, the bullbats
Diving out of the yellow sky
with their lonesome and jungly whistling,
I watched, as I've watched before, the waters send up their smoke signals
of blue mist,
And thought, for the first time,
I half-understood what they keep on trying to say.

But now I'm not sure.
Behind my back, the spider has got her instructions
And carries them out.
Flies drone, wind back-combs the marsh grass, swallows bank and climb.
Everything I can see knows just what to do,

Even the dragonfly, hanging like lapis lazuli in the sun . . .

I can't remember enough.

How the hills, for instance, at dawn in Kingsport
In late December in 1962 were black
against a sky
The color of pale fish blood and water that ran to white
As I got ready to leave home for the hundredth time,
My mother and father asleep,
my sister asleep,
Carter's Valley as dark as the inside of a bone
Below the ridge,
the first knobs of the Great Smokies
Beginning to stick through the sunrise,
The hard pull of a semi making the grade up U.S. 11W,
The cold with its metal teeth ticking against the window,
The long sigh of the screen door stop,
My headlights starting to disappear
in the day's new turning . . .

I'll never be able to.

Sunday, a brute bumblebee working the clover tops
Next to the step I'm sitting on,
sticking his huge head
Into each tiny, white envelope.
The hot sun of July, in the high Montana air, bastes a sweet glaze
On the tamarack and meadow grass.
In the blue shadows
moist curls of the lupine glide
And the bog lilies extinguish their mellow lamps . . .

Sunday, a *Let us pray* from the wind, a glint
Of silver among the willows.
                                        The lilacs begin to bleed
In their new sleep, and the golden vestments of morning
Lift for a moment, then settle back into place.
The last of the dog roses offers itself by the woodpile.
Everything has its work,
                                        everything written down
In a secondhand grace of solitude and tall trees . . .

August licks at the pine trees.
Sun haze, and little fugues from the creek.
Fern-sleep beneath the green skirt of the marsh.

I always imagine a mouth
Starting to open its blue lips
Inside me, an arm
                                curving sorrowfully over an open window
At evening, and toads leaping out of the wet grass.

Again the silence of flowers.
Again the faint notes of piano music back in the woods.
How easily summer fills the room.

The life of this world is wind.
Windblown we come, and windblown we go away.
All that we look on is windfall.
All we remember is wind.

Pickwick was never the wind . . .

It's what we forget that defines us, and stays in the same place,
And waits to be rediscovered.
Somewhere in all that network of rivers and roads and silt hills,
A city I'll never remember,
                                        its walls the color of pure light,
Lies in the August heat of 1935,
In Tennessee, the bottomland slowly becoming a lake.
It lies in a landscape that keeps my imprint
Forever,
            and stays unchanged, and waits to be filled back in.
Someday I'll find it out
And enter my old outline as though for the first time,

And lie down, and tell no one.

FROM

THE OTHER SIDE OF THE RIVER

(1984)

Lost Bodies

Last night I thought of Torri del Benaco again,
Its almond trees in blossom,
                                        its cypresses clothed in their dark fire,

And the words carved on that concrete cross

I passed each day of my life
In Kingsport going to town
                                        GET RIGHT WITH GOD / JESUS IS COMING SOON.

If I had it all to do over again
                                        I'd be a Medievalist.
I'd thoroughly purge my own floor.

Something's for sure in the clouds, but it's not for me,

Though all the while that light tips the fast-moving water,
East wind in a rush through the almond trees.

The cross was opposite Fleenor's Cabins below the hill
On U.S. 11W.
Harold Shipley told me, when I was twelve,
                                        he'd seen a woman undressed

In the back seat of a Buick, between two men,
                                        her cunt shaved clean,

In front of the motel office.
They gave him a dollar, he said, to stick his finger up there.

What can you say to that?
                                        everything Jesus promised

(My five senses waiting apart in their grey hoods,
Touching their beads,
                                    licking the ashes that stained their lips)

And someone to tell it to.

Torri del Benaco, on the east side of Lake Garda,
Was north past Peschiera and San Vigilio,
                                                        under the Bardolino hills.
I seldom went there, and remember it poorly.

One Sunday, I drove through town on my way to Riva at the top of the lake.
An east wind was blowing out toward the water,

Down through the vineyards, and down through the trees at the lake's edge.

I remember the cypress nods in its warm breath.
I remember the almond blossoms
                                                floating out on the waves, west to Salò.
I remember the way they looked there,
                                                     a small flotilla of matches.

I remember their flash in the sun's flare.

You've got to sign your name to something, it seems to me.
And so we rephrase the questions
Endlessly,
                hoping the answer might somehow change.

Still, a piece of his heart is not a piece of your heart,
Sweet Jesus, and never will be, but stays
A little window into the past,
                                        increasingly licked transparent
And out of shape.

When you die, you fall down,
                                        you don't rise up
Like a scrap of burnt paper into the everlasting.
Each morning we learn this painfully,
                        pulling our bodies up by the roots from their deep sleep.

Nobody takes that road now.
                                        The tourist cabins are gone,
And Harold, and Rose Dials
Who lived in a tarpaper shack just off the highway,
Nailed hard to the mountainside.
                                        And the two men and the Buick too,
Long gone down the Interstate
And the satellites that have taken us all from town.

Only the cross is still there, sunk deeper into the red clay
Than anyone could have set it.

And that luminous, nameless body whose flesh takes on
The mottoes we say we live by . . .

Of all the places around the lake,
                                        I've loved Sirmione best,
Its brilliant winks in the sun
And glassy exceptions like a trace in the mind.

Others stay in the memory like pieces of songs
You think you remember but don't,
                                        only a phrase here and there
Surfacing as it should, and in tune.

Gardone and Desenzano are like that, and Torri del Benaco.

Mostly what I remember is one garden, outside the town of Garda,
Between the lake's edge and the road:
Corn and beans, it looked like, and squash and finocchio.

All things that come to him come under his feet
In a glorious body,
                        they say. And why not?
It beats the alternative, the mighty working
Set to subdue the celestial flesh.

And does so, letting the grass go stiff, and the needles brown,

Letting the dirt take over. This is as far as it goes,
Where deer browse the understory and jays
                                                leap through the trees,

Where chainsaws
Whittle away at the darkness, and diesel rigs
Carry our deaths all night through the endless rain.

Lost Souls

From the bad eye and early morning
                                        you raise me
Unshuttered from the body of ashes
                                        you raise me
Out of the dust and moth light
                                   memory
Into the undertow of my own life
                                      you make me remember

I never dreamed of anything as a child.
I just assumed it was all next door,
                                      or day-after-tomorrow at least,
A different shirt I'd put on when the time was right.

It hasn't worked out that way.

My father wrote out his dreams on lined paper, as I do now,
And gave them up to the priest
                                   for both to come to terms with.
I give you mine for the same reason,

To summon the spirits up and set the body to music.

The last time I saw George Vaughan,
He was standing in front of my father's casket at the laying out,
One of the kindest men I've ever known.

When I was sixteen, he taught me the way to use a jackhammer,
                                        putting the hand grip
Into my stomach and clinching down,
Riding it out till the jarring became a straight line.

He taught me the way a shovel breathes,
And how the red clay gives away nothing.
He took my hand when my hand needed taking.

And I didn't even remember his name.

One evening in 1957 I found myself outside of Nashville,
                                        face down on the ground,
A straw in my mouth, the straw stuck deep
In the ginned heart of a watermelon,
                                the faces of five friends
Almost touching my face
As we sucked the sweet gin as fast as we could.

Over the green hinge of the Cumberland Plateau
The eyelash dusk of July was coming down
                                effortlessly, smooth as an oiled joint.
Agnes rolled over and looked up at the sky.
Her cousin, our host, rolled over and looked up at the sky.

What a life, he said. Jesus, he said, what a life.

Nobody needs to remember the Kingsport *Times-News*
In the summer of 1953,
                                        but I do,
Disguised to myself as a newspaperman on my slow way
To the city jail to check the drunk tank,
                                                                full summer and after supper,
Korea just over, the neon of Wallace's News and Parks-Belk
Lying along the sidewalk like tear sheets of tinted plastic,
Across Center and down to Freel's Drug,
                                                                  then left, and then left again
Into the blowing shadow and light
Under the elm trees,
The world and its disregard in the palm of my hand.

Nobody needs to remember the smell of bay rum
And disinfectant,
                                  the desperate grey faces
Of dirt farmers caught in the wrong dark at the wrong time,
Bib overalls sour with sweat and high water,
Brogans cracked and half broken,
                                                      the residue
Of all our illuminations and unnamed lives . . .
At least I thought that then.
And nobody needs to remember any of that,
                                                                      but I do.

What *does* one do with one's life? A shelf-and-a-half
Of magazines, pictures on all the walls
Of the way I was, and everyone standing next to me?
This one, for instance for instance for instance . . .

Nothing's like anything else in the long run.
Nothing you write down is ever as true as you think it was.

But so what? Churchill and I and Bill Ring
Will still be chasing that same dead pintail duck
down the same rapids in 1951
Of the Holston River. And Ted Glynn
Will be running too.
And 1951 will always be 1951.

A little curtain of flesh, Blake said,
For his own reasons . . .
And I had mine to draw it last night on the Wasatch Range
And pull it back as the sun rose
over the north fork
And blue weave of the Cumberlands.
It was June again, and 1964 again,
and I still wasn't there
As they laid her down and my father turned away,
I still imagine, precisely, into the cave of cold air
He lived in for eight more years, the cars
Below my window in Rome honking maniacally
O still small voice of calm . . .

Lonesome Pine Special

I was walking out this morning with rambling on my mind.

—SARA CARTER

There's a curve in the road, and a slow curve in the land,
Outside of Barbourville, Kentucky, on U.S. 25E,

I've always liked
                    each time I've passed it,
Bottomland, river against a ridge to the west,
A few farmhouses on each side of the road, some mailboxes
Next to a dirt lane that leads off through the fields.
Each time I'd think
                        How pleasant it must be to live here.

In Kingsport, when I was growing up,
Everyone seemed to go to Big Stone Gap, Virginia, up U.S. 23,
All the time.
                Everyone had an uncle or aunt there,
Or played golf, or traded cars.
They were always going up there
                                    to get married, or get liquor,
Or to get what was owed them
By someone they'd been in the service with.

Lone went up there more often than anyone else did,
Part of his territory for State Farm,
                                    somebody said,
Without much conviction.

When the talk turned to whiskey,
                                    and everyone dusted his best lie off,
We all knew, or thought we knew, where Lone went
With his funny walk and broken back
He could hit a golf ball a ton with,
                                    even if he did stand sideways
Like a man hauling a body out of the water,
Being the real owner, we thought, of that gas station out on the
  Jonesboro highway

You went to the back of
for a pint after 10 p.m.,
Lone getting richer and richer until the Moose Lodge
Started to take his business away
by doing it legal, and during the daylight.

So Lone went back, we all thought,
To stumping around the golf course, still
Hitting it sideways, still selling whatever he could
To anyone foolish enough to play him and pay him,
Old Lone, slicker than owl oil.

It was all so American,
The picket fence of wrought iron a hundred years old,
Lilacs at every corner of the lawned yard
in great heaps and folds,
A white house and wild alfalfa in scattered knots
Between the fence and the cracked sidewalk,
The wind from the Sawtooth Mountains
riffling the dust in slow eddies along the street
Near the end of June in Hailey, Idaho,
The house where Pound was born,
with its red maple floors
And small windows two blocks from Idaho 75,
Hemingway ten miles on up the same road between two evergreens,
Nobody noticing either place
as the cars went through town
All night and all day, going north, going south . . .

Another landscape I liked
Was south of Wytheville, Virginia, on U.S. 52
Just short of the Carolina line,
                                        a steel bridge over the New River,
Pasture on both sides of the road and woods on the easy slopes,
Big shrubs and trees lining the riverbanks like fur,
The road and the river both
Angling back toward the Iron Mountains,
The valley bulging out to the east
                                            in a graceful swirl,
The dead chestnut trees like grey candles
Wherever the woods began . . .

What is it about a known landscape
                                                that tends to undo us,
That shuffles and picks us out
For terminal demarcation, the way a field of lupine
Seen in profusion deep in the timber
Suddenly seems to rise like a lavender ground fog
At noon?
            What is it inside the imagination that keeps surprising us
At odd moments
                     when something is given back
We didn't know we had had
In solitude, spontaneously, and with great joy?

Today, at midsummer noon, I took the wooden floats
To the Yaak River, the small ones I'd carved from the larch
And cedar chips,
                     and loosed them downstream
To carry my sins away, as the palace guardians did each year at this time

In medieval Japan,
Where the river goes under the new bridge
                                        on County 508
And the first homesteaders took up their quarter sections.
From Sam Runyan's to Susie Speed's,
Through white water and rock and the tendrilous shade
Of the tamaracks,
                        out into rubbery blotches of sunlight,
The floats' shadows hanging beneath them like odd anchors
Along the pebbled bottom, the river slowing and widening,
The floats at great distances from one another
Past Binder's cabin under the black
                                    of the evergreen-covered dam
And over the falls and gone into foam and next year . . .

In the world of dirt, each tactile thing
                                        repeats the untouchable
In its own way, and in its own time.
Just short of Tryon, North Carolina, on U.S. 176,
Going south down the old Saluda Grade,
                                        kudzu has grown up
And over the tops of miles of oak trees and pine trees,
A wall of vines a hundred feet high, or used to be,
Into South Carolina,
That would have gone for a hundred more with the right scaffolding,
Rising out of the rock and hard clay in thin, prickly ropes
To snake and thread in daily measurable distances
Over anything still enough long enough,
                                        and working its way
Out of the darkness and overhang of its own coils
To break again and again

Into the sunlight, worthless and everywhere,
                                        breathing, breathing,
Looking for leverage and a place to climb.

It's true, I think, as Kenkō says in his *Idleness*,
That all beauty depends upon disappearance,
The bitten edges of things,
                         the gradual sliding away
Into tissue and memory,
                       the uncertainty
And dazzling impermanence of days we beg our meanings from,
And their frayed loveliness.

Going west out of Kalispell, Montana, on U.S. 2,
If you turned off at Kila,
                       and skirted the big slough
Where Doagie Duncan killed three men some seventy years ago
After a fight over muskrat hides,
Then turned south toward the timber
                                  and higher ground
On the dirt road to the Flathead Mine,
Past Sundelius' homestead and up toward Brown's Meadows,
Then swung down where the mine road
                                   branches right and doubles back,
You'd come through the thinning spruce and fir
And lodgepole pine to the suddenly open hillsides
And deep draws
                 of the Hog Heaven country
And start to see what I mean, the bunchgrass and bitterroot
And wild clover flattening under the wind
As you turned from the dirt road,
                              opened the Kansas gate

And began to follow with great care
The overgrown wagon ruts through the blowing field,
                                        the huge tamarack snag,
Where the tracks end and the cabin is,
Black in the sunlight's wash and flow
                                        just under the hill's crown,
Pulling you down like weight to the front door . . .

The cabin is still sizable, four rooms and the walls made
Of planed lumber inside,
                                        the outside chinked with mud
And cement, everything fifty years
Past habitation, the whole structure
                                        leaning into the hillside,
Windowless, doorless, and oddly beautiful in its desolation
And attitude, and not like
The cold and isolate misery it must have stood for
When someone lived here, and heard, at night,
This same wind sluicing the jack pines
                                        and ruined apple trees
In the orchard, and felt the immensity
Loneliness brings moving under his skin
Like a live thing, and emptiness everywhere like a live thing
Beyond the window's reach and fire's glare . . .

Whoever remembers that best owns all this now.
And after him it belongs to the wind again,
                                        and the shivering bunchgrass, and the seed cones.

There is so little to say, and so much time to say it in.

Once, in 1955 on an icy road in Sam's Gap, North Carolina,
Going north into Tennessee on U.S. 23,
I spun out on a slick patch
And the car turned once-and-a-half around,
Stopping at last with one front wheel on a rock
                                                                    and the other on air,
Hundreds of feet of air down the mountainside
I backed away from, mortal again
After having left myself
                                        and returned, having watched myself
Wrench the wheel toward the spin, as I'm doing now,
Stop and shift to reverse, as I'm doing now,
                                                               and back out on the road
As I entered my arms and fingers again
Calmly, as though I had never left them,
Shift to low, and never question the grace
That had put me there and alive, as I'm doing now . . .

Solo Joe is a good road.
It cuts southwest off Montana 508 above Blacktail Creek,
Crosses the East Fork of the Yaak River
                                                          and climbs toward Mount Henry.
Joe was an early prospector
Back in the days when everything came in by pack string
Or didn't come in at all.
                                        One spring he shot his pet cat
On the front porch with a rifle between the eyes
As she came through the cabin door.

He later explained she was coming for him
                                        but he got her first.
He drank deer's blood, it was said, and kept to himself,
Though one story has him a gambler later downriver near Kalispell.
Nobody lives there now,
But people still placer-mine in the summer, and camp out
Illegally on the riverbank.
No one knows anything sure about Joe but his first name
And the brown government sign that remembers him.
And that's not so bad, I think.
                                        It's a good road, as I say,
And worse things than that will happen to most of us.

The road in is always longer than the road out,
Even if it's the same road.
I think I'd like to find one
                                        impassable by machine,
A logging road from the early part of the century,
Overgrown and barely detectable.
I'd like it to be in North Carolina,
                                        in Henderson County
Between Mount Pinnacle and Mount Anne,
An old spur off the main track
The wagons and trucks hauled out on.
Blackberry brambles, and wild raspberry and poison ivy
Everywhere; grown trees between the faint ruts;
Deadfall and windfall and velvety sassafras fans
On both sides . . .
                                        It dips downhill and I follow it.
It dips down and it disappears and I follow it.

Two Stories

Tonight, on the deck, the lights
Semaphore up at me through the atmosphere,
Town lights, familiar lights
                                        pulsing and slacking off
The way they used to back on the ridge outside of Kingsport
Thirty-five years ago,
The moonlight sitting inside my head
Like knives,
                    the cold like a drug I knew I'd settle down with.
I used to imagine them shore lights, as these are, then,
As something inside me listened with all its weight
For the sea-surge and the sea-change.

There's a soft spot in everything
Our fingers touch,
                              the one place where everything breaks
When we press it just right.
The past is like that with its arduous edges and blind sides,
The whorls of our fingerprints
                                             embedded along its walls
Like fossils the sea has left behind.

This is a story I swear is true.

I used to sleepwalk. But only
On camping trips,
                              or whenever I slept outside.

One August, when I was eleven, on Mount LeConte in Tennessee,
Campfire over, and ghost story over,
Everyone still asleep, apparently I arose
From my sleeping bag,
                                        opened the tent flap, and started out on the trail
That led to the drop-off, where the mountainside
Went straight down for almost a thousand feet.
Half-moon and cloud cover, so some light
As I went on up the path through the rhododendron,
The small pebbles and split roots
                                                  like nothing under my feet.
The cliffside was half a mile from the campsite.
As I got closer,
                              moving blindly, unerringly,
Deeper in sleep than the shrubs,
I stepped out, it appears,
Onto the smooth lip of the rock cape of the cliff,
When my left hand, and then my right hand,
Stopped me as they were stopped
By the breathing side of a bear which woke me
And there we were,
                                    the child and the black bear and the cliff-drop,
And this is the way it went—
                                            I stepped back, and I turned around,
And I walked down through the rhododendron
And never looked back,
                                        truly awake in the throbbing world,
And I ducked through the low flap
Of the tent, so quietly, and I went to sleep
And never told anyone
Till years later when I thought I knew what it meant,
                                                                  which now I've forgot.

And this one is questionable,
Though sworn to me by an old friend
Who'd killed a six-foot diamondback about seven o'clock in the morning
(He'd found it coiled in a sunny place),
And threw it into a croker sack with its head chopped off,
and threw the sack in the back of a jeep,
Then left for his day's work
On the farm.
That evening he started to show the snake
To someone, and put his hand in the sack to pull it out.
As he reached in, the snake's stump struck him.
His wrist was bruised for a week.

It's not age,
nor time with its gold eyelid and blink,
Nor dissolution in all its mimicry
That lifts us and sorts us out.
It's discontinuity
and all its spangled coming between
That sends us apart and keeps us there in a dread.
It's what's in the rearview mirror,
smaller and out of sight.

What do you do when the words don't come to you anymore,
And all the embolisms fade in the dirt?
And the ocean sings in its hammock,
rocking itself back and forth?
And you live at the end of the road where the sky starts its dark decline?

The barking goes on and on
from the far hill, constantly
Sticking its noise in my good ear.

Goodbye, Miss Sweeney, goodbye.
I'm starting to think about the psychotransference of all things.
It's small bones in the next life.
It's small bones,
and heel and toe forever and ever.

The Other Side of the River

Easter again, and a small rain falls
On the mockingbird and the housefly,
on the Chevrolet
In its purple joy
And the TV antennas huddled across the hillside—

Easter again, and the palm trees hunch
Deeper beneath their burden,
the dark puddles take in
Whatever is given them,
And nothing rises more than halfway out of itself—

Easter with all its little mouths open into the rain.

There is no metaphor for the spring's disgrace,
No matter how much the rose leaves look like bronze dove hearts,
No matter how much the plum trees preen in the wind.

For weeks I've thought about the Savannah River,
For no reason,
                        and the winter fields around Garnett, South Carolina,
My brother and I used to hunt
At Christmas,
                        Princess and Buddy working the millet stands
And the vine-lipped face of the pine woods
In their languorous zigzags,
The quail, when they flushed, bursting like shrapnel points
Between the trees and the leggy shrubs
                                                into the undergrowth,

Everything else in motion as though under water,
My brother and I, the guns, their reports tolling from far away
Through the aqueous, limb-filtered light,
December sun like a single tropical fish
Uninterested anyway,
                                suspended and holding still
In the coral stems of the pearl-dusked and distant trees . . .

There is no metaphor for any of this,
Or the meta-weather of April,
The vinca blossoms like deep bruises among the green.

It's linkage I'm talking about,
                                        and harmonies and structures
And all the various things that lock our wrists to the past.

Something infinite behind everything appears,
                                                        and then disappears.

It's all a matter of how
you narrow the surfaces.
It's all a matter of how you fit in the sky.

Often, at night, when the stars seem as close as they do now, and as full,
And the trees balloon and subside in the way they do
when the wind is right,
As they do now after the rain,
the sea way off with its false sheen,
And the sky that slick black of wet rubber,
I'm fifteen again, and back on Mount Anne in North Carolina
Repairing the fire tower,
Nobody else around but the horse I packed in with,
and five days to finish the job.

Those nights were the longest nights I ever remember,
The lake and pavilion 3,000 feet below
as though modeled in tinfoil,
And even more distant than that,
The last fire out, the after-reflection of Lake Llewellyn
Aluminum glare in the sponged dark,
Lightning bugs everywhere,
the plump stars
Dangling and falling near on their black strings.

These nights are like that,
The silvery alphabet of the sea
increasingly difficult to transcribe,
And larger each year, everything farther away, and less clear,
Than I want it to be,
not enough time to do the job,

And faint thunks in the earth,
As though somewhere nearby a horse was nervously pawing the ground.

I want to sit by the bank of the river,
                                        in the shade of the evergreen tree,
And look in the face of whatever,
                                        the whatever that's waiting for me.

There comes a point when everything starts to dust away
More quickly than it appears,
                                        when what we have to comfort the dark
Is just that dust, and just its going away.

Twenty-five years ago I used to sit on this jut of rocks
As the sun went down like an offering through the glaze
And backfires of Monterey Bay,
And anything I could think of was mine because it was there
                                        in front of me, numinously everywhere,
Appearing and piling up . . .

So to have come to this,
                                remembering what I did do, and what I didn't do,
The gulls whimpering over the boathouse,
                                        the monarch butterflies
Cruising the flower beds,
And all the soft hairs of spring thrusting up through the wind,
And the sun, as it always does,
                                        dropping into its slot without a click,
Is a short life of trouble.

Homage to Claude Lorrain

I had a picture by him—a print, I think—on my bedroom wall
In Verona in 1959,
                    via Anzani n. 3.
Or maybe a drawing, a rigged ship in a huge sea,
Storm waves like flames above my bed.
It's lost between there and here now,
                                        and has been for years,
Trapped in the past's foliage, as so much else is
In spite of our constancy, or how
We rattle the branches and keep our lights on the right place.

The room had a vaulted ceiling and faced east.
The living room was a tower with skylights on four sides.
A third room sloped with the roof
                                        until it was two feet high at the far wall,
All of this part of a reconstructed attic, and washed white.

I lived there for two years,
                              one block from the Adige
Where seagulls, like little loaves of fresh bread,
Drifted and turned on its grey coils.
Between the sea fires of Claude Lorrain
                                        and the curled sheets of the river,
I burned on my swivel stool
Night after night,
                    looking into the future, its charred edges
Holding my life like a frame
I'd hope to fit into one day, unsigned and rigged for the deeps.

Mantova

Mantegna on all the walls,
The Mincio puddled outside the gates,
                                        clouds tattooed on its blue chest,
Mantova floats in the pigeon-light of late afternoon
Twenty-two years ago.
Rain shoots its white cuffs across the scene.

I remember a dream I had once in Mantova,
Everyone in it in full dress,
                              refectory hall,
Goblets and white linen.
At the near end of the table, heaped on a bronze salver
Like quail, all wishbone and delicate leg,
The roast children were served up.
                                    "You must try the thighs,"
My host said, his gloves still on.
                                  "You must try the thighs."

Half the sky full of rain, and half not,
Reeds under water pressure to stay still,
The river oncoming but not flashed,
Everything upside down,
                             the sky at rest underfoot.
Words, but who can remember?

What words does the sky know, or the clouds know?

On the wall of the summer house,
                                    where Giulio Romano left him,
The lion sips at the riverbank, and the trees provide.

Driving to Passalacqua, 1960

The road is a hard road,
                                        and the river is wadded and flattened out
Due west of Santa Maria dell'Ortolo.
Each morning I drove with its steady breathing right to my right,
Dawn like a courtier
With his high white hat just coming into the room,
Ponte Pietra cut in the morning gauze,
                                                            Catullus off to my left
Released in the labials of the sunlight,
Fire on the water,
                                  daylight striking its match
Wherever it pleased
Along the Adige and stitched cross-tiles of San Fermo . . .

What do I do with all this?
                                             Phlegethon
He must have crossed,
                                        Dante, I mean,
His cloak like a net as he glided and stepped over the stones.
I hurry on by, breakfast
In mind, and the day's duty, half-left at the *bivio*.
Our outfit was out in town,
                                             in hiding, spiked fence and three Chevrolets
In front when I pulled up for roll call
And the morning mail and settling in,
DiCenzo signed out for Udine, and Joe for Vienna.
All day the river burned by my desk
                                        as I sailed my boats down its licks for a foot or so.

Italian Days

1

Thinking again of a weekend trip to Ferrara,
Cosimo Tura on one wall,
                                        Miss d'Este long gone from the next,
I took from Verona once,
A place where the streets were as wide as Parisian boulevards,
The Po like a frayed rope out past the bulge of the dikes.

The weekend before I'd been to Merano and back,
And almost become a squib
                                        in the *Stars & Stripes*
When the helicopter's engine stopped
Thousands of feet above the Brenner highway,
And we began to slide sideways down the air
As quietly as a snowflake,
                                        the huge rotary blades above us
Circling like paddle churns in the wind

Languidly,
            the stillness abrupt, the plane
In a long slip like a scimitar curve toward the ground
Rising to meet us, its trees
Focusing automatically larger with each look
As though raised through a microscope,
The engine catching at last on its last turn,
Pine branches less than fifty feet below us,
                                                            the blade-slide bottoming out

As we started to rise and swing north
Up the Val d'Adige and into the emerald sundown

Outside Merano . . .
Back up out of darkness an hour later,
The houses beginning to flash on like matches below,
Left over Trento and left over Schio
and down, everyone out to supper,
The waitress admonishing Manzolin, "*Non si taglia la pasta.*"

Cut to Ferrara, and me
Threading my way out of town through bicycles, Vespas and runty Fiats
South to Ravenna and Rimini,
the lap of the Adriatic
And western Byzantium
In the long grasses of S. Apollinare in Classe,
The field stubble gold in the noon sun.

Cut to Verona, the town I always left from,
Work over, and Happy Hour,
Modugno on every phonograph
On Via Mazzini, "*Ciao, ciao, bambina . . .*"
It's 1959 and after supper,
Everyone disappearing like rain
From the streets and Caffè Dante, the fog in,
Can Grande skulking and disappearing in marble above his tomb

As I do along the cobblestones
He grins down on,
gone through the fog toward S. Anastasia
And the Due Torri, everything swaddled as though in newsprint,
The river off to the right like a licking sound,
Up past the Duomo,
then right and across the last bridge,
Where the beggar loomed in her burning chair.
Each night as I passed her
it took a hundred lire to put out the fire.

Up north, in the watersheds and rock slides of the Dolomites,
Snow has been leaving its same message
For thousands of years
                                        on the bark of the cedar trees.
There is no stopping the comings and goings in this world,
No stopping them, to and fro.

2

Palladio's buildings shone like the collar on someone's dog
In Vicenza, the only inscript in all the town.
For the rest, it was Goldstein patrolling the avenues
At sundown with hot hands.
                                        And Venezia, Lord of the Bees,
In the dark hives of the Hotel Artù with hot hands.
It was Charles with hot hands,
His fingers on this and that wherever he turned
In the bars of Little America.
It was weekend and off-duty and kicking the gong
In a foreign country,
                                        left foot and right foot.

Sister water, brother fire, gentle my way
Across,
          one foot on the river, one foot in the flames,
My lack of ability to remember it right.
The time we spotted the Vicentine,
For instance, it rained and dimpled all the way back,
With Grace in his lap and him driving,
Sneezing and making amends.
On alternate Sundays we'd drive to Soave and Asolo,
Padova and the Euganean Hills,
Always looking for the event,
                                        not knowing that we were it.

This was the world we lived in,
And couldn't get shut of.
                    And these were the rocks we walked on,
Milano, Certosa, footstep
                    after footstep echoing down the galleries,
Goldstein checking the nuns out,
Venezia settling like smoke at the unbitten center of things.
One Sunday after the Trattoria La Brera,
We went to Scuderi's place, his huge canvases
Stacked like Sheetrock against the wall.
                              "I have to keep them like this,"
He said, "to keep my life in order."
He died the next winter,
                    the heater electrocuting him in the bathtub.

Some nights, when the stars flash their gang codes,
And the fog slides in as cautiously as a bride
Across the steps the trees make
                         up from the sea,
And the gnatlight starts to solidify
Like a crust on the palm leaf and the pepper switch,
And the smell of the paper-whites
                         hangs like a June garden
Above the kitchen table,
Scuderi calls out my name
                    as I climb the six flights to his room
And stand in the doorway again,
Electric and redivivus in the world of light

He lived in inside his paintings for all those years,
Vaseline light
          through the slow filter of late November,
Acid light off the north Italian lakes,

Shorthand of light from the olive leaves
as they turn and tick in the wind,
Last light of the *dopoguerra* lifting Milan like a ship
In the Lombardy night outside his window
On top of the city wall,
bar light and aftermath,
Scuderi whitening to grain-out and then to blank,
Light like a sheet of paper
Everywhere, flat and unwrinkled and unreturnable.

3

At the end of the last word,
When night comes walking across the lake on its hands,
And nothing appears in the mirror,
or has turned to water
Where nothing walks or lies down,
What will your question be,
Whistling the dogs of mold in, giving them meat?
And what will it profit you?

No thought of that back then,
Bivouacked outside the castle above Marostica
Whose walls
downswept and pinioned the town like wings
In its coming-to-rest,
the town square
Blocked out like a chessboard black and white,
Black and white from up there,
Where the rook looked down on the knight's play.

What eschatology of desire
could move us in those days,
What new episiotomy of the word?

At San Gimignano, outside of town,
I did see that no one could last for good,
That no one could answer back from the other side.
Still, I'd like to think I've learned how to speak to them,
I'd like to think I know how to conjugate
"Can you hear me?" and "What?"

In Rome, on the Via Cassia,
there was opportunity enough
For that in the catacombs,
the lost bodies slipped in their slots
Like letters someone had never answered,
And then tossed out,
A chance to step back from the light
of the strung electric bulb,
And ask again if our first day in the dark
Is our comfort or signature.

Most of what I remember
Has nothing to do with any of that, it turns out:
A view from the Pinacoteca window across Siena
One morning in 1959
and out to the hillscapes and olive shine;
The way Piero della Francesca's *Madonna del Parto*
Was leaning against the wall
in Monterchi, and still unlit;
The eel fisherman that May twilight along the Mincio River.

But Scuderi did, and the helicopter did,
And the full moon like Borso's skull on the Zattere,
Fog smoking up from the humped lagoon;
and Eve coming out of Adam's rib

On San Zeno's doors in Verona,
her foot still stuck in his side;
And the morning we sat on the terrace,
Jim Gates and Tom Fucile and I,
In Bassano, the bowler of Monte Grappa across the valley,
Ghost hat on the head of northern Italy.

There is, in the orchards of Sommacampagna,
A sleet-like and tenuous iridescence that falls
Through the peach trees whenever it rains.
The blossoms parachute to the ground
So heavy and so distinct,
And the light above Riva spokes out from under the clouds
Like Blake,
the wires for the grapevines beading their little rainbows,
The cars planing by on the highway,
shooshing their golden plumes . . .

What gifts there are are all here, in this world.

Roma I

To start with, it looked abstract
that first year from the balcony
Over the Via del Babuino,
Local color as far as the eye could see,
and mumbled in slaps and clumps
Of gouaches constantly to itself,
A gentian snood of twilight in winter,
blood orange in spring,

And ten thousand yards of glass in the summer sky.
Wherever you looked in October, the night was jigged.

(In front of the Ristorante Bolognese,
Monica Vitti and Michelangelo Antonioni are having an aperitif,
Watched by a hundred people.
                                        On the marble plaque
On the building across the street from my room to the Polish patriot
Whose name escapes me forever,
The words start to disappear in the April nightswell.
The river of cars turns its small lights on,
                                  and everyone keeps on looking at everyone else.)

Rome in Rome? We're all leading afterlives
                                                  of one sort or another,
Wrapped in bird feathers, pecking away at our gathered seed,
The form inside the form inside.
And nothing's more common by now than the obelisk
At one end of the street
                                  and the stone boat at the other...
The smell of a dozen dinners is borne up
On exhaust fumes,
                              timeless, somehow, and vaguely reassuring.

Roma II

I looked long and long at my mother's miniature
The next year,
                        the year I lived on the east side
Of the church building that overlooked the Campo dei Fiori.
Her body had entered the oak grove.

By the river of five-sided leaves she had laid it down,
Hummingbird hard at the yellow shells of the sour grass,
Red throat in the light vouchsafed,
then quick hum to a marigold.

The poem is a self-portrait
always, no matter what mask
You take off and put back on.
As this one is, color of cream and a mouthful of air.
Rome is like that, and we are,
taken off and put back on.
Downstairs, in front of the *Pollarolla*,
The Irish poets are sketching themselves in,
and the blue awnings, and motorbikes.
They draw till we're all in, even our hands.

Surely, as has been said, emptiness is the beginning of all things.
Thus wind over water,
thus tide-pull and sand-sheen
When the sea turns its lips back . . .
Still, we stand by the tree whose limbs branch out like bones,
Or steps in the bronchial sediment.
And the masters stand in their azure gowns,
Sticks in their hands, palm leaves like birds above their heads.

Homage to Cesare Pavese

Death will come and it will have your eyes
From morning to morning, sleepless,
an old remorse.
Your eyes will be vain words, a silence

You'll see as you lean out to the mirror
Each day,
                    the one look that it has for everyone.

It will be like ooze from the sea,
Like stopping a vice
                                        and the sin. It will be like stopping the sin.
It will be the dead face in the mirror
Listening to shut lips.
It will descend silently,
                                        speechlessly into whirlpools.

Death will come and it will have your eyes,
Ridiculous vice
                              and the same look.
You are the great weariness.
You are scorched and burned back by the sea.
You say nothing,
                              and nobody speaks to you.

This is a balance sheet and the names don't count.
One nail on top of another,
                                             four nails make a cross.
Nothing can add to the past—
Woman is as woman does,
                                            and night is always the night.
With its black heart and its black hands it lays me down.

Cryopexy

Looming and phosphorescent against the dark,
Words, always words.
                    What language does light speak?
Vowels hang down from the pepper tree
                                        in their green and their gold.

❧

The star charts and galactic blood trails behind the eye
Where the lights are, and the links and chains are,
                                        cut wall through ascending wall,
Indigo corridors, the intolerable shine
                                        transgressing heaven's borders . . .

❧

What are the colors of true splendor,
                                        yellow and white,
Carnation and ivory, petal and bone?
Everything comes from fire.

❧

Glare and glare-white,
                    light like a plate of isinglass
Under the lid,
            currents of fox-fire between the layers,
And black dots like the blood bees of Paradise . . .

❧

Radiance comes through the eye
and lodges like cut glass in the mind,
Never vice versa,
Somatic and self-contained.

Like soiled stars from the night-blooming jasmine vine
Espaliered against the sky,
char flakes rise from their blank deeps
Through peach light and apricot
Into the endlessness behind the eye.

Blood clots, like numb houseflies, hang
In the alabaster and tracery,
icy detritus
Rocked in the swish and tug
of the eye's twice-turned and moonless tides.
Behind them, tourmaline thread-ladders
Web up through the nothingness,
the diamond and infinite glare . . .

Weightlessness underwrites everything
In the deep space of the eye,
the wash and drift of oblivion
Sifting the color out,
polishing, still polishing
Long after translucence comes.

One black, electric blot, blood-blown,
Vanishes like Eurydice
                                        away from the light's mouth
And under the vitreous bulge of the eye's hill,
Down, O down, down . . .

Clocking the slurs and backlit snow
In their dark descent:
A Vaseline-colored medicine cloud floats to the left,
A comet-like shadow-slur floats to the right
Through a different throb,
                                              the snow in its quartzed downfall.

Sometimes, in the saffron undercurrents
                                                                    trailing like Buddhist prayer robes
Across the eye,
                          clear eels and anemones
Bob and circle and sink back through the folds,
Caught in the sleeve of the curl's turn.

Across the eye's Pacific, stars
                                                  drop in the black water like pursed lips,
Islands and tiny boats
Dipping under the white lid of the strung horizon,
                                                          this one in amethyst, this one in flame.

T'ang Notebook

Fine clouds open their outfits
                                        and show us their buttons.
Moonlight widens the waves.
Step on your own song and listen to mine,
Not bitter like yours,
                                not flicked raw by lashes of dust.
Already, over Italy, the cold sun rises.

How I would like a mountain
                                        if I had means enough to live as a recluse.
I would like to renounce it all
And turn toward the ash-gold of flame
                                                mullioned between the palm fronds.

That constellation, with its seven high stars,
                                                is lifting its sword in the midnight.
I love you, dog, I love you.

Remain here and lengthen your days,
                                                Pilgrim,
Fame is a mist of grief on the river waves . . .

The low, wet clouds move faster than you do,
Snowed moon, your jade hair sleet
and grown thin.
All night I ask what time it is.

Stories of passion make sweet dust . . .
Sunset like a girl's robe falling away long ago . . .
An old song handles my heart . . .

Outside the side door, a luck-spider
huge in the flashlight's lamp,
Rappels down the air
to single a stitch and make her starred bed.
In the dark past the hemlock, something with small, bright wings
Has come from a great distance, and is tired
and wants to lie down.

Night spreads its handful of star-clusters and one eclipse
Above the palm tree.
There are shuddering birds and dead grasses
Wherever I turn my face.

The ten thousand starfish caught in the net of heaven
Flash at the sky's end.
Gulls settle, like grains of dust, on the black sand.

Lady of Light, Donna Dolorosa,
you drift like a skeleton
Through the night clouds.
The surf comes in and goes out like smoke.
Give me a sign,
show me the blessing pierced in my side.

This wind that comes in off the Pacific,
Where the color of mountains both is and is not,
ripples the distant marsh grass
And the grey doors of the sea.
The evening begins to close like a morning glory.
Like fear in a little boat,
the light slips under the sky.

When the mind is loosened and borne up,
The body is lightened
and feels it too could float in the wind,
A bell-sound between here and sleep.

A water egret planes down like a page of blank paper
Toward the edge of the noon sky.
Let me, like him, find an island of white reeds
To settle down on, under the wind, forgetting words.

Arkansas Traveller

On the far side of the water, high on a sandbar,
Grandfathers are lolling above the Arkansas River,
Guitars in their laps, cloth caps like Cagney down over their eyes.
A woman is strumming a banjo.
                                        Another adjusts her bow tie
And boiled shirtwaist.
And in the half-light the frogs begin from their sleep
To ascend into darkness,
Vespers recalibrate through the underbrush,
                                                        the insect choir
Offering its clear soprano
Out of the vaulted gum trees into the stained glass of the sky.

Almost ninety-five years to the day I saw
Ellison Smythe passed out
                                    on the back seat of an Oldsmobile 88
In the spring of 1952 in Biltmore Forest, N.C.,
Who then rose up from the dark of his sixteenth year
And said to the nothingness:
                                    Where are we,
Who's driving this goddamn thing?
My great-grandfather stepped off the boat
                                            from the archduchy of Upper Austria
And headed north to the territory.
And into another war
                            here, just past the Mississippi,
On the Arkansas.
                        I don't know that it was such a great blessing

Sending us to Arkansas,
But it was so regarded at the time, and we're grateful to Gen. Jackson.
Still, don't let me die as Grandmother did,
suddenly on a steamboat
Stuck fast on a sandbar unable to get to Little Rock.
And was four years later a volunteer captain
In the Confederacy,
and took a Minie ball in his palate
At Chickamauga he carried there till his death
Almost half a century afterward.
And wrote a poem back
To the widow of one of his men about a sure return
"Where life is not a breath,
Nor life's affections, transient fire . . . in heaven's light."
And was captured again,
and wounded again, confined for two years
At Rock Island prison.
And came back to Little Rock and *began his career.*
And died at sixty-six,
a ticket to Cuba stored flat in his jacket pocket.

When Jesus walked on the night grass
they say not even the dew trembled.
Such intricate catechisms of desire.
Such golden cars down the wrong side of the sky.

Each summer in Little Rock,
like a monk in his cell
Saying the lesson over and over

Until it is shining, all day I'd prove up my childhood till lights-out
Snapped on the fireflies that floated
Like miniature jellyfish
off the reefs of the sleeping porch
Whose jasmine-and-rose-scented air broke over me back and forth
Before I could count the half of them,
and settled me under.
This was before I was ten.
That year my grandfather, my look-alike on the sandbar, died,
The war ended, and nothing was ever the same way
Again.
His mantelpiece clock sits on my dresser now,
Still gilded and nineteenth-century.
Devotion, remember, is what counts.
Without it you're exiled, twisted and small.

The next morning we'd play golf,
four holes on the back side,
Trailing our footprints like paired bodies emptied and left out to dry
In the web of sunlight and wet grass
behind us over the clipped fairways,
My grandmother and I up before anyone else
Each day I was there,
the sun already a huge, hot thumb
At seven o'clock on our bare heads.
Later, its print still warm on my forehead,
Sunset like carrot juice down the left pane of the sky
Into the indeterminacy of somewhere else,
I'd roll the tarpaulin down and up
On the sleeping porch,
the frog-shrill and the insect-shrill

Threading out of the bushes
as palpable as a heartstring,
Whatever that was back then, always in memory . . .

To speak of the dead is to make them live again:
we invent what we need.
Knot by knot I untie myself from the past
And let it rise away from me like a balloon.
What a small thing it becomes.
What a bright tweak at the vanishing point, blue on blue.

To Giacomo Leopardi in the Sky

If you are become an eternal idea,
Refusing investiture in our pink rags,
wise beyond body and form,
Or if you housel elsewhere a different sun
In one of the other aethers,
from down here
Where our years are fanged and omnivorous,
Listen to what these words say, from one who remembers you.

July 17th, on the front deck
Looking out through the slats and palm leaves,
The ocean horizonless and sending out signals,
I start to unmarble
interminable spaces beyond it,

Silences so immense they sound like wind,
Like this wind that dismays me
With its calm
as it pulls the sheet of the night
Over my head.
How sweet it is to drown in such sure water.

Whenever I see you
On your left side through the clouds
Looking down on us,
our tongues tied, our friends all gone,
Our hearts and breaths with the air let out of them,
You make me bitter for being so much like you.

What day did I take this picture you have no part in?
1959, no leaves on the trees, late fall.
Ponte Pietra over the Adige.
Verona, early morning.
What purpose your brief drifting along my course?
You try to erase your tracks
but you're too far from the ground.
You've throbbed enough.
Everything on the earth is worth your sighs.

Never to see the light is best, you say,
who were made for joy,
Your neck of chalk like a vapor trail across the sky.

I know you're up there, hiding behind the noon light
And the crystal of space.
Down here,
In the lurch and gasp the day makes as it waits for you
In your black suit and mother-of-pearl,
The mail comes, the garbage goes,
the paired butterflies
Dip and swoop in formation,
Bees trail their tongues
and tiptoe around the circumferences
Of the melaleuca puffs,
Sucking the sweetness up, July 27th,
The hummingbird asleep on her branch,
the spider drawn up in flame.

You kept reading and reading,
Vowel over consonant
then three steps to the stars,
And there you languish,
outlined in flash points and solid geometry,
Epistle in tatters . . .

You doom us who see your face.
You force on us your sorrow:
So frail and vile throughout,
as ours is,
It assails the ear like paradise.

The moon goes up and goes down,
roused and quenched low.
You bend like a calling card away from the dawn.
You doom us who see your face.

It's the mind, not the body,
That bears us up and shines a light in our eyes:
If spirit is nothingness,
I'd rather the light came back than the light came on.

Noon, and you're there again on the other side of the sky.
Two kites have nested in the dry skirt
Of the palm tree
and scrape their voices like fingernails
Against the windowpane of the air
When they flutter down, quick fingers, to feed their chicks.
You'd like it on this side, I think.
Summer is everywhere, your favorite,
And dirt still crumbles and falls like small rain from the hand.
The wind blows in from the sea.
The girls are pretty and everyone is sad.

The night is clear and incised,
The moon like a gold record
above the houses and avocado grove,
And you're back,
floating behind the star's stitching,

Such fine thread to sip through.
Do you remember the pain of the way it was for you,
Teresa's song scratching the scab off your own youth
And approaching end,
The days not long enough, and the nights not long enough
For you to suffer it all?
                                        You'd do the same again, I'll bet,
And live the same life,
Paper umbrella above your head
To keep the snow off,
                                        the color of snowfall like curtains across your eyes.

Not one word has ever melted in glory not one.
We keep on sending them up, however,
As the sun rains down.
                                        You did it yourself,
All those nights looking up at the sky, wanting to be there
Away from the grief of being here
In the wrong flesh.
They must look funny to you now,
Rising like smoke signals into the infinite,
The same letter over and over,
                                                big o and little o.

August 15th, and ten days
And 1,700 miles from where we last spoke, less than a twitch
For you,
          seventy years into the past for me
As the crow flies and the weather burns.

And even here, like the hand of a drowning man, your own hand
Points out from behind the stars
still without urgency
The Bear and the dark waters
Each boat of flesh sets sail on . . .
Such hurt, and I turn the page
to this place, built in 1912
By someone who'd never heard your name
But knew your face on clear nights
over Mount Caribou
As you wheeled west, your mouth full of stars.

That's all I wanted to say.
Think of me now and then, as I think of you
When the moon's like a golden tick on the summer sky
Gorged with light:
you're part of my parts of speech.
Think of me now and then. I'll think of you.

Looking at Pictures

How many times have I come here
to look at these photographs
And reproductions of all I've thought most beautiful
In the natural world,
And tried to enter the tired bodies assembled in miniature?

St. Francis, for instance, who saw the fire in the pig's mouth,
And trees full of the drowned
who forgot to cross themselves.

Or the last half-page of the Verse of Light in Arabic
torn from the Koran,
Tacked like a terrible crystal this side of the reading lamp.
Beside it Adam and Eve in agony
Are ushered out through the stone gates of Paradise.

On the other side of the room
A Fra Angelico angel beats time on a tambourine:
Everything's music to his ears.
And Rothko has a black-on-red
Painting below it I'd sink through flat on my back
Endlessly down into nothingness . . .

But not now. Not now when the hound of the Pope's men
Is leaping, not now
when the banner of St. George
Dragontails out of the sky. Not now
When our fathers stand in their riding boots, arms crossed,
Trying to tell us something we can't quite hear,
our ears jugged like Kafka's.

The devil eats us, I know, but our arms don't touch his neck.
Help me remember, Madonna of Tenderness,
that everything slides away
Into him stealthily.

St. Francis is feeding the birds again.
And someone with wings and brown hair
is telling Mary something
Again in a different dress.

St. Anne and Château Noir,
The flute player from 2200 B.C.

Out of the Cyclades—St. Ignatius Loyola
                                                  would find no rope in all this
To cinch around himself. It's synaptical here,
And rearranged.

We stare at the backs of our own heads continually
Walking in cadence into the past,
Great-grandfathers before their suicides,
                                              Venice in sunshine, Venice in rain,
Someone standing in front of the sea
                                             watching the waves come in . . .

California Dreaming

We are not born yet, and everything's crystal under our feet.
We are not brethren, we are not underlings.
We are another nation,
                              living by voices that you will never hear,
Caught in the net of splendor
                                    of time-to-come on the earth.
We shine in our distant chambers, we are golden.

Midmorning, and Darvon dustfall off the Pacific
Stuns us to ecstasy,
                         October sun
Stuck like a tack on the eastern drift of the sky,
The idea of God on the other,
                                    body by body

Rinsed in the Sunday prayer-light, draining away
Into the undercoating and slow sparks of the west,
which is our solitude and our joy.

I've looked at this ridge of lights for six years now
and still don't like it,
Strung out like Good Friday along a cliff
That Easters down to the ocean,
A dark wing with ruffled feathers as far out as Catalina
Fallen from some sky,
ruffled and laid back by the wind,
Santa Ana that lisps its hot breath
on the neck of everything.

What if the soul indeed is outside the body,
a little rainfall of light
Moistening our every step, prismatic, apotheosizic?
What if inside the body another shape is waiting to come out,
White as a quilt, loose as a fever,
and sways in the easy tides there?
What other anagoge in this life but the self?
What other ladder to Paradise
but the smooth handholds of the rib cage?
High in the palm tree the orioles twitter and grieve.
We twitter and grieve, the spider twirls the honey bee,
Who twitters and grieves, around in her net,
then draws it by one leg
Up to the fishbone fern leaves inside the pepper tree
swaddled in silk
And turns it again and again until it is shining.

❧

Some nights, when the rock-and-roll band next door has quit playing,
And the last helicopter has thwonked back to the Marine base,
And the dark lets all its weight down
                                        to within a half inch of the ground,
I sit outside in the gold lamé of the moon
                                        as the town sleeps and the country sleeps
Like flung confetti around me,
And wonder just what in the hell I'm doing out here
So many thousands of miles away from what I know best.
And what I know best
                                has nothing to do with Point Conception
And Avalon and the long erasure of ocean
Out there where the landscape ends.
What I know best is a little thing.
It sits on the far side of the simile,
                                        the like that's like the like.

❧

Today is sweet stuff on the tongue.
The question of how we should live our lives in this world
Will find no answer from us
                                this morning,
Sunflick, the ocean humping its back
Beneath us, shivering out
                                wave after wave we fall from
And cut through in a white scar of healed waters,
Our wet suits glossed slick as seals,
                                        our boards grown sharp as cries.
We rise and fall like the sun.

Ghost of the Muse and her dogsbody
Suspended above the beach, November 25th,
Sun like a Valium disc, smog like rust in the trees.
White-hooded and friar-backed,
                                                            a gull choir eyeballs the wave reach.
Invisibly pistoned, the sea keeps it up,
                                                plunges and draws back, plunges and draws back,
Yesterday hung like a porcelain cup behind the eyes,
Sonorous valves, insistent extremities,
                                                                  the worm creeping out of the heart . . .

Who are these people we pretend to be,
                                                                  untouched by the setting sun?
They stand less stiffly than we do, and handsomer,
First on the left foot, and then the right.
Just for a moment we see ourselves inside them,
                                                                                      peering out,
And then they go their own way and we go ours,
Back to the window seat above the driveway,
Christmas lights in the pepper tree,
                                                            black Madonna
Gazing out from the ailanthus.
Chalk eyes downcast, heavy with weeping and bitterness,
Her time has come round again.

Piece by small piece the world falls away from us like spores
From a milkweed pod,
                                            and everything we have known,
And everyone we have known,
Is taken away by the wind to forgetfulness,
Somebody always humming,
                                                        California dreaming . . .

FROM

ZONE JOURNALS

(1988)

A Journal of English Days

(SEPTEMBER)

—Kensington Church Walk, St. Mary Abbots
Grey stone and dun through the mustard edges of chestnut leaves.
Inside, a funeral's going on and I back off
To sit on a wooden bench
Against a brick wall
                                        in the slick, unseasonable sunshine,
Trying to piece together
The way it must have been for someone in 1908
Fresh up from Italy,
A couple of books of his own poems in one hand
                                                                                and a dead galaxy
Set to go off in crystal inside his head.
Over the stained-glass windows in front of me,
In Kensington black and white,
                                                        Ancient Lights
Is nailed to the churchside stone,
The children trailing out of the false penumbra
                                                                    into the sun-screed in Indian file
Then in again, shrilling, in cadence, their little song.

—I'm back for a second look,
                                                but someone is meditating on last week's bench
In a full lotus. Now he touches his nose
With his right forefinger, and now
With his left.
                                His black shoes puddle beneath him

Like backs of mirrors he'll walk on tenderly
Over the flat-laid churchyard gravestones when he leaves.
But now he's back in position,
                                        hands cupped
In his lap, thumb end touching thumb end, his eyes closed—

One of those weightless, effortless late September days
As sycamore leaves
                              tack down the unresisting air
Onto the fire-knots of late roses
Still pumping their petals of flame
                                             up from the English loam,
And I suddenly recognize
The difference between the spirit and flesh
                                              is finite, and slowly transgressable . . .

(OCTOBER)

—October everywhere out of the sunlight
Onto the China jade of the blowing fields
Of Kensington Gardens—
                                      or else come down like wet lint
Over the Avon, soaking the glass.
It swivels my eyes that work me for grief and affliction
And pink my spirit, it guides my hand.

Fulke Greville lies in his stone boat in the church of St. Mary
In Warwickshire, not rippling the cold
Which clings like water drops to what was his face
On the other side of the light.

His kinsmen, Lords of the Bear and the Ragged Staff,
                                                            lie scattered around him,

Hermetically sealed in stone,
Who was friend to Elizabeth R and Sir Philip Sidney, ghost
In his own room now,
all passions heeled.

This afternoon I came up
Out of his Warwick dungeon
into the slow swish of the English rain,
Its bead curtain and lengths of chain
Strangely consoling after the iron artifacts
Hanging below like rib cages
and lungs in the torturous gloom.

The castle seemed to encircle me with its stone wings
And all of it lift
slightly at once, then settle back
As though the wind had died
That blows continuously under our feet
Holding up everything, then started again,
and what had sunk was risen,
I don't know, at least to where it began . . .

—October's a kind time,
The rain lying like loose bandages over the ground,
The white bounty of mushrooms thrusting their flesh up,
The comforting slide of darkness
edging like deep water
Back through the afternoon.
The sycamore trees in Lennox Gardens crisp and spray
In the wind, our discontent,
like Orpheus, singing elsewhere,
Charon, in slow motion, poling his empty boat
Cross-current, over the dark water

Into the different music of London traffic,
                                                            the coin still clenched in his teeth
The other side of the Thames . . .

Back in the Gardens, it's tag end of a skitterish day,
October 17th, Sir Philip dead
397 years today,
I watch the stiff papers scudding across the lawn,
Leaves heaped to vindicate speedily
The offices of the end,
                                                dogs nosing the moist-eared edges of things,
Noticing gradually
A larger darkness inching up through the dark
Like grass, that means to cover us all.
Across the way, the yellow moths of the window lights
Break from their blue cocoons.

—The trees stay green longer here, lacking
The clubbing frost that stuns them to glory.
                                                            Their leaves lie in limes and tans
Flocking the grass, vaguely pre-Cubist to me,
And blurred, without my glasses, arranged
In an almost-pattern of colors across the yard,
The same colors Cézanne once used in the same way
So often down in Provence.
                                                He died there today
Seventy-seven years ago, October 22nd, the fields and houses and trees
Still these colors and pure arrangements
Oozing out of the earth, dropping out of the sky
                                                            in memory of him each year
Everywhere, north and south . . .

He never painted the moon.
Never romantic enough,
                                        he saw what he saw in a white light.
Still, I remember it there, hanging like a doubloon
Over Puyricard, outside Aix, some fifteen years ago,
Godfrey and I in our yellow suits
                                                    vamping the landscape
Along the canal, first in its half, then two weeks later its full dress.
It's here now, powdering through the trees
                                                  as cars go by and drunks sing in the street.
The blue light from a TV swarms at the windowpanes
In one of the Dutch Georgians across the way.
He made us see differently, where the hooks fit, and the eyes go . . .
Nothing is ever finished.

—Up from the basement flat at 43A,
                                                        up past the Greek college,
Across Walton to Ovington Gardens
Then over to Brompton Road
And across,
                    left to the Oratory and right
Up under the chestnut trees to Ennismore Mews,
Up past the gardens and Prince's Gate
Across the main road and Rotten Row,
                                                          bicycle track
And long grass down to the Serpentine,
Ducks on the water, geese on the water, the paired swans
Imperious and the gulls
                                      neat on the slick edges,
Then backtrack and a right turn
To the west, across the road and into Kensington Gardens
And out to the chestnut and beech grove

As the dogs go by
                                        and the Punks noodle along
In their chrome stud belts and Technicolor hair.

What breeze-bristled cities the trees are,
Their lights snatched off and on,
                                                            streets cluttered with leaves.
The sky is scrubbed to a delft blue
                                                            in the present tense,
Segueing into grey and a future pearl.

I'm stuck here, unwilling to trace my steps back,
The month running down like a love affair
                                                                      inexorably to its close,
Sunday, October 30th, Pound's birthday ninety-eight years ago,
Everything lidded with grey, unporridgy clouds now,
Smooth as a slice of tin
                                                  or a flat rock in the street.
Like a bouffant hairdo of steel wool,
The limbs of a leafless chestnut tree are back-combed by the wind.
The English mind, he said, the cold soup of the English mind.
At Pisa it all came back
                                                  in a different light
In the wind-sear and sun-sear of the death cages,
Remembering Christmases in the country, the names
Of dead friends in the Tuscan twilight
                                                            building and disappearing across the sky.
Cold soup, cold soup,
Longwater color of pewter,
                                                       late grass green neon.

—*Short Riff for John Keats on His 188th Birthday*

Hopkins thought your verse abandoned itself
To an enervating luxury,
                                        a life of impressions
In fairyland, life of a dreamer,
And lacking the manly virtues of active thought.

Born on All Hallows' Eve, what other early interest
Can one assume,
                                that single, arterial drop of blood
On the clean sheet dispelling for good
                                                        a subsequent second,
Little black light magnet, imagination's Buddha . . .

(NOVEMBER)

—A *Traveler between life and death* . . .
Where is that line between sleep and sleep,
That line like a wind over water
Rippling toward shore,
                                        appearing and disappearing
In wind-rise and wind-falter—
That line between rain and sleet,
                                                    between leaf-bronze and leaf-drop—
That line where the river stops and the lake begins,
Where the black blackens
                                            and light comes out of the light . . .

Stone circle at Castlerigg,
                                            Cumbrian, Paleolithic chancel
Against the November mist and vault,
Mouth-mark of the invisible, air become breath
And ecclesiastical smoke . . .

Crows, like strings of black Christmas-tree lights, burn in the bare trees,
And silver Y moths—though soon to die—appear at dusk,

The night coming down, a dark snow
Piecemeal and hard across the moors
                                                  like the ashes of Paradise
3500 years ago,
                              Helvellyn and Thirlmere
Sluicing to charcoal down-valley, water and earth

And air all bleared to the same color, an indiscriminate estuary
Shoaling into the landscape, nobody here but me
Unspooling to nothingness,
                                        line after line after latched, untraceable line . . .

—November pares us like green apples,
                                                    circling under our skins
In long, unbroken spirals until
We are sweet flesh for the elements
                                                  surprised by the wind's shear
Curling down from the north of Wales
Like Occam's edge to Steeple Aston and Oxfordshire.

"Worst time of the year," he said,
                                              "leaves everywhere
And fresh cold to shiver your very seeds.
I've burned two piles already, Saturday morning yet"—
This in the Norman churchyard,
Grey flake and flame in a hushed mound on Delia Johnson,
                                                                  God Knows His Own,

Lead lines in the arteries for the first time, magpies
Hustling their double notes
                                          steadily, like oars in an oarlock,

Beechwoods and whitehorns, hawthorn and mountain ash
All burning down to bare ricks
Against the dropdraft of cold as winter circles and moves in . . .

—Chelsea Embankment, 5 p.m.: Whistler pastels squished
Down the fluted water, orange,
Tamarind, apricot,
jade on the slate slip of the river,
Tug-ducks moored at the mudbanks,
Southbank light-string reflections stretched like struck and vibrating pipes,
The Thames rung softly
cross-river, and always a different note
Under the Albert Bridge, the Chelsea and out through town—
Or star-colored steps that sink
Beneath the sharkskin of the current
down to the corridors
And bone-bossed gallery gates of the end.

—I keep coming back, like a tongue to a broken tooth,
Kensington Church Walk,
late afternoon,
Pigeons in bas-relief and frieze on the building's edge—
There is no sickness of spirit like homesickness
When what you are sick for
has never been seen or heard
In this world, or even remembered
except as a smear of bleached light
Opening, closing beyond any alphabet's
Recall to witness and isolate . . .

November's my favorite month,
the downside of autumn
And winter in first array, the sky

Constabled now and again
Over Kensington Gardens:
                                        north of the Serpentine,
A pale light on the bright side of the dark,
Everything starting to glide and refract,
                                                            moving just under water . . .

—Today is fire and solution, rack
                                                  of veins in the ruined trees,
A warm wind from the south and crows like mistletoe in the twist
And tuck of diluvial branches—

Stay out of the way and be conspicuous,
Step back and let your story, like water, go where it will,
Cut down your desires,
                                        alone, as you are, on the white heart of the earth.

—The sadness of Sunday train rides in the rain,
Little gardens and back yards
Bellied up to the buffed tracks,
Their wet laundry and broken toys beside TO LET signs,
Crushed Styrofoam cups
                                        small pockets of old ice turned out,

The joyless twitter of wheels
                                              and couplings turning and changing,
Whole centers of villages
Scooped out and fenced in for a high-rise or a car park,
Anguish of bitten trees, slow
Bull's-eyes of raindrops in flat, colorless water pools,

And all the south of England
Under the sponge,
                                  no one in sight but the yellow-slickered rail workers

Standing like patient, exotic birds
On the outskirts of Redhill, or upline from Haywards Heath,
One on one leg, as though poised for frogs,

The desolate, wax faces
Of young mothers gripping their children from side to side
In the fleshed, electric light,
                                        stunned by
Something they never asked for,
Something like somebody else's life, that they've been given,

Sadness of platforms, black umbrellas
Doleful on benches, half-opened, damp,
Tedious sense
Of expectation, the clouds
Continuing on for days past our destinations . . .

(DECEMBER)

—Noon like cicada wings,
                                        translucence remembered, half-sheets
Of light over light on the black stones
Of the crescent walk and bodices of the rhododendron,
Red eye of the whirring sun—
                                        December comes out of the ground
Shedding its skin on the bare trees,
And hovers above the northern sky
Wings like new glass,
                                wings like a thousand miles of new glass—

How sweet to think that Nature is solvency,
                                                    that something empirically true
Lies just under the dead leaves
That will make us anchorites in the dark

Chambers of some celestial perpetuity—
nice to think that,
Given the bleak alternative,
Though it hasn't proved so before,
and won't now
No matter what things we scrape aside—
God is an abstract noun.

—Flashback: a late September Sunday,
the V & A courtyard,
Holly and I at one end,
Bronze Buddha under some falling leaves at the other:
Weightlessness of the world's skin
undulating like a balloon
Losing its air around us, down drifting down
Through the faint hiss of eternity
Emptying somewhere else
O emptying elsewhere
This afternoon, skin
That recovers me and slides me in like a hand
As I unclench and spread
finger by finger inside the Buddha's eye . . .

—LONDON 1983

March Journal

—After the Rapture comes, and everyone goes away
Quicker than cream in a cat's mouth,
all of them gone

In an endless slipknot down the sky
                                        and its pink tongue
Into the black hole of Somewhere Else,

What will we do, left with the empty spaces of our lives
Intact,
        the radio frequencies still unchanged,
The same houses up for sale,
Same books unread,
                        all comfort gone and its comforting . . .

For us, the earth is a turbulent rest,
                                        a different bed
Altogether, and kinder than that—
After the first death is the second,
A little fire in the afterglow,
                              somewhere to warm your hands.

—The clean, clear line, incised, unbleeding,
Sharp and declarative as a cut
                                the instant before the blood wells out . . .

—March Blues
The insides were blue, the color of Power Putty,
When Luke dissected the dogfish,
                                        a plastic blue
In the whey
            sharkskin infenestrated:
Its severed tailfin bobbed like a wing nut in another pan
As he explained the dye job
                              and what connected with what,
Its pursed lips skewed and pointed straight-lined at the ceiling,
The insides so blue, so blue . . .

March gets its second wind,
starlings high shine in the trees
As dread puts its left foot down and then the other.
Buds hold their breaths and sit tight.
The weeping cherries
lower their languorous necks and nibble the grass
Sprout ends that jump headfirst from the ground,
Magnolia drums blue weight
next door when the sun is right.

—Rhythm comes from the roots of the world,
rehearsed and expandable.

—After the ice storm a shower of crystal down from the trees
Shattering over the ground
like cut glass twirling its rainbows,
Sunlight in flushed layers under the clouds,
Twirling and disappearing into the clenched March grass.

—Structure is binary, intent on a resolution,
Its parts tight but the whole loose
and endlessly repetitious.

—And here we stand, caught
In the crucifixal noon
with its bled, attendant bells,
And nothing to answer back with.
Forsythia purrs in its burning shell,
Jonquils, like Dante's angels, appear from their blue shoots.

How can we think to know of another's desire for darkness,
That low coo like a dove's
insistent outside the heart's window?

How can we think to think this?
How can we sit here, crossing out line after line,
Such five-finger exercises
                                        up and down, learning our scales,

And say that all quartets are eschatological
Heuristically
                    when the willows swim like medusas through the trees,
Their skins beginning to blister into a thousand green welts?
How can we think to know these things,
Clouds like full suds in the sky
                                                keeping away, keeping away?

—Form is finite, an undestroyable hush over all things.

A Journal of True Confessions

—Power rigs drift like lights out past the breakwater,
                                                            white, and fluorescent white,
The sea moving them up and down
In the burgeoning dawn,
                                        up and down,
White as they drift and flicker over the salmon run,

Engines cut, or cut back,
Trolling herring bait or flasher lures,
                                                    the sea moving them up and down,
The day's great hand unfolding
Its palm as the boats drift with the tide's drift:

All morning we slipped among them,
                                                    Ray at the boat's wheel

Maneuvering, baiting the double hooks, tying and cutting,
Getting the depth right,
                                        Mark and I
Watching the rods as their almost-invisible lines

Trailed through the boat's wake,
                                                    waiting for each to dip:
And when it came
We set the drag and played him,
                                                    the salmon jumping and silver,
Then settled like quick foil in the net's green . . .

Later, ground zero, the Strait of Juan de Fuca
                                                                  sliding the fog out
Uncharacteristically, sunlight letting its lines down
For a last run,
                        glint from the water like flecked scales,
Everything easing away, away,

Waves, and the sea-slack, sunset,
Tide's bolt shot and turned for the night,
The dark coming in,
                                    dark like the dogfish coming in
Under the island's eyelid, under and down.

—15 JULY 1984

—Lashed to the syllable and noun,
                                                        the strict Armageddon of the verb,
I lolled for seventeen years
Above this bay with its antimacassars of foam
On the rocks, the white, triangular tears
                                                sailboats poke through the sea's spun sheet,

Houses like wads of paper dropped in the moss clumps of the trees,
Fog in its dress whites at ease along the horizon,
Trying to get the description right.
                                        If nothing else,
It showed me that what you see
                                        both is and is not there,
The unseen bulking in from the edges of all things,
Changing the frame with its nothingness.

Its blue immensity taught me about subtraction,
Those luminous fingerprints
                                    left by the dark, their whorls
Locked in the stations of the pilgrim sun.
It taught me to underlook.
Turkey buzzards turn in their widening spins
                                                    over the flint
Ridged, flake-dried ground and kelp beds,
Sway-winged and shadowless in the climbing air.
Palm trees postcard the shoreline.
Something is added as the birds disappear,
                                                  something quite small
And indistinct and palpable as a stain
                                             of saint light on a choir stall.

—6 AUGUST 1984

—*I can write a simple, declarative English sentence,*
Mancini said,
              drinking a stinger and leaning back
In his green chair above the Arno.
                                        And not many can say that,
He added, running the peppermint taste

Around on his tongue.

Out on the river,

Down below Prato, the sun was lowering its burned body

Into the shadows.

Happy birthday, Lieutenant,

He quipped, and ordered another round.

Twenty-four years ago, and dog days, indeed, Fortunatus.

Six months later

(flash-forward across the Aegean),

Tell Laura I Love Her, PA'ed the ship's lounge, the Captain's arm

Around my shoulders, full moonlight and Jesus

everything in the sky

Was beautiful . . .

I ducked out and turned back down to Second Class,

His sweet invective lotioning my right ear.

And stingers that night as well, for hours out of Piraeus,

Mancini grinning like Ungaretti,

And then he said, What?

The stars are fastening their big buckles

and flashy night shoes,

Thunder chases its own tail down the sky,

My forty-ninth year, and all my Southern senses called to horn,

August night hanging like cobwebs around my shoulders:

How existential it all is, really,

the starting point always the starting point

And what's-to-come still being the What's-to-Come.

Some friends, like George, lurk in the memory like locusts,

while others, flat one-sided fish

Looking up, handle themselves like sweet stuff:

look out for them, look out for them.

—25 AUGUST 1984

—Cicadas wind up their one note to a breaking point.
The sunlight, like fine thread, opens and closes us.
The wind, its voice like grasshoppers' wings,
                                        rises and falls.
Sadness is truer than happiness.

Walking tonight through the dwarf orchard,
The fruit trees seem etched like a Dürer woodcut against the sky,
The odd fruit
          burined in bas-relief,
The moon with its one foot out of the clouds,
All twenty-one trees growing darker in a deepening dark.

When the right words are found I will take them in and be filled through with joy.
My mouth will be precious then,
                              as your mouth is precious.
If you want to hear me, you'll have to listen again.
You'll have to listen to what the wind says,
                                        whatever its next direction.

—9 SEPTEMBER 1984

—It's all such a matter of abstracts—
                              love with its mouth wide open,
Affection holding its hand out,
Impalpable to the impalpable—
No one can separate the light from the light.

They say that he comes with clouds,
The faithful witness,
               the first-begotten of the dead.
And his feet are like fine brass,
His voice the perpetual sound of many waters.

The night sky is darker than the world below the world,
The stars medieval cathedral slits from a long way.
This is the dark of the *Metamorphoses*
When sparks from the horses' hooves
showed us Persephone
And the Prince's car in its slash and plunge toward Hell.

Seventy-four years ago today,
Dino Campana, on the way back
From his pilgrimage on foot
To the holy chill of La Verna inside the Apennines
To kiss the rock where St. Francis received the stigmata,

Stopped in a small inn at Monte Filetto
And sat on a balcony all day
staring out at the countryside,
The hawks circling like lost angels against the painted paradise of the sky,
The slope below him
a golden painting hung from the walnut tree:

The new line will be like the first line,
spacial and self-contained,
Firm to the touch
But intimate, carved, as though whispered into the ear.

—25 SEPTEMBER 1984

—The dragon maple is shedding its scales and wet sides,
Scuffs of cloud bump past the Blue Ridge
looking for home,
Some nowhere that's somewhere for them,
The iris teeter and poke on their clubbed feet:
October settles its whole weight in a blue study.

I think of the great painters in light like this,
                                        Morandi's line
Drawn on the unredemptive air, Picasso's cut
Like a laser into the dark hard of the mystery,
Cézanne with his cross-tooth brush and hook,
And sad, immaculate Rothko,
                              whose line was no line at all,

His last light crusted and weighed down,
                                      holes within holes,
This canvas filled with an emptiness, this one half full . . .
Like the sky over Locust Avenue. Like the grass.

—5 OCTOBER 1984

—What disappears is what stays . . .
O'Grady stories abound.
                          Born one day later than I was, my alter ego,
He points at me constantly
Across the years
                   from via dei Giubbonari in Rome, spring 1965,
Asking me where the cadence is,
Dolce vitaed and nimbus-haired,
                                where's the measure we talked about?
His finger blurs in my eye.
Outside the picture,
                 the Largo looms in the bleached distance behind his back.

I look for it, Desmond, I look for it constantly
In the long, musical shape of the afternoon,
                                        in the slice of sunlight pulled
Through the bulge of the ash trees

Opening like a lanced ache in the front yard,
In the sure line the mockingbird takes
down from the privet hedge
And over the lawn where the early shade
Puddles like bass chords under the oak,
In the tangent of 4 p.m., in the uncut grass,
in the tangle and tongue-tie it smooths there . . .

But our lines seem such sad notes for the most part,
Pinned like reliquaries and stopgaps
to the cloth effigy of some saint
Laid out in the public niche
Of a mission or monastery—
St. Xavier, hear me,
St. Xavier, hear my heart,
Give my life meaning, heal me and take me in,
The dust like a golden net from the daylight outside
Over everything,
candles chewing away at the darkness with their numb teeth.

—19 OCTOBER 1984

—According to Freud, Leonardo da Vinci made up a wax paste
For his walks from which
he fashioned delicate animal figurines,
Hollow and filled with air.
When he breathed into them, they floated
Like small balloons, twisting and turning,
released by the air
Like Li Po's poems downriver, downwind
To the undergrowth and the sunlight's dissembling balm.
What Freud certainly made of this

Is one thing.
What does it mean to you,
Amber menagerie swept from his sun-struck and amber hands?

Giorgio Vasari told it first,
and told us this one as well:
A wine grower from Belvedere
Found an uncommon lizard and gave it to Leonardo,
Who made wings for it out of the skins
Of other lizards,
and filled the wings with mercury
Which caused them to wave and quiver
Whenever the lizard moved.
He made eyes, a beard and two horns
In the same way, tamed it, and kept it in a large box
To terrify his friends.
His games were the pure games of children,
Asking for nothing but artifice, beauty and fear.

—20 OCTOBER 1984

—Function is form, form function back here where the fruit trees
Strip to November's music,
And the black cat and the tortoiseshell cat
crouch and slink,
Crouch and slink toward something I can't see
But hear the occasional fateful rustlings of,
Where the last tomatoes seep
from their red skins through the red dirt,
And sweet woodruff holds up its smooth grey sticks
Like a room full of boys
all wanting to be excused at the same time:

The song of white lights and power boats,
the sails of August and late July devolve
To simple description in the end,
Something about a dark suture
Across the lawn,
something about the way the day snips
It open and closes it
When what-comes-out has come out
and burns hard in its vacancy,
Emerging elsewhere restructured and restrung,
Like a tall cloud that all the rain has fallen out of.

The last warm wind of summer
shines in the dogwood trees
Across the street, flamingoing berries and cupped leaves
That wait to be cracked like lice
Between winter's fingernails.
The season rusts to these odd stains
And melodramatic stutterings
In the bare spots of the yard, in the gutter angles
Brimming with crisp leftovers,
and gulled blooms in the rhododendrons,
Veneer, like a hard wax, of nothing on everything.

—3 NOVEMBER 1984

Night Journal

—I think of Issa, a man of few words:
The world of dew
Is the world of dew.

And yet . . .
And yet . . .

—Three words contain
all that we know for sure of the next life
Or the last one: Close your eyes.
Everything else is gossip,
false mirrors, trick windows
Flashing like Dutch glass
In the undiminishable sun.

—I write it down in visible ink,
Black words that disappear when held up to the light—
I write it down
not to remember but to forget,
Words like thousands of pieces of shot film
exposed to the sun.
I never see anything but the ground.

—Everyone wants to tell his story.
The Chinese say we live in the world of the ten thousand things,
Each of the ten thousand things
crying out to us
Precisely nothing,
A silence whose tune we've come to understand,
Words like birthmarks,
embolic sunsets drying behind the tongue.
If we were as eloquent,
If what we say could spread the good news the way that dogwood does,
Its votive candles
phosphorous and articulate in the green haze
Of spring, surely something would hear us.

—Even a chip of beauty
                                        is beauty intractable in the mind,
Words the color of wind
Moving across the fields there
                                                  wind-addled and wind-sprung,
Abstracted as water glints,
The fields lion-colored and rope-colored,
As in a picture of Paradise,
                                             the bodies languishing over the sky
Trailing their dark identities
That drift off and sieve away to the nothingness
Behind them
                    moving across the fields there
As words move, slowly, trailing their dark identities.

—Our words, like blown kisses, are swallowed by ghosts
Along the way,
                         their destinations bereft
In a rub of brightness unending:
How distant everything always is,
                                                        and yet how close,
Music starting to rise like smoke from under the trees.

—Birds sing an atonal row
                                           unsyncopated
From tree to tree,
                         dew chants
Whose songs have no words
                                              from tree to tree
When night puts her dark lens in,
One on this limb, two others back there.

—Words, like all things, are caught in their finitude.
They start here, they finish here

No matter how high they rise—
my judgment is that I know this
And never love anything hard enough
That would stamp me
and sink me suddenly into bliss.

A Journal of the Year of the Ox

—January,
the dragon maple sunk in its bones,
The sky grey gouache and impediment.
Pity the poor pilgrim, the setter-forth,
Under a sweep so sure,
pity his going up and his going down.

Each year I remember less.
This past year it's been
the Long Island of the Holston
And all its keening wires
in a west wind that seemed to blow constantly,
Lisping the sins of the Cherokee.

How shall we hold on, when everything bright falls away?
How shall we know what calls us
when what's past remains what's past
And unredeemed, the crystal
And wavering coefficient of what's ahead?

Thursday, purgatorial Thursday,
The Blue Ridge etched in smoke
through the leaded panes of the oak trees,
There, then not there,

A lone squirrel running the power line,
                                                neck bowed like a tiny buffalo:

The Long Island of the Holston,
                                                sacred refuge ground
Of the Cherokee Nation:
                                                nothing was ever killed there.
I used to cross it twice whenever I drove to the golf course.
Nobody tells you anything.

The ghost of Dragging Canoe
                                                settles like snowflakes on the limbs
Of the river bushes, a cold, white skin
That bleeds when it breaks.
                                                Everyone wants to touch its hem
Now that it's fallen, everyone wants to see its face.

What sifts us down through a blade-change
                                                stays hidden from us,
But sifts us the same,
Scores us and alters us utterly:
From somewhere inside and somewhere outside, it smooths us down.

Here's your Spook, Indaco said,
                                                sliding the imitation Sandeman's sherry figurine
Toward me along the bar, memento
And laughingstock of the 163rd,
                                                stamped out by the thousands
At Nove, two hours up the road.

It's usually a ceremony, all your colleagues
And fellow officers standing absurdly about
Happy you're leaving, and you too,
                                                            everyone half drunk
And hilarious in his cordovan shoes.

But not this time, Indaco wadding the paper sack up,
He and someone whose name I can't call back
                                                            letting me go for good, and glad of it:
I'd lost one document, I wore my hair long, I burned it by accident
And no one ever forgot.

Such small failures, such sleeveless oblivions
We passed through
                                        trying to get our lives to fit right
In what was available from day to day,
And art,
            and then the obvious end of art, that grace

Beyond its reach
                                    I'd see each night as I thumbed the Berensons
And argued with Hobart and Schneeman
                                                                    that what's outside
The picture is more important than what's in.
They didn't agree any more than Indaco had,

All of us hungering after righteousness
Like Paul Cézanne, we thought, in his constancy.
Or Aeneas with the golden bough
                                                            sweeping through Hell.
O we were luminous in our ignorance O we were true.

Form comes from form, it's said:
nothing is ever ended,
A spilling like shook glass in the air,
Water over water,
flame out of flame,
Whatever we can't see, whatever we can't touch,
unfixed and shining . . .

And today I remember nothing.
The sky is a wrung-out, China blue
and hides no meanings.
The trees have a pewter tinge and hide no meanings.
All of it hustles over me like a wind
and reminds me of nothing.

Nobody rises out of the ground in a gold mist.
Nobody slides like an acrobat
out of the endless atmosphere.
Nobody touches my face
Or hand.
Not a word is said that reminds me of anything

And O it is cold now by the fake Etruscan urn
And six miniature box bushes
nobody stands beside
In the real wind tightening its scarf
Around the white throats
of everyone who is not here.

The cold, almost solid, lies
Like snow outside
in the tufted spikes of the seed grass

And footprints we didn't leave
That cross the driveway and disappear up the front steps.

It's not the darkness we die of, as someone said,
                                        seamless and shut tight
As water we warm up and rock in,
But cold, the cold with its quartz teeth
And fingernails
                    that wears us away, wears us away

Into an afterthought.
                        Or a glint
Down there by the dwarf spruce and the squirrel run.
Or one of the absences who lips at the edge of understanding
Wherever I turn,
                    as pursed and glittering as a kiss.

—20 JANUARY 1985

—The sunset, Mannerist clouds
                                just shy of the Blue Ridge
Gainsay the age before they lose their blush
In the rising coagulation of five o'clock.
Two dark, unidentifiable birds
                                swoop and climb
Out of the picture, the white-slatted, red-roofed Munch house
Gathering light as the evening begins to clot.
The trees dissolve in their plenitude
                                    into a dark forest
And streetlights come on to stare like praying mantises down on us.

Next morning all's inside out,
                                the winter trees with their nervous systems
Snatched up and sparkless against the sky.

Light lies without desire on the black wires
And the white wires,
                                        the dead leaves sing like gnats,
Rising and settling back when the wind comes.
How does one deal with what is always falling away,
Returning diminished with each turn?
The grass knows, stunned in its lockjaw bed,
                                                                    but it won't tell.

—30 JANUARY 1985

—We stand at the green gates,
                                                    substitutes for the unseen
Rising like water inside our bodies,
Stand-ins against the invisible:
It's the blank sky of the page
                                                  —not the words it's never the words—
That backgrounds our lives:
It's you always you and not your new suit
That elicits solicitude:
The unknown repeats us, and quickens our in-between.

Winter is like that—abstract,
                                                  flat planes and slashes,
The Blue Ridge like a worm's back
Straight ahead,
                                    one skewed hump and then a smooth one,
Hallelujah of tree branches and telephone poles
In front, and a house or two and a nurse:
February music,
                                     high notes and a thin line strung
For us to cleave to, black notes
Someone is humming we haven't been introduced to:

Like the stone inside a rock,
the stillness of form is the center of everything,
Inalterable, always at ease.

—7 FEBRUARY 1985

—The rain, in its white disguise,
has nothing to say to the wind
That carries it, whose shoulders
It slips from giving no signal, aimlessly, one drop
At a time, no word
Or gesture to what has carried it all this way for nothing.

This is the disappearance we all dreamed of when young,
Without apology, tougher than water, no word
To anyone,
disguised as ourselves
And unrecognizable, unique
And indistinguishable from what we disappeared into.

—13 FEBRUARY 1985

—One, one and by one we all slip into the landscape,
Under the muddy patches,
locked in the frozen bud
Of the down-leafed rhododendron,
Or blurred in the echoing white of a rabbit's tail
Chalked on the winter's dark
in the back yard or the driveway.

One, one and by one we all sift to a difference
And cry out if one of our branches snaps
or our bark is cut.

The winter sunlight scours us,
The winter wind is our comfort and consolation.
We settle into our ruin

One, one and by one as we slip from clear rags into feathery skin
Or juice-in-the-ground, pooled
And biding its time
                    backwashed under the slick peach tree.
One, one and by one thrust up by the creek bank,
Huddled in spongy colonies,
                              longing to be listened to.

Here I am, here I am, we all say,
                              I'm back,
Rustle and wave, chatter and spring
Up to the air, the sweet air.
Hardened around the woodpecker's hole, under his down,
We all slip into the landscape, one, one and by one.

—25 FEBRUARY 1985

—Fever and ooze, fever and ooze:
Pronoun by pronoun, verb by irregular verb,
Winter grows great with spring: March:
                                        already something has let loose
Deep in the hidden undersprings
Of the year, looking for some way out: moss sings
At the threshold, tongues wag
                              down the secret valleys and dark draws
Under the sun-stunned grass:
What can't stop comes on, mewling like blood-rush in the ear,

Balancing over the sunken world:
fever and ooze, fever and ooze.

—9 MARCH 1985

—I used to sit on one of the benches along the Adige
In a small park upriver from S. Anastasia
from time to time
When I lived in Verona,
the Roman theater like lapped wings
On some seabird across the water
Unable to rise, half folded, half turned in the pocked air
The river spray threw up
on me and on it.
Catullus's seat—VALERI—was carved on top of the left-hand wing.
I used to try to imagine—delicious impossibility—
What it must have been like to be him,
his vowels and consonants
The color of bee wings hived in the bee-colored afternoons.
An iron-spiked and barbed-wire jut-out and overhang loomed
Just to my left.
I always sat as close to it as I could.

I remember a woman I saw there once,
in March,
The daylight starting to shake its hair out like torch flames
Across the river,
the season poised like a veiled bride,
White foot in its golden shoe
Beating the ground, full of desire, white foot at the white threshold.
She stared at the conched hillside
as though the season became her,
As though a threshold were opening

Somewhere inside her, no woman more beautiful than she was,
No song more insistent than the beat of that white foot,
As she stepped over,
                                        full of desire,
Her golden shoe like a sun in the day's deep chamber.
I remember the way she looked as she stood there,
                                                                        that look on her face.

—27 MARCH 1985

—Such a hustle of blue skies from the west,
                                                                the pre-Columbian clouds
Brooding and looking straight down,
The white plumes of the crab-apple tree
Plunging and streaming in their invisible headgear.

April plugs in the rosebud
                                              and its Tiffany limbs.
This earth is a plenitude, but it all twists into the dark,
The not no image can cut
Or color replenish.
                                       Not red, not yellow, not blue.

—9 APRIL 1985

—Draining the Great Valley of Southwest Virginia
                                                                  and Upper East Tennessee,
The Holston River cuts through the water gaps and the wind gaps
In the Stone Mountains and Iron Mountains
Northeast-southwest,
                                          a trellis pattern of feeder streams
Like a grid from Saltville in the north
To Morristown and Jefferson City in the south

Overlaying the uplifts and folds
                                        and crystalline highlands
That define and channel the main valley,
Clinch Mountain forming a western wall,
The Great Smokies and the Unakas dominant in the south.

In 1779 it took John Donelson from December till March
To go from Kingsport to Knoxville on it
By flatboat, a distance nowadays of two hours by car.
All of my childhood was spent on rivers,
The Tennessee and Hiwassee, the Little Pigeon,
The Watauga and Holston.
                                    There's something about a river
No ocean can answer to:
Leonardo da Vinci,
                        in one of his notebooks,
Says that the water you touch is the last of what has passed by
And the first of what's to come.

The Cherokee called it Hogoheegee,
                                            the Holston,
From its source in Virginia down to the mouth of the French Broad.
Donelson's flotilla to Middle Tennessee
From Fort Patrick Henry
                                —one of the singular achievements
In opening the West—
Began from the Long Island of the Holston, across
The river and upwind of the fort.
It took them four months, down the Holston and Tennessee,
Up the Ohio and Cumberland,
                                        to reach Nashville,
The Big Salt Lick, and the log cabins of settlement.

Intended by God's Permission, his journal said,
Through Indian ambush, death by drowning, death by fire,
Privation and frostbite,
                                        their clothes much cut by bullets,
Over the thirty miles of Muscle Shoals,
Loss of the pox-carrying boat and its twenty-eight people
Which followed behind in quarantine and was cut off,
Intercepted, and all its occupants
                                                    butchered or taken prisoner
Their cries distinctly heard by those boats in the rear,
Passage beyond the Whirl,
                                            the suckpool by Cumberland Mountain,
Slaughter of swans, slaughter of buffalo,
                                                            Intended by God's Permission . . .

Imagine them standing there
                                              in full headdress and harness
Having to give it all up,
                                        another agreement in blackface,
This one the Long Island of the Holston Peace Treaty,
Ending, the first time, the Cherokee Nation.
Imagine them standing very still,
Protecting their families, hoping to hang on to their one life.
Imagine the way they must have felt
                                                      agreeing to give away
What wasn't assignable,
The ground that everyone walked on,
                                                        all the magic of water,
Wind in the trees, sunlight, all the magic of water.

—18 APRIL 1985

—April, and mirror-slide of the fatal quiet,
Butterflies in a dark confusion over the flower's clenched cheeks,
The smell of chlorophyll
                                        climbing like desperation across my skin:
The maple is flocked, and the sky is choked with cloud tufts
That print a black alphabet
                                        along the hillsides and short lawns,
Block gutturals and half thoughts
Against the oily valves opening and closing in the leaves,
Edgy, autumnal morning,
April, stretched out at ease above the garden,
                                                            that rises and bows
To whatever it fancies:
Precious stones, the wind's cloth, Prester John or the boy-king of Babylon,
April,
        dank, unseasonable winter of the dead.

—27 APRIL 1985

—Visiting Emily Dickinson

We stood in the cupola for a while,
                                                JT, Joe Langland and I,
And then they left and I sat
Where she'd sat, and looked through the oak tree toward the hat factory
And down to the river, the railroad

Still there, the streets where the caissons growled
                                                                with their blue meat
Still there, and Austin and Sue's still there
Next door on the other side.
And the train station at the top of the hill.
                                                        And I sat there and I sat there

A decade or so ago
One afternoon toward the end of winter, the oak tree
Floating its ganglia like a dark cloud
                                        outside the window.
Or like a medusa hung up to dry.

And nothing came up through my feet like electric fire.
And no one appeared in a white dress
                                        with white flowers
Clutched in her white, tiny hands:
No voice from nowhere said anything
                                        about living and dying in 1862.

But I liked it there. I liked
The way sunlight lay like a shirtwaist over the window seat.
I liked the view down to the garden.
                                        I liked the boxwood and evergreens
And the wren-like, sherry-eyed figure

I kept thinking I saw there
                                as the skies started to blossom
And a noiseless noise began to come from the orchard—
And I sat very still, and listened hard
And thought I heard it again.
                                And then there was nothing, nothing at all,

The slick bodice of sunlight
                                smoothed out on the floorboards,
The crystal I'd turned inside of
Dissembling to shine and a glaze somewhere near the windowpanes,
Voices starting to drift up from downstairs,
                                        somebody calling my name . . .

—6 MAY 1985

—Ficino tells us the Absolute
Wakens the drowsy, lights the obscure,
                                                                revives the dead,
Gives form to the formless and finishes the incomplete.
What better good can be spoken of?

—9 MAY 1985

—In the first inch of afternoon, under the peach trees,
The constellations of sunlight
Sifting along their courses among the posed limbs,
It's hard to imagine the north wind
                                                        wishing us ill,
Revealing nothing at all and wishing us ill
In God's third face.
                                    The world is an ampersand,
And I lie in sweet clover,
                                            bees like golden earrings
Dangling and locked fast to its white heads,
Watching the clouds move and the constellations of light move
Through the trees, as they both will
When the wind weathers them on their way,
When the wind weathers them to that point
                                                                    where all things meet.

—15 MAY 1985

—For two months I've wanted to write about Edgar Allan Poe,
Who lived for a year where I live now
In 1826,
            the year that Mr. Jefferson died.
He lived, appropriately enough, at 13 West Range:
One room with a fireplace and bed,
                                                        one table and candlestick,

A small trunk and a washstand.
There's a top hat and a black hat box on the trunk lid.
There's a grey cape on the clothes rack
                                        and a bowl of mold-haired fruit
On the washstand.
                    There's a mirror and cane-back chair.

Over the door, in Latin, are bronze words
About the *Magni Poetae* which I don't believe
Any more now than I used to before I lived here.
Still, there's something about the place
                                        that draws me
A couple of times a week
To peer through the slab-glass door,
To knock twice with my left hand on the left doorjamb
Each time I go there,
                    hoping to call the spirits up
Or just to say hello.
                    He died in fear and away from home.

I went to his grave once in Baltimore,
                                        a young lieutenant
Intent on intensity.
I can't remember what I thought it meant to me then,
But can remember going back to the BOQ
To sit up most of the night
                    drinking red wine and reading a book of poems.
Here in Virginia when I visit his room and knock
Twice on the doorjamb, and look at the rump-sprung mattress,
The spirits come and my skin sings.
I still don't know why
                    but I think it's all right, and I like it.

—23 MAY 1985

—Horn music starts up and stutters uncertainly
out of the brown house
Across the street: a solo,
A duet, then three of them all at once, then silence,
Then up and back down the scale.
Sunday, the ninth of June, the morning
Still dull-eyed in its green kimono,
the loose, blown sleeves
Moving complacently in the wind.
Now there are two, then all three again
weaving a blurred, harmonic line
Through the oak trees and the dogwood
As the wind blows and the sheer nightgown of daylight glints.

Where was it I heard before
Those same runs and half-riffs
turned through a summer morning,
Come from one of the pastel buildings
Outside the window I sat in front of looking down
As I tried to practice my own scales
of invisible music
I thought I heard for hours on a yellow legal pad?
Verona, I think, the stiff French horn
Each weekend echoing my own false notes
and scrambled lines
I tried to use as decoys to coax the real things down
Out of the air they hid in and out of the pencils they hid in . . .

Silence again. For good, now,
I suspect, until next week,
arduous harmony,
Unalterable music our lives are measured by.
What will become of us, the Italian French horn player,

These players, me, all of us
trying to imitate
What we can't see and what we can't hear?
Nothing spectacular, I would guess, a life
Scored more or less by others,
smorzando here, *andante* there:
Only the music will stay untouched,
Moving as certainly as the wind moves,
invisible in the trees.

—12 JUNE 1985

—North wind flows from the mountain like water,
a clear constancy
Runneling through the grapevines,
Slipping and eddying over the furrows the grasses make
Between the heaves and slackening of the vine rows,
Easing and lengthening over the trees,
then smooth, flat
And without sound onto the plain below.
It parts the lizard-colored beech leaves,
Nudges and slithers around
the winter-killed cypress
Which stand like odd animals,
Brown-furred and hung from the sky,
backwashes against the hillsides
And nibbles my cheeks and hands
Where I stand on the balcony letting it scour me.
Lamentation of finches,
harangue of the sparrow,
Nothing else moves but wind in the dog-sleep of late afternoon . . .

Inside the self is another self like a black hole
Constantly dying, pulling parts of our lives
Always into its fluttery light,
                                        anxious as Augustine
For redemption and explanation:
No birds hang in its painted and polished skies, no trees
Mark and exclaim its hill lines,
                                        no grass moves, no water:

Like souls looking for bodies after some Last Judgment,
Forgotten incidents rise
                                        from under the stone slabs
Into its waxed air;
Grief sits like a toad with its cheeks puffed,
Immovable, motionless, its tongue like a trick whip
Picking our sorrows off, our days and our happiness;

Despair, with its three mouths full,
Dangles our good occasions, such as they are, in its grey hands,
Feeding them in,
                                        medieval and naked in their ecstasy;
And Death, a tiny o of blackness,
Waits like an eye for us to fall through its retina,
A minor irritation,
                                        so it can blink us back.

Nothing's so beautiful as the memory of it
Gathering light as glass does,
As glass does when the sundown is on it
                                        and darkness is still a thousand miles away.

Last night, in the second yard, salmon-smoke in the west
Back-vaulting the bats
                    who plunged and swooped like wrong angels
Hooking their slipped souls in the twilight,
The quattrocento landscape
                         turning to air beneath my feet,
I sat on the stone wall as the white shirts of my son and friend
Moved through the upper yard like candles
Among the fruit trees,
                    and the high voices of children
Sifted like mist from the road below
In a game I'd never played,
                         and knew that everything was a shining,
That whatever I could see was filled with the drained light
Lapping away from me quietly,
Disappearing between the vine rows,
                              creeping back through the hills,
That anything I could feel,
                         anything I could put my hand on—
The damasked mimosa leaf,
The stone ball on the gate post, the snail shell in its still turning—
Would burst into brilliance at my touch.
But I sat still, and I touched nothing,
                              afraid that something might change
And change me beyond my knowing,
That everything I had hoped for, all I had ever wanted,
Might actually happen.
                    So I sat still and touched nothing.

Six-thirty, summer evening, the swallow's hour
Over the vine rows:
                                        arrowing down the valley, banking back
And sliding against the wind, they feint
And rise, invisible sustenance disappearing
Out of the air:
                              in the long, dark beams of the farmhouse,
The termites and rhinoceros beetles bore in their slow lines
Under another sky:
                                        everything eats or is eaten.

I find myself in my own image, and am neither and both.
I come and go in myself
                                              as though from room to room,
As though the smooth incarnation of some medieval spirit
Escaping my own mouth and reswallowed at leisure,
Dissembling and at my ease.
The dove drones on the hillside,
                                                            hidden inside the dead pine tree.
The wasp drills through the air.
I am neither, I am both.
Inside the turtle dove is the turtle dove,
                                                                      a serious moan.
Inside the wasp we don't know, and a single drop of poison.

This part of the farmhouse was built in the fourteenth century.
Huge chains hold the central beam
                                                                and the wall together.
It creaks like a ship when the walls shift in the afternoon wind.

Who is it here in the night garden,
gown a transparent rose
Down to his ankles, great sleeves
Spreading the darkness around him wherever he steps,
Laurel corona encircling his red transparent headcap,
Pointing toward the Madonna?
Who else could it be,
voice like a slow rip through silk cloth
In disapproval? *Brother*, he says, pointing insistently,
A sound of voices starting to turn in the wind and then disappear as though
Orbiting us, *Brother, remember the way it was*
In my time: nothing has changed:
Penitents terrace the mountainside, the stars hang in their bright courses
And darkness is still the dark:
concentrate, listen hard,
Look to the nature of all things,
And vanished into the oncoming disappearing
Circle of voices slipstreaming through the oiled evening.

Hmmm . . . Not exactly transplendent:
Look to the nature of all things . . .
The clouds slide from the west to the east
Over the Berici Mountains, hiding the half of what he spoke of.
Wind is asleep in the trees,
weighing the shelled leaves down.
A radio comes and goes from a parked car below the hill.
What *is* it these children chant about
In their games?
Why are their voices so like those
I thought I heard just moments ago

Centrifugal in their extantsy?

Concentrate, listen hard . . .

A motor scooter whines up the hill road, toward the Madonna.

—9 JULY 1985

(CÀ PARUTA)

—All morning the long-bellied, two-hitched drag trucks
Have ground down the mountainside
loaded with huge, cut stone
From two quarries being worked
Some miles up the slope. Rock-drilled and squared-off,
They make the brakes sing and the tires moan,
A music of sure contrition that troubles our ears
And shudders the farmhouse walls.
No one around here seems to know
Where the great loads go or what they are being used for.
But everyone suffers the music,
We all sway to the same tune
when the great stones pass by,
A weight that keeps us pressed to our chairs
And pushes our heads down, and slows our feet.

Volcanic originally, the Euganean Hills
Blister a tiny part,
upper northeast, of the Po flood plain.
Monasteries and radar stations
Relay the word from their isolate concentration,
Grouped, as they are, like bread mold
and terraced like Purgatory.

Their vineyards are visible for miles,
                                                            cut like a gentle and green
Strip-mining curl up the steep slopes.
During the storm-sweeps out of the Alps,
From a wide distance they stand like a delicate Chinese screen
Against the immensity of the rain.

Outside my door, a cicada turns its engine on.
Above me the radar tower
Tunes its invisible music in:
                                                other urgencies tell their stories
Constantly in their sleep,
Other messages plague our ears
                                                    under Madonna's tongue:
The twilight twists like a screw deeper into the west.

Through scenes of everyday life,
Through the dark allegory of the soul
                                                            into the white light of eternity,
The goddess burns in her golden car
From month to month, season to season
                                                                high on the walls
At the south edge of Ferrara,
Her votive and reliquary hands
Suspended and settled upon as though under glass,
Offering, giving a gentle benediction:
Reality, symbol and ideal
                                            tripartite and everlasting
Under the bricked, Emilian sun.

Borso, the mad uncle, giving a coin to the jester Scoccola,
Borso receiving dignitaries
                                        or out hawking,
Or listening to supplications from someone down on his knees,
Or giving someone his due.
Borso d'Este, Duke of Ferrara and Modena, on a spring day
On horseback off to the hunt:
                                        a dog noses a duck up from a pond,
Peasants are pruning the vines back, and grafting new ones
Delicately, as though in a dance,
Ghostly noblemen ride their horses over the archway,
A child is eating something down to the right,
                                        a monkey climbs someone's leg . . .

Such a narrow, meaningful strip
                                        of arrows and snakes.
Circles and purple robes, griffins and questing pilgrims:
At the tip of the lion's tail, a courtier rips
A haunch of venison with his teeth;
At the lion's head,
                                        someone sits in a brushed, celestial tree.
What darkness can be objectified by this dance pose
And musician holding a dead bird
At each end of the scales?
                                        What dark prayer can possibly escape
The black, cracked lips of this mendicant woman on her pooled knees?
The shadowy ribbon offers its warnings up
                                        under the green eyes of heaven.

Up there, in the third realm,
                                        light as though under water
Washes and folds and breaks in small waves
Over each month like sunrise:
                                        triumph after triumph

Of pure Abstraction and pure Word, a paradise of white cloth
And white reflections of cloth cross-currented over the cars
With golden wheels and gold leads,
                                        all Concept and finery:
Love with her long hair and swans in trace,
Cybele among the Corybants,
Apollo, Medusa's blood and Attis in expiation:
All caught in the tide of light,
                                        all burned on the same air.

Is this the progression of our lives,
                                        or merely a comment on them?
Is this both the picture and what's outside the picture,
Or decoration opposing boredom
For court ladies to glance up at,
                                        crossing a tiled floor?
How much of what we leave do we mean to leave
And how much began as fantasy?
Questions against an idle hour as Borso looks to his hounds,
Virgo reclines on her hard bed
                                        under the dragon's heel,
And turreting over the green hills
And the sea, color of sunrise,
                                        the city floats in its marbled tear of light.

From my balcony, the intense blue of the under-heaven,
Sapphiric and anodyne,
                                        backdrops Madonna's crown.
Later, an arched stretch of cloud,
Like a jet trail or a comet's trail,
                                        vaults over it,

A medieval ring of Paradise.
Today, it's that same blue again, blue of redemption
Against which, in the vine rows,
                                                  the green hugs the ground hard.
Not yet, it seems to say, O not yet.

Heavy Italian afternoon: heat drives like a nail
Through the countryside,
                                        everything squirms
Or lies pinned and still in its shining.
On the opposite slope, Alfredo, his long, curved scythe
Flashing and disappearing into the thick junk weeds
Between the vine stocks, moves,
                                                  with a breathy, whooshing sound,
Inexorably as a visitation, or some event
The afternoon's about to become the reoccasion of:
St. Catherine catching the martyr's head
                                                              in her white hands;
St. Catherine urging the blades on
As the wheel dazzles and turns,
Feeling the first nick like the first rung of Paradise;
St. Catherine climbing, step by step,
The shattering ladder up
                                      to the small, bright hurt of the saved.

—25 JULY 1985
(CÀ PARUTA)

—Rilke, di Valmarana, the King of Abyssinia
And countless others once came to wash

At his memory, dipping their hands
                                        into the cold waters of his name,
And signing their own
In the vellum, nineteenth-century books
The Commune of Padova provided,
                                        each graced page
Now under glass in the fourteenth-century stone rooms
The poet last occupied.
We've come for the same reasons, though the great registers
No longer exist, and no one of such magnitude
Has been in evidence for some years.
                                        On the cracked, restored walls,
Atrocious frescoes, like those in an alcove of some trattoria,
Depict the Arcadian pursuits
He often wrote of,
                        dotted with puffy likenesses
Of the great man himself, intaglio prints of Laura
And re-creations of famous instances
In his life.
            Poems by devotees are framed and hung up
Strategically here and there.
In short, everything one would hope would not be put forth
In evidence on Petrarch's behalf.

Arquà Petrarca, the town he died in,
                                        and this is,
Dangles in folds and cutbacks
Down the mountainside,
                                medieval and still undisturbed
In the backwash he retired to, and the zone remains,
Corn, vineyards and fig orchards.
The town's on the other side of the hill, and unseen,
And from the second-floor balcony,
                                        southward across the Po Valley,

The prospect is just about
What he would have looked at,
                                        the extra roadway and house
Gracious and unobtrusive.
I ghost from room to room and try hard
To reamalgamate everything that stays missing,
To bring together again
                              the tapestries and winter fires,
The long walks and solitude
Before the damage of history and an odd fame
Unlayered it all but the one name and a rhyme scheme.
Marconi, Victor Emmanuel II, prince
And princess have come and gone.
                                        Outside, in the garden,
The hollyhocks and rose pips move quietly in the late heat.
I write my name in the dirt
                                  and knock twice as we leave.

Farfalla comes to my door frame,
                                        enters my window,
Swivels and pirouettes, white in the white sunlight,
Farfalla and bumblebee,
Butterfly, wasp and bumblebee
                                       together into the dark
Latitudes of my attic, then out
Again, all but la vespa,
The other two into the daylight, a different flower:
Vespa cruises in darkness,
                                 checking the corners out,
The charred crevices fit for her habitation, black
Petals for her to light on.

No clouds for four weeks, Madonna stuck
On the blue plate of the sky like sauce
                                        left out overnight,
Everything flake-red and dust-peppered,
Ants slow on the doorsill,
                              flies languishing on the iron
Railing where no wind jars them.
Dead, stunned heart of summer: the blood stills to a bell pull,
The cry from the watermelon truck
                                        hangs like a sheet in the dry air,
The cut grain splinters across the hillside.
All night the stalled dogs bark in our sleep.
All night the rats flutter and roll in the dark loft holes over our heads.

As St. Augustine tells us, whatever is, is good,
As long as it is,
                    even as it rusts and decays
In the paracletic nature of all things:
                                        transplendent enough,
I'd say, for our needs, if that's what he meant
Back there in the garden in that circle of voices
Widening out of the sunset and disappearing . . .

Dog fire: quick singes and pops
Of lightning finger the mountainside:
                                        the towers and deep dish
Are calling their children in, Madonna is calling her little ones

Out of the sky, such fine flames
To answer to and add up
                                        as they all come down from the dark.
In the rings and after-chains,
In the great river of language that circles the universe,
Everything comes together,
No word is ever lost,
                                no utterance ever abandoned.
They're all borne on the bodiless, glittering currents
That wash us and seek us out:
                                        there is a word, one word,
For each of us, circling and holding fast
In all that cascade and light.
Said once, or said twice,
                                        it gathers and waits its time to come back
To its true work:
                        concentrate, listen hard.

Enormous shadows settle across the countryside,
Scattered and misbegotten.
Clouds slide from the Dolomites
                                                as though let out to dry.
Sunset again: that same color of rose leaf and rose water.
The lights of another town
                                        tattoo their promises
Soundlessly over the plain.
I'm back in the night garden,
                                        the lower yard, between
The three dead fig trees,
Under the skeletal comb-leaves of the fanned mimosa branch,
Gazing at the Madonna,

The swallows and bats at their night work
And I at mine.
                                        No scooters or trucks,
No voices of children, no alphabet in the wind:
Only this silence, the strict gospel of silence,
                                                                                    to greet me,
Opened before me like a rare book.
I turn the first page
                                                  and then the next, but understand nothing,
The deepening twilight a vast vocabulary
I've never heard of.
I keep on turning, however:
                                                              somewhere in here, I know, is my word.

—3 AUGUST 1985
(CÀ PARUTA)

—A day licked entirely clean, the landscape resettled
Immeasurably closer, focused
And held still under the ground lens of heaven,
                                                                                        the air
As brittle as spun glass:
One of those days the sunlight stays an inch above,
                                                                                              or an inch inside
Whatever its tongue touches:
I can't remember my own youth,
That seam of red silt I try so anxiously to unearth:
A handful of dust is a handful of dust,
                                                                           no matter who holds it.
Always the adverb, always the ex-Etcetera . . .

—20 AUGUST 1985

—On my fiftieth birthday I awoke
In a Holiday Inn just east of Winchester, Virginia,
The companionable summer rain
stitching the countryside
Like bagworms inside its slick cocoon:
The memory of tomorrow is yesterday's story line:
I ate breakfast and headed south,
the Shenandoah
Zigzagging in its small faith
Under the Lee Highway and Interstate 81,
First on my left side, then on my right,
Sluggish and underfed,
the absences in the heart
Silent as sparrows in the spinning rain:

How do I want to say this?
My mother's mother's family
For generations has sifted down
This valley like rain out of Clarke County,
seeping into the red clay
Overnight and vanishing into the undergrowth
Of different lives as hard as they could.
Yesterday all of us went
to all of the places all of them left from
One way or another,
apple groves, scrub oaks, gravestones
With short, unmellifluous, unfamiliar names,
Cold wind out of the Blue Ridge,
And reason enough in the lowering sky for leaving
A weight so sure and so fixed . . .

And now it's my turn, same river, same hard-rock landscape
Shifting to past behind me.
What makes us leave what we love best?
What is it inside us that keeps erasing itself
When we need it most,
That sends us into uncertainty for its own sake
And holds us flush there
until we begin to love it
And have to begin again?
What is it within our own lives we decline to live
Whenever we find it,
making our days unendurable,
And nights almost visionless?
I still don't know yet, but I do it.

In my fiftieth year, with a bad back and a worried mind,
Going down the Lee Highway,
the farms and villages
Rising like fog behind me,
Between the dream and the disappearance the abiding earth
Affords us each for an instant.
However we choose to use it
We use it and then it's gone:
Like the glint of the Shenandoah
at Castleman's Ferry,
Like license plates on cars we follow and then pass by,
Like what we hold and let go,
Like this country we've all come down,
and where it's led us,
Like what we forgot to say, each time we forget it.

—25–29 AUGUST 1985

—Ashes know what burns,
clouds savvy which way the wind blows . . .
Full moon like a bed of coals
As autumn revs up and cuts off:
Remembering winter nights like a doused light bulb
Leaning against my skin,
object melting into the image
Under the quickly descending stars:
Once the impasse is solved, St. Augustine says, between matter and spirit,
Evil is merely the absence of good:
Which makes sense, if you understand what it truly means,
Full moon the color of sand now,
and still unretractable . . .

In a bad way,
I don't even know what I don't know,
Time like a one-eyed jack
whose other face I can't see
Hustling me on O hustling me on,
Dark of the moon, far side of the sun, the back half of the sky.
Time is memory, he adds:
It's all in the mind's eye,
where everything comes to one,
Conjecture, pure spirit, the evil that matter cannot present us—
As the sentence hides in the ink,
as cancer hides in the smoke,
As dark hides in the light,
Time hides in our pockets, not stirring, not weighing much.

—5 SEPTEMBER 1985

—Still, they tried it again, one last time,
In 1776, the Battle of Island Flats

Outside Fort Patrick Henry
on the Long Island of the Holston,
Dragging Canoe and Abraham
advancing quicker than frost
With their sworn braves through the countryside.

After a small skirmish between scouts and advance guards,
Dragging Canoe brought three hundred men
Into position along a quarter-of-a-mile
Fortified line of calm frontiersmen
and ended for all time
The Cherokee's mystic Nation
with streams of blood every way.

Never so much execution in so short a time
On the frontier.
Our spies really deserve the greatest applause.
We took a great deal of plunder and many guns.
We have a great reason to believe
They are pouring in greatest numbers upon us
and beg assistance of our friends.

Exaggeration and rhetoric:
Nothing was pouring on them, of course,
but history and its disaffection,
Stripping the vacuum of the Cherokee:
The Battle of Island Flats
Starts the inevitable exodus,
Tsali and the Trail of Tears . . .

—15 SEPTEMBER 1985

—Attention is the natural prayer of the soul . . .

September, the bed we lie in between summer and autumn,
Sunday in all the windows,
                                        the slow snow of daylight
Flaking the holly tree and the hedge panes
As it disappears in the odd milk teeth

The grass has bared, both lips back
                                                  in the cool suck of dusk.
Prayer wheels, ugly as ice, turn in our eyes:
                                                          verbs white, nouns white,
Adjectives white on white,
                                        they turn in our eyes:
Nothing is lost in my eyes in your eyes
                                                    nothing is lost
As the wheels whiffle and spin,
                                              conjunction and adverb
White in the white sky of our eyes,
                                                  ribbons luffing goodbye . . .

September butterflies, heavy with pollen, leaf down
In ones and pairs from the oak trees
                                                  through the dwarf orchard
And climb the gold-dusted staves of sunlight toward the south
Like notes from a lush music
                                          we always almost hear
But don't quite, and stutter into the understory next door.

Night now. Silence. The flowers redeem
Nothing the season can offer up,
                                              stars beginning to chink fast
Overhead, west wind

Shuffling the decks of the orchard leaves.
Silence again,
                    a fine ash, a night inside the night.

—29 SEPTEMBER 1985

—The shadows of leaves on the driveway and just-cut grass,
Blurred and enlarged,
                              riffle in short takes
As though stirred under water, a snicked breeze
Moving their makers cross-current and cross-grained across the pool
The daylight makes in the ash tree
                                        and the troubled oak.

These monochromatic early days of October
Throb like a headache just back of the eyes,
                                                  a music
Of dull, identical syllables
Almost all vowels,
                         ooohing and aaahing
As though they would break out in speech and tell us something.

But nothing's to be revealed,
It seems:
  each day the shadows blur and enlarge, the rain comes and comes back,
A dripping of consonants,
As though it too wanted to tell us something, something
Unlike the shadows and their stray signs,

Unlike the syllable the days make
Behind the eyes, cross-current and cross-grained, and unlike
The sibilance of oak tree and ash.
                                        What it wants to tell us

Is ecstasy and always,
Guttural words that hang like bats in the throat,
their wings closed, their eyes shut:

What it wants to tell us is damped down, slick with desire,
And unaccountable
to weather and its apostrophes,
Dark, sweet dark, and close to hand:
Inside its body, high on a branch, a bird
repeats the letters of its secret name
To everything, and everything listens hard.

—4 OCTOBER 1985

—Truth is the absence of falsehood,
beauty the absence of ugliness,
Jay like a stuffed toy in the pear tree,
Afternoon light-slant deep weight
diluting to aftermath on the lawn,
Jay immobile and fluffed up,
Cloud like a bass note, held and slow, now on the sunlight.
The disillusioned and twice-lapsed, the fallen-away,
Become my constituency:
those who would die back
To splendor and rise again
From hurt and unwillingness,
their own ash on their tongues,
Are those I would be among,
The called, the bruised by God, by their old ways forsaken
And startled on, the shorn and weakened.

There is no loneliness where the body is.
There is no Pyrrhic degeneration of the soul there,

Dragon maple like sunset,
scales fired in the noon's glare
Flaking and twisting when the wind spurts,
Sky-back a Cherokee blue,
scales winking and flashing.
The poem is written on glass
I look through to calibrate
the azimuth of sun and Blue Ridge,
Angle of rise and fall the season reconstitutes.
My name is written on glass,
The emptiness that form takes, the form of emptiness
The body can never signify,
yellow of ash leaves on the grass,
Three birds on the dead oak limb.
The heart is a spondee.

—12 OCTOBER 1985

—It is as though, sitting out here in the dwarf orchard,
The soul had come to rest at the edge of the body,
A vacancy, a small ache,
the soul had come to rest
After a long passage over the wasteland and damp season.
It is as though a tree had been taken out of the landscape.
It is as though a tree had been taken out
and moved to one side
And the wind blew where the tree had been
As though it had never blown there before,
or that hard.

Tomorrow the rain will come with its lucid elastic threads
Binding the earth and sky.
Tomorrow the rain will come
And the soul will start to move again,

Retracing its passage, marking itself
back to the center of things.
But today, in the blanched warmth of Indian summer,
It nudges the edge of the body,
The chill luminance of its absence
pulsing and deep,
Extraction the landscape illuminates in the body's night.

—22 OCTOBER 1985

—The season steps up,
repeating its catechism inside the leaves.
The dogwoods spell out their beads,
Wind zithers a *Kyrie eleison* over the power lines:
Sunday, humped up in majesty,
the new trench for the gas main
Thrums like a healing scar
Across the street, rock-and-roll
Wah-wahs from off the roof next door to Sylvia's house
just down the block:

The days peel back, maples kick in their afterburners,
We harry our sins
and expiations around the purgatorial strip
We're subject to, eyes sewn shut,
Rocks on our backs,
escaping smoke or rising out of the flame,
Hoping the angel's sword
unsullied our ashed foreheads,
Hoping the way up is not the way down,
Autumn firestorm in the trees,
autumn under our feet . . .

—29 OCTOBER 1985

—I have no interest in anything
but the color of leaves,
Yellow leaves drawing the light around them
Against the mumped clouds of an early November dusk—
They draw the light like gold foil
around their stiff bodies
And hang like Byzantium in the Byzantine sky.

I have no interest in anything
but the color of blood,
Blood black as a prayer book, flushed from my own body,
China black, lapping the porcelain:
somewhere inside me blood
Is drawing the darkness in,
Stipple by stipple into the darker waters beneath the self.

I have no interest in anything
but the color of breath,
Green as the meat-haunted hum of flies,
Viridian exocrine,
wisp of the wave-urge, jade
Calvary of the begotten sigh,
Alpha of everything, green needle and green syringe.

—11 NOVEMBER 1985

—"If you licked my heart, you'd die,
poisoned by gall and anxiousness."
I read that last night in my first dream.

In the next, the leaves fell from the trees,
the stars fell from the sky
Like snowflakes, slowly and vast:

As I walked through the lightfall, my footprints like small, even voids
Behind me,
                    the color of starflakes settling on everything,
Light up to my ankles, then up to my knees,
I moved effortlessly through the splendor drifting around me
Until I became a dot,
                              then grained out into light,
The voids of my footprints still sunk, hard-edged and firm, where I'd
    passed.

In my last dream, just before sunrise,
I showed slides, two slides at a time,
                                        of the Resurrection, one
A painting, the other a photograph.
Much later, I showed the Five Sorrows of the Virgin,
One at a time,
            three prayers of intercession and the Assumption of St. John . . .

The subject matter is not the persona, it's the person:
"If you licked my heart, you'd die,
                                        poisoned by gall and anxiousness."

Today, in mid-November's ocher afternoon light,
All's otherworldly,
                    my neighbor rolling his garbage carts to the curb,
My son repacking the tulip bulbs in their black beds:
What stays important is what we don't know and what we are not,
For nothing and nothing make nothing.

—20 NOVEMBER 1985

—All my life I've stood in desire:
                                    look upon me and leave me alone,

Clear my windows and doors of flies
And let them be, taking no heed of them: I abide
In darkness, it is so small and indivisible,
A full food, and more precious than time:

Better to choose for your love what you can't think,
better
To love what may be gotten and held,
And step above what can be cast out and covered up:
The shorter the word, the more it serves the work of the spirit:
Tread it down fast,
have it all whole, not broken and not undone.

—28 NOVEMBER 1985

—Last day of November, rain
Stringy and almost solid,
incessantly gathering darkness around it
At one in the afternoon across
the Long Island of the Holston:
Up-island, steam from the coal gasification plant
Of Tennessee Eastman Corporation melds
With the cloud cover and rain cover
halfway up Bays Mountain—
Sycamore trees, with their mace-like and tiny pendants
And chimes, bow out toward the south sluice of the South Fork
Where I stand, a twentieth-century man on ground
Holy for over ten thousand years:
Across the river, the burial sites
have been bulldozed and slash-stacked
Next to Smith Equipment Company;
Behind me, the chain-linked and barbed-wire fence

Cuts under the power pylon
from one side of the island to the other,
Enclosing the soccer fields;
Rain is continuous as I turn
From the grey, cataracted eye
of a television set
Caught in a junk-jam of timber and plastic against the bank,
And walk back to the footbridge
I'd crossed the river on an hour and a half before:
Next to it, off to the left,
A rectangular block of marble, backed by slab-stone,
Had been inscribed:
Long Island of the Holston
Sacred Cherokee Ground Relinquished by Treaty
Jan. 7, 1806.
3.61 Acres Returned
To the Eastern Band of Cherokee Indians by
The City of Kingsport on July 16, 1976:
Wolf Clan, Blue Clan, Deer Clan, Paint Clan, Wild Potato Clan,
Long Hair Clan, Bird Clan:

Steam stacks, sycamores, brush harbor,
rain like the river falling . . .

—5 DECEMBER 1985

—Late afternoon, blue of the sky blue
As a dove's neck, dove
Color of winter branches among winter branches,
Guttural whistle and up,
December violets crooked at my feet,
Cloud-wedge starting to slide like a detached retina

Slanting across the blue
inaction the dove disappears in.

Mean constellations quip and annoy
next night against the same sky
As I seek out, unsuccessfully,
In Luke's spyglass Halley's comet and its train of ice:
An ordered and measured affection is virtuous
In its clean cause
however it comes close in this life.
Nothing else moves toward us out of the stars,
nothing else shines.

—12 DECEMBER 1985

—*I am poured out like water.*
Who wouldn't ask for that *lightning strike*,
the dog's breath on your knee
Seductive and unrehearsed,
The heart resoftened and made apt for illumination,
The body then taken up and its ghostly eyes dried?
Who wouldn't ask for that light,
that liquefaction and entry?

The pentimento ridgeline and bulk
Of the Blue Ridge emerge
behind the vanished over-paint
Of the fall leaves across the street,
Cross-hatched and hard-edged, deep blue on blue.
What is a life of contemplation worth in this world?
How far can you go if you concentrate,
how far down?

The afternoon shuts its doors.
The heart tightens its valves,
                                        the dragon maple sunk in its bones,
The grass asleep in its wheel.
The year squeezes to this point, the cold
Hung like a lantern against the dark
                                                  burn of a syllable:
I roll it around on my tongue, I warm its edges . . .

—25 DECEMBER 1985

Light Journal

To speak the prime word and vanish
                                                  into the aneurysm
Unhealed and holding the walls open,
Trip and thump of light
                                   up from the fingernails and through
The slack locks and stripped vessels
At last to the inarticulation of desire . . .

What did I think I meant then, Greece, 1959:
                                                            Beauty is in the looking for it,
The light here filtered through silk,
The water moving like breathing,
Moving in turn to the tide's turn,
                                             black thread through the water weave.

Whatever it was, I still mean it.

Everyone stands by himself
on the heart of the earth,
Pierced through by a ray of sunlight:
And suddenly it's evening.

It's odd what persists
slip-grained in the memory,
Candescent and held fast,
Odd how for twenty-six years the someone I was once has stayed
Stopped in the columns of light
Through S. Zeno's doors,
trying to take the next step and break clear . . .

A Journal of One Significant Landscape

April again. Aries comes forth
and we are released
Into the filter veins and vast line
Under the elm and apple wood.
The last of the daffodils
Sulphurs the half-jade grass
against the arbor vitae.

Better the bodying forth,
better the coming back.
I listen to what the quince hums,

Its music filling my ear
                    with its flushed certitude.
Wild onion narrows the latitudes.

I pale and I acquiesce.
                    Gravity empties me
Stem by stem through its deep regalia,
Resplendent and faintly anodyne,
The green of my unbecoming
                    urging me earthward.

I long to escape through the white light in the rose root,
At ease in its clean, clear joy:
Unlike the spring flowers, I don't unfold, one petal
                    after another, in solitude—
Happiness happens, like sainthood, in spite of ourselves.

The day dies like a small child,
                    blushed and without complaint,
Its bedcovers sliding quietly to the floor.
How still the world's room holds,
                    everything stemming its breath
In exhilaration and sadness.

Halfway through May and I am absolved,
A litter of leaves like half notes
                    held tight in the singing trees.
Against the board fence, the candle tips of the white pines

Gutter and burn, gutter and burn
                                        on the blue apse of the sky.

How do we get said what must be said,
Seep of the honeysuckle like bad water, yellow
And slick, through the privet hedge,
                                        tiger iris opening like an eye
Watching us steadily now, aware that what we see

In its disappearance and inexactitude
Is not what we think we see.
                                        How does one say these things?
The sheathed beaks of the waxed magnolia
Utter their couched syllables,

Shhh of noon wind mouthing the last word.
Deep in the crevices and silk ravines of the snow rose,
Under the purple beards at the lily's throat,
                                        silence stocks its cocoon:
Inside, in its radiance,
                                        the right answer waits to be born.

Truthful words are not beautiful,
                                        beautiful words not truthful,
Lao-tzu says. He has a point.
Nor are good words persuasive:
The way of heaven can do no real harm,
                                        and it doesn't contend.

Beginning of June, clouds like medieval banderoles
Out of the sky's mouth
                                        back toward the east,
Explaining the painting as Cimabue once did
In Pisa, in tempera,
                                    angels sending the message out

In those days. Not now, down here
Where the peaches swell like thumbs, and the little apples and pears
Buzz like unbroken codes on the sun's wire,
                                                                their secret shoptalk
The outtakes we would be privy to,

But never are, no matter how hard we look at them or listen.
Still, it's here in its gilt script,
                                            or there, speaking in tongues.
One of the nondescript brown-headed black birds that yawp
And scramble in and out of the trees
                                                        latches me with his lean eye

And tells me I'm wasting my time,
                                                    something I'm getting used to
In my one life with its one regret
I keep on trundling here
                                        in order to alter it.
You're wasting your time, he tells me again. And I am.

It is not possible to read the then in the now.
It is not possible to see the blood in the needle's eye,
Sky like a sheet of carbon paper
                                                repeating our poor ills

On the other side.
We must be good to each other.

Like a developing photograph,
the dawn hillsides appear
Black-and-white then green then rack-over into color
Down-country along the line,
House and barn as the night blanks
away into morning's fixer . . .

Like dreams awaiting their dreamers, cloud-figures step forth
Then disappear in the sky, ridgelines are cut,
grass moans
Under the sun's touch and drag:
With a sigh the day explains itself, and reliefs into place . . .

Like light bulbs, the pears turn on,
birds plink, the cow skull spins and stares
In heaven's eye, sunshine
Cheesecloths the ground beside the peach trees.
The dragon maple shivers its dry sides . . .

I put down these memorandums of my affections,
As John Clare said,
memory through a secondary
Being the soul of time
and life the principal but its shadow,
July in its second skin glistering through the trees . . .

For the Heavenly Father desires that we should see,
Ruysbroeck has told us,
and that is why
He's ever saying to our innermost spirit one deep
Unfathomable word,
and nothing else . . .

Thus stone upon stone,
And circle on circle I raised eternally:
So step after step
I drew back in sure ascension to Paradise,

Someone once wrote about Brunelleschi—
Giovanbattista Strozzi,
Vasari says—when he died
Vaulting the double dome of S. Maria del Fiore
In Florence,
which everyone said was impossible.

Paolo Uccello, on the other hand, once drew
The four elements as animals:
a mole for earth,
A fish for water, a salamander for fire, and for air
A chameleon which lives on air
and thus will assume whatever color.

In his last days, secluded inside his house, he stayed up
All night in his study, his wife said,
intent on perspective.
O what a lovely thing perspective is, he'd call out.

August thrusts down its flushed face,
disvectored at the horizon.

How is the vanishing point
when you look at it hard?
How does it lie in the diamond zones?
What are the colors of disappearance,
pink and grey,
Diamond and pink and grey?
How are they hard to look at?

September's the month that moves us
out of our instinct:
As the master said:
for knowledge, add something every day,
To be wise, subtract . . .
This is the season of subtraction,

When what goes away is what stays,
pooled in its own grace,
When loss isn't loss, and fall
Hangs on the cusp of its one responsibility,
Tiny erasures,
palimpsest over the pear trees.

Somewhere inside the landscape
Something reverses.
Leaf lines recoil, the moon switches

Her tides, dry banks begin to appear
In the long conduits
                                        under the skin and in the heart.

I listen to dark October just over the hill,
I listen to what the weeds exhale,
                                                            and the pines echo,
Elect in their rectitude:
The idea of emptiness is everything to them.
                                                                        I smooth myself, I abide.

Chinese Journal

In 1935, the year I was born,
                                                    Giorgio Morandi
Penciled these bottles in by leaving them out, letting
The presence of what surrounds them increase the presence
Of what is missing,
                                        keeping its distance and measure.

The purple-and-white spike plants
                                                            stand upright and spine-laced,
As though poised to fight by keeping still.
Inside their bristly circle,
The dwarf boxwood
                                        flashes its tiny shields at the sun.

Under the skylight, the Pothos plant
Dangles its fourteen arms
                                        into the absence of its desire.
Like a medusa in the two-ply, celadon air,
Its longing is what it grows on,
                                        heart-leaves in the nothingness.

To shine but not to dazzle.
Falling leaves, falling water,
                                        everything comes to rest.

What can anyone know of the sure machine that makes all things work?
To find one word and use it correctly,
                                        providing it is the right word,
Is more than enough:
An inch of music is an inch and a half of dust.

Night Journal II

The breath of What's-Out-There sags
Like bad weather below the branches,
                                        fog-sided, Venetian,
Trailing its phonemes along the ground.
                                        It says what it has to say
Carefully, without sound, word
After word imploding into articulation

And wherewithal for the unbecome.
I catch its drift.

And if I could answer back,
If once I had a cloudier tongue,
what would I say?
I'd say what it says: nothing, with all its verities
Gone to the ground and hiding:
I'd say what it says now,
Dangling its language like laundry between the dark limbs,
Just hushed in its cleanliness.

The absolute night backs off.
Hard breezes freeze in my eyelids.
The moon, stamped horn of fool's gold,
Answers for me in the arteries of the oak trees.
I long for clear water, the silence
Of risk and deep splendor,
the quietness inside the solitude.
I want its drop on my lip, its cold undertaking.

FROM

XIONIA

(1990)

Silent Journal

Inaudible consonant inaudible vowel
The word continues to fall
                    in splendor around us
Window half shadow window half moon
                                        back yard like a book of snow
That holds nothing and that nothing holds
Immaculate text
            not too prescient not too true

Bicoastal Journal

Noon light on the jacaranda fans
Colorless sheen,
            and distant figures disincarnate
Every so often among the trunks.
Red beards of the eucalyptus pips.
Squall line backing and filling
                        over the ocean's floor,
Waves folding and splayed flat.
Three sparrows bob at the feeder, two crows bring down rain.

Rain gone, sun perched on pine limb.
Birds bathe in an ashtray.
Ocean appalled above the kelp beds,
As though softer there.

Up here, glister of water bead,
                                        ants edging the ponds and lakes
Swelling the tabletop.
Here come the crows again, and the doves. Here come the gulls.

The contemplative soul goes out and comes back with marvelous
   quickness—
Or bends itself, as it were,
                                    into a circle, Richard of St. Victor says.
Or gathers itself, as it were,
In one place and is fixed there motionless
Like birds in the sky, now to the right, now to the left . . .

There are six kinds of contemplation,
                                                St. Victor adds:
Imagination, and according to imagination only;
Imagination, according to reason; reason
According to imagination;
                                    reason according to reason;
Above, but not beyond, reason;
                                        above reason, beyond reason.

First month, third day, 32 degrees.
Overcast afternoon,
                              cloud cover moving from west to east
As slow as my imagination.
Squirrels flick through the bare branches of oak trees.
Sitting outside is like sitting under the ocean:

The white pines undulate
as though looked at through sea wash:
Some wind ripples by, like a current.

I'd rather be elsewhere, like water
hugging the undergrowth,
Uncovering rocks and small windfall
Under the laurel and maple wood.
I'd rather be loose fire
Licking the edges of all things but the absolute
Whose murmur retoggles me.
I'd rather be memory, touching the undersides
Of all I ever touched once in the natural world.

December Journal

God is not offered to the senses,
St. Augustine tells us,
The artificer is not his work, but is his art:
Nothing is good if it can be better.
But all these oak trees look fine to me,
this Virginia cedar
Is true to its own order
And ghosts a unity beyond its single number.
This morning's hard frost, whose force is nowhere absent, is nowhere
present.
The undulants cleanse themselves in the riverbed,
The mud striders persevere,
the exceptions provide.

I keep coming back to the visible.
                                        I keep coming back
To what it leads me into,
The hymn in the hymnal,
The object, sequence and consequence.
By being exactly what it is,
It is that other, inviolate self we yearn for,
Itself and more than itself,
                                    the word inside the word.
It is the tree and what the tree stands in for, the blank,
The far side of the last equation.

Black and brown of December,
                                        umber and burnt orange
Under the spoked trees, front yard
Pollocked from edge feeder to edge run,
Central Virginia beyond the ridgeline spun with a back light
Into indefinition,
                        charcoal and tan, damp green . . .

Entangled in the lust of the eye,
                                    we carry this world with us wherever we go,
Even into the next one:
Abstraction, the highest form, is the highest good:
Everything's beautiful that stays in its due order,
Every existing thing can be praised
                                        when compared with nothingness.

The seasons roll from my tongue—
Autumn, winter, the *integer vitae* of all that's in vain,
Roll unredeemed.
                                        Rain falls. The utmost
Humps out to the end of nothing's branch, crooks there like an inchworm,
And fingers the emptiness.
December drips through my nerves,
                                                            a drumming of secondary things
That spells my name right,
                                                  heartbeat
Of slow, steady consonants.
Trash cans weigh up with water beside the curb,
Leaves flatten themselves against the ground
                                                                        and take cover.

How are we capable of so much love
                                                            for things that must fall away?
How can we utter our mild retractions and still keep
Our wasting affection for this world?
                                                            Augustine says
This is what we desire,
The soul itself instinctively desires it.
                                                            He's right, of course,
No matter how due and exacting the penance is.
The rain stops, the seasons wheel
Like stars in their bright courses:
                                                      the cogitation of the wise
Will bind you and take you where you will not want to go.
Mimic the juniper, have mercy.

The tongue cannot live up to the heart:
Raise the eyes of your affection to its affection
And let its equivalents
                    ripen in your body.
Love what you don't understand yet, and bring it to you.

From somewhere we never see comes everything that we do see.
What is important devolves
                    from the immanence of infinitude
In whatever our hands touch—
The other world is here, just under our fingertips.

Georg Trakl Journal

Sunday, first day of summer,
The whites of my eyes extinguished
                    in green and blue-green,
The white sleep of noon
Settling, a fine powder,
                    under the boxweed and overgrowth.
Windless, cloudless sky.
Odor of amethyst, odor of mother-of-pearl.
Beyond the mulched beds,
The roses lie open like a tear in the earth's side.
St. Thomas, if he were here,
                    would put his hand just there.

Never forget where your help comes from.
Last year, and the year before,
                    the landscape spoke to me
Wherever I turned,

Chook-chook and interlude chook-chook and interlude
As I sat in the orchard,
Fricatives and labials, stops and chords
falling like sequins inside the shadows
The jack pines laid at my feet,
Little consonants, little vowels
For me to place on my tongue,
for me to utter and shine from.

Now silence. Now no forgiveness.
Not even a syllable
Strays through the fevered window
Or plops like a toad in the tall grass.
The afternoon
Dissolves in my mouth,
The landscape dwindles and whispers like rice through my dry fingers.
Now twilight. Now the bereft bodies
Of those who have never risen from the dead glide down
Through the dwarf orchard
And waver like candle flames
under the peach trees and go out.

Night, and the arbor vitae, like nuns,
Bow in their solitude,
stars hang like tiny crosses
Above the ash trees,
Lamenting their nakedness.
Haloes of crystal thorns
Parachute out of the sky.
The moon, like a broken mouth,
Cloistered, in ruins, the vanished landscape,
Keep their vows, their dark patience.
Nothing says anything.
Nothing says nothing.

Language Journal

Late February, five o'clock: the cantaloupe-colored light,
Light of martyrs and solitaries,
Lies like a liquid on the trees
                                                    as though ladled there.
Jerome,
               at large in a light like this,
Cold Mountain and Paul of Thebes
Drifting like small flames back toward the sun,
Would feel at ease
                                    momentarily
In their uninterruptible avenue and dance.
The cars slide past on their golden wheels
Down Locust.
                              The joggers go by and grain into radiance.

The leaves of the rhododendron
                                                         dangle like reliquaries,
Gilded and stained in their little piles
As though spurted upon
                                              by the cleave from a saint's head,
The surface of everything
Hovering above itself in an expiation of held breath
As the body of afternoon is borne back to the hills.
Sunday, stub-end of winter,
                                                    baroque in its seal and dazzle,
Despair like an underpainting across the landscape,
These days we define ourselves inside,
These afternoons of last light
                                                      through which we all depend.

Maybe the theorists are right:
everything comes from language,
The actual web of root and rain
Is just an afterimage
pressed on the flyleaf of a book,
This first, pale envelope of forsythia unglued
By the March heat
only a half-thought apostrophe
And not the flesh of experience:
Nothing means anything, the slip of phrase against phrase
Contains the real way our lives
Are graphed out and understood,
the transformation of adverb
To morpheme and phoneme is all we need answer to.

But I don't think so today,
unless the landscape is language
Itself, which it isn't.
The water beads necklaced across the bare branch of this oak tree
Have something to say now
but not about syllables,
For water they are, and to water they shall return.
Out of sight, out of earshot, along the vertical axis
Of meaning,
the music of what's real,
The plainsong of being, is happening all the while.
The verb that waits for us in the trees
is reconstruct, not deconstruct:
The sound of one hand clapping is the sound of one hand clapping.

Umbria mistica . . . What I remember is how
I remember it:
                                        from Spello to Collepino across to Assisi
Over the humpback whole of Monte Subasio,
Bird bone and twig dry,
                                                    dust swirls like ghosts of penitents
Working the switchbacks and hairpins down to the sanctuary,
The cowl of mid-August heat
                                                            like cloth on our bodies:
Who couldn't hallucinate in such an ascetic landscape?
Seductive as pain, sharp-edged as guilt,
Its deprivations are palpable in the sunlight:
Nothing's so sweet as self-denial,
                                                                nothing so bountiful . . .

What is it we never can quite put our finger on
Inside the centricity of surface
                                                            that foregrounds and drains
The abstracts we balance our lives by?
Whatever it is, the language is only its moan.
Whatever it is, the self's trace
                                                            lingers along it
Much in the way that lies live in lines,
That air's in the atmosphere and wine's in this grape I pick now
From the vine beside me,
                                                      Perugia darkening out of sight,
Assisi darkening out of sight,
Raggio verde cutlassing down
                                                            as it must have done before.

To be of use, not to be used by,
the language sighs,
The landscape sighs, the wide mouth
Of March sighs at the ear of evening,
Whose eye has that look of eternity in its gaze.
To be of use,
look of eternity in its gaze,
Not to be used by . . .
This English is not the King's English,
it doesn't dissemble.
If anything means nothing, nothing means anything,
Full moon in the sky
Like a golden period.
It doesn't dissemble.

Late March, spring's loop in a deep regress,
Sunlight like polyurethane
on the concrete blocks
And the driveway's asphalt curve . . .
I step through the alphabet
The tree limbs shadow across the grass,
a dark language
Of strokes and ideograms
That spells out a different story than we are used to,
A story with no beginning and no end,
a little one.
I leave it and cross the street.
I think it's a happy story,
and not about us.

May Journal

Notes from the provinces always start
With the weather—
it is no different here, the sunlight
Sweeping the high May afternoon with its golden broom,
The tulips flashing themselves
Like badges before our interrogatory eyes,
The whole floor of being
dustless and unencumbered,
The crystal a simile the landscape half shines through,
Image within the image, the word as world as well
As note of music,
a touchiness along the bone.

Then they go on to talk about
the death of the soul
(Though not in so many words) or the death of the heart
In terms of the new season—
an iris, say, with its blue ear
Cocked to the pulse beat of what's-to-come.
Today's note, from Charlottesville, has nothing of that, though
Iris is in abundance
And onion and rhododendron metaphor wildly.
This is a message with no message
apart from its meaning,
The landscape awake in its first fire and finery.

The visible world is nothing more than a trompe l'oeil
By someone wanting a moment's peace
From the knowledge that Paradise
is what we live in

And not a goal to yearn for, I read once in a book
(Or something to that effect), and it sounds right to me:
That which was lost has not been found,
                                        shelter is not transcendence,
Someone has written elsewhere,
I'm sure, though I haven't found it back here in the dwarf orchard,
Peach blossoms starting to pink their wings
                                        where nothing's about to fall.

What is it in all myth
                        that brings us back from the dead?
What is it that jump-starts in verisimilitude
And ends up in ecstasy,
That takes us by both hands
                              from silence to speechlessness?
What is it that brings us out of the rock with such pain,
As though the sirens had something to say to us after all
From their clover and green shore,
                                    the words of their one song
Translatable, note by note?
As though the inexpressible were made inexpressible . . .

A Journal of Southern Rivers

What lasts is what you start with.
What hast thou, O my soul, with Paradise, for instance,
Is where I began, in March 1959—
                                    my question has never changed,
Always the black angel asleep on my lips,
                                        always
The dove's moan in the mimosa tree,

The blue faces of the twice transfigured
closing their stone eyes.

Love for the physical world,
a liquid glory,
Instead of a struck eternity
Painted and paralyzed
at this end and the other,
Always the black angel asleep on my lips,
always
The dove's moan in the mimosa tree,
The blue faces of the twice transfigured
closing their stone eyes.

We walk with one foot in each world,
the isness of everything
Like a rock in each shoe, the way, and along-the-way.

Overcast, south wind,
Montana early July,
fire in the barrel stove,
Bull thistle, yarrow and red clover
Adamant on the old trail.
Two jacksnipe scurry in single file across the yard.
One calls from the marsh.

Cold, rainy Thursday.
If being is Being, as Martin Heidegger says,
There is no other question,

nothing to answer to,
That's worth the trouble.
In awe and astonishment we regain ourselves in this world.
There is no other.

The whole moon and the whole sky are reflected
in a dewdrop in the grass.
The depth of the drop is the height of the moon.

Everything fades away beyond the self,
warped or plumb.
The dry summer grass is frail as hair.
How admirable are the insects that understand the ways of heaven,
The *selva illuminata*
that jacklights us now and then,
The nearness of nothingness,
The single spirit that lies at the root of all things.

One August starts to resemble another,
so many years laid bare
Under a sky like water.
The sounds of summer are everywhere:
At fifty-two, how hard it still is
to face all and not shirk.
How many lives must one have,
How many chances, before the right one is played out?

How can we trust the sure, true words
written in blue ink?
Does the amber remember the pine?

September thunder lays down
its pre-attack barrage
From the other side of the Blue Ridge.
The clouds darken, layer by layer,
Muzzle-flash of the lightning
singeing their undersides.
The landscape opens itself
Inch by inch to the sparks
and soothing rounds of the rain.

How easily one thing comes and another passes away.
How soon we become the acolytes
Of nothing and nothing's altar
redeems us and makes us whole
Now for the first time,
And what we are is what we are not,
ecstatic and unknown.
What lasts is what you start with.

Whose shadows are dancing upside down in the southern rivers?
Fifty-two years have passed
like the turning of a palm . . .

China Journal

North wind like a fine drill
                                        sky Ming porcelain for a thousand miles
The danger of what's-to-come is not in its distance
Two inches can break the heart

(GREAT WALL)

Halfway to Chengdu; past noon.
Against the brown riprap and scree grass,
Two peach trees in blossom,
                                        speechless from daybreak till now.

(JIALING RIVER)

Sky color of old steam
                                        the power that moves what moves
Moves as the Buddha moves unmoving
                                        great river goes eastward

(LESHAN)

The emperor's men are dust-red from eternity,
Quince tree pale cinnabar in the field.

Invisible as dewdrops in the afterlife, time thumbs us,
Not lightly here, but not lightly there.

(XI'AN)

Local Journal

November in afterpiece,
transitional showdown,
Commedia dell'arte of months.
Above the morning, fast-running clouds
Scuttle and rain, then snow,
then break to a backdrop of Venetian blue.
Wind spills from the trees.
How much, thrums Expiation, half
Asleep in the wings, *how much will it all add up to?*

Always the same answer out of the clouds,
always the same sigh.

The void exists, and enters heaven with the infinite breath,
Pythagoras said,
beginning first in the numbers:
Those who have come for punishment must then be punished,
Don't dandle, don't speak in the dark.

Objects do not exist,
by convention sweet, by convention bitter.

Still, you could have fooled me,
my left hand in the juniper bush

At three in the afternoon,
My right with the pruning shears
Cutting the sticks of the rhododendron back.

Later,

Trailing the garbage cans to the curb,
Solace of river rock, raw rood of the power pole.
Such oleaginous evenings . . .

Time is another country.

If you don't expect the unexpected,

you'll never find it.

A hundred mountains and not one bird,
A thousand paths and no sign:
Winter along the James River:

a shawl of bare trees

Damasks the far bank, a boat
Knocks at its mooring post.

No one comes forth. Nothing steps

Into the underbrush or rises out of the frame.

No wind, no shudder:

water and sky, water and sky.

The four seasons are unforgiving,

no news, no news:

A small reward, but I accept it.
For over a half century I've waited in vain.
Wind and cloud, sunset and dusk—

they all know where to go.

You can't escape the attention of what you can't see.

December's the denouement,
                    short steps to the solstice.
Last sun. Against the mauve hills,
Winter branches smolder, burst into flame, then die out.
At one glance, autumn is gone.
Brake lights from a stalled car shine like dog's eyes through the trees.
Heaven and earth are darkened to fine ash.
                              To fine ash and a white coal.

Last Journal

Out of our own mouths we are sentenced,
                    we who put our trust in visible things.

Soon enough we will forget the world.
                    And soon enough the world will forget us.

The breath of our lives, passing from this one to that one,
Is what the wind says, its single word
                    being the earth's delight.

Lust of the tongue, lust of the eye,
                    out of our own mouths we are sentenced . . .

FROM

CHICKAMAUGA

(1995)

Sitting Outside at the End of Autumn

Three years ago, in the afternoons,
                    I used to sit back here and try
To answer the simple arithmetic of my life,
But never could figure it—
This object and that object
Never contained the landscape
                    nor all of its implications,
This tree and that shrub
Never completely satisfied the sum or quotient
I took from or carried to,
                    nor do they do so now,
Though I'm back here again, looking to calculate,
Looking to see what adds up.

Everything comes from something,
                    only something comes from nothing,
Lao Tzu says, more or less.
Eminently sensible, I say,
Rubbing this tiny snail shell between my thumb and two fingers.
Delicate as an earring,
                    it carries its emptiness like a child
It would be rid of.
I rub it clockwise and counterclockwise, hoping for anything
Resplendent in its vocabulary or disguise—
But one and one make nothing, he adds,
                    endless and everywhere,
The shadow that everything casts.

Reading Lao Tzu Again in the New Year

Snub end of a dismal year,
                                        deep in the dwarf orchard,
The sky with its undercoat of blackwash and point stars,
I stand in the dark and answer to
My life, this shirt I want to take off,
                                                    which is on fire . . .

Old year, new year, old song, new song,
                                                        nothing will change hands
Each time we change heart, each time
Like a hard cloud that has drifted all day through the sky
Toward the night's shrugged shoulder
                                                    with its epaulet of stars.

Prosodies rise and fall.
                                    Structures rise in the mind and fall.
Failure reseeds the old ground.
Does the grass, with its inches in two worlds, love the dirt?
Does the snowflake the raindrop?

I've heard that those who know will never tell us,
                                                                and heard
That those who tell us will never know.
Words are wrong.
Structures are wrong.
                                    Even the questions are compromise.

Desire discriminates and language discriminates:
They form no part of the essence of all things:
each word
Is a failure, each object
We name and place
leads us another step away from the light.

Loss is its own gain.
Its secret is emptiness.
Our images lie in the flat pools of their dark selves
Like bodies of water the tide moves.
They move as the tide moves.
Its secret is emptiness.

Four days into January,
the grass grows tiny, tiny
Under the peach trees.
Wind from the Blue Ridge tumbles the hat
Of daylight farther and farther
into the eastern counties.

Sunlight spray on the ash limbs.
Two birds
Whistle at something unseen, one black note and one interval.
We're placed between now and not-now,
held by affection,
Large rock balanced upon a small rock.

Under the Nine Trees in January

Last night's stars and last night's wind
Are west of the mountains now, and east of the river.
Here, under the branches of the nine trees,
how small the world seems.

Should we lament, in winter, our shadow's solitude,
Our names spelled out like snowflakes?
Where is it written, *the season's decrease diminishes me*?

Should we long for stillness,
a hush for the trivial body
Washed in the colors of paradise,
Dirt-colored water-colored match-flame-and-wind-colored?

As one who has never understood the void,
should I
Give counsel to the darkness, honor the condor's wing?
Should we keep on bowing to
an inch of this and an inch of that?

The world is a handkerchief.
Today I spread it across my knees.
Tomorrow they'll fold it into my breast pocket,
white on my dark suit.

After Reading Wang Wei, I Go Outside to the Full Moon

Back here, old snow like lace cakes,
Candescent and brittle now and then through the tall grass.
Remorse, remorse, the dark drones.

The body's the affliction,
No resting place in the black pews of the winter trees,
No resting place in the clouds.

Mercy upon us, old man,
You in the China dust, I this side of my past life,
Salt in the light of heaven.

Isolate landscape. World's grip.
The absolute, as small as a poker chip, moves off,
Bright moon shining between pines.

Easter 1989

March is the month of slow fire,
                                        new grasses stung with rain,
Cold-shouldered, white-lipped.
Druidic crocus circles appear
Overnight, morose in their purple habits,
                                                        wet cowls
Glistening in the cut sun.

Instinct will end us.
The force that measles the peach tree
                                        will divest and undo us.
The power that kicks on
                              the cells in the lilac bush
Will tumble us down and down.
Under the quince tree, purple cross points, and that's all right

For the time being,
                         the willow across the back fence
Menacing in its green caul.
When the full moon comes
                                 gunning under the cloud's cassock
Later tonight, the stations
Will start to break forth like stars, their numbers flashing and then some.

Belief is a paltry thing
                           and will betray us, soul's load scotched
Against the invisible:
We are what we've always thought we were—
Peeling the membrane back,
                                  amazed, like the jonquil's yellow head
Butting the nothingness—
                                in the wrong place, in the wrong body.

The definer of all things
                              cannot be spoken of.
It is not knowledge or truth.
We get no closer than next-to-it.
Beyond wisdom, beyond denial,
                                    it asks us for nothing,
According to Pseudo-Dionysus, which sounds good to me.

Nubbly with enzymes,
The hardwoods gurgle and boil in their leathery sheaths.
Flame flicks the peony's fuse.
Out of the caves of their locked beings,
                                                            fluorescent shapes
Roll the darkness aside as they rise to enter the real world.

Reading Rorty and Paul Celan One Morning in Early June

In the skylight it's Sunday,
A little aura between the slats of the Venetian blinds.
Outside the front window,
                                            a mockingbird balances
Gingerly on a spruce branch.
At the Munch house across the street,
Rebecca reads through the paper, then stares at her knees
On the front porch.
                                    Church bell. Weed-eater's cough and spin.

From here, the color of mountains both is and is not,
Beginning of June,
Haze like a nesting bird in the trees,
The Blue Ridge partial,
                                        then not partial,
Between the staff lines of the telephohe wires and pine tips
That sizzle like E.T.'s finger.
Mid-nineties, and summer officially still three weeks away.

If truth is made and not found,
what an amazing world
We live in, more secret than ever
And beautiful of access.
Goodbye, old exits, goodbye, old entrances, the way
Out is the way in at last,
Two-hearted sorrow of middle age,
substanceless blue,
Benevolent anarchy to tan and grow old with.

If sentences constitute
everything we believe,
Vocabularies retool
Our inability to measure and get it right,
And languages don't exist.
That's one theory. Here's another:
Something weighs on our shoulders
And settles itself like black light
invisibly in our hair . . .

Pool table. Zebra rug.
Three chairs in a half circle.
Buck horns and Ca' Paruta.
Gouache of the Clinchfield station in Kingsport, Tennessee.
High tide on the Grand Canal,
San Zeno in late spring
Taken by "Ponti" back in the nineteenth century.
I see the unknown photographer
under his dark cloth. Magnesium flash.
Silence. I hear what he has to say.

June 3rd, heat like Scotch tape on the skin,
Mountains the color of nothing again,
then something through mist.
In Tuscany, on the Sette Ponti, Gròpina dead-ends
Above the plain and the Arno's marauding cities,
Columns eaten by darkness,
Cathedral unsentenced and plugged in
To what's-not-there,
windows of alabaster, windows of flame.

Cicada

All morning I've walked about,
opening books and closing books,
Sitting in this chair and that chair.
Steady drip on the skylight,
steady hum of regret.
Who listens to anyone?
Across the room, bookcases,
across the street, summer trees.

Hear what the book says:
This earthly light
Is a seasoning, tempting and sweet and dangerous.
Resist the allurements of the eye.
Feet still caught in the toils of this world's beauty,
resist
The gratifications of the eye.

Noon in the early September rain.
A cicada whines,
his voice
Starting to drown through the rainy world,
No ripple of wind,
no sound but his song of black wings,
No song but the song of his black wings.

Such emptiness at the heart,
such emptiness at the heart of being,
Fills us in ways we can't lay claim to,
Ways immense and without names,
husk burning like amber
On tree bark, cicada wind-bodied,
Leaves beginning to rustle now
in the dark tree of the self.

If time is water, appearing and disappearing
In one heliotropic cycle,
this rain
That sluices as through an hourglass
Outside the window into the gutter and downspout,
Measures our nature
and moves the body to music.

The book says, however,
time is not body's movement
But memory of body's movement.
Time is not water but the memory of water:
We measure what isn't there.
We measure the silence.
We measure the emptiness.

Tennessee Line

Afternoon overcast the color of water
                                        smoothed by clouds
That whiten where they enter the near end of the sky.
First day of my fifty-fifth year,
Last week of August limp as a frayed rope in the trees,
Yesterday's noise a yellow dust in my shirt pocket
Beneath the toothpick,
                        the .22 bullet and Amitone.

Sounds drift through the haze,
The shadowless orchard, peach leaves dull in the tall grass,
No wind, no bird shudder.
Green boat on the red Rivanna.
                                Rabbit suddenly in place
By the plum tree, then gone in three bounds.
Downshift of truck gears.

In 1958, in Monterey, California,
I wrote a journal of over one hundred pages
About the Tennessee line,
About my imagined unhappiness,
                                and how the sun set like a coffin
Into the grey Pacific.
How common it all was.
                        How uncommon I pictured myself.

Memento scrivi, skull-like and word-drunk,
                                        one hundred fourteen pages
Of inarticulate self-pity

Looking at landscape and my moral place within it,
The slurry of words inexorable and dark,
The ethical high ground inexorable and dark
I droned from
                    hoping for prescience and a shibboleth . . .

I remember the word and forget the word
                                        although the word
Hovers in flame around me.
Summer hovers in flame around me.
The overcast breaks like a bone above the Blue Ridge.
A loneliness west of solitude
Splinters into the landscape
                              uncomforting as Braille.

We *are* our final vocabulary,
                              and how we use it.
There is no secret contingency.
There's only the rearrangement, the redescription
Of little and mortal things.
There's only this single body, this tiny garment
Gathering the past against itself,
                                  making it otherwise.

Looking Outside the Cabin Window, I Remember a Line by Li Po

The river winds through the wilderness,
Li Po said
          of another place and another time.

It does so here as well, sliding its cargo of dragon scales
To gutter under the snuff
                    of marsh willow and tamarack.

Mid-morning, Montana high country,
Jack snipe poised on the scarred fence post,
Pond water stilled and smoothed out,
Swallows dog-fighting under the fast-moving storm clouds.

Expectantly empty, green as a pocket, the meadow waits
For the wind to rise and fill it,
                    first with a dark hand
Then with the rain's loose silver
A second time and a third
                    as the day doles out its hours.

Sunlight reloads and ricochets off the window glass.
Behind the cloud scuts,
                    inside the blue aorta of the sky,
The River of Heaven flows
With its barge of stars,
                    waiting for darkness and a place to shine.

We who would see beyond seeing
                    see only language, that burning field.

Mid-winter Snowfall in the Piazza Dante

Verona, late January . . .
                    Outside the caffè,
The snow, like papier-mâché, settles
Its strips all over Dante's bronze body, and holds fast.

Inside, a grappa
In one hand, a double espresso in the other,
I move through the room, slowly,
                    from chessboard to chessboard.

It's Tuesday, tournament night.
Dante's statue, beyond the window, grows larger and whiter
Under the floodlights
                    and serious Alpine snowfall.

In here I understand nothing,
                    not the chess, not the language,
Not even the narrow, pointed shoes the men all wear.
It's 1959. It's ten-thirty at night. I've been in the country for one week.

The nineteenth-century plush
                    on the chairs and loveseats
Resonates, purple and gold.
Three boards are in play in the front room, one in the bar.

My ignorance is immense,
                    as is my happiness.
Caught in the glow of all things golden
And white, I think, at twenty-three, my life has finally begun.

At a side table, under
The tulip-shaped lamps, a small group drinks to a wedding:
"*Tutti maschi*," the groom toasts,
                    and everyone lifts his full glass.

The huge snowflakes like soft squares
Alternately black and white in the flat light of the piazza,
I vamp in the plush and gold of the mirrors,
                    in love with the world.

That was thirty years ago.
I've learned a couple of things since then
                                                  not about chess
Or plush or all things golden and white.

Unlike a disease, whatever I've learned
Is not communicable.
                                  A singular organism,
It does its work in the dark.

Anything that we think we've learned,
                                                  we've learned in the dark.
If there is one secret to this life, it is this life.
This life and its hand-me-downs,
                                             bishop to pawn 4, void's gambit.

Sprung Narratives

What were we thinking of,
                                       where were we trying to go,
My brother and I,
That March afternoon almost forty-five years ago,
Up U.S. 11W,
Snow falling, aged ten and eight,
                                             so many miles from anyone we knew?

Past Armour Drug, the Civic Auditorium, Brooks Circle
And up the four-lane highway,
Past cornfield and sedgebrush field,
                                               past the stone diner and Hillcrest,
Then up the mountain,

Five miles in the late snow,
unsure of our whereabouts.

Home, of course, parents abstract with dread,
Three months in a new town,
Second World War just over
Some six months before,
home to the only home we knew.
Or would know from that day on.
We'd missed the bus. We didn't know what else we should do.

Half-hallowed, half-hand-me-down,
our adolescence loomed
At walk's end, eager to gather us.
We let it.
And learned to dance with it, cumbersome, loath, in our arms.
And learned its numbers.
And learned its names.

How impossible now to reach it,
No matter how close we come
driving by in the car—
That childhood,
That landscape we pictured ourselves a no-cut part of
For good—
each time we revisit it.

Returned to the dwarf orchard,
Pilgrim,
Sit still and lengthen your lines,

Shorten your poems and listen to what the darkness says
With its mouthful of cold air.

Midnight, cloud-scatter and cloud-vanish,
sky black-chill and black-clear,
South wind through the March-bare trees,
House shadows and hedge shadows.
It's your life. Take it.
Next month, next year, who knows where you will be.

It's Saturday night,
summer of 1963,
The Teatro Farnese in Rome.
For 150 lire,
it's Sordi and Gassman
In Mario Monicelli's *La Grande Guerra.*

Alberto Sordi and Vittorio Gassman, World War I
And the north Italian front.
Such unwilling heroes!
Sordi a Roman, Gassman a conscript from the Veneto,
Each speaking his dialect,
each speaking, to my ears, as though in tongues.

But not to the *romanacci*
howling in recognition,
Sending each *stronzo*, each *fijo de na mignota*,
Back at the screen in an ecstasy
Of approval. "Who *are* you?" it asks.
Semmo l'anima de li mortacci tui . . .

Who knows what the story line
                                                became, what happened to happen
At movie's end. What's brought back
Is not the occasion but its events,
                                                the details
Surrounding it that nicked us.

The world is a language we never quite understand,
But think we catch the drift of.
                                                Speaking in ignorance
And joy, we answer
What wasn't asked, by someone we don't know, in strange tongues,

Hoping to get the roll right—
Across the Tiber,
                                past Belli and Dante, off to supper
Scorching the kamikaze Fiats,
A li mortacci tui, brutto zozzo, v'a fa'un culo . . .

After it's over, after the last gaze has shut down,
Will I have become
The landscape I've looked at and walked through
Or the road that took me there
                                                or the time it took to arrive?

How are we balanced out,
                                            by measure, number and weight
As the Renaissance had it,
The idea of God with a compass or gold protractor in his hand?
Lovely to think so,
                                the landscape and journey as one . . .

Seventeen years in Laguna Beach—
Month after month the same weather,
                                        year after year the same blue
Stretched like a tent-half above our heads.
Even the rain was predictable
When it rounded the Isthmus on Catalina
                                        and curtained ashore.

Even the waves seemed laid back
And cool,
        tweaking the beaches with their tremulous sighs
Of smooth self-satisfaction,
Barely filling the tide pools,
                                languishing back and forth
Between moon-pull and earth-pull.

The walkway unwound along the cliffs
Overlooking all this,
                        and dipped to the pale shoreline
Like an Ace bandage. Down it I went
Each afternoon that I could,
Down to the burning sand,
                                down to the lid of the ocean's great blind eye.

Always the same ghost-figures
Haunting the boardwalk, the basketball courts and the beach.
Always the same shades
                            turning their flat, cocoa-buttered faces
Into the sun-glare,
Pasty, unchangeable faces,
                                unchangeable bodies impatient, unfulfilled.

I walked among them, booted, black-jacketed, peering
Unsurreptitiously into
                                        whatever was recognizable.
I never knew anyone.
The sea with its one eye stared. I stared.
For seventeen years we both stared
                                                as they turned like blank souls toward the sun.

This text is a shadow text.
Under its images, under its darkened prerogatives,
Lie the lines of youth,
                                        golden, and lipped in a white light.
They sleep as their shadows move

As though in a dream,
                                        disconnected, unwished-upon.
And slightly distorted. And slightly out of control.
Their limbs gleam and their eyelids gleam,
                                                                under whose soft skin
The little dances and paroxysms leap and turn.

Spot, pivot and spin . . . Spot, pivot and spin . . .
                                                                        Esposito breaks
From the black-robed, black-cordovaned
Body of student priests
                                        and feints down the wave-tongued sand
Like a fabulous bird where the tide sifts out and in.

His cassock billows and sighs
As he sings a show tune this morning at Ostia,
Rehearsing the steps and pirouettes
                he had known by heart once
Last year in another life.

Behind him, like small fists,
                the others open and close
Around the two German girls
Whose father has laid on and paid for
Their trip to the beach with American priests-to-be

Who drink at his *birreria* on Via della Croce.
                September, still 1963.
Two months from now, Jerry Jacobson
Will burst through the door
Of my tiny apartment on Via del Babuino

And tell me that President Kennedy has been shot.
Two months.
                But for now Esposito
Relives his turns and stage days,
The priests remember or reinvent,
                Maria Luisa

And Astrid pretend
                their charms will never dissolve or die back
In marriage and motherhood,
And I, the teacher of noun and verb
                in a language they can't quite understand,
Hum with Esposito and covet their golden hair.

Something surrounds us we can't exemplify, something
Mindless and motherless,
                                        dark as diction and twice told.
We hear it at night.
Flake by flake,
                        we taste it like tinfoil between our teeth.

Under the little runnels of snow,
                                                  under the mist
Settling like moonlight
Over the orchard,
                              under the grasses and black leaves,
In its hush, in its sky width, it takes our breath away.

How small it is, and remote,
                                          like a photograph from a friend's album
Of the house he lived in as a child.
Or our house seen from next door
Through the bathroom window,
                                                  a curtain pushed to one side.
How barren the porch looks, how forlorn the rosebushes.

Inside the front room, there are different lights in different places.
Different cars block the driveway.
Where has the tree gone
                                        that feathered the summer air with music?
Where is the white throat
That settled the dark, and that darkness settled itself inside?

The valley has been filled in
                                          with abandoned structures.

New roads that have been bypassed
By newer roads
                                        glint in the late sun and disappear.
As the twilight sinks in
Across the landscape,
                                                        lights come on like the lights next door . . .

Seeing the past so
                                        diminishes it and us too,
Both of us crowding the ghost ramp
And path along the strawberry patch and peanut field,
Down through the hemlocks and apple trees
Behind the house,
                                        into the black hole of history.

What's left?
                              A used leaf shredder, empty begonia pots,
Some memory like a dot
Of light retreating, smaller and sharper with each glance,
Nobody left to remember it
But us,
            half hidden behind a bathroom window curtain? I guess so.

Broken English

Spring like smoke in the fruit trees,
Ambulance siren falling away
                                                    through the thick grass.
I gaze at the sky and cut lines from my long poem.

What matters we only tell ourselves.

Without the adjective there is no evil or good.

All speech pulls toward privacy
                                        and the zones of the infinite.

Better to say what you mean than to mean what you say.

Without a syntax, there is no immortality.

Truth's an indefinite article.
When we live, we live for the last time,
                                                as Akhmatova says,
One *the* in a world of *a*.

Chickamauga

Dove-twirl in the tall grass.
                                    End-of-summer glaze next door
On the gloves and split ends of the conked magnolia tree.
Work sounds: truck back-up-beep, wood tin-hammer, cicada, fire horn.

History handles our past like spoiled fruit.
Mid-morning, late-century light
                                        calicoed under the peach trees.
Fingers us here. Fingers us here and here.

The poem is a code with no message:
The point of the mask is not the mask but the face underneath,
Absolute, incommunicado,
                                        unhoused and peregrine.

The gill net of history will pluck us soon enough
From the cold waters of self-contentment we drift in
One by one
            into its suffocating light and air.

Structure becomes an element of belief, syntax
And grammar a catechist,
Their words what the beads say,
                                        words thumbed to our discontent.

Blaise Pascal Lip-syncs the Void

It's not good to be complete.
It's not good to be concupiscent,
                                        caught as we are
Between a the and a the,
Neither of which we know and neither of which knows us.
It's not good to be sewn shut.

There's change and succession in all things, Pascal contends,
But inconstancy, boredom and anxiety condition our days.

Neither will wash for him, though,
since nature is corrupt.
That's why we love it.
That's why we take it, unwinnowed,
Willingly into our hearts.

December. 4 p.m.
Chardonnay-colored light-slant
Lug weight in the boned trees.
Squirrel dead on the Tarmac.
Boom-boxing Big Foot pickup trucks
Hustle down Locust,
light pomegranate pink grapefruit then blood.
We take it into our hearts.

The Silent Generation

Afternoons in the backyard, our lives like photographs
Yellowing elsewhere,
in somebody else's album,
In secret, January south winds
Ungathering easily through the black limbs of the fruit trees.

What was it we never had to say?
Who can remember now—
Something about the world's wrongs,
Something about the way we shuddered them off like rain
In an open field,
convinced that lightning would not strike.

We're arm in arm with regret, now left foot, now right foot.
We give the devil his due.
We walk up and down in the earth,
                                        we take our flesh in our teeth.
When we die, we die. The wind blows away our footprints.

An Ordinary Afternoon in Charlottesville

Under the peach trees, the ideograms the leaves throw
Over the sun-prepped grass read
Purgatio, illuminatio, contemplatio,
Words caught in a sweet light endurable,
                                        unlike the one they lead to,
Whose sight we're foundered and fallowed by.

Meanwhile, the afternoon
                                fidgets about its business,
Unconcerned with such immolations,
Sprinkle of holy grit from the sun's wheel,
                                        birds combustible
In the thin leaves incendiary—
Fire, we think, marvellous fire, everything starts in fire.

Or so they say. We like to think so
Ourselves, feeling the cold
                                glacier into the blood stream
A bit more each year,
Tasting the iron disk on our tongues,
Watching the birds oblivious,
                                hearing their wise chant, *hold still, hold still*...

Mondo Angelico

Fish never sleep.
                Aquatic angels,
They drift in the deep ether of all their rectitude,
Half dark, half flicker of light
At the eye's edge,
                their shadows shadows of shadows—

Under the blue spruce,
Under the skunkweed and onion head,
Under the stump,
                the aspergillum of the dew-rose,
They signal and disappear.

Like lost thoughts,
                they wouldn't remember us if they could,
Hovering just out of touch,
Their bodies liminal, their sights sealed.
Always they disregard us
                with a dull disregard.

Mondo Henbane

The journey ends between the black spiders and the white spiders,
As Blake reminds us.
                For now,
However, pain is the one thing that fails to actualize
Where the green-backed tree swallows dip
                and the wood ducks glide

Over the lodgepole's soft slash.
Little islands of lime-green pine scum
Float on the pot-pond water.
                                        Load-heavy bumblebees
Lower themselves to the sun-swollen lupine and paintbrush throats.

In the front yard, a half mile away,
                                        one robin stretches his neck out,
Head cocked to the ground,
Hearing the worm's hum or the worm's heart.
Or hearing the spiders fly,
                              on their fiery tracks, through the smoke-choked sky.

Miles Davis and Elizabeth Bishop Fake the Break

Those two dark syllables, *begin*,
                                        offer no sustenance,
Nor does this pale squish of September sunlight unwound
Across the crabgrass.

The silence is cold, like an instrument in the hand
Which cannot be set aside,
Unlike our suffering, so easy, so difficult.

Still, the warmth on our skin is nice,
                                        and the neighbor's pears,
Late pears, dangle like golden hourglasses above our heads.

"It's just description," she said,
                                        "they're all just description."

Meaning her poems . . . Mine, too,
The walleye of morning's glare
lancing the landscape,
The dogwood berries as red as cinnamon drops in the trees,
Sunday, the twenty-ninth of September, 1991.

From the top . . . Beginning in ignorance, we stick to the melody—
Knowledge, however, is elsewhere,
a tune we've yet to turn to,
Its syllables scrubbed in light, its vestibules empty.

Peccatology

As Kafka has told us,
sin always comes openly:
It walks on its roots and doesn't have to be torn out.

How easily it absolves itself in the senses,
However, in Indian summer,
the hedge ivy's star-feet
Treading the dead spruce and hemlock spurs,
The last leaves like live coals
banked in the far corners of the yard,
The locust pods in Arabic letters, right to left.

How small a thing it becomes, nerve-sprung
And half electric,
deracinated, full of joy.

East of the Blue Ridge, Our Tombs Are in the Dove's Throat

Late Sunday in Charlottesville.
We cross our arms like effigies, look up at the sky
And wait for a sign of salvation—
                    as Lorca has taught us to say,
Two and two never make four down here,
They always make two and two.

Five crows roust a yellow-tailed hawk from the hemlock tree next door,
Black blood spots dipping and blown
Across the relentless leeching
                    the sun pales out of the blue.

We'd like to fly away ourselves, pushed
Or pulled, into or out of our own bodies,
                    into or out of the sky's mouth.
We'd like to disappear into a windfall of light.

But the numbers don't add up.
Besides, a piece of jar glass
                    burns like a star at the street's edge,
The elbows and knuckled limb joints of winter trees,
Shellacked by the sunset, flash and fuse,
Windows blaze
                    and the earthly splendor roots our names to the ground.

As Our Bodies Rise, Our Names Turn into Light

The sky unrolls like a rug,
                                        unwelcoming, gun-grey,
Over the Blue Ridge.
Mothers are calling their children in,
                                                        mellifluous syllables, floating sounds.
The traffic shimmies and settles back.

The doctor has filled his truck with leaves
Next door, and a pair of logs.
                                            Salt stones litter the street.
The snow falls and the wind drops.
How strange to have a name, any name, on this poor earth.

January hunkers down,
                                        the icicle deep in her throat—
The days become longer, the nights ground bitter and cold,
Single grain by single grain
Everything flows toward structure,
                                                    last ache in the ache for God.

Still Life with Spring and Time to Burn

Warm day, early March. The buds preen, busting their shirtwaists
All over the plum trees. Blue moan of the mourning dove.
It's that time again,
                                    time of relief, time of sorrow
The earth is afflicted by.
We feel it ourselves, a bright uncertainty of what's to come

Swelling our own skins with sweet renewal, a kind of disease
That holds our affections dear
                                    and asks us to love it.
And so we do, supposing
That time and affection is all we need answer to.
But we guess wrong:

Time will append us like suit coats left out overnight
On a deck chair, loose change dead weight in the right pocket,
Silk handkerchief limp with dew,
                                    sleeves in a slow dance with the wind.
And love will kill us—
Love, and the winds from under the earth
                                    that grind us to grain-out.

With Simic and Marinetti at the Giubbe Rosse

Where Dino Campana once tried to sell his sad poems
Among the tables,
Where Montale settled into his silence and hid,
Disguised as himself for twenty years,
The ghosts of Papini and Prezzolini sit tight
With Carlo Emilio Gadda
                                    somewhere behind our backs.

Let's murder the moonlight, let's go down
On all fours and mewl like the animals and make it mean what it means.
Not even a stir.
Not even a breath across the plates of *gnocchi* and roast veal.
Like everything else in Florence, that's part of the past,
The wind working away away kneading the sea so muscles . . .

Those who don't remember the Futurists are condemned to repeat them.
We order a grappa. We order a mineral water.
Little by little, the lucid, warm smile of the moon
Overflowed from the torn clouds.
Some ran.
A cry was heard in the solitude of the high plains.
Simic e Wright sulla traccia. La luna ammazzata.

To the Egyptian Mummy in the Etruscan Museum at Cortona

Wrapped like a sprained ankle from head to toe,
locked in glass
In an inconceivable country,
Spun on the sprung reflections caught in a stranger's eye
Year after year,
you would not imagine yourself if you could,
Peninsulaed as you are, and rare.

Outside the window, sun rains on the Middle Ages.
An upupa pecks in the tall grass.
Under the stone walls and stone towers,
the hillside unravels its tapestry,
A picnic in spring's green fire: one man's asleep and a young girl
Claps time for her brother who hand-dances with his dog.

One half-expects, say, Guidoriccio da Fogliano
In full regalia,
Or Malatesta, at least, at large from the Marches,
To climb the gut-twisted road through the quicksilver glint and tufa stone
Toward the south gate and you,
pale messenger from the wordless world . . .

Leonardo, Vasari says,
would purchase the caged, white doves
As he walked through the market sprawl of San Lorenzo
In order to set them free. I'll do
The same thing for you, unlatching this landscape, the vine rows and
olive trees,
Till its wingspread shrinks to a radiance.
Look. Already it's getting smaller.

With Eddie and Nancy in Arezzo at the Caffè Grande

Piero in wraps, the True Cross *sotto restauro,*
Piazza desolate edge
Where sunlight breaks it,
desolate edge
Where sunlight pries it apart.
A child kicks a soccer ball. Another heads it back.

The Fleeting World, Po Chü-i says, short-hops a long dream,
No matter if one is young or old—
The pain of what is present never comes to an end,
Lightline moving inexorably
West to east across the stones,
cutting the children first, then cutting us.

Under the archways, back and forth among the tables,
The blind ticket seller taps and slides.
Lotteria di Foligno, Lotteria di Foligno,
he intones,
Saturday, mid-May, cloud bolls high cotton in the Tuscan sky.
One life is all we're entitled to, but it's enough.

Watching the Equinox Arrive in Charlottesville, September 1992

2:23 p.m.

The season glides to a click.
Nobody says a word
From where I sit, shadows dark flags from nothing's country,
Birds in the deep sky, then not,
Cricket caught in the outback between a grass spear and a leaf.
The quince bush
Is losing its leaves in the fall's early chemotherapy,
And stick-stemmed spikes of the lemon tree
Spink in the sun.
Autumnal outtakes, autumnal stills . . .

Mockingbird, sing me a song.
Back here, where the windfall apples rot to the bee's joy,
Where the peach sheaths and pear sheaths piebald and brindle,
Where each year the orchard unlearns
everything it's been taught,
The weekend's rainfall
Pools its untroubled waters,
Doves putter about in the still-green limbs of the trees,
Ants inch up the cinder blocks and lawn spiders swing from the vines.
You've got to learn to unlearn things, the season repeats.
For every change there's a form.

Open your mouth, you are lost, close your mouth, you are lost,
So the Buddhists say.
They also say,

Live in the world unattached to the dust of the world.
Not so easy to do when the thin, monotonous tick of the universe
Painfully pries our lips apart,
                                        and dirties our tongues
With soiled, incessant music.
Not so easy to do when the right front tire blows out,
Or the phone rings at 3 a.m.
                                        and the ghost-voice says, "It's 911, please hold."
They say, enter the blackness, the form of forms. They say,
No matter how we see ourselves, sleeping and dreaming see us as light.

Still, there's another story,
                                        that what's inside us is what's outside us:
That what we see outside ourselves we'll soon see inside ourselves.
It's visible, and is our garment.
Better, perhaps, to wear that.
Better to live as though we already lived the afterlife,
Unattached to our cape of starred flesh.
But Jesus said,
                        Lift up the stone and you will find me,
Break open a piece of wood, I'm there.
It's hard to argue with that,
Hard to imagine a paradise beyond what the hand breaks.

For every force there's a change.
Mouthful of silence, mouthful of air,
                                                sing me your tune.
The wind leaves nothing alone.
How many times can summer turn to fall in one life?
Well you might ask, my old friend,
Wind-rider, wind-spirit, seeking my blood out,
                                                        humming my name.

Hard work, this business of solitude.
Hard work and no gain,
Mouthful of silence, mouthful of air.
Everything's more than it seems back here. Everything's less.

Like migrating birds, our own lives drift away from us.
How small they become in the blank sky, how colorful,
On their way to wherever they please.
We keep our eyes on the ground,
                                        on the wasp and pinch bug,
As the years grind by and the seasons churn, north and south.
We keep our eyes on the dirt.
Under the limp fins of the lemon tree, we inhabit our absence.
Crows cross-hatch and settle in,
                                        red birds and dust sparrows
Spindle and dart through the undergrowth.
We don't move. We watch, but we don't move.

Waiting for Tu Fu

Snip, snip goes wind through the autumn trees.
I move my bed to the battlefront,
                                        dead leaves like a blanket of moth bodies
Up to the necks of the cold grasses.
It crunches like pecan shells underfoot.
It crinks my back where I lie
                                        gazing into the beaten artifice
Of gold leaf and sky.

How vast the clouds are, how vast as they troll and pass by.
Splendid and once-removed, like lives, they never come back.

Does anyone think of them?
Everything's golden from where I lie.
Even the void
Beyond the void the clouds cross.
Even the knowledge that everything's fire,
and nothing ever comes back.

All that was yesterday, or last week,
Or somebody else's line of talk.
Words rise like mist from my body,
Prayer-smoke, a snowy comfort.
The Greek-thin hammered gold artifacts
and glazed inlay
Of landscape and sky
Accept it as incense, for they are used to such things.

What have you done with your life,
you've asked me, as you've asked yourself,
What has it come to,
Carrying us like a barge toward the century's end
And sheer drop-off into millennial history?
I remember an organ chord one Sunday in North Carolina.
I remember the smell of white pines,
Vitalis and lye soap.

O we were pure and holy in those days,
The August sunlight candescing our short-sleeved shirt fronts,
The music making us otherwise.
O we were abstract and true.
How could we know that grace would fall from us like shed skin,
That reality, our piebald dog, would hunt us down?

The seasons reshuffle and set me.
Cattle as large as clouds
                    lumber across my mind's sky
And children rise in the wind
Like angels over the lake, sad cataracted eye—

I remember cutting its surface once in a green canoe,
Eye that saw everything, that now sees nothing at all . . .

Where is my life going in these isolate outlands,
You questioned once in a verse.
I ask the same thing,
                    wreckage of broken clouds too far to count,
The landscape, like God, a circle whose center is everywhere
And circumference nowhere,
Dead end of autumn, everything caught between stone-drift and stone.

Black winter bird flocks side-wheel
From tree lung to grief-empty tree lung,
                                        lawn furniture
Imprints, unsat in. It's late.
Darkness, black phosphorus, smokes forth in the peaches and white pines.
The pile driver footing the new bridge
Cuts off, the bird flocks cough up and out.

I've read *Reflections in Autumn*,
                    I've been through the Three Gorges, I've done Chengdu . . .
Much easier here to find you out,
A landscape yourself by now,
Canebrake and waterbrake, inviolable in the memory.
Immortals, you once said, set forth again in their boats.
White hair, white hair. Drift away.

Still Life with Stick and Word

April is over. May moon.
How many more for my regard,
                                        hundreds, a handful?
Better not trouble the dark water due north of north.
Better to concentrate on something close, something small.
This stick, for instance. This word.

Next week. Back in the same chair.
And here's the stick
                        right where I dropped it, deep in the grass.
Maple, most likely, fuzz-barked and twice-broken, spore-pocked
With white spots, star charts to ford the river of heaven.
Warm wood. Warm wind from the clouds.

Inside now. The word is *white*.
It covers my tongue like paint—
                                        I say it and light forms,
Bottles arise, emptiness opens its corridors
Into the entrances and endless things that form bears.
White, great eviscerator.

Out into absence. Night chair.
Rose constellations rise
                            up from the shed and sad trees,
White yips in the dog dark that mirror the overburn.
A slide of houselight escapes through the kitchen window.
How unlike it is. How like.

Looking West from Laguna Beach at Night

I've always liked the view from my mother-in-law's house at night,
Oil rigs off Long Beach
Like floating lanterns out in the smog-dark Pacific,
Stars in the eucalyptus,
Lights of airplanes arriving from Asia, and town lights
Littered like broken glass around the bay and back up the hill.

In summer, dance music is borne up
On the sea winds from the hotel's beach deck far below,
"Twist and Shout," or "Begin the Beguine."
It's nice to think that somewhere someone is having a good time,
And pleasant to picture them down there
Turned out, tipsy and flushed, in their white shorts and their turquoise
 shirts.

Later, I like to sit and look up
At the mythic history of Western civilization,
Pinpricked and clued through the zodiac.
I'd like to be able to name them, say what's what and how who got where,
Curry the physics of metamorphosis and its endgame,
But I've spent my life knowing nothing.

Looking Again at What I Looked At for Seventeen Years

Quick pink; Soutine meat-streaks in the west,
Ocean grey drop cloth underfoot;
                                        peroxided gums—
Memory's like that, mixed metaphors, time's drone and gouache

Hovering near the horizon, black
Instinct filling the edges in, resplendent with holes.

We have it for text and narrative—
                                        nothing is new,
Remembrance, both nerve-net and nerve-spring,
The connection of everything with everything else
(Like absences the sea fills),
Constructs us and deconstructs us, world's breath, world's body.

Down there, for instance, just past the security lights
The hotel fans, wave-hollows build and dispense, surf sighs
And the unseen undertow
Sucks it away to where it's unreachable for good
Until it all comes back . . .
                                It's like that.

Looking Across Laguna Canyon at Dusk, West-by-Northwest

I love the way the evening sun goes down,
                                        orange brass-plaque, life's loss-logo,
Behind the Laguna hills and bare night-wisps of fog.
I love the way the hills empurple and sky goes nectarine,
The way the lights appear like little electric fig seeds, the wet west
Burnishing over into the indeterminate colors of the divine.

Like others, I want to pour myself into the veins of the invisible
at times like this,
                        becoming all that's liquid and moist.

Like Dionysus, I'd enter the atmosphere, spread and abandon—
They'd have to look for me elsewhere then,
Trickle of light extinguished in the Pacific, dark sluice, dark sluice line.

Venexia I

Too much at first, too lavish—full moon
Jackhammering light-splints along the canal, gondola beaks
Blading the half-dark;
Moon-spar; backwash backlit with moon-spark . . .

Next morning, all's otherwise
With a slow, chill rainfall like ragweed
                    electric against the launch lights,
Then grim-grained, then grey.
This is the water-watch landscape, the auto-da-fé.

Such small atrocities these days between the columns,
Such pale seductions and ravishments.
Boats slosh on the crushed canal, gulls hunch down, the weather rubs us
    away.
From here it's a long walk home.

Listen, Venice is death by drowning, everyone knows,
City of masks and minor frightfulness, October city
Twice sunk in its own sad skin.
How silently the lagoon
                    covers our footsteps, how quickly.

Along the Zattere, the liners drift huge as clouds.
We husband our imperfections, our changes of tune.
When water comes for us, we take it into our arms—
What's left's affection, and that's our sin.

Venexia II

Acqua alta, high water,
                                        sea gull anchored like Rimbaud's boat
Among the detritus, stuffed plastic food sacks bobbing like corks
Under Our Lady's stone-stern gaze,
                                                            Venezia, Serenissima . . .
Tide-slosh nibbles our shoe tops, then stumbles them under.

These are the dark waters, dark music
That scours us, that empties us out
                                                            only to fill us back by inches
With sweet, invisible plentitude,
Notes of astonishment, black notes to leave our lives by.

The Angel of Death, with her golden horn and her golden robe,
Rocks on the gondola's prow,
                                                  rain-dazzled, lashed at ease.
Under the rainfall's doom date,
She shines in her maritime solitude, she slides in splendor.

Outside the window, Rio San Polo churns and squalls.
The *traghetto*'s light
Burns like a homing Cathar soul
                                                        over the slack tide
Descending the greened Salute's steps.

This is the terminate hour, its bell
Tumbling out of Santa Maria Gloriosa dei Frari,
Last link in the chain of Speculation,
                                                              pulling us under.
Water is what it comes from, water is where it goes.

FROM

BLACK ZODIAC

(1997)

Apologia Pro Vita Sua

1

How soon we come to road's end—
Failure, our two-dimensional side-kick, flat dream-light,
Won't jump-start or burn us in,

Dogwood insidious in its constellations of part-charred cross points,
Spring's via Dolorosa
                                        flashed out in a dread profusion,
Nowhere to go but up, nowhere to turn, dead world-weight,

They've gone and done it again,
                                                    dogwood,
Spring's sap-crippled, arthritic, winter-weathered, myth limb,
Whose roots are my mother's hair.

Landscape's a lever of transcendence—
                                                            jack-wedge it here,
Or here, and step back,
Heave, and a light, a little light, will nimbus your going forth:

The dew bead, terminal bead, opens out
                                                              onto a great radiance,
Sun's square on magnolia leaf
Offers us entrance—
                                      who among us will step forward,

Camellia brown boutonnieres
Under his feet, plum branches under his feet, white sky, white noon,
Church bells like monks' mouths tonguing the hymn?

Journal and landscape
—Discredited form, discredited subject matter—
I tried to resuscitate both, breath and blood,
                                        making them whole again

Through language, strict attention—
Verona mi fe', disfecemi Verona, the song goes.
I've hummed it, I've bridged the break

To no avail.
                April. The year begins beyond words,
Beyond myself and the image of myself, beyond
Moon's ice and summer's thunder. All that.

The meat of the sacrament is invisible meat and a ghostly substance.
I'll say.
          Like any visible thing,
I'm always attracted downward, and soon to be killed and assimilated.

Vessel of life, it's said, vessel of life, brought to naught,
Then gathered back to what's visible.
That's it, fragrance of spring like lust in the blossom-starred orchard,

The shapeless shape of darkness starting to seep through and emerge,
The seen world starting to tilt,
Where I sit the still, unwavering point
                                    under that world's waves.

How like the past the clouds are,
Building and disappearing along the horizon,
Inflecting the mountains,
                                        laying their shadows under our feet

For us to cross over on.
Out of their insides fire falls, ice falls,
What we remember that still remembers us, earth and air fall.

Neither, however, can resurrect or redeem us,
Moving, as both must, ever away toward opposite corners.
Neither has been where we're going,
                                                    bereft of an attitude.

Amethyst, crystal transparency,
                                            Maya and Pharaoh ring,
Malocchio, set against witchcraft,
Lightning and hailstorm, birthstone, savior from drunkenness.

Purple, color of insight, clear sight,
Color of memory—
                                violet, that's for remembering,
Star-crystals scattered across the penumbra, hard stars.

Who can distinguish darkness from the dark, light from light,
Subject matter from story line,
                                            the part from the whole
When whole is part of the part and part is all of it?

Lonesomeness. Morandi, Cézanne, it's all about lonesomeness.
And Rothko. Especially Rothko.
Separation from what heals us
                                        beyond painting, beyond art.

Words and paint, black notes, white notes.
Music and landscape; music, landscape and sentences.
Gestures for which there is no balm, no intercession.

Two tone fields, horizon a line between abysses,
Generally white, always speechless.
Rothko could choose either one to disappear into. And did.

Perch'io no spero di tornar giammai, ballatetta, in Toscana,
Not as we were the first time,
                                        not as we'll ever be again.
Such snowflakes of memory, they fall nowhere but there.

Absorbed in remembering, we cannot remember—
Exile's anthem, O stiff heart,
Thingless we came into the world and thingless we leave.

Every important act is wordless—
                                        to slip from the right way,
To fail, still accomplishes something.
Even a good thing remembered, however, is not as good as not
    remembering at all.

Time is the source of all good,
time the engenderer
Of entropy and decay,
Time the destroyer, our only-begetter and advocate.

For instance, my fingernail,
so pink, so amplified,
In the half-dark, for instance,
These force-fed dogwood blossoms, green-leafed, defused,
limp on their long branches.

St. Stone, say a little prayer for me,
grackles and jay in the black gum,
Drowse of the peony head,
Dandelion globes luminous in the last light, more work to be done . . .

2

Something will get you, the doctor said,
don't worry about that.
Melancholia's got me,
Pains in the abdomen, pains down the left leg and crotch.

Slurry of coal dust behind the eyes,
Massive weight in the musculature, dark blood, dark blood.
I'm sick and tired of my own complaints,

This quick flick like a compass foot through the testicle,
Deep drag and hurt through the groin—
Melancholia, black dog,
everyone's had enough.

Dew-dangled, fresh-cut lawn grass will always smell like a golf course
Fairway to me, Saturday morning, Chuck Ross and I
Already fudging our scores down,
happy as mockingbirds in deep weeds,

The South Fork of the Holston River
Slick as a nickel before its confluence behind our backs
At Rotherwood with the North Fork's distant, blurred thunder,

Our rounds in the seventies always including mulligans,
Nudged lies, "found" lost balls, some extraordinary shots
And that never-again-to-be-repeated
teen-age false sense of attainment.

One summer, aged 16, I watched—each night, it seemed—my roommate,
A college guy, gather his blanket up, and flashlight,
And leave for his rendezvous with the camp cook—
he never came back before dawn.

Some 40 years later I saw him again for the first time
Since then, in a grocery store, in the checkout line,
A cleric from Lexington, shrunken and small. Bearded even.

And all these years I'd thought of him, if at all, as huge
And encompassing,
Not rabbit-eyed, not fumbling a half-filled brown sack,
dry-lipped, apologetic.

In 1990 we dragged Paris
—back on the gut again after 25 years—
The Boulevard Montparnasse,
La Coupole, the Select, you know, the Dôme, the Closerie de Lilas,

Up and down and back and forth.
Each night a Japanese girl would take a bath at 4 a.m.
In the room above ours,
each night someone beat his wife

In a room above the garage outside our window.
It rained all day for ten days.
Sleeplessness, hallucination, O City of Light . . .

What sane, impossible reason could Percy Heath have made up
To talk to me, drunk, white and awe-struck,
—And tone-deaf to boot—
that night at the Carmel Mission?

But talk he did, uncondescending, feigning interest,
As Milt Jackson walked by and John Lewis walked by,
Gerry Mulligan
Slouched in one corner, Paul Desmond cool in an opposite one.

October, 1958, Monterey Jazz Festival,
First advisors starting to leave the Army Language School for South
Vietnam,
The Pacific's dark eyelid
beginning to stir, ready to rise and roll back . . .

During World War II, we lived in Oak Ridge, Tennessee,
Badges and gates, checkpoints, government housing, government rules.
One house we lived in was next door to a two-star admiral.

I learned a couple of things in the three-plus years we lived in Oak Ridge,
One from my first (and only) paper route, the second
After my first (and only) breaking-and-entering.

One thing I learned, however, I didn't know what to do with:
Death is into the water, life is the coming out.
I still don't, though nothing else matters but that, it seems,
nothing even comes close.

Elm Grove, Pine Valley and Cedar Hill,
what detritus one remembers—
The one-armed soldier we spied on making out in the sedge grass
With his red-haired girl friend behind the Elm Grove playground,

For instance, in 1944 . . . I was nine, the fourth grade . . .
I remember telling Brooklyn, my best friend,
my dick was stiff all night.
Nine years old! My dick! All night!

We talked about it for days,
Oak Ridge abstracted and elsewhere,
—D-Day and Normandy come and gone—
All eyes on the new world's sun king,
its rising up and its going down.

It's Wednesday afternoon, and Carter and I are on the road
For the Sullivan County National Bank Loan Department,
1957, Gate City and Southwest Virginia.

We're after deadbeats, delinquent note payers, in Carter's words.
Cemetery plots—ten dollars a month until you die or pay up.
In four months I'll enter the Army, right now I'm Dr. Death,

Riding shotgun for Carter, bringing more misery to the miserable.
Up-hollow and down-creek, shack after unelectrified shack—
The worst job in the world, and we're the two worst people in it.

Overcast afternoon, then weak sun, then overcast again.
A little wind
whiffles across the back yard like a squall line
In miniature, thumping the clover heads, startling the grass.

My parents' 60th wedding anniversary
Were they still alive,
5th of June, 1994.
It's hard to imagine, I think, your own children grown older than you
ever were, I can't.

I sit in one of the knock-off Brown-Jordan deck chairs we brought from
California,
Next to the bearded grandson my mother never saw.
Some afternoon, or noon, it will all be over. Not this one.

3

June is a migraine above the eyes,
Strict auras and yellow blots,
                                        green screen and tunnel vision,
Slow ripples of otherworldliness,

Humidity's painfall drop by drop.
Next door, high whine of the pest exterminator's blunt machine.
Down the street, tide-slap of hammer-and-nail,
                                        hammer-and-nail from a neighbor's roof.

I've had these for forty years,
                                        light-prints and shifting screed,
Feckless illuminations.
St. John of the Cross, Julian of Norwich, lead me home.

It's good to know certain things:
What's departed, in order to know what's left to come;
That water's immeasurable and incomprehensible

And blows in the air
Where all that's fallen and silent becomes invisible;
That fire's the light our names are carved in.

That shame is a garment of sorrow;
That time is the Adversary, and stays sleepless and wants for nothing;
That clouds are unequal and words are.

I sense a certain uncertainty in the pine trees,
Seasonal discontent,
                                        quotidian surliness,
Pre-solstice jitters, that threatens to rattle our equilibrium.

My friend has lost his larynx,
My friend who in the old days, with a sentence or two,
Would easily set things right,

His glasses light-blanks as he quoted a stanza from Stevens or Yeats
Behind his cigarette smoke.
Life's hard, our mutual third friend says . . . It is. It is.

Sundays define me.
                                        Born on a back-lit Sunday, like today,
But later, in August,
And elsewhere, in Tennessee, Sundays dismantle me.

There is a solitude about Sunday afternoons
In small towns, surrounded by all that's familiar
And of necessity dear,

That chills us on hot days, like today, unto the grave,
When the sun is a tongued wafer behind the clouds, out of sight,
And wind chords work through the loose-roofed yard sheds,
                                                                                a celestial music . . .

There is forgetfulness in me which makes me descend
Into a great ignorance,
And makes me to walk in mud, though what I remember remains.

Some of the things I have forgotten:
Who the Illuminator is, and what he illuminates;
Who will have pity on what needs have pity on it.

What I remember redeems me,
                                        strips me and brings me to rest,
An end to what has begun,
A beginning to what is about to be ended.

What are the determining moments of our lives?
                                                        How do we know them?
Are they ends of things or beginnings?
Are we more or less of ourselves once they've come and gone?

I think this is one of mine tonight,
The Turkish moon and its one star
                                        crisp as a new flag
Over my hometown street with its dark trash cans looming along the curb.

Surely this must be one. And what of me afterwards
When the moon and her sanguine consort
Have slipped the horizon? What will become of me then?

Some names are everywhere—they are above and they are below,
They are concealed and they are revealed.
We call them wise, for the wisdom of death is called the little wisdom.

And my name? And your name?
                                        Where will we find them, in what pocket?

Wherever it is, better to keep them there not known—
Words speak for themselves, anonymity speaks for itself.

The Unknown Master of the Pure Poem walks nightly among his roses,
The very garden his son laid out.
Every so often he sits down. Every so often he stands back up . . .

Heavy, heavy, heavy hangs over our heads. June heat.
How many lives does it take to fabricate this one?
Aluminum pie pan bird frightener
                                        dazzles and feints in a desultory breeze

Across the road, vegetable garden mojo, evil eye.
That's one life I know for sure.
Others, like insects in amber,
                                        lie golden and lurking and hidden from us.

Ninety-four in the shade, humidity huge and inseparable,
Noon sun like a laser disk.
The grackle waddles forth in his suit of lights,
                                        the crucifixion on his back.

Affection's the absolute
                    everything rises to,
Devotion's detail, the sum of all our scatterings,
Bright imprint our lives unshadow on.

Easy enough to say that now, the hush of late spring
Hung like an after-echo

Over the neighborhood,
                    devolving and disappearing.

Easy enough, perhaps, but still true,
Honeysuckle and poison ivy jumbling out of the hedge,
Magnolia beak and white tongue, landscape's off-load, love's lisp.

ENVOI

What we once liked, we no longer like.
What we used to delight in settles like fine ash on our tongues.
What we once embraced embraces us.

Things have destinies, of course,
On-lines and downloads mysterious as the language of clouds.
My life has become like that,

Half uninterpretable, half new geography,
Landscapes stilled and adumbrated, memory unratcheting,
Its voice-over not my own.

Meanwhile, the mole goes on with its subterranean daydreams,
The dogs lie around like rugs,
Birds nitpick their pinfeathers, insects slick down their shells.

No horizon-honing here, no angst in the anthill.
What happens is what happens,
And what happened to happen never existed to start with.

Still, who wants a life like that,
No next and no before, no yesterday, no today,
Tomorrow a moment no one will ever live in?

As for me, I'll take whatever wanes,
The loosening traffic on the straightaway, the dark and such,
The wandering stars, wherever they come from now, wherever they go.

I'll take whatever breaks down beneath its own sad weight—
The paintings of Albert Pinkham Ryder, for instance,
Language, the weather, the word of God.

I'll take as icon and testament
The daytime metaphysics of the natural world,
Sun on tie post, rock on rock.

Poem Half in the Manner of Li Ho

All things aspire to weightlessness,
                                        some place beyond the lip of language,
Some silence, some zone of grace,

Sky white as raw silk,
                        opening mirror cold-sprung in the west,
Sunset like dead grass.

If God hurt the way we hurt,
                                he, too, would be heart-sore,
Disconsolate, unappeasable.

Li Ho, the story goes, would leave home
Each day at dawn, riding a colt, a servant boy
                                                walking behind him,

An antique tapestry bag
Strapped to his back.
When inspiration struck, Ho would write
The lines down and drop them in the bag.
At night he'd go home and work the lines up into a poem,
No matter how disconnected and loose-leafed they were.
His mother once said,
"He won't stop until he has vomited out his heart."

And so he did.
Like John Keats,
He died believing his name would never be written among the Characters.
Without hope, he thought himself—that worst curse—unlucky.
At twenty-seven, at death's line, he saw a man come
In purple, driving a red dragon,
A tablet in one hand, who said,
"I'm here to summon Li Ho."
Ho got from his bed and wept.
Far from the sick room's dragon-dark, snow stormed the passes,
Monkeys surfed the bo trees
and foolish men ate white jade.

How mournful the southern hills are,
how white their despair
Under December's T'ang blue blank page.

What's the use of words—there are no words
For December's chill redaction,
for the way it makes us feel.

We hang like clouds between heaven and earth,
                                        between something and nothing,
Sometimes with shadows, sometimes without.

Meditation on Form and Measure

A palm print confirms the stars, but what confirms the hand?
Out of any two thoughts I have, one is devoted to death.
Our days an uncertainty, a chaos and shapeless,
All that our lives are
                        blurs down, like a landscape reflected in water.
All stars are lights, all lights are not stars.

13 July, buck robin dry-preens on lodge pole branch,
North sky racked-over to stone-washed blue,
Star-wheels in whiteout,
One cloud over Caribou as though spray-painted there,
Doe bird tail-up under stained glass Venetian footbridge.

Spruce-cloister abbeyesque, trees monk-like and shadow-frocked,
Grouse in the dark folds,
Sunlight pale cross through the thick branches,
Male grouse twice-graced in a sacrificial strut,
                                                fantailed, away
From something hidden and too young, lord down the dead log.

The moon, like some albino black hole, draws the light in,
The crescent moon, falling and golden,
And darkens the sky around it erupting in stars,

Word stars, warrior stars, word warriors
                                                                                assembling
Accents and destinies, moon drawing the light inside.

Time and light are the same thing somewhere behind our backs.
And form is measure.
                                        Without measure there is no form:
Form and measure become one.
Time and light become one somewhere beyond our future.
Father darkness, mother night,
                                                            one and one become one again.

Now, in their separateness, however, they sizzle and hum,
Sweet, self-destructive music
That cradles our bodies and turns them
Back to an attitude, a near-truth
Where measure is verbal architecture
                                                                        and form is splendor.

Immodestly, we pattern ourselves against the dead,
Echoes and mirrors, distant thunder,
Those fabulous constellations
                                                            we gaze at but can't explain.
Our lives reflections of shadows, cries
Echoes of echoes, we live among ghosts, sighting and sizing,

Hawk like a circling scrap of ash on the thermal's flame,
Gray jay non grata at feeder trough,

Barn swallows veering like fighter planes
out of the overcast,
La Traviata incongruous
Inside from the boom box tape, bird snarl and aria.

Memory is a cemetery
I've visited once or twice, white
ubiquitous and the set-aside
Everywhere under foot,
Jack robin back on his bowed branch, missus tucked butt-up
Over the eggs,
clouds slow and deep as liners over the earth.

My life, like others' lives, has been circumscribed by stars.
O vaghe stelle dell'orso,
beautiful stars of the Bear,
I took, one time, from a book.
Tonight, I take it again, that I, like Leopardi, might
One day immerse myself in its cold, Lethean shine.

Poem Almost Wholly in My Own Manner

Where the Southern cross the Yellow Dog
In Moorhead, Mississippi,
my mother sheltered her life out

In Leland, a few miles down US 82,
unfretted and unaware,
Layered between history and a three-line lament

About to be brought forth
on the wrong side of the tracks
All over the state and the Deep South.

We all know what happened next,
blues and jazz and rhythm-and-blues,
Then rock-and-roll, then sex-and-drugs-and-rock-and-roll, lick by lick

Blowing the lanterns out—and everything else—along the levees:
Cotton went west, the music went north
and everywhere in between,

Time, like a burning wheel, scorching along by the highway side,
Reorganizing, relayering,
turning the tenants out.

9 p.m. August sky eleemosynary, such sweet grief,
Music the distant thunder chord
that shudders our lives.

Black notes. The black notes
That follow our footsteps like blood from a cut finger.
Like that.

Fireflies, slow angel eyes,
nod and weave,
Tracking our chary attitudes, our malevolent mercies.

Charity, sometimes, we have,
appearing and disappearing
Like stars when nightwash rises through us.

(Hope and faith we lip-sync,
                    a dark dharma, a goat grace,
A grace like rain, that goes where rain goes.)

Discreetly the evening enters us,
                    overwhelms us,
As out here whatever lifts, whatever lowers, intersects.

Interstices. We live in the cracks.
Under Ezekiel and his prophesies,
                    under the wheel.

Poetry's what's left between the lines—
                    a strange speech and a hard language,
It's all in the unwritten, it's all in the unsaid . . .

And that's a comfort, I think,
                    for our lack and inarticulation.
For our scalded flesh and our singed hair.

But what would Robert Johnson say,
                    hell-hounded and brimstone-tongued?
What would W. C. Handy say,

Those whom the wheel has overturned,
                    those whom the fire has,
And the wind has, unstuck and unstrung?

They'd say what my mother said—
                    a comfort, perhaps, but too cold
Where the Southern cross the Yellow Dog.

Meditation on Summer and Shapelessness

We have a bat, one bat, that bug-surfs
our late-summer back yard
Just as the fireflies begin
To rise, new souls, toward the August moon.
Flap-limbed, ungathered,
He stumbles unerringly through them,
Exempt as they feint and ascend to their remission—
Light, Catharist light;
Brightness to brightness where I sit
on the back brink of my sixth decade,
Virginia moon in the cloud-ragged, cloud-scutted sky,
Bat bug-drawn and swallow-crossed, God's wash.

One comes to understand
Candide and Tiberius,
Sour saints, aspiring aphasiacs,
Recluses and anchorites,
Those whom the moon's pull and the moon's
hydrointerpretation
Crumble twice under,
Those hard few for whom the Eagle has never landed.
Out here, all's mythic, medieval, or early A.D.
One half expects
Raymond of Toulouse or Hadrian to step forth,
Resplendent and otherwise, out of the hedge row or arborvitae.
One half hopes, moon's gun with a dead bead.

I never quite got it, what they meant,
                                        but now I do,
Waking each morning at dawn,
Or before, some shapeless, unfingerprintable dread
On me like cold-crossed humidity,
Extinction shouldering, like a season, in from my dreamscape.
Without my glasses, the light around the window shade
Throbs like an aura, so faint
At first, then luminous with its broken promises—
Feckless icon, dark reliquary.
Mortality hunches, like fine furniture, crowding the room.

Rising, feeding the dogs, bringing the newspaper in,
Somehow should loosen things up.
It doesn't, of course.
                        There's still the pill to be taken,
And then another, eye drops,
Toothbrush and toothpaste,
                              reflection of someone older and strange
Constantly in the mirror,
Breakfast and then the day's doom, long-leafed
And everywhere,
Shadowing what I look at, shadowing what I see.
The News, then supper, then back to the black beginning.

Après-dog days, dead end of August,
Summer a holding pattern,
                              heat, haze, humidity
The mantra we still chant, the bell-tick our tongues all toll.
Whatever rises becomes a light—

Firefly and new moon,
Star and star and star chart
                                        unscrolled across the heavens
Like radioactive dump sites bulb-lit on a map.
Whatever holds back goes dark—
The landscape and all its accoutrements, my instinct, my hands,
My late, untouchable hands.

Summer's crepuscular, rot and wrack,
Rain-ravaged, root-ruined.
Each August the nightscape inserts itself
                                        another inch in my heart,
Piece and a piece, piecemeal, time's piecework.
August unedges and polishes me, water's way.
Such subtle lapidary.
Last lights go out in the next-door house,
                                        dogs disappear,
Privet and white pine go under, bird-squelch and frog-shrill.
To be separate, to be apart, is to be whole again.
Full night now and dust sheet—
                                        the happy life is the darkened life.

The Appalachian Book of the Dead

Sunday, September Sunday . . . Outdoors,
Like an early page from The Appalachian Book of the Dead,
Sunlight lavishes brilliance on every surface,
Doves settle, surreptitious angels, on tree limb and box branch,
A crow calls, deep in its own darkness,
Something like water ticks on
Just there, beyond the horizon, just there, steady clock . . .

Go in fear of abstractions . . .

Well, possibly. Meanwhile,
They *are* the strata our bodies rise through, the sere veins
Our skins rub off on.
For instance, whatever enlightenment there might be
Housels compassion and affection, those two tributaries
That river above our lives,
Whose waters we sense the sense of

late at night, and later still.

Uneasy, suburbanized,
I drift from the lawn chair to the back porch to the dwarf orchard
Testing the grass and border garden.
A stillness, as in the passageways of Paradise,
Bell jars the afternoon.

Leaves, like *ex votos*, hang hard and shine
Under the endlessness of heaven.
Such skeletal altars, such vacant sanctuary.

It always amazes me
How landscape recalibrates the stations of the dead,
How what we see jacks up

the odd quotient of what we don't see,
How God's breath reconstitutes our walking up and walking down.
First glimpse of autumn, stretched tight and snicked, a bad face lift,
Flicks in and flicks out,

a virtual reality.
Time to begin the long division.

Umbrian Dreams

Nothing is flat-lit and tabula rasaed in Charlottesville,
Umbrian sackcloth,
                    stigmata and *Stabat mater*,
A sleep and a death away,
Night, and a sleep and a death away—
Light's frost-fired and Byzantine here,
                              aureate, beehived,
Falling in Heraclitean streams
Through my neighbor's maple trees.
There's nothing medieval and two-dimensional in our town,
October in full drag, Mycenaean masked and golden lobed.

Like Yeats, however, I dream of a mythic body,
Feathered and white, a landscape
                              horizoned and honed as an anchorite.
(Iacopo, hear me out, St. Francis, have you a word for me?)
Umbrian lightfall, lambent and ichorous, mists through my days,
As though a wound, somewhere and luminous,
                                        flickered and went out,
Flickered and went back out—
So weightless the light, so stretched and pained,
It seems to ooze, and then not ooze, down from that one hurt.
You doubt it? Look. Put your finger there. No, there. You see?

October II

October in mission creep,
                         autumnal reprise and stand down.
The more reality takes shape, the more it loses intensity—

Synaptic uncertainty,
Electrical surge and quick lick of the minus sign,
Tightening of the force field
Wherein our forms are shaped and shapes formed,
                                        wherein we pare ourselves to our attitudes . . .

Do not despair—one of the thieves was saved; do not presume—one of
    the thieves was damned,
Wrote Beckett, quoting St. Augustine.
It was the shape of the sentence he liked, the double iambic pentameter:
It is the shape that matters, he said.
Indeed, shape precludes shapelessness, as God precludes Godlessness.
Form is the absence of all things. Like sin. Yes, like sin.

It's the shape beneath the shape that summons us, the juice
That spreads the rose, the multifoliate spark
                                                        that drops the leaf
And darkens our entranceways,
The rush that transfigures the maple tree,
                                            the rush that transubstantiates our lives.
October, the season's signature and garnishee,
October, the exponential negative, the plus.

Lives of the Saints

1

A loose knot in a short rope,
My life keeps sliding out from under me, intact but
Diminishing,
              its pattern becoming patternless,
The blue abyss of everyday air

Breathing it in and breathing it out,
                                        in little clouds like smoke,
In little wind strings and threads.

Everything that the pencil says is erasable,
Unlike our voices, whose words are black and permanent,
Smudging our lives like coal dust,
                                        unlike our memories,
Etched like a skyline against the mind,
Unlike our irretrievable deeds . . .
The pencil spills everything, and then takes everything back.

For instance, here I am at Hollywood Boulevard and Vine,
Almost 60, Christmas Eve, the flesh-flashers and pimps
And inexhaustible Walk of Famers
                                        snubbing their joints out,
Hoping for something not-too-horrible to happen across the street.
The rain squall has sucked up and bumped off,
The palm fronds dangle lubriciously.
                                        Life, as they say, is beautiful.

2

One week into 1995, and all I've thought about
Is endings, retreads,
                        the love of loss
Light as a locket around my neck, idea of absence
Hard and bright as a dime inside my trouser pocket.
Where is the new and negotiable,
The undiscovered snapshot,
                                    the phoneme's refusal, word's rest?

Remember, face the facts, Miss Stein said.
                                                And so I've tried,

Pretending there's nothing there but description, hoping emotion shows;
That that's why description's there:
The subject was never smoke,
                                        there's always been a fire.
The winter dark shatters around us like broken glass.
The morning sky opens its pink robe.

All explorers must die of heartbreak.
                                                Middle-aged poets, too,
Wind from the northwest, small wind,
Two crows in the ash tree, one on an oak limb across the street.
Endless effortless nothingness, January blue:
Noteless measureless music;
                                        imageless iconography.
I'll be the lookout and listener, you do the talking . . .

3

Chinook, the January thaw;
                                        warm wind from the Gulf
Spinning the turn-around and dead leaves
Northeast and southeast—
I like it under the trees in winter,
                                        everything over me dead,
Or half-dead, sky hard,
Wind moving the leaves around clockwise, then counterclockwise too.

We live in a place that is not our own . . .
                                                I'll say . . . Roses rot
In the side garden's meltdown, shrubs bud,
The sounds of syllables altogether elsewhere rise
Like white paint through the sun—
                                        familiar only with God,

We yearn to be pierced by that
Occasional void through which the supernatural flows.

The plain geometry of the dead does not equate,
Infinite numbers, untidy sums:
We believe in belief but don't believe,
                                        for which we shall be judged.
In winter, under the winter trees—
A murder of crows glides over, some thirty or more,
To its appointment,
                        sine and cosine, angle and arc.

4

The winter wind re-nails me,
                                respirations of the divine
In and out, a cold fusion.
Such dire lungs.
The sun goes up and the sun goes down,
                                        small yelps from the short weeds.
Listen up, Lord, listen up.
The night birds sleep with their wings ajar.
                                        Black branches, black branches.

Al poco giorno ed al gran cerchio d'ombra—
A little light and a great darkness,
Darkness wherein our friends are hid,
                                        and our love's gone wrong.
If death is abstract (force through pure, illusory space),
May I be put, when the time comes, in the dwelling of St. John
As I wrest myself from joy
                                into the meta-optics of desire.

Posteriori Dei . . .
God's back, love's loss, light's blank the eye can accommodate

And the heart shelve,
world's ever-more-disappearing vacancy
Under the slow-drag clouds of heaven
The landscape absorbs and then repents of,
clouds ponderous as a negative
Nothing can keep from moving.

5

The afternoon is urban, and somewhat imaginary,
Behind the snowfall, winter's printout
And self-defense, its matrix and self-design.
All afternoon
The afternoon was ordinary
And self-perpetuating behind its Chinese screen.
But it was urban, and actual, in the long run.

In dread we stay and in dread depart . . .
Not much wrench room.
The 13th century knew this, a movable floor—
Here's bad and There's worse.
Outside the door, demons writhed just under the earth's crust,
Outside the door,
and licensed to govern in God's name.
On the street, the ride-bys and executions lip-chant and sing.

Contemplative, cloistered, tongue-tied,
Zen says, watch your front.
Zen says, wherever you are is a monastery.
The afternoon says, life's a loose knot in a short rope.
The afternoon says,
show me your hands, show me your feet.
The lives of the saints become our lives.
God says, watch your back.

Christmas East of the Blue Ridge

So autumn comes to an end with these few wet sad stains
Stuck to the landscape,
                                        December dark
Running its hands through the lank hair of late afternoon,
Little tongues of the rain holding forth
                                                        under the eaves,
Such wash, such watery words . . .

So autumn comes to this end,
And winter's vocabulary, downsized and distanced,
Drop by drop
Captures the conversation with its monosyllabic gutturals
And tin music,
                              gravelly consonants, scratched vowels.

Soon the camel drivers will light their fires, soon the stars
Will start on their brief dip down from the back of heaven,
Down to the desert's dispensation
And night reaches, the gall and first birth,
The second only one word from now,
                                                    one word and its death from right now.

Meanwhile, in Charlottesville, the half-moon
Hums like a Hottentot
                                       high over Monticello,
Clouds dishevel and rag out,
The alphabet of our discontent
Keeps on with its lettering,
                                            gold on the black walls of our hearts . . .

Negatives II

One erases only in order to write again . . .

You don't know what you don't know,
We used to say in the CIC in Verona—
Negative space, negative operability
To counterposition the white drift of the unknown.
You can't see what you can't see.

It's still the best advice, but easy to overlook
As winter grinds out its cigarette
Across the landscape.
                                        February.
Who could have known, in 1959, the balloon would not go up?
Who could have seen, back then, the new world's new disorder?

John Ruskin says all clouds are masses of light, even the darkest ones.
Hard to remember that these overcast afternoons,
Midweek, ash-black and ash-white,
                                                            negative shapes sketched in
And luminous here and there in loose interstices
Elbowed and stacked between earth and sky.

Hard to remember that as the slipstream of memory shifts
And shutters, massing what wasn't there as though it were.
Where are the secret codes these days for nuking the Brenner Pass?
And the Run, and the Trieste Station?
Like sculptured mist, sharp-edged and cut into form, they slide on by.

One only writes in order to erase again . . .

Lives of the Artists

1

Learn how to model before you learn to finish things,
Michelangelo hisses . . .
                                        Before you bear witness,
Be sure you have something that calls for a witnessing,
I might add—
Don't gloss what isn't assignable or brought to bear,
Don't shine what's expendable.

March in the northern south. Hard ides-heat
Bangs through the branches of winter trees,
                                                            thumps the gauges
Needling green and immodestly
Out of the dead leaves, out of their opium half-dreams.
Willows, medusa-hooded and bone-browed, begin to swim up
Through their brown depths, wasps revive
                                                            and plants practice their scales.

In Poussin's apocalypse,
                                        we're all merely emanations sent forth
From landscape's hell-hung heart-screen—
Some flee through the dust, some find them a bed in the wind's scorched
   mouth,
Some disappear in flame . . .
                                            As I do this afternoon
Under the little fires in the plum tree, white-into-white-into-white,
Unidentified bird on a limb, lung-light not of this world.

2

When you have died there will be nothing—
No memory of you will remain,
                                        not even a trace as you walk
Aimlessly, unseen, in the fitful halls of the dead,
Sappho warns us. She also writes:
The moon has set, and the Pleiades—
                                                in the deep middle of the night
The time is passing . . .

How is it that no one remembers this?
                                                Time's ashes, *I lie alone.*
So simple, so simple, so unlike the plastic ticking Christ
Who preyed on us we prayed to—
Such eucharistic side-bars, such saint-shortened anomalies
Under the dull stained glass,
                                        down the two-lane and four-lane highways.
Pain enters me drop by drop.

The two plum trees, like tired angels, have *dropped their wings at their sides.*
I walk quietly among the autumn offerings
Dark hands from the underworld
Push up around me,
                        gold-amber cups
and bittersweet, nightshade, indulgences from the dead.
I walk quietly and carefully on their altar,
                                                among their prayers.

3

We all rise, if we rise at all, to what we're drawn by,
Big Smoke, simplicity's signature,
Last untranslatable text—

The faithful do not speak many words . . .

What's there to say,

Little smoke, cloud-smoke, in the plum trees,
Something's name indecipherable

rechalked in the scrawled branches.

Everything God possesses, it's been said, *the wise man already has.*
Some slack, then, some hope.
Don't give the word to everyone,
The gift is tiny, the world made up
Of deceivers and those who are deceived—

the true word

Is the word about the word.

Celestial gossip, celestial similes
(Like, like, like, like, like)
Powder the plum blossoms nervously, invisibly,

the word

In hiding, unstirred. The facts,
The bits of narrative,

glow, intermittent and flaked.

The sins of the uninformed are the first shame of their teachers.

4

Jaundicing down from their purity, the plum blossoms
Snowfall out of the two trees
And spread like a sheet of mayflies

soundlessly, thick underfoot—

I am the silence that is incomprehensible,
First snow starts drifting down from the sky,

late fall in the other world;

I am the utterance of my name.

Belief in transcendence,
belief in something beyond belief,
Is what the blossoms solidify
In their fall through the two worlds—
The imaging of the invisible, the slow dream of metaphor,
Sanction our going up and our going down, our days
And the lives we infold inside them,
our *yes* and *yes.*

Good to get that said, tongue of cold air
Licking the landscape,
snuffing the flame in the green fuse.
I am the speech that cannot be grasped.
I am the substance and the thing that has no substance,
Cast forth upon the face of the earth,
Whose margins we write in,
whose one story we tell, and keep on telling.

5

There's nothing out there but light,
the would-be artist said,
As usual just half right:
There's also a touch of darkness, everyone knows, on both sides of both horizons,
Prescribed and unpaintable,
Touching our fingertips whichever way we decide to jump.
His small palette, however, won't hold that color,
though some have, and some still do.

The two plum trees know nothing of that,
Having come to their green grief,
their terrestrial touch-and-go,
Out of grace and radiance,

Their altered bodies alteration transmogrified.
Mine is a brief voice, a still, brief voice
Unsubject to change or the will to change—
                                        might it be restrung and rearranged.

But that is another story.
                                Vasari tells us
An earlier tale than Greek of the invention of painting,
How Gyges of Lydia
Once saw his own shadow cast
                                    by the light of a fire
And instantly drew his own outline on the wall with charcoal . . .
Learn to model before you learn how to finish things.

Deep Measure

Shank of the afternoon, wan weight-light,
Undercard of a short month,
                                    February Sunday . . .
Wordlessness of the wrong world.
In the day's dark niche, the patron saint of What-Goes-Down
Shuffles her golden deck and deals,
                                        one for you and one for me . . .

And that's it, a single number—we play what we get.
My hand says measure,
                                doves on the wire and first bulb blades
Edging up through the mulch mat,
Inside-out of the winter gum trees,
A cold harbor, cold stop and two-step, and here it comes,

Deep measure,
deep measure that runnels beneath the bone,
That sways our attitude and sets our lives to music;
Deep measure, down under and death-drawn:
Pilgrim, homeboy of false time,
Listen and set your foot down,
listen and step lightly.

Thinking of Winter at the Beginning of Summer

Milton paints purple trees. Avery.
And Wolf Kahn too.
I've liked their landscapes,
Nightdreams and daymares,
pastures and woods that burn our eyes.
Otherwise, why would we look?
Otherwise, why would we stretch our hands out and gather them in?

My brother slides through the blue zones in enormous planes.
My sister's cartilage, ash and bone.
My parents rock in their blackened boats
back and forth, back and forth.
Above the ornamental cherries, the sky is a box and a glaze.
Well, yes, a box and a glaze.

Pulled from despair like a bad tooth,
I see my roots, tiny roots,
glisten like good luck in the sun.
What we refuse defines us,
a little of this, a little of that.

The light stays fool's gold for a long time.
The light stays fool's gold for a long time.

—FOR WINTER WRIGHT

Jesuit Graves

Midsummer. Irish overcast. Oatmeal-colored sky.
The Jesuit pit. Last mass
For hundreds whose names are incised on the marble wall
Above the gravel and grassless dirt.
Just dirt and the small stones—
how strict, how self-effacing.

Not suited for you, however, Father Bird-of-Paradise,
Whose *plumage of far wonder* is not formless and not faceless,
Whatever you might have hoped for once.
Glasnevin Cemetery, Dublin, 3 July 1995.
For those who would rise to meet their work,
that work is scaffolding.

Sacrifice is the cause of ruin.
The absence of sacrifice is the cause of ruin.
Thus the legends instruct us,
North wind through the flat-leaved limbs of the sheltering trees,
Three desperate mounds in the small, square enclosure,
souls God-gulped and heaven-hidden.

P. Gerardus Hopkins, 28 July 1844–8 June 1889, Age 44.
And then the next name. And then the next,
Soldiers of misfortune, lock-step into a star-colored tight dissolve,

History's hand-me-ons. But you, Father Candescence,
You, Father Fire?
                    Whatever rises comes together, they say. They say.

Meditation on Song and Structure

I love to wake to the *coo coo* of the mourning dove
At dawn—
            like one drug masking another's ill effects,
It tells me that everything's all right when I know that everything's wrong.
It lays out the landscape's hash marks,
                              the structures of everyday.
It makes what's darkened unworkable
For that moment, and that, as someone once said, is grace.
But this bird's a different story.

Dawn in the Umbrian hills.
In the cracks of the persian blinds, slim ingots of daylight stack and drip.
This bird has something to say—
                         a watery kind of music,
Extended improvisations, liquid riffs and breaks—
But not to me, pulled like a dead weight
From the riptide of sleep, not to me,
Depression's darling, history's hand job, not to me . . .

Twice, now, I've heard the nightingale.
                              First in the first light
Of a dust-grey dawn,
And then at midnight, a week later,

Walking my friend to the parking lot
In Todi, moon vamping behind the silted cloud mounds,
A pentimento of sudden illumination,
Like bird work or spider work.
Senti, my friend said, *Shhh*,

È l'usignolo, the nightingale,
As bird and bird song drifted downhill,
easy as watershine,
Ripply and rock-run.
Silence. No moon, no motorbike, no bird.
The silence of something come and something gone away.
Nightingale, ghost bird, ghost song,
Hand that needles and threads the night together,
light a candle for me.

Swallows over the battlements
and thigh-moulded red tile roofs,
Square crenelations, Guelph town.
Swallows against the enfrescoed backdrop of tilled hills
Like tiny sharks in the tinted air
That buoys them like a tide,
arrested, water-colored surge.
Swallows darting like fish through the alabaster air,
Cleansing the cleanliness, feeding on seen and the unseen.

To come back as one of them!
Loose in the light and landscape-shine,
language without words,
Ineffable part of the painting and ignorant of it,
Pulled by the lunar landswell,

Demi-denizen of the godhead
Spread like a golden tablecloth wherever you turn—
Such judgment, such sweet witch-work.

This mockingbird's got his chops.
Bird song over black water—
Am I south or north of my own death,
                                        west or east of my final hurt?
In North Carolina, half a century ago,
Bird song over black water,
Lake Llewellyn Bibled and night-colored,
                                        mockingbird
Soul-throated, like light, a little light in great darkness.

Zodiac damped, then clicked off,
                                        cloud-covering-heaven.
Bird song over black water.
I remember the way the song contained many songs,
As it does now, the same song
Over the tide pool of my neighbor's yard, and mine's slack turning,
Many songs, a season's worth,
Many voices, a light to lead back
                                        to silence, sound of the first voice.

Medieval, prelatic, why
Does the male cardinal sing that song, *omit, omit*,
From the eminence of the gum tree?
What is it he knows,
                        silence, *omit, omit*, silence,

The afternoon breaking away in little pieces,
Siren's squeal from the bypass,
The void's tattoo, *Nothing Matters*,
mottoed across our white hearts?

Nature abhors originality, according to Cioran.
Landscape desires it, I say,
The back yard unloading its cargo of solitudes
Into the backwash of last light—
Cardinal, exhale my sins,
help me to lie low and leave out,
Remind me that vision is singular, that excess
Is regress, that more than enough is too much, that
compression is all.

Sitting at Dusk in the Back Yard After the Mondrian Retrospective

Form imposes, structure allows—
the slow destruction of form
So as to bring it back resheveled, reorganized,
Is the hard heart of the enterprise.
Under its camouflage,
The light, relentless shill and cross-dresser, pools and deals.
Inside its short skin, the darkness burns.

Mondrian thought the destructive element in art
Much too neglected.
Landscape, of course, pursues it savagely.
And that's what he meant:
You can't reconstruct without the destruction being built in;

There is no essence unless
nothing has been left out.

Destruction takes place so order might exist.
Simple enough.
Destruction takes place at the point of maximum awareness.
Orate sine intermissione, St. Paul instructs.
Pray uninterruptedly.
The gods and their names have disappeared.
Only the clouds remain.

Meanwhile, the swallows wheel, the bat wheels, the grackles begin their business.
It's August.
The countryside
Gathers itself for sacrifice, its slow
fadeout along the invisible,
Leaving the land its architecture of withdrawal,
Black lines and white spaces, an emptiness primed with reds and blues.

Black Zodiac

Darkened by time, the masters, like our memories, mix
And mismatch,
and settle about our lawn furniture, like air
Without a meaning, like air in its clear nothingness.
What can we say to either of them?
How can they be so dark and so clear at the same time?
They ruffle our hair,
they ruffle the leaves of the August trees.
Then stop, abruptly as wind.

The flies come back, and the heat—

what can we say to them?

Nothing is endless but the sky.
The flies come back, and the afternoon
Teeters a bit on its green edges,

then settles like dead weight

Next to our memories, and the pale hems of the masters' gowns.

Those who look for the Lord will cry out in praise of him.
Perhaps. And perhaps not—

dust and ashes though we are,

Some will go wordlessly, some
Will listen their way in with their mouths
Where pain puts them, an inch-and-a-half above the floor.
And some will revile him out of love

and deep disdain.

The gates of mercy, like an eclipse, darken our undersides.
Rows of gravestones stay our steps,

August humidity

Bright as auras around our bodies.
And some will utter the words,

speaking in fear and tongues,

Hating their garments splotched by the flesh.
These are the lucky ones, the shelved ones, the twice-erased.

Dante and John Chrysostom
Might find this afternoon a sidereal roadmap,
A pilgrim's way . . .

You might too

Under the prejaundiced outline of the quarter moon,
Clouds sculling downsky like a narrative for *whatever comes,*
What *hasn't happened to happen yet*
Still lurking behind the stars,
                                        31 August 1995 . . .
The afterlife of insects, space graffiti, white holes
In the landscape,
                    such things, such avenues, lead to dust
And handle our hurt with ease.
Sky blue, blue of infinity, blue
                                        waters above the earth:
Why do the great stories always exist in the past?

The unexamined life's no different from
                                                  the examined life—
Unanswerable questions, small talk,
Unprovable theorems, long-abandoned arguments—
You've got to write it all down.
Landscape or waterscape, light-length on evergreen, dark sidebar
Of evening,
            you've got to write it down.
Memory's handkerchief, death's dream and automobile,
God's sleep,
            you've still got to write it down,
Moon half-empty, moon half-full,
Night starless and egoless, night blood-black and prayer-black,
Spider at work between the hedges,
Last bird call,
            toad in a damp place, tree frog in a dry . . .

We go to our graves with secondary affections,
Second-hand satisfaction, half-souled,
                                        star charts demagnetized.
We go in our best suits. The birds are flying. Clouds pass.
Sure we're cold and untouchable,
                                    but we harbor no ill will.
No tooth tuned to resentment's fork,
                                        we're out of here, and sweet meat.
Calligraphers of the disembodied, God's word-wards,
What letters will we illuminate?
Above us, the atmosphere,
The nothing that's nowhere, signs on, and waits for our beck and call.
Above us, the great constellations sidle and wince,
The letters undarken and come forth,
Your X and my X.
                        The letters undarken and they come forth.

Eluders of memory, nocturnal sleep of the greenhouse,
Spirit of slides and silences,
                                Invisible Hand,
Witness and walk on.
Lords of the discontinuous, lords of the little gestures,
Succor my shift and save me . . .
All afternoon the rain has rained down in the mind,
And in the gardens and dwarf orchard.
                                        All afternoon
The lexicon of late summer has turned its pages
Under the rain,
                        abstracting the necessary word.
Autumn's upon us.

The rain fills our narrow beds.
Description's an element, like air or water.
                                                                That's the word.

China Mail

It's deep summer east of the Blue Ridge.
Temperatures over 90 for the twenty-fifth day in a row.
The sound of the asphalt trucks down Locust Avenue
Echoes between the limp trees.
                                                    Nothing's cool to the touch.

Since you have not come,
The way back will stay unknown to you.
And since you have not come,
                                                  I find I've become like you,
A cloud whose rain has all fallen, adrift and floating.

Walks in the great void are damp and sad.
Late middle age. With little or no work,
                                                              we return to formlessness,
The beginning of all things.
Study the absolute, your book says. But not too hard,

I add, just under my breath.
Cicadas ratchet their springs up to a full stop
                                                                in the green wings of the oaks.
This season is called white hair.
Like murdered moonlight, it keeps coming back from the dead.

Our lives will continue to turn unmet,
                                                           like Virgo and Scorpio.

Of immortality, there's nothing but old age and its aftermath.
It's better you never come.
How else would we keep in touch, tracing our words upon the air?

Disjecta Membra

1

Back yard, dry flower half-border, unpeopled landscape
Stripped of embellishment and anecdotal concern:
A mirror of personality,
                    unworldly and self-effacing,
The onlooker sees himself in,
                         a monk among the oak trees . . .
How silly, the way we place ourselves—the struck postures,
The soothing words, the sleights-of-hand
                              to hoodwink the Paraclete—
For our regard; how always the objects we draw out
To show ourselves to effect
(The chiaroscuro of character we yearn for)
Find us a shade untrue and a shade untied.
                              Bad looking glass, bad things.

Simplify, Shaker down, the voice drones.
Out of the aether, disembodied and discontent,
No doubt who *that* is . . .
                    Autumn prehensile from day one,
Equinox pushing through like a cold front from the west,
Drizzle and dropped clouds, wired wind.
It's Sunday again, brief devotions.

We look down, dead leaves and dead grass like a starry sky
From inside out.
Simplify, open the emptiness, divest—
The trees do, each year milking their veins
Down, letting the darkness drip in,
I.V. from the infinite.

Filing my nails in the Buddha yard.
Ten feet behind my back, like slow, unsteady water,
Backwash of traffic spikes and falls off,
Zendo half-hunched through the giant privet,
shut sure as a shell.
Last cat's-eyes of dew crystal and gold as morning fills the grass.
Between Buddha-stare and potting shed,
Indian file of ants. Robin's abrupt arrival
And dust-down.
Everything's one with everything else now,
Wind leaf-lifter and tuck-in,
Light giving over to shadow and shadow to light.

I hope for a second chance where the white clouds are born,
Where the maple trees turn red,
redder by half than where
The flowers turned red in spring.
Acolyte at the altar of wind,
I love the idleness of the pine tree,
the bright steps into the sky.
I've always wanted to lie there, as though under earth,
Blood drops like sapphires, the dark stations ahead of me

Like postal stops on a deep journey.
I long for that solitude,
                                        that rest,
The bed-down and rearrangement of all the heart's threads.

What nurtures us denatures us and will strip us down.
Zen says, stand by the side of your thoughts
As you might stand by the bank of a wide river.
                                                                Dew-burdened,
Spider webs spin like little galaxies in the juniper bush,
Morning sunlight corpus delicti
                                                sprawled on the damp pavement.
Denatures us to a nub.
And sends us twisting out of our back yards into history.
As though by a wide river,
                                          water hustling our wants away,
And what we're given, and what we hope to be absolved of . . .
How simply it moves, how silently.

Death's still the secret of life,
                                              the garden reminds us.
Or vice-versa. It's complicated.
Unlike the weed-surge and blossom-surge of early fall,
Unlike the insect husks in the spider's tracery,
Crickets and rogue crows gearing up for afternoon sing-along.
The cottontail hides
                                    out in the open, hunched under the apple tree
Between the guillotine of sunlight and guillotine of shade
Beyond my neighbor's hedge.
                                               The blades rise and the blades fall,

But rabbit sits tight. Smart bun.
Sit tight and hold on. Sit tight. Hold on.

Love is more talked about than surrendered to. Lie low,
Meng Chiao advises—
                                        beauty too close will ruin your life.
Like the south wind, it's better to roam without design.
A lifetime's a solitary thread, we all learn,
                                                        and needs its knot tied.
Under the arborvitae,
The squirrels have buried their winter dreams,
                                                        and ghosts gather, close to home.
My shadow sticks to the trees' shadow.
There is no simile for this,
                                        this black into black.
Or if there is, it's my penpoint's drop of ink slurred to a word.
Of both, there soon will be not a trace.

With what words, with what silence—
Silence becoming speechlessness,
                                                words being nothing at all—
Can we address a blade of grass, the immensity of a snowflake?
How is it that we presume so much?
                                                There are times, Lord, there are times . . .
We must bite hard into the 21st century,
We must make it bleed.
October approaches the maple trees with its laying-on of hands,
Red stains in the appled west,
                                                red blush beginning to seep through

Just north of north, arterial headway, cloud on cloud.
Let it come, Lord, let it come.

2

If I could slide into a deep sleep,
I could say—to myself, without speaking—why my words embarrass me.

Nothing regenerates us, or shapes us again from the dust.
Nothing whispers our name in the night.
Still must we praise you, nothing,
still must we call to you.

Our sin is lack of transparency.

November is dark and doom-dangled,
fitful bone light
And suppuration, worn wrack
In the trees, dog rot and dead leaves, watch where you're going . . .

Illegibility. Dumb fingers from a far hand.

When death completes the number of the body, its food
Is weeping and much groaning,
and stranglers come, who roll
Souls down on the dirt . . .
And thus it is written, and thus believed,
Though others have found it otherwise.

The restoration of the nature of the ones who are good
Takes place in a time that never had a beginning.

Well, yes, no doubt about that.
One comes to rest in whatever is at rest, and eats
The food he has hungered for.
The light that shines forth there, on that body, does not sink.

This earth is a handful of sleep, eyes open, eyes shut,
A handful, just that—

There is an end to things, but not here.
It's where our names are, hanging like flesh from the flame trees.

Still, there are no flame points in the sky—

There are no angels, there is no light
At just that point where one said,
                                        this is where light begins.

It dies out in me.

The word is inscribed in the heart.
                                        It is beyond us,
The heart, that changeling, word within word.

Compulsive cameo, God's blue breath
So light on the skin, so infinite,

Why do I have to carry you, unutterable?
Why do you shine out,
                              lost penny, unspendable thing,

Irreversible, unappeasable, luminous,
Recoursed on the far side of language?

Tomorrow's our only hiding place,
November its last address—
                                                        such small griefs, such capture.

Insurmountable comforts.
And still I carry you. And still you continue to shine out.

Substance. And absence of all substance.
God's not concerned for anything, and has no desire.

Late at night we feel,
                                                insensate, immaculata,
The cold, coercive touch of nothing, whose fingerprints
Adhere like watermarks to the skin—

Late at night, our dark and one refuge.

Life is a sore gain, no word, no world.
Eternity drips away, inch by inch, inside us,
December blitzing our blind side,
                                                                white-tongued and anxious.

That's it. Something licks us up.

December. Blood rolls back to its wound.
God is a scattered part,
                                                    syllable after syllable, his name asunder.

No first heaven, no second.

Winter sun is a killer,
late light bladed horizon-like
Wherever you turn,
arteried, membraned, such soft skin.

Prayers afflict us, this world and the next:

Grief's an eclipse, it comes and it goes.
Photographs show that stars are born as easily as we are.
Both without mercy.

Each leads us away, leads us away.

Guilt is a form in itself.
As is the love of sentences
That guilt resides in, then darkens.
It is as certain.
It is as unregenerative. It is as worn.

Everything terminal has hooks in eternity.
Marsh grass, for instance. Foxfire.
Root work and come-betweens,
the Lord's welkin and Lord's will,

As some say in these parts not out loud.

In the bare tines of the lemon tree,
Thorns bristle and nubs nudge,
limbs in a reverie of lost loads.
This life is our set-aside, our dry spot and shelter.

When slant-light crisps up,
and shatters like broken lime glass
Through the maple trees, in December,
Who cares about anything but weights and absolutes?

Write up, it's bad, write down, it's still bad.
Remember, everyone's no one.

The abyss of time is a white glove—
take it off, put it on,
Finger by finger it always fits,
Buttons mother-of-pearl, so snug, such soft surroundings.

Lord of the broken oak branch,
Lord of the avenues,
Tweak and restartle me, guide my hand.

3

Whatever it was I had to say,
I've said two times, and then a third.
An object for light to land on,
I'm one-on-one with the visible
And shadowy overhang.
It's Christmas Eve, and the Pleiades
Burn like high altar host flames
scrunched in the new moon sky—
Their earthly, votive counterparts flash and burst in the spruce trees
And Mrs. Fornier's window.
It's 9:10 and I'm walking the dogs down Locust Avenue.
It's a world we've memorized by heart:
Myopic constellations, dog's bark,
bleak supplicants, blood of the lamb . . .

Unfinished, unable, distracted—
How easily we reproach ourselves for our lives lived badly,
How easily us undo.
Despair is our consolation, sweet word,
                                        and late middle age
And objectivity dulled and drear.
Splendor of little fragments.
Rilke knew one or two things about shame and unhappiness
And how we waste time and worse.
I think I'm starting to catch on myself.
                                        I think I'm starting to understand
The difference between the adjective and the noun.

Dead moth, old metaphysician, cross-backed, Christ's arrowhead, look,
I'll tell you one thing—
Inch by inch, everyday, our lives become less and less.
Obsessive and skinless, we shrink them down.
And here's another—
                        a line of poetry's a line of blood.
A cross on the back is like a short sword in the heart,
December sun in a fadeaway, cloud under cloud
Over the Blue Ridge,
                        just there, just west of Bremo Bluff.
Okay, I'll keep my mouth shut and my eyes fast on the bare limbs of the fruit trees.
A line in the earth's a life.

O well the snow falls and small birds drop out of the sky,
The back yard's a winding sheet—
                                                            winter in Charlottesville,
Epiphany two days gone,
Nothing at large but Broncos, pickups and 4x4s.
Even the almost full moon
                                                is under a monochrome counterpane
Of dry grey.
                    Eve of St. Agnes and then some, I'd say,
Twenty-three inches and coming down.
The Rev. Doctor Syntax puts finger to forehead on the opposite wall,
Mancini and I still blurred beside him, Mykonos, 1961,
The past a snowstorm the present too.

The human position—anxiety's afterlife, still place—
Escapes us.
                    We live in the wind-chill,
The what-if and what-was-not,
The blown and sour dust of just after or just before,
The metaquotidian landscape
                                                    of soft edge and abyss.
How hard to take the hard day and ease it in our hearts,
Its icicle and snowdrift and
                                                its wind that keeps on blowing.
How hard to be as human as snow is, or as true,
So sure of its place and many names.
It holds the white light against its body, it benights our eyes.

The poem uncurls me, corrects me and croons my tune,
Its outfit sharp as the pressed horizon.
                                        Excessive and honed,
It grins like a blade,
It hums like a fuse,
                        body of ash, body of fire,
A music my ear would be heir to.
I glimpse it now and then through the black branches of winter trees.
I hear its burn in the still places.
Halfway through January, sky pure, sky not so pure,
World still in tucker and bib.
Might I slipstream its fiery ride,
                                    might I mind its smoke.

Is *this* the life we long for,
                              to be at ease in the natural world,
Blue rise of Blue Ridge
Indented and absolute through the January oak limbs,
Turkey buzzard at work on road-kill opossum, up
And flapping each time
A car passes and coming back
                                  huge and unfolded, a black bed sheet,
Crows fierce but out of focus high up in the ash tree,
Afternoon light from stage left
Low and listless, little birds
Darting soundlessly back and forth, hush, hush?
                                                Well, yes, I think so.

Take a loose rein and a deep seat,
John, my father-in-law, would say
To someone starting out on a long journey, meaning, take it easy,
Relax, let what's taking you take you.
I think of landscape incessantly,
mountains and rivers, lost lakes
Where sunsets festoon and override,
The scald of summer wheat fields, light-licked and poppy-smeared.
Sunlight surrounds me and winter birds
doodle and peck in the dead grass.
I'm emptied, ready to go. Again
I tell myself what I've told myself for almost thirty years—
Listen to John, do what the clouds do.

FROM

APPALACHIA

(1998)

Stray Paragraphs in February, Year of the Rat

East of town, the countryside unwrinkles and smooths out
Unctuously toward the tidewater and gruff Atlantic.
A love of landscape's a true affection for regret, I've found,
Forever joined, forever apart,
                                        outside us yet ourselves.

Renunciation, it's hard to learn, is now our ecstasy.
However, if God were still around,
                                        he'd swallow our sighs in his nothingness.

The dregs of the absolute are slow sift in my blood,
Dead branches down after high winds, dead yard grass and undergrowth—
The sure accumulation of all that's not revealed
Rises like snow in my bare places,
                                        cross-whipped and openmouthed.

Our lives can't be lived in flames.
Our lives can't be lit like saints' hearts,
                                        seared between heaven and earth.

February, old head-turner, cut us some slack, grind of bone
On bone, such melancholy music.
Lift up that far corner of landscape,
                                        there, toward the west.
Let some of the deep light in, the arterial kind.

Stray Paragraphs in April, Year of the Rat

Only the dead can be born again, and then not much.
I wish I were a mole in the ground,
                                        eyes that see in the dark.

Attentive without an object of attentiveness,
Unhappy without an object of unhappiness—
Desire in its highest form,
                                        dog prayer, diminishment . . .

If we were to walk for a hundred years, we could never take
One step toward heaven—
                                        you have to wait to be gathered.

Two cardinals, two blood clots,
Cast loose in the cold, invisible arteries of the air.
If they ever stop, the sky will stop.

Affliction's a gift, Simone Weil thought—
The world becomes more abundant in severest light.

April, old courtesan, high-styler of months, dampen our mouths.

The dense and moist and cold and dark come together here.

The soul is air, and it maintains us.

Basic Dialogue

The transformation of objects in space,
                    or objects in time,
To objects outside either, but tactile, still precise . . .
It's always the same problem—
Nothing's more abstract, more unreal,
                    than what we actually see.
The job is to make it otherwise.

Two dead crepe-myrtle bushes,
                    tulips petal-splayed and swan-stemmed,
All blossoms gone from the blossoming trees—the new loss
Is not like old loss,
Winter-kill, a jubilant revelation, an artificial thing
Linked and lifted by pure description into the other world.

Self-oblivion, sacred information, God's nudge—
I think I'll piddle around by the lemon tree, thorns
Sharp as angel's teeth.
                    I think
I'll lie down in the dandelions, the purple and white violets.
I think I'll keep on lying there, one eye cocked toward heaven.

April eats from my fingers,
                    nibble of dogwood, nip of pine.
Now is the time, Lord.
Syllables scatter across the new grass, in search of their words.
Such minor Armageddons.
Beside the waters of disremembering,
                    I lay me down.

Star Turn

Nothing is quite as secretive as the way the stars
Take off their bandages and stare out
At the night,
                    that dark rehearsal hall,
And whisper their little songs,
The alpha and beta ones, the ones from the great fire.

Nothing is quite as gun shy,
                                        the invalid, broken pieces
Drifting and rootless, rising and falling, forever
Deeper into the darkness.
Nightly they give us their dumb show, nightly they flash us
Their message and melody,
                                        frost-sealed, our lidless companions.

A Bad Memory Makes You a Metaphysician, a Good One Makes You a Saint

This is our world, high privet hedge on two sides,
                                                            half-circle of arborvitae,
Small strip of sloped lawn,
Last of the spring tulips and off-purple garlic heads
Snug in the cutting border,
Dwarf orchard down deep at the bottom of things,
                                                            God's crucible,
Bat-swoop and grab, grackle yawp, back yard . . .

This is our landscape,
Bourgeois, heartbreakingly suburban;
                    these are the ashes we rise from.
As night goes down, we watch it darken and disappear.
We push our glasses back on our foreheads,
                    look hard, and it disappears.

In another life, the sun shines and the clouds are motionless.
There, too, the would-be-saints are slipping their hair shirts on.
But only the light souls can be saved;
Only the ones whose weight
                    will not snap the angel's wings.
Too many things are not left unsaid.
If you want what the syllables want, just do your job.

In the Kingdom of the Past, the Brown-Eyed Man Is King

It's all so pitiful, really, the little photographs
Around the room of places I've been,
And me in them, the half-read books, the fetishes, this
Tiny arithmetic against the dark undazzle.
Who do we think we're kidding?

Certainly not our selves, those hardy perennials
We take such care of, and feed, who keep on keeping on
Each year, their knotty egos like bulbs
Safe in the damp and dreamy soil of their self-regard.
No way we bamboozle them with these

Shrines to the woebegone, ex votos and reliquary sites
One comes in on one's knees to,

The country of *what was*, the country of *what we pretended to be*,
Cruxes and intersections of all we'd thought was fixed.
There is no guilt like the love of guilt.

Passing the Morning Under the Serenissima

Noon sun big as a knuckle,
                                        tight over Ponte S. Polo,
Unlike the sighting of Heraclitus the Obscure,
Who said it's the width of a man's foot.
Unable to take the full
                                "clarity" of his fellow man,
He took to the mountains and ate grasses and wild greens,
Aldo Buzzi retells us.

Sick, dropsical, he returned to the city and stretched out on the ground
And covered his body with manure
To dry himself out.
                              After two days of cure, he died,
Having lost all semblance of humanity, and was devoured by dogs.
Known as "the weeping philosopher," he said one time,
The living and the dead, the waked and the sleeping, are the same.

Thus do we entertain ourselves on hot days, Aldo Buzzi,
Cees Nooteboom, Gustave Flaubert,
The flies and nameless little insects
                                                    circling like God's angels
Over the candy dish and worn rug.
The sun, no longer knuckle or foot,
                                                    strays behind June's flat clouds.
Boats bring their wild greens and bottled water down the Republic's
        shade-splotched canals.

Venetian Dog

Bad day in Bellini country, Venetian dog high-stepper
Out of Carpaccio and down the street,
                                        tail like a crozier
Over his ivory back.
A Baron Corvo bad day, you mutter, under your short breath.

Listen, my friend, everything works to our disregard.
Language, our common enemy, moves like the tide against us,
Fortune's heel upwind
                        over Dogana's golden universe
High in the cloud-scratched and distant sky.

Six p.m. Sunday church bells
Flurry and circle and disappear like pigeon flocks,
Lost in the sunlight's fizzle and fall.
The stars move as well against us.
                                    From pity, it sometimes seems.

So what's the body to do,
                        caught in its web of spidered flesh?
Venetian dog has figured his out, and stands his ground,
Bristled and hogbacked,
Barking in cadence at something that you and I can't see.
                                                        But

For us, what indeed, lying like S. Lorenzo late at night
On his brazier, lit from above by a hole in the sky,
From below by coals,
                        his arm thrown up,
In Titian's great altarpiece, in supplication, what indeed?

In the Valley of the Magra

In June, above Pontrèmoli, high in the Lunigiana,
The pollen-colored chestnut blooms
                                        sweep like a long cloth
Snapped open over the bunched treetops
And up the mountain as far as the almost-Alpine meadows.
At dusk, in the half-light, they appear
Like stars come through the roots of the great trees from another sky.
Or tears, with my glasses off.
                                    Sometimes they seem like that
Just as the light fades and the darkness darkens for good.

Or that's the way I remember it when the afternoon thunderstorms
Tumble out of the Blue Ridge,
And distant bombardments muscle in
                                        across the line
Like God's solitude or God's shadow,
The loose consistency of mortar and river stone
Under my fingers where I leaned out
Over it all,
            isolate farm lights
Starting to take the color on, the way I remember it . . .

Returned to the Yaak Cabin, I Overhear an Old Greek Song

Back at the west window, Basin Creek
Stumbling its mantra out in a slurred, midsummer monotone,
Sunshine in planes and clean sheets

Over the yarrow and lodgepole pine—
We spend our whole lives in the same place and never leave,
Pine squirrels and butterflies at work in a deep dither,
Bumblebee likewise, wind with a slight hitch in its get-along.

Dead heads on the lilac bush, daisies
Long-legged forest of stalks in a white throw across the field
Above the ford and deer path,
Candor of marble, candor of bone—
We spend our whole lives in the same place and never leave,
The head of Orpheus bobbing in the slatch, his song
Still beckoning from his still-bloody lips, bright as a bee's heart.

Ars Poetica II

I find, after all these years, I am a believer—
I believe what the thunder and lightning have to say;
I believe that dreams are real,
                                        and that death has two reprisals;
I believe that dead leaves and black water fill my heart.

I shall die like a cloud, beautiful, white, full of nothingness.

The night sky is an ideogram,
                                        a code card punched with holes.
It thinks it's the word of what's-to-come.
It thinks this, but it's only The Library of Last Resort,
The reflected light of The Great Misunderstanding.

God is the fire my feet are held to.

Cicada Blue

I wonder what Spanish poets would say about this,
Bloodless, mid-August meridian,
Afternoon like a sucked-out, transparent insect shell,
Diffused, and tough to the touch.
Something about a labial, probably,
something about the blue.

St. John of the Cross, say, or St. Teresa of Avila.
Or even St. Thomas Aquinas,
Who said, according to some,
"All I have written seems like straw
Compared to what I have seen and what has been revealed to me."
Not Spanish, but close enough,
something about the blue.

Blue, I love you, blue, one of them said once in a different color,
The edged and endless
Expanse of nowhere and nothingness
hemmed as a handkerchief from here,
Cicada shell of hard light
Just under it, blue, I love you, blue . . .

We've tried to press God in our hearts the way we'd press a leaf in a book,
Afternoon memoried now,
sepia into brown,
Night coming on with its white snails and its ghost of the Spanish poet,
Poet of shadows and death.
Let's press him firm in our hearts, O blue, I love you, blue.

All Landscape Is Abstract, and Tends to Repeat Itself

I came to my senses with a pencil in my hand
And a piece of paper in front of me.
                                                            To the years
Before the pencil, O, I was the resurrection.
Still, who knows where the soul goes,
Up or down,
                        after the light switch is turned off, who knows?

It's late August, and prophets are calling their bears in.

The sacred is frightening to the astral body,
As is its absence.
                        We have to choose which fear is our consolation.
Everything comes *ex alto,*
We'd like to believe, the origin and the end, or
Non-origin and the non-end,
                                        each distant and inaccessible.

Over the Blue Ridge, the whisperer starts to whisper in tongues.

Remembered landscapes are left in me
The way a bee leaves its sting,
                                        hopelessly, passion-placed,
Untranslatable language.
Non-mystical, insoluble in blood, they act as an opposite
To the absolute, whose words are a solitude, and set to music.

All forms of landscape are autobiographical.

Opus Posthumous

Possum work, world's windowlust, lens of the Byzantine—
Friday in Appalachia.
Hold on, old skeletal life,
                                        there's more to come, if I hear right.
Still, even the brightest angel is darkened by time,
Even the sharpest machine
                                          dulled and distanced by death.

Wick-end of August, wicked once-weight of summer's sink and sigh.

September now, set to set foot on the other side,
Hurricanes sprouting like daisy heads around her lap.
We know where she's been. We know
What big secret she keeps,
                                          so dark and dungeoned, and wish her well,
Praying that she will whisper it to us
                                                  just once, just this once.

The secret of language is the secret of disease.

Quotations

Renoir, whose paintings I don't much like,
Says what survives of the artist is the feeling he gives by means of objects.
I do like that, however,
The feeling put in as much as the feeling received
To make a work distinctive,
Though I'm not sure it's true,
                                            or even it's workable.

When Chekhov died, he died at dawn,
a large moth circling the lamp,
Beating its pressed wings.
Placed in a zinc casket, the corpse, labeled *Fresh Oysters*,
Was sent to Moscow in a freight car from Germany.
His last words were, *Has the sailor left?*
I am dying, Ich sterbe.

My breath is corrupt, my days are extinct, the graves are ready for me,
Job says. *They change the night into day—*
The light is short because of darkness . . .
I have said to corruption,
thou art my father, to the worm,
Thou art my mother and my sister—
They shall go down to the bars of the pit,
when our rest together is in the dust.

That's all. There's nothing left after that.
As Meng Chiao says,
For a while the dust weighs lightly on my cloak.

The Appalachian Book of the Dead II

Late Saturday afternoon in Charlottesville.
Columbus Day,
Windless, remorseless Columbus Day,

Sunlight like Scotch tape
Stuck to the surfaces of west-worn magnolia leaves.
Children are playing their silly games
Behind the back yard,
toneless, bell-less Columbus Day.

Despair's a sweet meat I'd hang a fang in once or twice,
Given the go-ahead.
And where's October's golden and red,
Where is its puff of white smoke?
Another page torn off
The Appalachian Book of the Dead,
Indifferent silence of heaven,
Indifferent silence of the world.

Jerusalem, I say quietly, Jerusalem,
The altar of evening starting to spread its black cloth
In the eastern apse of things—
the soul that desires to return *home*, desires its own destruction,
We know, which never stopped anyone,
The fear of it and dread of it on every inch of the earth,
Though light's still lovely in the west,
billowing, purple and scarlet-white.

Indian Summer II

As leaves fall from the trees, the body falls from the soul.
As memory signs transcendence, scales fall from the heart.
As sunlight winds back on its dark spool,
November's a burn and an ache.

A turkey buzzard logs on to the late evening sky.
Residual blood in the oak's veins.
Sunday. Recycling tubs like flower bins at the curb.

Elsewhere, buried up to her armpits,
                                        someone is being stoned to death.
Elsewhere, transcendence searches for us.
Elsewhere, this same story is being retold by someone else.

The heavenly way has been lost,
                                        no use to look at the sky.
Still, the stars, autumnal stars, start to flash and transverberate.
The body falls from the soul, and the soul takes off,
                                        a wandering, moral drug.

This is an end without a story.
This is a little bracelet of flame around your wrist.
This is the serpent in the Garden,
                                        her yellow hair, her yellow hair.

We live in two landscapes, as Augustine might have said,
One that's eternal and divine,
                                        and one that's just the back yard,
Dead leaves and dead grass in November, purple in spring.

Autumn's Sidereal, November's a Ball and Chain

After the leaves have fallen, the sky turns blue again,
Blue as a new translation of Longinus on the sublime.
We wink and work back from its edges.
                                        We walk around

Under its sequence of metaphors,
Looking immaculately up for the overlooked.
Or looking not so immaculately down for the same thing.

If there's nothing going on, there's no reason to make it up.
Back here, for instance, next to the cankered limbs of the plum trees,
We take a load off.
                                        Hard frost on the grass blades and wild onion,
Invisibly intricate, so clear.
Pine needles in herringbone, dead lemon leaves, dead dirt.
The metaphysical world is meaningless today,

South wind retelling its autobiography
                                                                      endlessly
Through the white pines, somesuch and susurration, shhh, shhh . . .

The Writing Life

Give me the names for things, just give me their real names,
Not what we call them, but what
They call themselves when no one's listening—
At midnight, the moon-plated hemlocks like unstruck bells,
God wandering aimlessly elsewhere.
                                                                Their names, their secret names.

December. Everything's black and brown. Or half-black and half-brown.
What's still alive puts its arms around me,
                                                                      amen from the evergreens
That want my heart on their ribbed sleeves.
Why can't I listen to them?
                                                    Why can't I offer my heart up
To what's in plain sight and short of breath?

Restitution of the divine in a secular circumstance—
Page 10, The Appalachian Book of the Dead,
                                        the dog-eared one,
Pre-solstice winter light laser-beaked, sun over Capricorn,
Dead-leaf-and-ice-mix grunged on the sidewalk and driveway.
Short days. Short days. Dark soon the light overtakes.
                                                Stump of a hand.

Reply to Wang Wei

The dream of reclusive life, a strict, essential solitude,
Is a younger hermit's dream.
Tuesday, five days till winter, a cold, steady rain.
White hair, white heart. The time's upon us and no exit
East of the lotus leaves.
                        No exit, you said, and a cold, steady rain.

Indeed.
      All those walks by the river, all those goodbyes.
Willows shrink back to brown across Locust Avenue,
The mountains are frost and blue
                              and fellow travellers.
Give you peace, you said, freedom from ten thousand matters.
And asked again, does fame come only to the ancients?

At the foot of the southern mountains, white clouds pass without end,
You wrote one time in a verse.
                            They still do, and still without end.
That's it. Just wanted to let you know it hasn't changed—no out, no end,
And fame comes only to the ancients, and justly so,
Rain turning slowly to snow now then back into rain.

Everywhere everywhere, you wrote, something is falling,
The evening mist has no resting place.
What time we waste, wasting time.
                                        Still, I sit still,
The mind swept clean in its secret shade,
Though no monk from any hill will ever come to call.

Giorgio Morandi and the Talking Eternity Blues

Late April in January, seventy-some-odd degrees.
The entry of Giorgio Morandi in The Appalachian Book of the Dead
Begins here, without text, without dates—
A photograph of the master contemplating four of his objects,
His glasses pushed high on his forehead,
                                             his gaze replaced and pitiless.

The dove, in summer, coos sixty times a minute, one book says.
Hard to believe that,
                              even in this unseasonable heat,
A couple of them appearing and silent in the bare tree
Above me.
                Giorgio Morandi doesn't blink an eye
As sunlight showers like sulphur grains across his face.

There is an end to language.
                              There is an end to handing out the names of things,
Clouds moving south to north along the Alleghenies
And Blue Ridge, south to north on the wind.
Eternity, unsurprisingly, doesn't give this a take.
Eternity's comfortless, a rock and a hard ground.

Now starless, Madonnaless, Morandi
Seems oddly comforted by the lack of comforting,
A proper thing in its proper place,
Landscape subsumed, language subsumed,
                                        the shadow of God
Liquid and indistinguishable.

Drone and Ostinato

Winter. Cold like a carved thing outside the window glass.
Silence of sunlight and ice dazzle.
                                        Stillness of noon.
Dragon back of the Blue Ridge,
Landscape laid open like an old newspaper, memory into memory.

Our lives are like birds' lives, flying around, blown away.
We're bandied and bucked on and carried across the sky,
Drowned in the blue of the infinite,
                                        blur-white and drift.
We disappear as stars do, soundless, without a trace.

Nevertheless, let's settle and hedge the bet.
                                        The wind picks up, clouds cringe,
Snow locks in place on the lawn.
Wordless is what the soul wants, the one thing that I keep in mind.
One in one united, bare in bare doth shine.

"It's Turtles All the Way Down"

I snap the book shut. February. Alternate sky.
Tiny gobbets like pyracantha beans on the mock crab-apple trees.
None of this interests me.

Mercy is made of fire, and fire needs fire, another book says.
It also says, to get to God, pull both your feet back—
One foot from out of this life, one foot from the other.

Outside, I walk off-cadence under the evergreens,
Ground needles bronzed and half mythic, as though from a tomb,
5:20 winter lightfall sifted and steeped through medium yellow.

What God is the God behind the God who moves the chess pieces,
Borges wondered.
                                        What mask is the mask behind the mask
The language wears and the landscape wears, I ask myself.

O, well, I let the south wind blow all over my face.
I let the sunshine release me and fall all over my face.
I try not to think of them stopping.

Half February

St. Valentine's. Winter is in us.
Hard to be faithful to summer's bulge and buzz
                                                                        in such a medicine.
Hard to be heart-wrung
And sappy in what's unworkable and world-weary.
Hard to be halt and half-strung.

All of us, more or less, are unfaithful to something.
Solitude bears us away,
Approaches us in the form of a crescent, like love,
And bears us away
Into its icy comforting, our pain and our happiness.

I saw my soul like a little silkworm, diligently fed,
Spinning a thread with its little snout,
Anna Garcias wrote in the sixteenth century.
And who can doubt her,
Little silkworm in its nonbeing and nothingness.

Nothing like that in these parts these days—
The subject for today, down here, is the verb "to be,"
Snow falling, then sleet, then freezing rain,
St. Catherine nowhere in evidence, her left side opened, her heart
    removed,
All the world's noise, all its hubbub and din,
                                        now chill and a glaze.

Back Yard Boogie Woogie

I look out at the back yard—
                        sur le motif, as Paul Cézanne would say,
Nondescript blond winter grass,
Boxwood buzz-cut still dormant with shaved sides, black gum tree
And weeping cherry veined and hived against the afternoon sky.

I try to look at landscape as though I weren't there,
                                        but know, wherever I am,
I disturb that place by breathing, by my heart's beating—

I only remember things that I think I've forgot,
Lives the color of dead leaves, for instance, days like dead insects.

Most of my life is like that,
scattered, fallen, overlooked.
Back here, magenta rosettes flock the limbs of the maple trees,
Little thresholds of darkness,
Late February sunlight indifferent as water to all the objects in it.

Only perfection is sufficient, Simone Weil says.
Whew...
Not even mercy or consolation can qualify.
Good thing I've got this early leaf bristle in my hand.
Good thing the cloud shadows keep on keeping on, east-by-northeast.

The Appalachian Book of the Dead III

Full moon illuminated large initial for letter M,
Appalachian Book of the Dead, 22 February 1997—
La luna piove, the moon rains down its antibiotic light
Over the sad, septic world,
Hieroglyphs on the lawn, supplicant whispers for the other side,
I am pure, I am pure, I am pure...

The soul is in the body as light is in the air,
Plotinus thought.
Well, I wouldn't know about that, but
La luna piove, and shines out in every direction—
Under it all, disorder, above,
A handful of stars on one side, a handful on the other.
Whatever afflictions we have, we have them for good.

Such Egyptology in the wind, such raw brushstrokes,
Moon losing a bit from its left side at two o'clock.
Still, light mind-of-Godish,
                                        silent deeps where seasons don't exist.
Surely some splendor's set to come forth,
Some last equation solved, declued and reclarified.
South wind and a long shine, a small-time paradiso . . .

Opus Posthumous II

Sitting as though suspended from something, cool in my deck chair,
Unlooked-on, otherworldly.
There is no acquittal, there is no body of light and elegy.
There is no body of fire.

It is as though an angel had walked across the porch,
A conflagration enhanced, extinguished, then buried again,
No pardon, no nourishment.
It's March, and starvelings feed from my mouth.

Ubi amor, ibi oculus,
                                love sees what the eye sees
Repeatedly, more or less.
It certainly seems so here, the gates of the arborvitae
The gates of mercy look O look they feed from my mouth.

Body Language

The human body is not the world, and yet it is.
The world contains it, and is itself contained. Just so.
The distance between the two
Is like the distance between the *no* and the *yes*,
                                        abysmal distance,
Nothing and everything. Just so.

This morning I move my body like a spring machine
Among the dormant and semi-dead,
The shorn branches and stubbed twigs
                                        hostile after the rain,
Grumpy and tapped out as go-betweens.
Blossoming plum tree coronal toast, cankered and burned.

When body becomes the unbody,
Look hard for its certitude, inclusive, commensurate thing.
Look for its lesson and camouflage.
Look hard for its leash point and linkup.
The shadow of the magnolia tree is short shrift for the grass.

I move through the afternoon,
                                        autumnal in pre-spring,
October-headed, hoarfrost-fingered.
The body inside the body is the body I want to come to—
I see it everywhere,
Lisping and licking itself, breaking and entering.

"When You're Lost in Juarez, in the Rain, and It's Eastertime Too"

Like a grain of sand added to time,
Like an inch of air added to space,
                                        or a half-inch,
We scribble our little sentences.
Some of them sound okay and some of them sound not so okay.
A grain and an inch, a grain and an inch and a half.

Sad word wands, desperate alphabet.

Still, there's been no alternative
Since language fell from the sky.
Though mystics have always said that communication is languageless.
And maybe they're right—
                                the soul speaks and the soul receives.
Small room for rebuttal there . . .

Over the Blue Ridge, late March late light annunciatory and visitational.

Tonight, the comet Hale-Bopp
                                    will ghost up on the dark page of the sky
By its secret juice and design from the full moon's heat.
Tonight, some miracle will happen somewhere, it always does.
Good Friday's a hard rain that won't fall,
Wild onion and clump grass, green on green.

Our mouths are incapable, white violets cover the earth.

The Appalachian Book of the Dead IV

High-fiving in Charlottesville.
Sunset heaped up, as close to us as a barrel fire.
Let's all go down to the river,
there's a man there that's walking on the water,
On the slow, red Rivanna,
He can make the lame walk, he can make the dumb talk,
and open up the eyes of the blind.
That dry-shod, over-the-water walk.

Harbor him in your mind's eye, snub him snug to your hearts.

They'll have to sing louder than that.
They'll have to dig deeper into the earbone
For this one to get across.
They'll have to whisper a lot about the radiant body.
Murmur of river run, murmur of women's voices.
Raised up, without rhyme,
the murmur of women's voices.
Good luck was all we could think to say.

Dogwood electrified and lit from within by April afternoon late-light.

This is the lesson for today—
narrative, narrative, narrative . . .
Tomorrow the sun comes back.
Tomorrow the tailings and slush piles will turn to gold
When everyone's down at the river.
The muscadines will bring forth,
The mountain laurel and jack-in-heaven,
while everyone's down at the river.

Early Saturday Afternoon, Early Evening

Saturday. Early afternoon. High
Spring light through new green,
                                        a language, it seems, I have forgotten,
But which I'll remember soon enough
When the first pages are turned
                                        in The Appalachian Book of the Dead.
The empty ones. The ones about the shining and stuff.

Father darkness, mother abyss,
                                        the shadow whispered,
Abolish me, make me light.
And so it happened. Rumor of luminous bodies.
The face on the face of the water became no face.
The words on the page of the book became a hush.
                                                            And luminous too.

These things will come known to you,
                                              these things make soft your shift,
Alliteration of lost light, aspirate hither-and-puff,
Afternoon undervoices starting to gather and lift off
In the dusk,
            Red Rover, Red Rover, let Billy come over,
Laughter and little squeals, a quick cry.

"The Holy Ghost Asketh for Us with Mourning and Weeping Unspeakable"

Well, sainthood's a bottomless pity,
                                          as some wag once said, so

Better forget about that.
I'd rather, in any case, just sit here and watch the rose bleed.
I'd rather it it than me.
For that's how the world proceeds, I've found out,
some blood and a lot of *watch.*

Still, I like to think of them there in their gold gowns and hair shirts,
Missing whatever was lost or lopped
Their last time around,
its absence revealing a pride of place.
I like to think of their tender flesh
Just healed, or just beginning to heal,
syrupy, sweet like that.

Whatever has been will be again,
unaltered, ever-returning.
Serenity of the rhododendron, pink and white,
Dark cinnamon, pink and white,
Azaleas opening in their own deep sleep. Ours too.
After-rupture of tulip border, and
white light in the green.

Unseen, unlistened to, unspoken of.
Salvation.
Light is, light is not, light is—
However you look at it, the heaven of the contemplatives is a hard gig.
Thrones and Dominions they'd drift among.
The landscape and wild chestnut will not remember them.

The Appalachian Book of the Dead V

Half-asleep on the back deck,
low wasp-hum of power mower
Ebbing and coming back from next door,
Aggressive shadows of maple leaves
crabbing across the shy sunlight
Languishing apprehensively over the fresh-stained pine boards.
Half-silence, 5 p.m. traffic tide, half-silence, violin tone scales.

So, where do we go from here,
Indoors now, great rush of wheels in my head, it is spring—
Vacancy, earth life, remains out there,
somewhere in the machine.
Waiting for something to come—anything—and mushroom,
I think of myself as a hare, as Virginia Woolf once said,
stilled, expecting moon-visitors.

When your answers have satisfied the forty-two gods,
When your heart's in balance with the weight of a feather,
When your soul is released like a sibyl from its cage,
Like a wind you'll cross over,
not knowing how, not knowing where,
Remembering nothing, unhappening, hand and foot.

The world's a glint on the window glass,
The landscape's a flash and fall,
sudden May rain like a sleet spill
On the tin roof, no angel, night dark.
Eternity puddles up.
And here's the Overseer, blue, and O he is blue . . .

Star Turn II

How small the stars are tonight, bandannaed by moonlight,
How few and how far between—
Disordered and drained, like highlights in Dante's death mask.
Or a sequined dress from the forties
                                        —hubba-hubba—
Some sequins missing, some sequins inalterably in place.

Unlike our lives, which are as they are.
Unlike our imagined selves, which are as we'll never become,
Star-like and shining,
Everyone looking up at, everyone pointing there, O there,
Masked and summering in,
                              each one a bright point, each one a dodged eclipse.

After Reading T'ao Ch'ing, I Wander Untethered Through the Short Grass

Dry spring, no rain for five weeks.
Already the lush green begins to bow its head and sink to its knees.

Already the plucked stalks and thyroid weeds like insects
Fly up and trouble my line of sight.

I stand inside the word *here*
                                        as that word stands in its sentence,
Unshadowy, half at ease.

Religion's been in a ruin for over a thousand years.
Why shouldn't the sky be tatters,
lost notes to forgotten songs?

I inhabit who I am, as T'ao Ch'ing says, and walk about
Under the mindless clouds.
When it ends, it ends. What else?

One morning I'll leave home and never find my way back—
My story and I will disappear together, just like this.

Remembering Spello, Sitting Outside in Prampolini's Garden

In and out of the shy, limp leaves of the grape arbor,
Song birds slither and peel back.

High in the Umbrian sky, the ghosts
Of true saints pinwheel and congregate like pale, afternoon clouds
Ready to jump-start the universe,

The Gates of Propertius—so they say—
cream-porphyry at the west of town,
Monte Subasio north-northwest.

It's getting late. The white dog has buried her bits of bread and
The early apricots start to shine,
forty-watt bulbs
Against the sundowned and mottled plain.

No word for time, no word for God, landscape exists outside each,
But stays, incurable ache, both things,

And bears me out as evening darkens and steps forth,
my body snug in my life
As a gun in its carrying case,
As an old language, an old address.

I sit in my plastic lawn chair,
unearthly and dispossessed,
My eyes on the turning stars.
Like a Roman statue, I watch everything and see nothing.

Just under the surface of the earth,
The traffic continues to glide by
all night with its lights off.

American Twilight

Why do I love the sound of children's voices in unknown games
So much on a summer's night,
Lightning bugs lifting heavily out of the dry grass
Like alien spacecraft looking for higher ground,
Darkness beginning to sift like coffee grains
over the neighborhood?

Whunk of a ball being kicked,
Surf-suck and surf-spill from traffic along the bypass,
American twilight,
Venus just lit in the third heaven,
Time-tick between "Okay, let's go," and "This earth is not my home."

Why do I care about this? Whatever happens will happen
With or without us,
                                        with or without these verbal amulets.
In the first ply, in the heaven of the moon, a little light,
Half-light, over Charlottesville.
Trees reshape themselves, the swallows disappear, lawn sprinklers do the
    wave.

Nevertheless, it's still summer: cicadas pump their boxes,
Jack Russell terriers, as they say, start barking their heads off,
And someone, somewhere, is putting his first foot, then the second,
Down on the other side,
                                        no hand to help him, no tongue to wedge its weal.

The Appalachian Book of the Dead VI

Last page, The Appalachian Book of the Dead,
                                                                        full moon,
No one in anyone's arms, no lip to ear, cloud bank
And boyish soprano out of the east edge of things.
Ball-whomp and rig-grind stage right,
Expectancy, quivering needle, at north-northwest.

And here comes the angel with her drum and wings. Some wings.
Lost days, as Meng Chiao says, a little window of words
We peer through darkly. Darkly,
Moon stopped in cloud bank, light slick for the chute and long slide,
No lip, no ear.
                                Distant murmur of women's voices.

I hear that the verb is facilitate. To facilitate.
Azure. To rise. To rise through the azure. Illegible joy.

No second heaven. No first.
I think I'll lie here like this awhile, my back flat on the floor.
I hear that days bleed.
                    I hear that the right word will take your breath away.

Landscape as Metaphor, Landscape as Fate and a Happy Life

August. Montana. The black notebook open again.
Across the blue-veined, dune-flattened, intimate blank of the page,
An almost-unseeable winged insect has set forth
On foot.
          I think I'll track his white trail.

—To set one's mind on the ink-line, to set one's heart on the dark
Unknowable, is far and forlorn, wouldn't you say?

Up here, our lives continue to lift off like leaf spores in the noon-wash,
Spruce trees and young hemlocks stand guard like Egyptian dogs
At the mouth of the meadow,
Butterflies flock like angels,
                              and God knees our necks to the ground.

—Nevertheless, the stars at midnight blow in the wind like high cotton.
There is no place in the world they don't approach and pass over.

Wind lull, midmorning, tonight's sky
                                    light-shielded, monkish and grand
Behind the glare's iconostasis, yellow poppies
Like lip prints against the log wall, the dead sister's lunar words
Like lip prints against it, this is as far as it goes . . .

—The sun doesn't shine on the same dog's back every day.
Only you, Fragrant One, are worthy to judge us and move on.

Opus Posthumous III

Mid-August meltdown, Assurbanipal in the west,
Scorched cloud-towers, crumbling thrones—
The ancients knew to expect a balance at the end of things,
The burning heart against the burning feather of truth.
                                                                                    Sweet-mouthed,
Big ibis-eyed, in the maple's hieroglyphs, I write it down.

All my life I've looked for this slow light, this smallish light
Starting to seep, coppery blue,
                                             out of the upper right-hand corner of things,
Down through the trees and off the back yard,
Rising and falling at the same time, now rising, now falling,
Inside the lapis lazuli of late afternoon.

Until the clouds stop, and hush.
Until the left hedge and the right hedge,
                                                            the insects and short dogs,
The back porch and barn swallows grain-out and disappear.
Until the bypass is blown with silence, until the grass grieves.
Until there is nothing else.

FROM

NORTH AMERICAN BEAR

(1999)

Step-children of Paradise

Dark of the moon, bear's tail through triage of winter trees,
Back yard a deep
                    tabula rasa, where to begin?

With or without language, there's always room for another life.
We've downloaded this one into an anxious indeterminacy,
Doing a little of this and a little of that,
As time, the true dissolver, eats away at our fingertips,
Leaving us memory and its end game,
                                        blurred star chart in the black light.

When the world has disappeared, someone will have to carry us,
Unseen and nightlong.
                              When the world has disappeared, amigo,
Somebody's got to pick up the load.
Rainy Saturday, January doldrums, toothache
Like a saint's call in my mouth, unavoidable, up and down.

We live our lives like stars, unconstellated stars, just next to
Great form and great structure,
                                        ungathered, uncalled upon.

Thinking About the Night Sky, I Remember a Poem by Tu Fu

Drifting, drifting, a single gull between sky and earth,
He said of himself, alone at night on the Yangtze.

Bent grasses and gentle wind.
And asked where his name was
Among the poets.
No answer, moon's disk on the great river.

People have free-fallen for thousands of miles through the distances of the heart,
Snowfall like starbursts
in the porch light's snap and slow freeze.
Such big flakes, such sure descent.
Black window of night behind the arborvitae,
bright grass and slender brocade.

Where there's smoke, there's ash.
Useless to let the mind grind down
To what's beyond it.
I'll set my sights on something small. I'll finish this poem,
This one that's not about the stars,
but what's between them.

North American Bear

Early November in the soul,
a hard rain, and dusky gold
From the trees, late afternoon
Squint-light and heavy heart-weight.
It's always downleaf and dim.
A sixty-two-year-old, fallow-voiced, night-leaning man,
I stand at ease on the blank sidewalk.
Unhinder my habitat, starlight, make me insoluble;
Negative in my afterscape,
sidle the shadow across my mouth.

Random geometry of the stars,
random word-strings
As beautiful as the alphabet.
Or so I remember them,
North American Bear,
Orion, Cassiopeia and the Pleiades,
Stitching their syntax across the deep North Carolina sky
A half-century ago,
The lost language of summer nights, the inarticulate scroll
Of time
pricked on its dark, celestial cylinder.

What is it about the stars we can't shake?
What pulse, what tide drop
Pulls us like vertigo upward, what
Height-like reversal urges us toward their clear deeps?
Tonight, for instance,
Something is turning behind my eyes,
something unwept, something unnamable,
Spinning its line out.
Who is to say the hijacked heart has not returned to its cage?
Who is to say some angel has not
breathed in my ear?

I walk in the chill of the late autumn night
like Orpheus,
Thinking my song, anxious to look back,

My vanished life an ornament, a drifting cloud, behind me,
A soft, ashen transcendence
Buried and resurrected once, then time and again.
The sidewalk unrolls like a deep sleep.
Above me the stars, stern stars,
Uncover their faces.
                                        No heartbeat on my heels, no footfall.

The season approaches us, dead leaves and withered grasses
Waxed by the wind wherever you look,
                                                            the clear night sky
Star-struck and star-stung, that constellation, those seven high stars,
General Ke-Shu lifting his sword, the Chinese say.
Or one of them said,
One at the Western Front as part of his army, without doubt.
I almost can see him myself,
                                                  long-sword over the Bear's neck,
His car wheel-less, darkness sifting away like a sandstorm to the west.

Some of these star fires must surely be ash by now.
I dawdle outside in the back yard,
Humming old songs that no one cares about anymore.
The hat of darkness tilts the night sky
Inch by inch, foot by black foot,
                                                      over the Blue Ridge.
How bright the fire of the world was, I think to myself,
Before white hair and the ash of days.
I gaze at the constellations,
                                                forgetting whatever it was I had to say.

The sidewalk again, unrolling grey and away. 9 p.m.
A cold wind from the far sky.
There is a final solitude I haven't arrived at yet,
Weariness like a dust in my throat.
                                        I simmer inside its outline,
However, and feel safe, as the stars spill by, for one more night
Like some medieval journeyman enfrescoed with his poem in his hand,
Heaven remaining my neighborhood.
And like him, too, with something red and inviolate
                                                        under my feet.

If You Talk the Talk, You Better Walk the Walk

The Buddhist monk hears all past
                                  and all future in one stroke of the temple bell,
And pries the world out from a pinpoint.
Or grinds it down from immensity to a wheat grain.
Those are his footprints, there by the monastery wall.
This is the life he rejected, written around us—

Incessant rain, slip-stitch vocabulary of winter trees
And winter dreadlocks on half-abandoned garden stalks
Long deconstructed, so
                              familiar and comforting
We don't understand a word.
Another February morning at the heart of the world.

The country we live in's illegible, impossible of access.
We climb, like our deepest selves, out of it forever.

Upward, we think, but who knows.
                                        Are those lights stars or the flametips of hell?
Who knows. We dig in and climb back up.
Wind shear and sleight-of-hand, hard cards, we keep on climbing.

St. Augustine and the Arctic Bear

China moon in the northeast, egg-like, 9:10 p.m.
There is no story here, only the moon
                                                  and a few script-stars,
Everything headed due west on its way through heaven,
Constellations like silver combs with their shell inlays,
Darkness like a sweet drink on the tongue.

No story, perhaps, but something's trying to get told,
Though not by me.
                                  Augustine said that neither future
Nor past exists, as one is memory, the other expectation.
When expectation becomes memory, I'd hasten to add,
We'll live in the past, a cold house on a dark street.

However, he also said,
None fall who will lift their eyes.
And said that time, in essence, remains a body without form.
On the other hand, the arctic bear,
Like time invisible in its element,
                                             has form to burn,

But does not do so, and keeps his eyes
                                                  fixed on the black water.

As I do, wherever I find it,
Bubba's bateau and his long pole
                                        always at my back,
A lap and a noisome breeze.
Formless and timeless, he wears my heart on his hard sleeve.

Sky Diving

Clear night after four days' rain,
                                moon brushed and blanched, three-quarters full.
Arterial pulse of ground lights and constellations.

I've talked about one thing for thirty years,
                                                and said it time and again,
Wind like big sticks in the trees—
I mean the still, small point at the point where all things meet;
I mean the form that moves the sun and the other stars.

What a sidereal jones we have!
                                        Immensity fills us
Like moonrise across the night sky, the dark disappears,
Worlds snuff, nothing acquits us,
And still we stand outside and look up,
                                            look up at the heavens and think,

Such sidebars, such extra-celestial drowning pools
To swallow us.
                Let's lie down together. Let's open our mouths.

FROM

A SHORT HISTORY OF THE SHADOW

(2002)

Looking Around

I sit where I always sit, in back of the Buddha,
Red leather wing chair, pony skin trunk
                                        under my feet,
Skylight above me, Chinese and Indian rugs on the floor.
1 March, 1998, where to begin again?

Over there's the ur-photograph,
                    Giorgio Morandi, glasses pushed up on his forehead,
Looking hard at four objects—
Two olive oil tins, one wine bottle, one flower vase,
A universe of form and structure,

The universe constricting in front of his eyes,
                                        angelic orders
And applications scraped down
To paint on an easel stand, some in the frame, some not.
Bologna, my friend, Bologna, world's bite and world's end.

It's only in darkness you can see the light, only
From emptiness that things start to fill,
I read once in a dream, I read in a book
                                        under the pink
Redundancies of the spring peach trees.

Old fires, old geographies.
In that case, make it old, I say, make it singular

In its next resurrection,
White violets like photographs on the tombstone of the yard.

Each year it happens this way, each year
Something dead comes back and lifts up its arms,
puts down its luggage
And says—in the same costume, down-at-heels, badly sewn—
I bring you good news from the other world.

One hand on the sun, one hand on the moon, both feet bare,
God of the late
Mediterranean Renaissance
Breaststrokes across the heavens.
Easter, and all who've been otherwised peek from their shells,

Thunderheads gathering at the rear
abyss of things,
Lightning, quick swizzle sticks, troubling the dark in-between.
You're everything that I'm not, they think,
I'll fly away, Lord, I'll fly away.

April's agnostic and nickel-plated and skin deep,
Glitter and bead-spangle, haute couture,
The world its runway, slink-step and glide.
Roll the stone slowly as it vogues and turns,
roll the stone slowly.

Well, that was a month ago. May now,
What's sure to arrive has since arrived and been replaced,

Snick-snack, lock and load, grey heart's bull's-eye,
A little noon music out of the trees,
a sonatina in green.

Spring passes. Across the room, on the opposite wall,
A 19th-century photograph
Of the Roman arena in Verona. Inside,
stone tiers and stone gate.
Over the outer portico, the ghost of Catullus at sky's end.

The morning and evening stars never meet,
nor summer and spring:
Beauty has been my misfortune,
hard journey, uncomfortable resting place.
Whatever it is I have looked for
Is tiny, so tiny it can dance in the palm of my hand.

This is the moment of our disregard—
just after supper,
Unseasonable hail in huddles across the porch,
The dogs whimpering,
thunder and lightning eddying off toward the east,
Nothing to answer back to, nothing to dress us down.

Thus do we slide into our disbelief
and disaffection,
Caught in the weeds and understory of our own lives,
Bad weather, bad dreams.
Proper attention is our refuge now, our perch and our praise.

So? So. The moon has its rain-ring auraed around it—
The more that we think we understand, the less we see,

Back yard becoming an obelisk
Of darkness into the sky,
                                        no hieroglyphs, no words to the wise.

Looking Around II

Pale sky and one star, pale star,
Twilight twisting down like a slow screw
Into the balsa wood of Saturday afternoon,
Late Saturday afternoon,
                                        a solitary plane
Eating its way like a moth across the bolt of dusk
Hung like cheesecloth above us.

Ugo would love this, Ugo Foscolo,
                                                    everything outline,
Crepuscular, still undewed,
Ugo, it's said, who never uttered a commonplace,
His soul transfixed by a cypress tree,
The twilight twisted into his heart,
Ugo, immortal, unleavened, when death gave him fame and rest.

Tonight, however's, a different story,
                                                    flat, uninterrupted sky,
Memorial Day,
Rain off, then back again, a
Second-hand light, dishcloth light, wrung out and almost gone.
9:30 p.m.,

Lightning bugs, three of them, in my neighbor's yard,
leaping beyond the hedge.

What can I possibly see back here I haven't seen before?
Is landscape, like God, a Heraclitean river?
Is language a night flight and sea-change?
My father was born Victorian,
knee-pants and red ringlets,
Sepia photographs and desk drawers
Vanishing under my ghostly touch.

I sit where I always sit,
knockoff Brown Jordan plastic chair,
East-facing, lingering late spring dusk,
Virginia privet and honeysuckle in full-blown bloom and too sweet,
Sky with its glazed look, and half-lidded.
And here's my bat back,
The world resettled and familiar, a self-wrung sigh.

César Vallejo, on nights like this,
His mind in a crash dive from Paris to South America,
Would look from the Luxembourg
Gardens or some rooftop
For the crack, the tiny crack,
In the east that separates one world from the next,
this one from
That one I look for it too.

Now into June, cloverheads tight, Seurating the yard,
This land-washed *jatte* fireflied and Corgied.
How sweet familiarity is,
With its known bird songs,
                                        its known smudges.
Today, as Machado said, is every day and all days.
A little wind from the southwest, a little wind in the apple tree.

And dusk descending, or dusk rising,
Sky flat as a sheet, smooth as bedclothes on a dead woman's bed.
It's always this way at 9 p.m.,
Half moon like a cleaved ox wheel
In miniature,
Machado smooth as a night bird half-asleep in the gum tree.

Crepuscularum. The back yard etched in and scored by
Lack of light.
What's dark gets darker against the shrinking, twilit sky,
Hedgerow and hemlock and maple tree.
A couple of lightning bugs.
Dog bark and summer smell.
                                        Mosquitos. The evening star.

Been rode hard and put up wet, someone said to me once
In Kalispell, meaning,
                                        I hope I'm being used for a higher good,
Or one I'm not aware of.
Dino Campana could have said that.
Said it and meant, Lord, that's it. And please turn off the light.
And he did.

Looking Around III

August. Cloud-forest Chinese Ming screen
Beyond the south meadow and up the attendant feeder hills.
No wind and a steady rain.
Raven squawk and swallow bank,
                                        screen shift at meadow mouth.
I find I have nothing to say to any of this.

Northwest Montana under the summer's backlash and wet watch.
The tall marsh grass kneels to their bidding.
The waters of Basin Creek pucker their tiny lips,
                                                            their thousand tiny lips.
The clouds shatter and the clouds re-form.
I find I have nothing to say to any of this.

Osip Mandelstam, toward the end of his short, word-fiery life,
Said heaven was whole, and that flowers live forever.
He also said what's ahead of us is only someone's word—
We were born to escort the dead, and be escorted ourselves.
Down by the creek bank, the sound that the water makes is almost human.

Down by the creek bank, the water sound
Is almost like singing, a song in praise of itself.
The light, like a water spider, stretches across the backwash.
Under the big spruce at the channel's bend,
                                                    someone's name and dates
Mirror the sky, whose way, like Mandelstam's, was lost in the sky.

Last night like spider light webbed and still in the tall grass,
Twin fawns and a doe at the salt lick,
Hail-battered marigolds and delphinium against the cabin wall,
Coyote about to trot out
Behind the diversion ditch and head for his breakfast.

I don't understand how white clouds can cover the earth.
I don't understand how a line of verse can fall from the sky.
I don't understand how the meadow mouth
                                                            opens and closes.
I don't understand why the water keeps saying yes, O, yes.
I don't understand the black lake that pools in my heart.

Late afternoon and long shadows across the deer ford,
Mt. Henry volcanic and hushed against the west sky and cloud clot.
Dante, according to Mandelstam,
Was not descriptive, was never descriptive, his similes
Exposing the inner image of the structure's force—

Birds were a pilgrimage, for instance, rivers political.
Cloud and cloud-flow having their way,
                                                        cloud-rags and cloud-rugs
Inching across the upper meadow, now the lower.
Inside the image inside the image is the image, he might have added,
Crystalline, pristine. But he didn't.

I sit where I always sit,
                                        northwest window on Basin Creek,
A homestead cabin from 1912,
Pine table knocked together some 30 years ago,

Indian saddle blanket, Peruvian bedspread
And Mykonos woven rug
                                        nailed up on the log walls.

Whose childhood is this in little rectangles over the chair?
Two kids with a stringer of sunfish,
Two kids in their bathing suits,
                                             the short shadows of evergreens?
Under the meadow's summer coat, forgotten bones have turned black.
O, not again, goes the sour song of the just resurrected.

To look hard at something, to look through it, is to transform it,
Convert it into something beyond itself, to give it grace.
For over 30 years I've looked at this meadow and mountain landscape
Till it's become iconic and small
And sits, like a medieval traveller's triptych,
                                                            radiant in its disregard.

All morning the donors have knelt, in profile, where the creeks meet,
The thin spruce have listened to what the rustle is, and nodded—
Like coyote's ears, they're split in the wind.
Tonight, after 10 p.m., the moon will varnish everything
With a brilliance worthy, wherever that is, of Paradise.

Citronella

Moonlight blank newsprint across the lawn,
Three-quarters moon, give or take,
                                                  empty notebook, no wind.
When it's over it's over,

Cloud crossing moon, half-clear sky, then
candle-sputter, shadow-crawl.

Well, that's a couple of miles down the road,
he said to himself,
Watching the moonlight lacquer and mat.
Surely a mile and then some,
Watching the clouds come and the clouds go.

Citronella against the tiny ones, the biters,
Sky pewter-colored and suddenly indistinct now—
Sweet smell of citronella,
beautiful, endless youth.
The book of moonlight has two pages and this one's the first one.

Forsake me not utterly,
Beato immaculato,
and make me marvellous in your eyes.

If This Is Where God's At, Why Is That Fish Dead?

If God is the one and infinite,
If God is the clear-cut and cloudless sky,
Powers, Dominions,
If God is a bed and a held breath,
You have a reason, my friend, to be inquisitive.

The morning smells like Milan, autumnal Milan, fog
And a fine rain in the trees,
huge plane leaves stuck on the sidewalks
Throughout the Sforza gardens,

Villa Guastalla calm as a ship
through the part-brown park and the mist.

The Japanese say we live in twelve pictures thrown from the floating world,
Where sin is a ladder to heaven.
Or has been. Or can be.

First light in the east last light in the west and us in between,
Lives marginal at best
and marginally brought to bear.
But that's okay, given the star-struck alternative.
Remember us in the ghost hour remember us in our need.

It's Dry for Sure, Dry Enough to Spit Cotton

Afternoon, summer half-gone, autumn half-here, strange day,
Most of the grass dead, blue-grey cloud shelf
Thickening down from the west,
yard light
Like the inside of a diving bell not yet in deep water.

The afternoon's got our number.
If only the rain
Would come and wash it off our foreheads.
If only the rain would come, unstrung through the hard weeds,
And wash us—sprung syllables, little eternities,

The rain with its thick fingers, the rain which will fill us
As slowly as hair grows, as slowly as fingernails—
Immaculate as the Jordan, Lord, Giovanni Battista

Out of the hills, hands faith-faint,
huge as all nothingness.

Where the sky disappears, the horizon spurts like a needle.
We all have death's birthmark on our faces,
sometimes red, sometimes unseeable.

If My Glasses Were Better, I Could See Where I'm Headed For

Autumn is over us, leaf blowers
Whine in the wind, vans wail, the heart makes scurrying sounds
As though preparing itself to start out on a long journey.
It wants to carry us with it, safe in its damp folds.
It wants to carry us, one by one.

Birds split and the ants go south.
The weevils turn in their sleep inside the red doors of the trunk.
Housefly and bumblebee carcasses drain in the sun.
Words stuttered by hand.
Gates of mercy.
Time after time.

As for me,
I'll put on the pilgrim slippers some of these days
There, where all things are forgot.
Till then, I'll see that the grass gets mowed.
Till then, I'll check out the cloud's drift, and the season's drift,
And how the days move, one at a time,
always at night, and always in my direction.

Lost Language

October, and leaves fall down. One feels the world go by.
First frost. And a licking sound
Just under the earth,
                                        great wheels, or a sluice of some sort.
Sunlight thin as Saran Wrap.
A licking sound, the suck and bump of something against something.

One lives one's life in the word,
One word and a syllable, word and one syllable.
As though ice and its amulets could rise and rest us.
Whatever it is we look for is scattered, apart.

I have a thirst for the divine,
                                                  a long drink of forbidden water.
I have a hankering for the dust-light, for all things illegible.
I want to settle myself
Where the river falls on hard rocks,
                                                            where no one can cross,
Where the star-shadowed, star-colored city lies, just out of reach.

Mondo Orfeo

Three-quarters moon, last of November,
                                                                  5 o'clock afternoon.
Acolytes of the tactile, servants of the articulate,
The infinite festers in our bones—
Sundown, and a drained blue from the sky so long,
                                                                        ghost whispers, lost voices,
Dry wind in dry grass, our bitter song.

Our song resettles no rocks, it makes no trees move, it
Has come to nothing, this sour song, but it's all we've got
And so we sing it
                                        being ourselves
Matter we have no choice in.
Zone wind, wind out of Thrace were we elsewhere, which we're not,

But would be, oak trees still standing where he left them, Orpheus,
Whose head-bobbing river tongue has no stop,
                                                                                whose song has no end.

For us, however, it's box canyon and bad weather and what-comes-next.
It's wind-rasp.
                                    It's index finger to puckered lips. It's Saint Shush.

In Praise of Thomas Hardy

Each second the earth is struck hard
                                                            by four and a half pounds of sunlight.
Each second.
Try to imagine that.
                                        No wonder deep shade is what the soul longs for,
And not, as we always thought, the light.
No wonder the inner life is dark.
Sounding, and sicced on like a dog,
                                                            they all go down and devolve,
Vowel-dancing, heart-sick,
Hoping for realignment and a space that won't shine.

Unlike the October moon, Apached and blade-dazzled, smalled
Down the western sky
                                            into Ovidian intersect

With time and its ghostly renderings.
Unlike the leaves of the ash tree, moon-treated and hanging on
For one day longer or so.
Unlike our shrunk selves, dripping like washing on the line.

Is

Transcendence is a young man's retreat,
                                        and resides in a place
Beyond place, vasty, boundless.
It hums, unlike the beauty of the world,
                                        without pause, without mercy.

If it's an absence, it's we who are absent, not it.
If it's past cold and colorless,
                              it's we who are colorless, not it.
If it stays hidden, it's we who hide.

March is our medicine,
                         we take it at morning, we take it at night.
It, too, is colorless, it, too, is cold and past tense.
But it's here, and so are we.

Each waits for deliverance.
March, however, unlike ourselves, knows what to expect—
April again in his Joseph coat.

The seasons don't care for us. For them,
                                        transcendence is merely raiment,
And never a second thought.
Poor us, they think, poor us in our marly shoes,
                                              poor us in our grass hair.

Polaroids

Since landscape's insoluble,
Then loath at last light I leave the landfall, soft and gone.
Or it leaves me.
                    I've got a tune in my head I can't let go,
Unlike the landscape, heavy and wan,
Sunk like a stone in the growing night,
Snuffed in the heart like a candle flame that won't come back.

Our world is of little moment, of course, but it *is* our world.
Thus it behooves us to contemplate,
                                        from time to time,
The *weight of glory* we should wish reset in our hearts,
About the things which are seen,
                                        and things which are not seen,
That corresponds like to like,
The stone to the dark of the earth, the flame to the star.

Those without stories are preordained to repeat them,
I saw once in the stars.
                              Unclear who underwrote *that*,
But since then I've seen it everywhere
I've looked, staggering
Noon light and night's meridian wandering wide and the single sky.
And here it is in the meadow grass, a brutish script.

We tend to repeat what we don't know
Instead of the other way around—
                                        thus mojo, thus misericordia,

Old cross-work and signature, the catechism in the wind.
We tend to repeat what hurts us, things, and ghosts of things,
The actual green of summer, and summer's half-truth.
We tend to repeat ourselves.

One longs for order and permanence,
An order as in the night sky just north of Mt. Caribou,
Permanence like the seasons,
                                        coming in, going out,
Watchman and wanderer. There's been no cure, however, and no
Ecstasy in transcendent form, so
Don't look for me here, incipient, now, in the artifice.

Florence is much on my mind, gold leaf and golden frame,
Infinite background of the masters—
Mayfire of green in the hills,
                                        watchtower and Belvedere,
The Arno, as Dino said, like a dithering snake,
Sad swipe of forgetfulness.
Last chance, a various universe.

A few more rising and setting suns.
Always the spike of the purple lupin, always the folded hands of the dog
    rose.
Childhood, gentle monk.
His eye extinguished,
                                someone's red-gold heart-mouth has sealed his lips.
No wind in the evergreens, no singer, no lament.
Summer surrounds us, and wordless, O blue cathedral.

A few more sorrowful scenes.
The waters murmur, shadows are moist in the upper meadow.
Silence wide as a wasteland through the black streets of the forest.
Over the white eyelids of the dead,
                                        white clover is blossoming.
Late snow like a fallen city shimmers the mountain's riprap and stare.
Unmullioned window, stained light.

The lapis lazuli dragonflies
                                        of postbelief, rising and falling near
The broken slab wood steps, now one by one, now in pairs,
Are not the dragonflies of death with their blue-black eyes.
These are the tiny ones, the stems, the phosphorescent,
Rising and falling like drowned playthings.
They come and they disappear. They come back and they disappear.

Horizon-hump of pine bristles on end toward the south,
Breath-stealer, cloudless drop cloth
Of sky,
        the great meadow beneath like a mirror face down in the earth,
Accepting nothing, giving it back.
We'll go, as Mandelstam tells us, into a growing numbness of time,
Insoluble, as long as landscape, as indistinct.

Nostalgia

Always it comes when we least expect it, like a wave,
Or like the shadow of several waves,
                                        one after the next,
Becoming singular as the face

Of someone who rose and fell apart at the edge of our lives.

Breaks up and re-forms, breaks up, re-forms.
And all the attendant retinue of loss foams out
Brilliant and sea-white, then sinks away.

Memory's dog-teeth,
                    lovely detritus smoothed out and laid up.

And always the feeling comes that it was better then,
Whatever *it* was—
                    people and places, the sweet taste of things—
And this one, wave-borne and wave-washed, was part of all that.

We take the conceit in hand, and rub it for good luck.

Or rub it against the evil eye.
And yet, when that wave appears, or that wave's shadow, we like it,
Or say we do,
            and hope the next time

We'll be surprised again, and returned again, despite the fact

The time will come, they say, when the weight of nostalgia,
                                                            that ten-foot spread
Of sand in the heart, outweighs
Whatever living existence we drop on the scales.

May it never arrive, Lord, may it never arrive.

A Short History of the Shadow

Thanksgiving, dark of the moon.
Nothing down here in the underworld but vague shapes and black holes,
Heaven resplendent but virtual
Above me,
                trees stripped and triple-wired like Irish harps.
Lights on Pantops and Free Bridge mirror the eastern sky.
Under the bridge is the river,
                                the red Rivanna.
Under the river's redemption, it says in the book,
It says in the book,
Through water and fire the whole place becomes purified,
The visible by the visible, the hidden by what is hidden.

Each word, as someone once wrote, contains the universe.
The visible carries all the invisible on its back.
Tonight, in the unconditional, what moves in the long-limbed grasses,
                                                what touches me
As though I didn't exist?
What is it that keeps on moving,
                                a tiny pillar of smoke
Erect on its hind legs,
                        loose in the hollow grasses?
A word I don't know yet, a little word, containing infinity,
Noiseless and unrepentant, in sift through the dry grass.
Under the tongue is the utterance.
Under the utterance is the fire, and then the only end of fire.

Only Dante, in Purgatory, casts a shadow,
L'ombra della carne, the shadow of flesh—
                                                            everyone else *is* one.
The darkness that flows from the world's body, gloomy spot,
Pre-dogs our footsteps, and follows us,
                                                            diaphanous bodies
Watching the nouns circle, and watching the verbs circle,
Till one of them enters the left ear and becomes a shadow
Itself, sweet word in the unwaxed ear.
This is a short history of the shadow, one part of us that's real.
This is the way the world looks
In late November,
                              no leaves on the trees, no ledge to foil the lightfall.

No ledge in early December either, and no ice,
La Niña unhosing the heat pump
                                                  up from the Gulf,
Orange Crush sunset over the Blue Ridge,
No shadow from anything as evening gathers its objects
And eases into earshot.
Under the influx the outtake,
                                              Leon Battista Alberti says,
Some lights are from stars, some from the sun
And moon, and other lights are from fires.
The light from the stars makes the shadow equal to the body.
Light from fire makes it greater,
                                    there, under the tongue, there, under the utterance.

River Run

In spite of armchair and omelette,
In spite of the daily paradise and quid pro quo,
Like Lorca, I wait for
                                        the things of the other side,
A little river of come and go,
A heartbeat of sorts, a watch tick, a splash in the night.

Wherever I turn, everything looks unworldly
Already,
                the stars in their empty boxes, the lights
Of the high houses glowing like stones
Through the thrones of the trees,
                                                            the river hushed in a brown study.

What isn't available is always what's longed for,
It's written, erased, then written again.
                                                                    Thus Lost and Unknown,
Thus Master of the Undeciphered Parchment, thus Hail and Farewell.
It's not the bullet that kills you, as the song goes,
                                                                                it's the hole.
It's not the water you've got to cross, it's the river.

Appalachian Lullaby

In Kingsport, high on the ridge,
                                                            night is seeping out of the Cumberlands
And two-steps the hills, shadows in ecstasy across the sky—

Not dark, not dark, but almost,
deep and a sweet repose.

Under the washed-red mimosa spikes,
under the blue backwash
Of evening, under the gun
Of mother-prayer and expectation, gently the eyelids close.

My sister and mother and father, each
In a separate room,
stay locked in a private music and drift away, night
And day, drift away.

I hear the gates of my life snick shut,
Air kisses,
kisses from some place that I've never been, but will be from.
Snick snick through the Red Sea, snick snick toward the promised land.

Someone is turning the lights out.
The darkness is mine,
Time, slow liquid, like a black highway in front of me
Somewhere, no headlights, somewhere.

Hello goodbye hello. Works and days.
We come, we hang out, we disappear.
There are stars above us that can't be counted,
and can't be counted on.

Gently the eyelids close.
Not dark, not dark. But almost.
Drift away. And drift away.
A deep and a sweet repose.

Relics

After a time, Hoss, it makes such little difference
What anyone writes—
Relics, it seems, of the thing
are always stronger than the thing itself.
Palimpsest and pentimento, for instance, saint's bones
Or saint's blood,
Transcendent architecture of what was possible, say,
once upon a time.

The dogwoods bloom, the pink ones and the white ones, in blots
And splotches across the dusk.
Like clouds, perhaps. Mock clouds
In a mock heaven,
The faint odor of something unworldly, or otherworldly,
Lingering in the darkness, then not.
As though some saint had passed by the side yard,
the odor of Paradise,

As Aldo Buzzi has it,
Odor of Heaven, the faithful say.
And what is this odor like? someone who'd smelled it was asked once.
He had no answer, and said,
"It doesn't resemble any flower or any bloom or spice on this earth.
I wouldn't know how to describe it."
Lingering as the dark comes on.

St. Gaspare Del Bufalo was one of these fragrant saints,
Buzzi continues,
St. Gaspare, who walked in the rain without an umbrella and still stayed dry.

Miraculous gift.
He knew, he added, one of the saint's relatives, a pianist,
who served him an osso buco once
In a penthouse in Milan.

Let's see. A cold spring in Charlottesville,
End of April, 2000—
If you can't say what you've got to say in three lines,
better change your style.
Nobody's born redeemed, nobody's moonlight, golden fuse in the deadly trees.
White wind through black wires,
humming a speech we do not speak.
Listen for us in the dark hours, listen for us in our need.

Why, It's as Pretty as a Picture

A shallow thinker, I'm tuned
to the music of things,
The conversation of birds in the dusk-damaged trees,
The just-cut grass in its chalky moans,
The disputations of dogs, night traffic, I'm all ears
To all this and half again.

And so I like it out here,
Late spring, off-colors but firming up, at ease among half things.
At ease because there is no overwhelming design
I'm sad heir to,
At ease because the dark music of what surrounds me
Plays to my misconceptions, and pricks me, and plays on.

It is a kind of believing without belief that we believe in,
This landscape that goes
no deeper than the eye, and poises like
A postcard in front of us
As though we'd settled it there, just so,
Halfway between the mind's eye and the mind, just halfway.

And yet we tend to think of it otherwise. Tonight,
For instance, the wind and the mountains and half-moon talk
Of unfamiliar things in a low familiar voice,
As though their words, however small, were putting the world in place.
And they are, they are,
the place inside the place inside the place.

The postcard's just how we see it, and not how it is.
Behind the eye's the other eye,
and the other ear.
The moonlight whispers in it, the mountains imprint upon it,
Our eyelids close over it,
Dawn and the sunset radiate from it like Eden.

Nine-Panel Yaak River Screen

Midmorning like a deserted room, apparition
Of armoire and table weights,
Oblongs of flat light,
the rosy eyelids of lovers
Raised in their ghostly insurrection,
Decay in the compassed corners beating its black wings,
Late June and the lilac just ajar.

Where the deer trail sinks down through the shadows of blue spruce,
Reeds rustle and bow their heads,
Creek waters murmur on like the lamentation of women
For faded, forgotten things.
And always the black birds in the trees,
Always the ancient chambers thudding inside the heart.

Swallow pure as a penknife
                                        slick through the insected air.
Swallow poised on the housepost, beakful of mud and a short straw.
Swallow dun-orange, swallow blue,
                                                    mud purse and middle arch,
Home sweet home.
Swallow unceasing, swallow unstill
At sundown, the mother's shade over silver water.

At the edge of the forest, no sound in the grey stone,
No moan from the blue lupin.
The shadows of afternoon
                                        begin to gather their dark robes
And unlid their crystal eyes.
Minute by minute, step by slow step,
Like the small hand on a clock, we climb north, toward midnight.

I've made a small hole in the silence, a tiny one,
Just big enough for a word.
And when I rise from the dead, whenever that is, I'll say it.
I can't remember the word right now,

But it will come back to me when the northwest wind
                                                  blows down off Mt. Caribou
The day that I rise from the dead, whenever that is.

Sunlight, on one leg, limps out to the meadow and settles in.
Insects fall back inside their voices,
Little fanfares and muted repeats,
Inadequate language of sorrow,
                                    inadequate language of silted joy,
As ours is.
The birds join in. The sunlight opens her other leg.

At times the world falls away from us
                                         with all its disguises,
And we are left with ourselves
As though we were dead, or otherwised, our lips still moving,
The empty distance, the heart
Like a votive little-red-wagon on top of a child's grave,
Nothing touching, nothing close.

A long afternoon, and a long rain begins to fall.
In some other poem, angels emerge from their cold rooms,
Their wings blackened by somebody's dream.
The rain stops, the robin resumes his post.
                                              A whisper
Out of the clouds and here comes the sun.
A long afternoon, the robin flying from post back to post.

The length of vowel sounds, by nature and by position,
Count out the morning's meters—
                    birdsong and squirrel bark, creek run,
The housefly's languor and murmurous incantation.
I put on my lavish robes
And walk at random among the day's
                    dactyls and anapests,
A widening caesura with each step.

I walk through my life as though I were a bookmark, a holder of place,
An overnight interruption
                    in somebody else's narrative.
What is it that causes this?
What is it that pulls my feet down, and keeps on keeping my eyes
                    fixed to the ground?
Whatever the answer, it will start
                    the wolf pack down from the mountain,
The raven down from the tree.

Time gnaws on our necks like a dog
                    gnaws on a stew bone.
It whittles us down with its white teeth,
It sends us packing, leaving no footprints on the dust-dour road.
That's one way of putting it.
Time, like a golden coin, lies on our tongue's another.
We slide it between our teeth on the black water,
                    ready for what's next.

The white eyelids of dead boys, like flushed birds, flutter up
At the edge of the timber.

Domestic lupin Crayolas the yard.
                                                            Slow lopes of tall grasses
Southbound in the meadow, hurled along by the wind.
In wingbeats and increments,
The disappeared come back to us, the soul returns to the tree.

The intermittent fugues of the creek,
                                                            saying yes, saying no,
Master music of sunlight
And black-green darkness under the spruce and tamaracks,
Lull us and take our breath away.
                                                            Our lips form fine words,
But nothing comes out.
Our lips are the messengers, but nothing can come out.

After a day of high winds, how beautiful is the stillness of dusk.
Enormous silence of stones.
Illusion, like an empty coffin, that something is missing.
Monotonous psalm of underbrush
                                                            and smudged flowers.
After the twilight, darkness.
After the darkness, darkness, and then what follows that.

The unborn own all of this, what little we leave them,
St. Thomas's hand
                                        returning repeatedly to the wound,
Their half-formed mouths irrepressible in their half-sleep,
Asking for everything, and then some.

Already the melancholy of their arrival
Swells like a sunrise and daydream
                                        over the eastern ridge line.

Inside the pyrite corridors of late afternoon,
Image follows image, clouds
Reveal themselves,
                        and shadows, like angels, lie at the feet of all things.
Chambers of the afterlife open deep in the woods,
Their secret hieroglyphics suddenly readable
With one eye closed, then with the other.

One star and a black voyage,
                                drifting mists to wish on,
Bullbats and their lullaby—
Evening tightens like an elastic around the hills.
Small sounds and the close of day,
As if a corpse had risen from somewhere deep in the meadow
And walked in its shadows quietly.

The mouth inside me with its gold teeth
Begins to open.
No words appear on its lips,
                                no syllables bubble along its tongue.
Night mouth, silent mouth.
Like drugged birds in the trees,
                                angels with damp foreheads settle down.
Wind rises, clouds arrive, another night without stars.

The Wind Is Calm and Comes from Another World

Overcast August morning.
                                        A little rain in the potholes,
A little shade on the shade.
The world is unconversational, and bides its own sweet time.
What you see is what you see, it seems to say, but we
Know better than that,
                                   and keep our eyes on the X, the cloud-ridden sky.

Heliotrope, we say, massaging its wings. Heliotrope.

Summer Mornings

Over the hill, the river's glib.
                                        In multiple tongues,
It's got a line of talk for anyone who wants it.
Lonely summer morning. Dwarf willows,
Black corners, a safe shadow for anyone who wants it.

What the river says isn't enough.
The scars of unknowing are on our cheeks,
                                                  those blank pages.
I'll let the wind speak my piece.
I'll let the Vocalissimo lay me down,
                                             and no one else.

There is out here, on summer mornings, a kind of light,
silky and rare,
That drapes through the evergreens
Every so often when clouds from the northwest glacier across
The sun and disintegrate.

A light like the absence of light it is so feral and shy.
A pentimento, even.
It is as though it dreamed us out of its solitude.
It is as though we're glazed here,
unasked for, unremembering.

It's Monday back there in the land of the Chickasaws.
The white clouds stumble upon each other, and pile up
Like mountains of faithlessness,
As clouds will, on a summer morning,
forgetting nothing, as clouds do.

Bright Monday. Unbearable light in the evergreens.
Dark river beneath it,
threading the eye of the underworld.
Above, on the great current of air,
The clouds drift on to their appointed stations, as clouds will do.

Odor of propane, nervous rustling of aspen leaves,
Summer morning unravelling silently through the woods.
The long body of the Hunter Gracchus sails by on its black water.
Late, golden July.

Time, like a swallow's shadow cutting across the grass,
Faint, darker, then faint again,
Imprints our ecstasy, and scores us.
And time will finish this, not I, and write it out,
as only time can.

The river rises in the mind, but empties nowhere,
Its hair naked in naked branches.
Spiders swing through my heart,
the moons of Jupiter turn and shine,
The river slides on its flaming wheel

And sings on summer mornings,
as though to croon itself to sleep.
And mumbles a kind of nothingness,
River that flows everywhere, north and south, like the wind
And never closes its eye.

Cloud skiff, like early snowfall, on the move from the west
Over Mt. Henry and my shoulder.
St. Pablo, patron of horses, appears through his wounds.
Hoofprints in khaki-colored dust.
Horseman salve our sins.

Summer morning. Gun-grey sky.
Rust keeps nibbling away at the edges of our lives.
Under the roots of the pine trees,
under the thunder,
Lightning is tracking our footprints, one leg at a time.

Bird life. An unappeasable bird life.
Saint's flesh melting into the flames below the brazier.
Sky flat and blank as parchment,
Wordless, encrypted blue,
                    God's endgame, summer morning.

The secret language of butterflies.
The short shadows of those
                    who will not rise from the dead.
The broken dream-cries of angels half-dazed in the woods.
The adjective and the noun.

Via Negativa

If a man wants to be sure of his road,
he must close his eyes and walk in the dark.

ST. JOHN OF THE CROSS

In Southwest Virginia, just this side of Abingdon,
The mountains begin to shoulder up,
The dogwoods go red and leaf-darkened,
And leftover roadside wildflowers neon among the greens—
Early October, and Appalachia dyes her hair.
What is it about the southern mountains
                    that vacuums me out,
That seems to hold me on an invisible flame until I rise up and veer
Weightless and unrepentant?
The great valley pours into Tennessee, the ridges like epaulets
To the north, landscape in pinks-and-greens
                    off to the south.

How pretty to think that gods abound,

and everything stays forgotten,

That words are dust, and everyone's lip that uttered them is dust,
Our line of discomfort inalterable, sun-struck,
From not-ness into not-ness,
Our prayers—like raiment, like char scraps—rising without us
Into an everlasting,

which goes on without us,

Blue into blue into blue—
Our prayers, like wet-wrung pieces of glass,
Surf-spun, unedged and indestructible and shining,
Our lives a scratch on the sky,

painless, beyond recall.

I never remember going out at night, full moon,
Stalking the yard in California the way I do here,
First frost

starting to sort its crystals out, moon shadows

Tepid and underslung on the lawn.
I don't remember—although I should—the emptiness
That cold brings, and stillness brings.
I never remember remembering the odd way
Evergreens have in night light

of looming and floating,

The way the spirit, leaving your mouth, looms too and floats
In front of you like breath,

leading the way as it disappears in the darkness.

Long journey, short road, the saying goes,
Meaning our lives,
                                        meaning the afterlife of our nights and days
During our sleepwalk through them.
The verbal hunger, the narrowness
Between the thing itself and the naming of the thing
Coils like a tapeworm inside us
                                                        and waits to be filled.
Our lives continue on course, and reject all meaning,
Each of us needing his martyrdom,
                                                              each of us needing that hard love.
We sink to our knees like Sunday, we rise and we sink again.
There is no pardon for this.

Bottomless water, heart's glass.
Each year the autumn comes that was not supposed to be
Back in the garden without language,
Each year, dead leaves like words
                                                            falling about our shoulders,
Each year, same words, same flash and gold guise.
So be it. The Angel of the Serpent That Never Arrives
Never arrives, the gates stay shut
                                                           under a shine and a timelessness.
On Locust Avenue the fall's fire
Collapses across the lawn,
The trees bear up their ruin,
                                      and everything nudges our lives toward the coming ash.

Nostalgia II

January, moth month,
                        crisp frost-flank and fluttering,
Verona,
Piazza Brà in the cut-light,
                            late afternoon, mid-winter,
1959,
Roman arena in close-up tonsured and monk robed
After the snowfall.

Behind my back, down via Mazzini, the bookstore
And long wooden table in whose drawer
Harold will show me, in a month or so,
                                        the small books
From Vanni Scheiwiller, *All'insegna del pesce d'oro*,
That will change my life,
Facsimiles, A *Lume Spento*, and *Thrones*, full blown, in boards.

Made in Verona. Stamperia Valdonega.
That's how it all began, in my case,
                                    Harold and I
Ghosting the bookstores and bars,
Looking for language and a place to stand that fit us,
The future, like Dostoevsky, poised
To read us the riot act.
                        And it did. And it's been okay.

Body and Soul

(FOR COLEMAN HAWKINS)

The world's body is not our body,
although we'd have it so.
Our body's not infinite, although
This afternoon, under the underwater slant-shine
Of sunlight and cloud shadow,
It almost seems that way in the wind,
a wind that comes
From a world away with its sweet breath and its tart tongue
And casts us loose, like a cloud,
Heaven-ravaged, blue pocket, small change for the hand.

I used to think the power of words was inexhaustible,
That how we said the world
was how it was, and how it would be.
I used to imagine that word-sway and word-thunder
Would silence the Silence and all that,
That words were the Word,
That language could lead us inexplicably to grace,
As though it were geographical.
I used to think these things when I was young.
I still do.

Some poems exist still on the other side of our lives,
And shine out,
but we'll never see them.
They are unutterable, in a language without an alphabet.
Unseen. World-long. Bone music.
Too bad. We'd know them by heart
if we could summer them out in our wounds.

Too bad. Listening hard.
Clouds, of course, are everywhere, and blue sky in between.
Blue sky. Then what comes after the blue.

Our lives, it turns out, are still-lifes, glass bottles and fruit,
Dead animals, flowers,
                                        the edges of this and that
Which drop off, most often, to indeterminate vacancy.
We're beautiful, and hung up to dry.
                                                        Outside the frame,
Mountains are moving, rivers flash, a cloud-scrumbled sky.
Field-patches nudge up to comfort us.
A train crosses a trestle.
Across the room, someone gets up and rearranges the things.

Insubstantial as smoke, our words
Drum down like fingertips across the page,
                                                                leaving no smudge or mark.
Unlike our purloined selves, they will not rise from the dead.
Unlike our whimpers and prayers, they lie low and disappear.
This word, that word, all fall down.
How far from heaven the stars are,
                                                        how far the heart from the page.
We don't know what counts—
It's as simple as that, isn't it,
                                                we just don't know what counts.

Mid-winter in Charlottesville,
                                                    soul-shunt and pat-down, crumbs
Snow-flecked across the back yard, then gone on the sun's tongue.
These are the four lessons I have learned,
One from Martha Graham,
                                                three others from here and there—

Walk as though you'd been given one brown eye and one blue,
Think as though you thought best with somebody else's brain,
Write as though you had in hand the last pencil on earth,
Pray as though you were praying with someone else's soul.

Body and Soul II

(FOR COLEMAN HAWKINS)

The structure of landscape is infinitesimal,
Like the structure of music,
                                        seamless, invisible.
Even the rain has larger sutures.
What holds the landscape together, and what holds music together,
Is faith, it appears—faith of the eye, faith of the ear.
Nothing like that in language,
However, clouds chugging from west to east like blossoms
Blown by the wind.
                              April, and anything's possible.

Here is the story of Hsuan Tsang.
A Buddhist monk, he went from Xian to southern India
And back—on horseback, on camel-back, on elephant-back, and on foot.
Ten thousand miles it took him, from 629 to 645,
Mountains and deserts,
In search of the Truth,
                              the heart of the heart of Reality,
The Law that would help him escape it,
And all its attendant and inescapable suffering.
                                                            And he found it.

These days, I look at things, not through them,
And sit down low, as far away from the sky as I can get.

The reef of the weeping cherry flourishes coral,
The neighbor's back porch lightbulbs glow like anemones.
Squid-eyed Venus floats forth overhead.
This is the half hour, half-light, half-dark,
when everything starts to shine out,
And aphorisms skulk in the trees,
Their wings folded, their heads bowed.

Every true poem is a spark,
and aspires to the condition of the original fire
Arising out of the emptiness.
It is that same emptiness it wants to reignite.
It is that same engendering it wants to be re-engendered by.
Shooting stars.
April's identical,
celestial, wordless, burning down.
Its light is the light we commune by.
Its destination's our own, its hope is the hope we live with.

Wang Wei, on the other hand,
Before he was 30 years old bought his famous estate on the Wang River
Just east of the east end of the Southern Mountains,
and lived there,
Off and on, for the rest of his life.
He never travelled the landscape, but stayed inside it,
A part of nature himself, he thought.
And who would say no
To someone so bound up in solitude,
in failure, he thought, and suffering.

Afternoon sky the color of Cream of Wheat, a small
Dollop of butter hazily at the western edge.
Getting too old and lazy to write poems,
I watch the snowfall

From the apple trees.
Landscape, as Wang Wei says, softens the sharp edges of isolation.
Don't just do something, sit there.
And so I have, so I have,
                                        the seasons curling around me like smoke,
Gone to the end of the earth and back without a sound.

FROM

BUFFALO YOGA

(2004)

Landscape with Missing Overtones

The sun has set behind the Blue Ridge,
And evening with its blotting paper
                                                            lifts off the light.
Shadowy yards.   Moon through the white pines.

Portrait of the Artist by Li Shang-Yin

My portrait is almost finished now
                                                            in the Book of White Hair.
Sunset over the Blue Ridge.
Puce floating cloud.
                                        A minute of splendor is a minute of ash.

Buffalo Yoga

Everything's more essential in northern light, horses
Lie down in the dry meadow,
Clouds trail, like prairie schooners,
                                                            across the edge of the left horizon,
Swallows jackknife and swan dive,
Bees blip and flies croon, God with his good ear to the ground.

Everything's more severe, wind
At a standstill and almost visible in the tamaracks,

Golden sap on the lodgepole pine
mosaicked and Byzantine
Inside the day's cupola,
Cuneiform characters shadowed across the forest floor.

Everything seems immediate,
like splinters of the divine
Suddenly flecked in our fingertips,
Forbidden knowledge of what's beyond what we can just make out,
Saw grass blades in their willingness to dazzle and bend,
Mnemonic waters, jack snipe, nightjar.

God's ghost taps once on the world's window,
then taps again
And drags his chains through the evergreens.
Weather is where he came from, and to weather returns,
His backside black on the southern sky,
Mumbling and muttering, distance like doomsday loose in his hands.

The soul, as Mallarmé says, is a rhythmical knot.
That form unties. Or reties.
Each is its own music,
The dark spider that chords and frets, unstringing and stringing,
Instrument, shadowy air-walker,
A long lamentation,
poem whose siren song we're rocked by.

An article isn't the last word, although we'd like it so.
Always there will be others,
                                        somewhere along the narrow road
That keeps on disappearing
                                        just there, in the mountains.

As soon as I sat down, I forgot what I wanted to say.
Outside, the wind tore through the stiff trees
Like rips through fabric.
                                    The bored hum of a lawn mower
Ebbed and flowed, white horse standing still in the near meadow,
No word in my ear, no word on the tip of my tongue.
It's out there, I guess,
Among the flowers and wind-hung and hovering birds,
And I have forgotten it,
                                    dry leaf on a dry creek.
Memory's nobody's fool, and keeps close to the ground.

All my life I've listened for the dark speech of silence,
And now, every night,
I hear a slight murmur, a slow rush,
My blood setting out on its long journey beyond the skin.

Earlier lives are restlessly playing hide-and-seek
Among the bog lilies and slough grass.
In this late light, the deer seem a sort of Georg Trakl blue.
The pond dims, the lonely evening pond.

A dead face appears at the window, then disappears.
The sky returns to its room,
                    monk birds pull up their hoods.

This is how the evening begins,
                    arranging its black pieces
Across the landscape.
Enormous silence, like wind, blows south through the meadow grasses.
Everything else holds its breath.
Stars begin to appear as the night sky
                    sets out its own pieces, the white ones.
Its moves are not new, but they are inexorable, and cold.

The sun, like a golden octopus
                    out from its reef
Of clouds, or the clouds themselves, so transubstantiationally strange
In summer weather,
Or what's left of the evergreens in their stern vestments,
It's never the same day twice.

A poem is read by the poet, who then becomes
That poem himself
For a little while,
                    caught in its glistening tentacles.
The waters of deep remembering
Wash over him, clouds build up,

As do the shadowy pools
                    under the evergreens.
Later, the winds of forgetfulness
Blow in from a thousand miles away

And the poet starts to write.
This is the way the day moves,
                                        and the sparks from its wheels.

He didn't have much to say, he thought,
                                        but knew at least how to say it.
Cold comfort. Sunday,
The clouds in their summer whites,
The meadow a Paris green,
                                        black and tan of the trees.
Sundays are no good, he thought, Sundays are all used up.
Poor miter, poor chasuble.

Mondays are worse still. Tuesday's the one,
                                        inanimate Tuesday,
So gentle, so pacified.
They flutter like flames, like feathers, from the brown calendars of the past.
Each of us has his day when the wind stops, and the clouds stop,
When everything grinds down and grains out.
Let mine be a Tuesday, he thought.
                                        Let mine be always day-after-tomorrow.

Everything tends toward circumference, it seems—the world,
This life, and no doubt the next,
                                        dependence and dear dread,
Even the universe in its spare parts.
                                        As for me,
I'm ringed like a tree, stealthily, year by year, moving outward.

Time wears us down and away
Like bootheels, like water on glass,
like footfalls on marble stairs,
Step by slow step until we are edgeless and smoothed out.

And childhood is distant, as distant as the rings of Saturn.

Let loose of my hand, Time, just this once,
And walk behind me along the corridor, the endless one,
That leads to the place I have to go.

There's no erasing the false-front calligraphy of the past.
There's no expunging the way the land lies, and its windfall glare.
I never did get it right.

When the great spider of light unspools her links and chains,
May the past be merciful,
the landscape have pity on me—
Forgive me my words, forgive me my utterances.

The water is saying yes and yes in the creekbed.
Clouds have arrived, and last night's moon,
full moon, is a memory.
The wind picks its way through the tight trees
Slowly, as though not to break something.
Marsh snipe on top of the blue spruce.
Nothing in nature says no.

Like tiny ghost dancers, the lupine and Indian paintbrush
Stand still and send back their messages
Through the canyons and black arroyos under the earth.
White horses shade down the deer.
Out of the dank doors in the woods,
                    angels emerge with their bronze foreheads.

And always, beneath the sunlit trees,
The easy breath-pull of moss,
                    gondolas on the black canals
Ferrying back and forth
                just under the forest floor
The shadows of those who go, and the shadows of those who stay,
Some standing, some sitting down.

Duckweed lies flat on the green water.
The white flags of two deer
                rattle across the meadow.
Transparent riders appear through the spruce trees and set off for the south.
I stand on the near edge of the marsh and watch them disappear.
Like them, I would gladly close my mouth
                        and whisper to no one.

Wind whirls, and dust flies up in eddies.
Flowers rise up and fall,
                trees buckle, and rise back up and fall.
Summer saddens and grows hot.

Bull snipe cackles in marsh mud.
Hawk corkscrews above the meadow,
                                        then dwindles out in the overcast.
Sun back, then swallowed for good.

The world is dirty and dark.
Who thought that words were salvation?
                                        We drift like water.
Whose life is it anyway?

A misericordia in the wind,
                                        summer's symphony
Hustling the silence horizonward,
Black keys from Rimbaud's piano in the Alps struck hard,
Then high tinkles from many white ones.
Then all of it gone to another room of the sky.

Thus do we pass our mornings,
                                        or they pass us, waving,
In dark-colored clothes and sad farewells,
The music of melancholy short shrift on their tongues,
Slow sift for the hourglass.
Emptiness fills our fields,
                                        new flowers rise from the dead.

The itchings for ultimate form,
                                        the braiding of this and that
Together in some abstract design
Is what we're concerned about,
A certain inevitability, a certain redress.
And so we wait for afternoon, and a different weather.

We wait for the consolation of the commonplace,
The belt of light to buckle us in.
We wait for the counterpart,
                                        the secretive music
That only we can hear, or we think that only we can hear.
Long afternoons.
                        Long afternoons and long, difficult evenings.

Wind from the northwest,
                                        spilling over the edge from Canada.
Big wind. Many steps.
Red bug on the windowpane. This side.
                                                        Nothing's bothering him
As everything vertical outside
Bends left a lot, then less, then a lot.
                                                    Red feet, red wings,
A journey beyond the wide world's end, transparent, upside down,
A kind of feckless gesture, like words
We travel back and forth to, one by one,
                                                        down low and out of the wind.

American midnight, the full moon
Starting its dip behind the mountains.
                                                    Fluttery shapes,
Fatal as angels in the shadowy corners of the mind,
Flatter the landscape.
Everything seems to coalesce and disintegrate
At once,
        a formal attribute of moonlight, one half
Of which we see, one half of which we maneuver not to see.

No longer interested in
                                        the little deaths of fixed forms,
Their bottled formaldehyde,
We follow the narrow road that disappears in the mountains,
We follow the stations of the tongue,
Arc and trailhead,
                                  the blaze on the tree.
Look for us soon on the other side
Where the road tumbles down,
                                                curving into the invisible city.

Outside, as it does one time each year,
The long body of the Hunter Gracchus sails by on the black water
Between the evergreens.
                                        Odor of endlessness. Odor of boat tar.
Dwindling shouts in the twilight. Rustle of aspen leaves.
Woodsmoke. Night birds. Dark linen.

The morning darkens. A wind from the north, winter wind,
Harassing the blue lips
                                        of lupine and cornflower.
Like souls of the half-begotten, dead mosses fold their stiff hands.
The trees continue their slow dismemberment and fall.
If there were graves up here
                                             they would open at your feet,
The mother appearing in summer and sweet decay.

The natural world, out of whose wounds the supernatural
Rises, and where it longs to return,

Shifts in its socket from time to time
                                        and sparks come forth.
These are the cracks, the hyphens of light, the world relinquishes
Briefly, then stanches with human dust.
And that's what's waiting for you in the far meadow,
                                        there, where the line's lunar linkup lurks.

The soul starts to talk to itself in the deep sleep of summer.
Under the light-flocked, mismatched spruce boughs,
It begins to know each other.
                                        The lonely half looks up at the sky,
The other stares at the dirt.
Who knows what they have to say,
                                        their voices like just-strung electric wire,
Constant, unhearable, but live to a single touch.

All guilt and dull ache,
                              we sit in stillness and think of forgotten things.
The stained glare of angel wings,
Radiant Sundays,
Austere, half-opened chambers of the half-opened heart,
Sun-clustered meadow,
The soul surrounding it,
                              a shimmering, speechless lash of light.

Dismantling the damaged bridge,
                                        Crash found a water ouzel's nest
Made wholly of moss.
I asked him had he ever seen one, he nodded yes.

I asked him had he ever seen one walk
underwater, and he nodded yes.
Over or under, to walk in water is a wondrous thing,
I thought.
Then thought of Tom, just dead in a foreign land,
And wanted to be an ouzel myself and walk
under the North Atlantic
And bring him back, and lay him in the stiff, mossy bed
Forever, above the water,
to walk in which is a wondrous thing
In either world, in either station.

Wind lull, and drifting mid-mountain clouds.
Shadows, like huge toads, consume themselves.
Horses lie down
In the mute meadow, birds hold their tongues
As morning prepares itself for the downdraft and broken spoke,
The descent of fiery wheels.
God's chosen walk close to the wall.

Clear-cuts take on a red glow as the dark begins to shut down.
Last pass of the barn swallow,
last lisp of the lingering clouds.
The generator coughs off. Lights out.
Stillness and no echoes, as though a body gathered itself
For a deep journey.
Occasional flicks from the flat and widening stars.
No shank, no shadow.

Footsteps faint through the thickening trees.
And the sound of two hands clapping,
                    a not unholy music.

Heat-quivering avenues cascade from the clouds,
                    and half-remembered
Faces roll back, stripped of their foliage,
To haunt their bodies, ghost-gazed and newly peregrine.
Unshod, uncreased, the feet of the recently resurrected
Pass over the dusty passageways
                    of afternoon, and leave no prints.
Out of the evergreens, one song and a bitter sigh.

How beautiful summer is,
                    unclottable darkness
Seeping across the landscape
Like blood from a hemophiliac.
How strong the heart is to entertain such loveliness.
How stringent the stars are,
                    spreading their welcome across the sky.
Passport stamped, the barrier lifting, how easily one is gathered.

The stars seem like window lights tonight,
                    or streetlights left on to comfort the dead
Unrolling their intergalactic curio maps
This side of midnight.
Their journey is long, and one without amenities.
Mother of Poverty, turn a blind eye on them, let them pass.

Past midnight's the other side,
north and south, down-ladder to dawn.
In the slick, cold corridors of the end, it is not our friend.
It's where our echoes reside.
It's what we have to pass through,
re-hearing each word we've ever uttered,
Listening one last time to the star-stung sound of our little voices.

The sky is hardening, color of pewter,
and ladles its wind
Like watery broth through the pine trees.
Who knows the heart of another's heart?
Our lives are the length of a struck match,
And our days are sure to end in a dark confusion.

Where the deer trail sinks down in the August shade of the pine trees,
There, on the other side of the creek,
Sapsucker off-rhythm drums
in the lodgepole and tamarack.
A knocking, as though he would enter,
Or exit, something
Dimmed and wind-whipped, riddled with wormways.

The blue flowers of summer
Turn toward us on their stiff stalks their sinister faces.
Something red dies out in us,
and closes its eyelids.
I want to become a horseman, a Mongol rider.

I want to become the black of the sapsucker's wing,
An absence of all color,
                    a feathery geography.

Chortle, and stuttering half-lilt, of an unknown bird.
They are burying Tom in West Virginia in a couple of days.
Butterfly yo-yoing back and forth above the short flowers.

White horse and mule and fjord horse
                    at grass in the glistering field.
They are burying Tom in West Virginia on Monday next.
Hum and hiccup of generator, hum of the creek.

Black dog and golden dog at large in the meadow marsh.
They are burying Tom in West Virginia, and that is that,
Butterfly back at the dandelion,
                    as cosmopolitan as the weed.

Like memory, night is kind to us,
Erasing idle details.
                    Circumference, for instance. Or linearity.
Astronomy starts to make some sense, and verticality.
Like sediment, inch after inch, we rise toward the stars.

The formalist implications of the afterlife
Seem to reveal, so far,
                    one star and a black voyage

To rediscover our names,
Our real names, imperishably inscribed in the registry of light,
From which all letters befall.

And that suits me for the time being,
Afternoon's alphabet beginning to firm up in the field,
Such radiant lettering.
If one only knew the name he was practicing for,
It would be easily there.

The world is a magic book, and we its sentences.
We read it and read ourselves.
We close it and turn the page down
And never come back,
Returned to what we once were before we became what we are.
This is the tale the world tells, this is the way it ends.

Buffalo Yoga Coda I

Low deck, Montana sky
color of cold Confederate uniforms,
High water in all the creeks, trees down
From wind and wet, beginning of June,
Snow yesterday, hard rain and hard frost, three bags full,
Whitecaps and white river, welcome back,
The tamaracks whisper and the lodgepole and the sough.

I slip the word in my shirt pocket: Time.
To warm it, to keep it dark, to keep it back from Forever.
I fold it in half and hold it there.

Like the cicada, however, it leaves its body and goes about its business,
Slick shell, such beautiful wings,
A corpse to reckon with.
Memento mori, perhaps.

That which we leave unspoken is like the hail from last night's storm
Still clustered and white
in the shadowy tall grass, as yet unreached by the sun.
Like unuttered words, they disappear
One by one in the light,
crystal and golden for an instant, then nothing at all.
Like everything else not done or not chosen.
Like all that's liquid and overlooked,
what we don't give, what we don't take.

Bullbat's back,
high up and almost unseeable in the morning's glare,
Swallows a hyperkinetic singsong down below.
I daydream about a pierced, medieval vision,
a suppuration of wounds,
A spurting of blood,
One ladle, two quick and endless gulps.
St. Catherine of Siena, drink something from me.

Like the patch of late snow each one of us has left in his heart
Hoarding some hurt or other,
some wind chime of vague consequence,
The world has a caked and cold spot for the self-deceived,

No matter how much they glitter and spark in the sleeved sunfall.
Theirs is the dark inheritance of the doubly dead.
For them the snuffed flame, the Fifteenth Station of the Cross.

Like intercessionary prayers to Purgatory,
Our little whines and our simperings
Flutter into the weather.
No wonder no answer is all we ever get, no wonder.

The purple violets are just back in the long grass.
You don't hear a peep from them,
Intent, as they are, on doing whatever it is they're here to do.
Look how low they lie in the wind,
how pursed their lips are.

In the high house of oblivion, there are many windows.
Through one of them, a light like the light
Now sliding across the meadow slides,
burst and perpetual.
One knows it from old frames of celluloid, exposed some,
That scorch like a wood flame, a hard light

That does not illuminate, but outlines and silhouettes.
Inside its panes the snow falls,
defining and flame-colored snow.
Through all the rest, no light shines,
Silence breeds and recalibrates, no waters whiffle, no wind.

Night fog, denser and denser.
Above it, an endlessness,
flight path for the newly received.
Or so they want to believe, their poor hands like poor flags in the distance.
Down here, however, it's difficult.
Down here, it's a different story.
This world, no thought of the other.

We'd like the fog to drift and rise, but it hugs the ground.
Like words we meant to say, but didn't.
We'd like to tell the departed to come back,
to say we're sorry for what we didn't say.
If, in fact, they're up there.
If, in fact, they're not still here,
still hugging the ground like the fog, like us.

I think I'll lie down just here for a while,
the sun on my cheek,
The wind like grass stems across my face,
And listen to what the world says,
the luminous, transubstantiated world,
That holds me like nothing in its look.

Buffalo Yoga Coda II

If, as Kafka says, the hunting dogs,
At play in the stone courtyard,
Will catch the hare no matter,
regardless of how it may be flying

Already now through the dark forest,
Then it must stay itself with just these trees,
                                                            and their bright passage,
Those marks and punctuations before the sentence ends,
Before, in short, and black as a bible,
                                                      the period closes in.

If, on the other hand, the hunting dogs,
                                                        now at play
In the stone courtyard,
Never arrive, the story becomes less classical.
And the hare, however fast,
                                            will always be slow enough
To outlast the ending, which presupposes the source
Of story and story line,
Which cannot be doubted, and so the period snaps in place.

And thus one parable becomes another, the sun,
As it must, continues its chords and variations,
The waters lisp in the speckled woods,
The deer put their tentative feet,
                                                  one forward, one back,
On the dead pine needles and dead grass,
Then turn like Nijinsky out of the sunlight and up the hill.
When Tolstoy met Chekhov, Chekhov says,
                                                      they spoke of immortality, what else.

Outside the outhouse doorframe, dewbows, a spatter of
Word-crystals, little eternities,
                                              each one of them,
Syllable, syllable, one handful of sleep, then two.

The long body of the Hunter Gracchus,
needle on Kafka's compass,
Slides through the upper meadow out of the south-southwest
As it does each year,
Ceaselessly circumnavigating
Our lives,
always true north, the black river just inches above the ground,
Time's sluice and time's undertow,
On its way to Mt. Caribou, and on toward the northern lights.

The dove finds no olive leaf,
so it slips back to the darkness inside the ark,
He wrote toward the end of his short, pain-dominant life.
And who would say otherwise?
There was a bird in the room, he wrote,
Each of his limbs as tired as a whole human being.
Whoever heard of a dying man drinking?
he asked, unable to do so himself.
And who would ask otherwise?

Late spring in the upper northwest,
first day of summer and the lilac just out,
Pale purple and dark purple
Over the white of the propane tank in back of the cabin.
The lilac is wonderful, isn't it? he wrote once,
Even when dying it drinks,
like a fish you might say.
Pale purple and dark purple,
And green of the underleaf, and green of the meadow.

I take down the thin book of All I Will Ever Know,
And find them, the one entry,
Three tiny words, three poised and tail-lifted scorpions.

Inadequate to the demands
imagination has settled upon me,
I listen to what the landscape says,
And all that it fails to say, and what the clouds say, and the light,
Inveterate stutterer.
Not much this morning, it turns out,
Odor of lilac like a south wind
Suddenly through the open window, swallow twaddle
Inelegant under the raw eaves.

Kafka appears in a splotch of sunlight
beyond the creek's course,
Ready, it seems, to step off the *via dolorosa* he's walked through the dark
forest.
I offer him bread, I offer him wine and soft cheese,
But he stands there, hands in his pockets,
Shaking his head no, shaking his head,
unable, still,
To speak or eat or to drink.
Then raises his right hand and points to the lilacs,
smiles, and changes back into sunlight.

Buffalo Yoga Coda III

Late morning on the cusp of the world,
Clouds beginning to burble and build
                                        across the southern skyline,
Susurration of waters,
Sunlight settling like a giant bird
Soundlessly over the meadow,
                                  feathery touches at the edges of things.

The raven is yakking and looking for somewhere to land,
                                                    the restless raven,
Begetter of aches and many wounds,
Malicious informant, *boia* of the airy blue.
One tree's not good enough;
                                 he tries another and then a third.
He's got his bright eye on me.

Under the low hum of the sweet bees,
Under the hair-heavy hoof of the warrior ant,
Under the towering shadows he must go through,
                                                and surface from,
Under the beetle's breast and the grub's,
The future is setting its table,
                               its cutlery dark, its mirrors anxious and blank.

Can sunlight rustle across the skin?
Can dew fall upon the eye?

Can lamentations of the unborn grieve in the wind?
Can alien constellations comfort the sore children?
Can the hands of the dead rise?
Can God untwist all that he's twisted?
Can horizons steal our breath?
Can we take back the borrowed dust we've given away?
Can the right word ring, O my, forever in the ear?
Can a selfish song be its own praise?

These are the simulacra of our days,
                                        the June clouds
Like Navajo rugs on heaven's floor,
Grey-black in the underwarp,
Dullness of distance in the shadowless corridors
Down through the forest,
                                lilacs deglazed and past repair,
Pine squirrels riding the grub line from thicket to windowsill and back.

Humdrum and extracurricular,
                                the waters turn from our touch, the grass yields,
And all the spidery elegance of afternoon
Lays down its weary body,
Legs tucked and dimmed some,
                                        unbidden and warm at our feet.
It's somebody's birthday, the 27th of June.
Sitting outside on the new-laid steps, I sharpen my pencil

To rig up his elegy,
Which this is, at least in part, and mine as well, I guess,

If the road he takes to return here
Is Koo Koo Boyd or Solo Joe,
French Garver or Basin Creek;
And if, in the Indian paintbrush sundown, the sound
He hears is the bullbat or summer snipe,
then this is for both of us.

A fine rain and a fine mist,
return of the great blue heron
To Porcupine and its upper reaches, above the creek bridge.
How beautiful summer is,
with all its creatures and all its weather,
Sunblade for just a second, then back in its scabbard of clouds,
Robins and rain continuing to pierce and pick at the earth,
Great blue at the top of the last larch,
eye ready for his turn.

Last legs of the lilac, but here come the lupine and bear grass,
The paintbrush and yarrow stalks.
Black ants work the underground,
freelancing among the stones and clay lumps,
Their slighter cousins hard and orderly at the weeds.

Two whitetail does, flags up, at romp in the near meadow,
One snipe in a sexual dive and collapse
just there, in the marsh slough,
Moose at the salt block,
East-inching shadows like black tongues licking themselves up.

I think I'll lie down just here for a while,
the sun on my cheek,
The wind like grass stems across my face,
And listen to what the world says,
the luminous, transubstantiated world,
That holds me like nothing in its look.

The Gospel According to St. Someone

Reflected radiance, moon envy, we hang outside
Ourselves like bats,
clothed in our flash dreams.
Sunset soaks down to the last leaves of the autumn trees.
Under our heads, the world is a long drop and an ache.
Above us, the sky forks,
great road to the left, great road to the right.

Someone will come and walk on his hands
through the dry grass to the altar.
Someone will take the wafer, someone will take the wine
And walk back through the gravestones.
Succor us, someone,
Let us drink from your mouth and let us eat from your tongue.

Eternal penny, counterfeit truth, score us and pay us off.
Buried November, read us our rites.
Salvation, worry our sins.
Awake, we all share the same world,
asleep, we're each in our own.
Lay me down, Lord, let me sleep.

Homage to Mark Rothko

I tried their ways for a little while,
But wasn't at ease with them, they
                                        not bringing me to the revealed.
Still, I kept on praising them.
I cast my body upon the earth.
I cast my body upon the waters,
                                        and kept on praising them all.
The glories refused to shelter me,
Nothing explained, nothing brought to bear.
I tried their ways for a little while,
                                        but nothing was ever revealed.

We enter the fields of memory and devotion.
Allow me, as Paul Celan says,
                                        to thank you from there—
Landscape, this world, this poor earth
Under the sun, holding nothing back,
This almost-nature that goes from light to light, that melts
The gold coin between our teeth,
That raises, like water, the shadow of the wound
                                                        up to our necks.
Allow me to thank you from all the language there is in that.

Early December, autumn's ragtag and cockamamie end.
Next door, Doctor Dave's got his pickup truck at the raked leaf pile,
Bird feeders float like flying saucers
                                        suddenly through the trees,
Plaster Madonna and wood-cut edge of the Blue Ridge

Zoomed in by the bare branches.
Turkey buzzards and crows
                                        drifting like lint on the Piedmont sky,
December, ragtag and gypsy day.
Allow me to thank you from all that's missing in all of that.

Form cannot deconstruct or be annihilated, you said.
The communion of saints,
                                        desire and its aftermath,
Chalice and chasuble, bread and wine—
Just sonar of purification, imprints,
                                                pretty tomfoolery.
Whatever *it* is, it's beyond all this, you said.
                                                And painting and language and music.
Stars are the first pages, you said, in The Book of Unknowing.
Behind them are all the rest.
Form is eternal and exists unwreckable, past repair, you said.

In the light that shines without shadow,
                                                    our hiding place.
Comfort metastasizes.
Wintering in. Wintering in to distance and wordlessness.
Comfort blackens the X rays.
                                            Echoes, deep subtractions.
Wretched the body dependent upon the body.
Wretched the flesh and the soul therein.
I tried to give form to the formless,
                                                and speech to the unspeakable.
To the light that shines without shadow, I gave myself.

Portrait of the Artist in a Prospect of Stone

Here is a photograph of George Mancini and me
On Hydra, the 23 March, 1961.
We're out on the breakwater.
                                        An American girl named Merle
Is next to George, who's reading a newspaper. Eric,
An Englishman, and Le Grand Danois
Are next to her.
    Feta, the dog, stands foursquare and panting in the cold Aegean sun.
I'm at the far end, looking at George,
Sunglasses, white socks, and desert boots,
                                                    Lieutenant's last morning.
Axel Jensen, outside the frame's edge, is up the rock-warped hill.
He's writing a first novel.
About his days with the Tuareg nomads in Algeria.
Or maybe Morocco. It's hard to remember everything.

Do I remember the would-be American novelist
Rewriting Proust for the middle west?
                                                Just out of the Air Force,
He'd spent a year on the island, sleeping with some musician's wife,
Also, it turned out, American.
I, of course, loved all of this.
What else was a 25-year-old,
                                        Armied and under wraps for years,
Supposed to fall in love with?
Back in Verona, that army was looking for me.
Security violation, a missing classified document.
Ciccolella, our G-2, would tell my colonel,
                                                "We don't come down on our own."

Meanwhile, I sat in the almost-April Greek sunshine
Romancing expatriates,
hoping for my turn to become like one of them.

Mancini remembers less than I.
Or says he does,
Patmos just to the east, where much was revealed to John.
The winds out of Asia ride hard herd on the waves.
Narrative's narrative is seldom as slick as it purports to be,
We know, but what is this red paint print above our heads?
Ricordo di Roma, thumb smear
by Mary who did the oil painting
There on the wall from the photograph on Via del Babuino.
You're blocking my view of God,
Tom said to his ex-intended,
Camel caravans moving like Bergman across the sand dunes,
Gods bright in the bright Aegean air.
Axel dreams of his Berber robes,
I dream, in my white socks, of permanent leave,
And Greece, a sleep and forget-me-not, is long, and has no dreams.

Listen, memory's got a hard heart and a soft head.
Whatever light the eye sees, the heart says dark, dark, dark.
Nothing is ever lost, I once said.
That was untrue,
I know now, the past a hiding place
Beyond recall or recovery, no matter our wants or our diligence.
Whatever is gone is gone,
Settling like sand dollars under memory's eyelid,
Down to the darkness where nothing stirs,
nothing except the heart,
That eyeless fish, drifting on slow, invisible currents

Beneath a blue hopscotch of islands where,
up above,
Somebody young and undiminished assembles a few friends
Along a breakwater in the sun.
Then one of them takes a camera out.

Rosso Venexiano

And here is a photograph of me taking a photograph
Of Holly and me. In 1969, I think,
In Venice,
Timothy Hennessey's wretched painting
Behind us, the ornate Venetian mirror throwing us back
Spotted, rejuvenate, shelved in two.

And that's not half bad, I'd say,
Chihuly downstairs, and Luke Hodgkin, *acqua alta*
Finally out the door,
the schifo from the trattoria
Flushed through the ground floor hallway's side rooms,
The lettuce flats and cardboard wine boxes
sucked back toward Malamocco.

End of March, thirty-three years ago.
Across the water, in S. Sebastiano, the Veronesi
Are arc-lit and scaffolded,
The Phantom Turk, square-rigged ghost ship,
still moored on the Grand Canal
In front of Palazzo Guggenheim.

Or so we imagined it,
Corvo at large on the damp streets,

Pound on his daily constitutional, as I've said before,
Exhuming the Zattere and Innocenti,
Fluttering candlelike guttering light
At night in the windows high up in Palazzo Barbaro.

Our altered and unreal lives.
How silly it all was, how delicious,
Palazzo this and Palazzo that,
Guardi and Canaletto from every bridge and opening,
The gold-domed Dogana a harsh relief in the winter sun.
Nobody sat on the steps that year,
not I, not anyone.

What else is bereft in the camera's lens, or the mirror's eye?
People, of course, and the future; Campo S. Polo:
Sabo, co fa scuro, Gran Balo Macabro, the poster announced.
Lord, the detritus.
Write, the voice said. *For whom?* came the response.
For the dead whom thou didst love, came the instant reply.

And will they read me?
Aye, for they return as posterity, the voice answered one last time.
Red of Titian's *Assumption*, red of the Doge's fingernail,
Blood red of the *Serenissima*,
Lagoon light, sunset and cloud blaze,
red of the Cardinal entourage.

Arrivederci Kingsport

It's all Interstate anymore,
the sedge fields Ted Glynn and I
Would shoot doves on. Or underwater.

The Country Music Highway, out of the hollers and backwash
Of southeastern Kentucky, old U.S. 23,
Has carried the boys to a different demarcation,
Their voices like field mice in the 21st-century wind.

Goodbye to that stuff,
The late '40s and early '50s and adolescence,
Dolores Urquiza and Clara Hall
                                        —memory's music just out of tune—
Drifting in their 7th-grade frocks across the Civic Auditorium floor.
Goodbye to Sundays, and band practice,
                                                the backseats of cars,
Goodbye to WKPT and everybody's song.

Jesus, it's all still a fist of mist
That keeps on cleaning my clock,
                                        tick-tock, my youth, tick-tock, my youth,
Everything going away again and again toward the light.
Who will remember Christina Marsh and Bobby Step,
                                                            now that I'm gone?
Who will remember the frog famine,
Now that the nameless roads
                                      have carried us all from town?

Midsummer in 1951,
                        the censer gone,
The call-and-response both gone, how far away is that?
A life unremarkable, but one which was remarked,
It turns out. Without consolation, it seemed,
                                                    adolescence,
The summer seeped to its end,
The sweet smoke of the past like bandages
                                                on all our imagined wounds.

And once upon a time, in the long afternoons of autumn,
The boys and girls would lay them down
in the bitter weeds
And watch the hidden meanderings
Of stars in their luminous disguise,
that ill-invested blue.
Is there reprieve for this act?
Is there reprieve for such regard?
Not in this life, and not in the next.

Well, yes, but beside the point.
And what is the point?
The point is the drawn-out landfall
From Chestnut Ridge to Moccasin Gap.
The point is U.S. 11W disappearing
In front of us and behind our backs,
the winter winds
And the clouds that dog our footsteps, out west and back east.

And so the dance continues,
Boots Duke and Jackie Imray,
Bevo and Kay Churchill,
Jim Churchill and Nancy Sims,
Name after name dropping into the dark waters of day-before-yesterday.
Champe Bachelder and Karen Beall,
Bill Ring and Sarah Lou,
Slow dance, the music coming up again.

Goodnight, sweetheart, well, it's time to go.
Ta-ta-ta-ta-tum, Goodnight, sweetheart, well, it's time to go,
the soft-aired, Tennessee night
Gathers its children in its cupped hands.

Time has its covenant, and who's to say that it is unjust.
We make our sad arrangements.
                                        The sky clears, the sun sets.
No matter the words, we never forget our own song.

January II

A cold draft blows steadily from a crack in the window jamb.
It's good for the soul.
For some reason, I think of monuments in the high desert,
                                        and what dissembles them.

We're all born with a one-way ticket, of course,
Thus do we take our deaths up on our shoulders and walk and walk,
Trying to get back.

We'd like to move as the water moves.
We'd like to cover the earth
                                        the way the wind covers the earth.
We'd like to burn our way there, like fire.

It's not in the cards.
Uncertainty harbors us like winter mist—
                                        the further we go, the deeper it gets.
Sundown now, and wind from the northwest.

The month is abandoned.
                                        Volvos go wandering to and fro
Like lost polar bears. The landscape is simple and brown.
The future's behind us, panting, lolling its black tongue.

Homage to Giorgio Morandi

You, of all the masters, have been the secret sharer
Of what's most important,
                                        exclusion,
Until the form is given us out of what has been given,
And never imposed upon,
Scrape and erase, scrape and erase
                                                until the object comes clear.

I well remember the time I didn't visit you
In Bologna, 1964,
                                the year you died.
Bob Koffler and Wolf Kahn went, Mary and all the rest of us
Remaining in Rome. What a mistake.
The next thing we heard was your *coccodrillo* in the *Daily American.*

And now you've become iconic, as only is right,
Grizzano and atelier,
                                    permanent as a pair of finger rings
On your worldwide hands.
The farther out of the picture you go, the greater it grows.
The farther out of our lives you go, *la stessa storia.*

And now you have become an eternal occasion.
The less in view, the more your presence
Surrounds us,
                            and concentrates our tick-tock attention.
How proper it is we see you most where you are not,
Among your objects.
                                    This bottle, for instance, this vase.

Bologna made you and Bologna undid you in the scheme of things.
It never mattered to you.
How little we knew about your life,
how little we knew about anything,
The Roman nights so florid and opposite of all that you stood for.
We bathed in our own dark waters,
you dabbled your brush in yours.

The would-be artist's credo—
He keeps to himself
and doesn't play well with others—
Found short shrift on your star chart.
Still, no serious time for anything but your work,
You looked as hard as anyone ever looked,
then left it out.

My Own Little Civil War

I come from the only county in Tennessee that did not secede
Throughout the entire Civil War,
Sullivan County,
Rock-ribbed, recalcitrant, Appalachian cornerstone.
My kinfolk were otherwise,
Arkansans and Mississippians,
Virginians and Tarheels.
Still, I was born just a half mile from Shiloh churchyard,
And had a relative, the family story goes, who served there,
Confederate quartermaster,
who took the occasion, that first day,
To liberate many bills

From Union coffers as the Johnnys swept through to the river,
And never replaced them when the Bluebellies swept back
And through the following afternoon.

My great-grandfather Wright left VMI to join up
With Lee and the Army of Northern Virginia
Somewhere near Richmond,
                                        and ended up,
Lucky lad, a staff officer in the general's command.
Who knows how many letters that took?
After the war he went back to Lexington, with Lee,
The general to Washington College and immortality,
Capt. Wright at the far end of town,
                                                  still marching away the lost cause.
Marse Robert has his horse and white tomb
Under the oak trees.
My great-grandfather has his name in a long thin line
Of others who were Captains of the Corps of Cadets,
                                                              too little, boys, too late.

My great-grandfather Penzel, four years in the country,
Saddled up in 1861 in Little Rock
With the Capital City Guards
                                         and struck out for Tennessee.
His name is last on the list, carved in print on an obelisk,
In front of a civic building somewhere near downtown.
Like just about everyone else, he finished the war as a captain,
Enduring the raw campaigns
                                        of southeast Tennessee,
Chickamauga, two years in Rock Island prison, deep
Wounds in his mouth and elsewhere,
Then back, like all the others, into the thick of it.

A long way for a country boy,
slaveless, and no stake in it,
From the green hills of Bohemia.

There are letters from Isaac Wright,
Bladen County, North Carolina,
1856,
To his son near Lafayette Courthouse, Red River, Arkansas,
A dozen or so, I cannot decipher.
Political
And familial, about President Franklin Pierce,
Wishing that John C. Calhoun
were still alive and president
Instead, and the Constitutional rights of the South
Established with greater force,
and greater clarity.
"I fear that we shall yet have difficulties with our Northern Brethren."
And then the price of negroes,
Nearby farms, the fear of high water,
the price of cotton, always the price of cotton.
Then "love to Elizabeth, my son, and you and the children."

All this from the documents
left by my great-aunt Marcella,
A folder that also holds,
Inexplicably, my grandmother's marriage license
And one short sketch, so titled, of the Fulton and Nowland families.
So much for all that . . .
However, wrapped in wax paper,
Among the letters, is another small envelope
Containing a lock, so called,
of Robert E. Lee's hair,

Sent by him to the wife of the lucky lad from VMI . . .
That's it, my own little Civil War—
                                        a lock of hair,
A dozen unreadable letters,
An obit or two,
And half the weight and half-life
                                        of a half-healed and hurting world.

Sun-Saddled, Coke-Copping, Bad-Boozing Blues

Front porch of the first cabin, with Luke.
July, most likely, and damp, both of us wearing rubber boots.
Just out of the photograph, beyond the toe of my left foot,
The railing where Tim and I, one afternoon,
                                        carved our poor initials
While working on verses for his song, "Stockman's Bar Again, Boys."
Both song and singer are gone now, and the railing too.

We all sang in the chorus
                                        back in L.A., in the recording studio,
Holly and I and Bill Myers and Kelly and Johnny Rubinstein.
Such joyful music, so long ago,
                                        before the coke crash and the whiskey blows.
Sun-soured Montana daydreams,
Los Angeles and its dark snood so soft on the neck.
Lie still I'm working on it lie still.

Billy Mitchell's just come by, somebody stole his tools,
Leland Driggs has shot an elk and broke the county's rules.
Sweet Dan Kelly's on his Cat, watch out and back away,
Snuffy Bruns is feeding squirrels and Crash is bucking hay.

Big John Phelan's got outside a half a fifth of gin,
We've all gone and gotten drunk in Stockman's Bar again.

Dead frequency, Slick, over and out.
It's mostly a matter of what kind of noise you make.
American Hot Wax, for instance, and "Stand by Your Man"—
George Jones, type-casting for sure.
And music, always music—keyboard and guitar, violin,
Anything with a string.
Your band was called Fun Zone, you up front,
Poncher on drums, Wolfie on bass, and Johnny R. at the piano.

And others. Until the lights went out.
Renaissance boy,
With coke up your nose and marijuana in your eye,
We loved you the best we could, but nobody loved you enough.
Except Miss Whiskey.
You roll in your sweet baby's arms now, as once you said you would,
And lay your body down,
in your meadow, in the mountains, all alone.

—TIM MCINTIRE (1944–1986)

In Praise of Han Shan

Cold Mountain and Cold Mountain became the same thing in the mind,
The first last seen
slipping into a crevice in the second.

Only the poems remained,
scrawled on the rocks and trees,
Nothing's undoing among the self-stung unfolding of things.

FROM

SCAR TISSUE

(2006)

Appalachian Farewell

Sunset in Appalachia, bituminous bulwark
Against the western skydrop.
An Advent of gold and green, an Easter of ashes.

If night is our last address,
This is the place we moved from,
Backs on fire, our futures hard-edged and sure to arrive.

These are the towns our lives abandoned,
Wind in our faces,
The idea of incident like a box beside us on the Trailways seat.

And where were we headed for?
The country of Narrative, that dark territory
Which spells out our stories in sentences, which gives them an end
and beginning . . .

Goddess of Bad Roads and Inclement Weather, take down
Our names, remember us in the drip
And thaw of the wintry mix, remember us when the light cools.

Help us never to get above our raising, help us
To hold hard to what was there,
Orebank and Reedy Creek, Surgoinsville down the line.

Last Supper

I seem to have come to the end of something, but don't know what,
Full moon blood orange just over the top of the redbud tree.
Maundy Thursday tomorrow,
then Good Friday, then Easter in full drag,
Dogwood blossoms like little crosses
All down the street,
lilies and jonquils bowing their mitred heads.

Perhaps it's a sentimentality about such fey things,
But I don't think so. One knows
There is no end to the other world,
no matter where it is.
In the event, a reliquary evening for sure,
The bones in their tiny boxes, rosettes under glass.

Or maybe it's just the way the snow fell
a couple of days ago,
So white on the white snowdrops.
As our fathers were bold to tell us,
it's either eat or be eaten.
Spring in its starched bib,
Winter's cutlery in its hands. Cold grace. Slice and fork.

The Silent Generation II

We've told our story. We told it twice and took our lumps.
You'll find us here, of course, at the end of the last page,
Our signatures scratched in smoke.

Thunderstorms light us and roll on by.
Branches bend in the May wind,
But don't snap, the flowers bend and do snap, the grass gorps.

And then the unaltered grey,
Uncymbaled, undrumrolled, no notes to set the feet to music.
Still, we pull it up to our chins; it becomes our lives.

Garrulous, word-haunted, senescent,
Who knew we had so much to say, or tongue to say it?
The wind, I guess, who's heard it before, and crumples our pages.

And so we keep on, stiff lip, slack lip,
Hoping for words that are not impermanent—small words,
Out of the wind and the weather—that will not belie our names.

The Wrong End of the Rainbow

It must have been Ischia, Forio d'Ischia.
Or Rome. The Pensione Margutta. Or Naples
Somewhere, on some dark side street in 1959

With What's-Her-Name, dear golden-haired What's-Her-Name.
Or Yes-Of-Course
In Florence, in back of S. Maria Novella,
And later wherever the Carabinieri let us lurk.

Milano, with That's-The-One, two streets from the Bar Giamaica.
Venice and Come-On-Back,
three flights up,
Canal as black as an onyx, and twice as ground down.

Look, we were young then, and the world would sway to our sway.
We were riverrun, we were hawk's breath.
Heart's lid, we were center's heat at the center of things.

Remember us as we were, amigo,
And not as we are, stretched out at the wrong end of the rainbow,
Our feet in the clouds,
                    our heads in the small, still pulse-pause of age,

Gazing out of some window, still taking it all in,
Our arms around Memory,
Her full lips telling us just those things
                    she thinks we want to hear.

A Field Guide to the Birds of the Upper Yaak

A misty rain, no wind from the west,
Clouds close as smoke to the ground,
                    spring's fire, like a first love, now gone to ash,
The lives of angels beginning to end like porch lights turned off
From time zone to time zone,
                    our pictures still crooked on the walls,
Our prayer, like a Chinese emperor, always two lips away,
Our pockets gone dry and soft with lint.
Montana morning, a cold front ready to lay its ears back.

If I were a T'ang poet, someone would bid farewell
At this point, or pluck a lute string,
                    or knock on a hermit's door.
I'm not, and there's no one here.

The iconostasis of evergreens across the two creeks
Stands dark, unkissed and ungazed upon.
Tonight, it's true, the River of Heaven will cast its net of strung stars,
But that's just the usual stuff.
                                        As I say, there's no one here.

In fact, there's almost never another soul around.
There are no secret lives up here,
                                        it turns out, everything goes
Its own way, its only way,
Out in the open, unexamined, unput upon.
The great blue heron unfolds like a pterodactyl
Over the upper pond,
                                two robins roust a magpie,
Snipe snipe, the swallows wheel, and nobody gives a damn.

A Short History of My Life

Unlike Lao-tzu, conceived of a shooting star, it is said,
And carried inside his mother's womb
For 62 years, and born, it's said once again, with white hair,
I was born on a Sunday morning,
                                        untouched by the heavens,
Some hair, no teeth, the shadows of twilight in my heart,
And a long way from the way.
Shiloh, the Civil War battleground, was just next door,
The Tennessee River soft shift at my head and feet.
The dun-colored buffalo, the sands of the desert,
Gatekeeper and characters,
                                    were dragon years from then.

Like Dionysus, I was born for a second time.
From the flesh of Italy's left thigh, I emerged one January
Into a different world.
                                        It made a lot of sense,
Hidden away, as I had been, for almost a life.
And I entered it open-eyed, the wind in my ears,
The slake of honey and slow wine awake on my tongue.
Three years I stood in S. Zeno's doors,
                                                        and took, more Rome than Rome,
Whatever was offered me.
The snows of the Dolomites advanced to my footfalls.
The lemons of Lago di Garda fell to my hands.

Fast-forward some forty-five years,
                                                    and a third postpartum blue.
But where, as the poet asked, will you find it in history?
Alluding to something else.
Nowhere but here, my one and only, nowhere but here.
My ears and my sick senses seem pure with the sound of water.
I'm back, and it's lilac time,
The creeks running eastward unseen through the dank morning,
Beginning of June. No light on leaf,
No wind in the evergreens, no bow in the still-blonde grasses.
The world in its dark grace.
                                             I have tried to record it.

Confessions of a Song and Dance Man

The wind is my music, the west wind, and cold water
In constant motion.
                                    I have an ear

For such things, and the sound of the goatsucker at night.
And the click of twenty-two cents in my pants pocket
That sets my feet to twitching,
                                        that clears space in my heart.

"We are nothing but footmen at the coach of language,
We open and close the door."
                                        Hmmm two three, hmmm two three.
"Only the language is evergreen,
                                        everything else is seasonal."
A little time step, a little back-down on the sacred harp.
"Language has many mothers, but only one father."

The dying *narcissus poeticus* by the cabin door,
Bear grass, like Dante's souls,
                                        flame-flicked throughout the understory,
The background humdrum of mist
Like a Chinese chant and character among the trees,
Like dancers wherever the wind comes on and lifts them . . .

The stillness of what's missing
                                        after the interwork's gone,
A passing sand step, a slow glide and hush to the wings—
A little landscape's a dangerous thing, it seems,
Giving illusion then taking it back,
                                        a sleight of hand tune
On a pennywhistle, but holding the measure still, holding the time.

A God-fearing agnostic,
                                        I tend to look in the corners of things,

Those out-of-the-way places,
The half-dark and half-hidden,
                                                  the passed-by and over-looked,
Whenever I want to be sure I can't find something.
I go out of my way to face them and pin them down.

Are you there, Lord, I whisper,
                                                  knowing he's not around,
Mumble *kyrie eleison*, mumble O three-in-none.
Distant thunder of organ keys
In the fitful, unoccupied
                                        cathedral of memory.
Under my acolyte's robes, a slip-step and glide, slip-step and a glide.

Red-winged blackbird balancing back and forth on pond reed,
Back and forth then off then back again.
What is it he's after,
                                   wing-hinge yellow and orange,
What is it he needs down there
In snipe country, marsh-muddled,
                                                       rinsed in long-day sunlight?

The same thing I need up here, I guess,
A place to ruffle and strut,
                                          a place to perch and sing.
I sit by the west window, the morning building its ruins
In increments, systematically, across the day's day.

Make my bed and light the light,
                                             I'll be home late tonight, blackbird, bye-bye.

College Days

Mooresville, North Carolina, September 1953.
Hearts made of stone, doodly wop, doodly wop, will never break... I
Should have paid more attention, *doodly wop, doodly wop,*
To the words and not just the music.
Stonestreet's Cafe,
                    the beginning of what might be loosely called
My life of learning and post-adolescent heartbreak-without-borders.
All I remember now is four years of Pabst Blue Ribbon beer,
A novel or two, and the myth of Dylan Thomas—
American lay by, the academic chapel and parking lot.
O, yes, and my laundry number, 597.

What does it say about me that what I recall best
Is a laundry number—
                    that only reality endures?
Hardly. Still, it's lovely to hope so,
That speculation looms like an ever-approaching event
Darkly on the horizon,
                    and bids us take shelter,
Though, like Cavafy's barbarians, does not arrive.
That's wishful thinking, Miguel,
But proper, I guess,
                    to small rooms and early morning hours,
Where juke joints and clean clothes come in as a second best.
Is sin, as I said one time, more tactile than a tree?

Some things move in and dig down
                              whether you want them to or not.
Like pieces of small glass your body subsumes when you are young,

They exit transformed and easy-edged
Many years later, in middle age, when you least expect them,
And shine like Lot's redemption.
College is like this, a vast, exact,
                                        window of stained glass
That shatters without sound as you pass,
Year after year disappearing, unnoticed and breaking off.
Gone, you think, when you are gone, thank God. But look again.
Already the glass is under your skin,
                                        already the journey's on.

There is some sadness involved, but not much.
                                        Nostalgia, too, but not much.
Those years are the landscape of their own occasions, nothing lost,
It turns out, the solemn sentences metabolized
Into the truths and tacky place mats
We lay out
          when custom demands it.
That world becomes its own image, for better or worse
—the raven caws, the Weed-Eater drones—
And has no objective correlative to muscle it down.
It floats in the aether of its own content,
                                        whose grass we lie on,
Listening to nothing. And to its pale half brother, the nothingness.

Bedtime Story

The generator hums like a distant *ding an sich*.
It's early evening, and time, like the dog it is,
                                        is hungry for food,

And will be fed, don't doubt it, will be fed, my small one.
The forest begins to gather its silences in.
The meadow regroups and hunkers down
                                        for its cleft feet.

Something is wringing the rag of sunlight
                                        inexorably out and hanging.
Something is making the reeds bend and cover their heads.
Something is licking the shadows up,
And stringing the blank spaces along, filling them in.
Something is inching its way into our hearts,
                              scratching its blue nails against the wall there.

Should we let it in?
                    Should we greet it as it deserves,
Hands on our ears, mouths open?
Or should we bring it a chair to sit on, and offer it meat?
Should we turn on the radio,
                              should we clap our hands and dance
The Something Dance, the welcoming Something Dance?
                              I think we should, love, I think we should.

Transparencies

Our lives, it seems, are a memory
                              we had once in another place.
Or are they its metaphor?
The trees, if trees they are, seem the same,
                                        and the creeks do.
The sunlight blurts its lucidity in the same way,

And the clouds, if clouds they really are,
still follow us,
One after one, as they did in the old sky, in the old place.

I wanted the metaphor, if metaphor it is, to remain
always the same one.
I wanted the hills to be the same,
And the rivers too,
especially the old rivers,
The French Broad and Little Pigeon, the Holston and Tennessee,
And me beside them, under the stopped clouds and stopped stars.
I wanted to walk in that metaphor,
untouched by time's corruption.

I wanted the memory adamantine, never-changing.
I wanted the memory amber,
and me in it,
A figure among its translucent highlights and swirls,
Mid-stride in its glittery motions.
I wanted the memory cloud-sharp and river-sharp,
My place inside it transfiguring, ever-still,
no wind and no wave.

But memory has no memory. Or metaphor.
It moves as it wants to move,
and never measures the distance.
People have died of thirst in crossing a memory.
Our lives are summer cotton, it seems,
and good for a season.
The wind blows, the rivers run, and waves come to a head.
Memory's logo is the abyss, and that's no metaphor.

Morning Occurrence at Xanadu

Swallows are flying grief-circles over their featherless young,
Night-dropped and dead on the wooden steps.
The aspen leaves have turned grey,
                                        slapped by the hard, west wind.

Someone who knows how little he knows
Is like the man who comes to a clearing in the forest,
                                                            and sees the light spikes,
And suddenly senses how happy his life has been.

The Minor Art of Self-defense

Landscape was never a subject matter, it was a technique,
A method of measure,
                        a scaffold for structuring.
I stole its silences, I stepped to its hue and cry.

Language was always the subject matter, the idea of God
The ghost that over my little world
Hovered, my mouthpiece for meaning,
                                        my claw and bright beak . . .

Scar Tissue

What must be said can't be said,
It looks like; nobody has a clue,
                                    not even, it seems, the landscape.

One hears it in dreams, they say,
Or out of the mouths of oracles, or out of the whirlwind.

I thought I heard it, a whisper, once,
In the foothills of the Dolomites,
                                        night and a starless sky,
But who can remember, a black night, a starless sky,
Blurred voice and a blurred conceit.

It takes a crack in the membrane,
                                        a tiny crack, a stain,
To let it come through; a breath, a breath like a stopped sigh
From the land of foreign tongues.
It is what it has to say, sad stain of our fathers.

Whatever is insignificant has its own strength,
Whatever is hidden, clear vision.
Thus the ant in its hide-and-seek,
                                        thus the dung beetle,
And all the past weight of the world it packs on its back.

The insect world has no tongue to let loose, and no tongue to curb,
Though all day and all night it cries out.
Who says we shouldn't listen to them?
Who says we shouldn't behave ourselves as they do,
                                                no noise but for one purpose?

Whatever the root sees in the dark is infinite.
Whatever the dead see is the same.
Listen, the rivers are emptying
                                        under our feet,
Watched over by all the waters of the underworld.

Why does one never tire of looking out at the obvious?
The merely picturesque
                                        is good for a day or so,
The ugly fascinates for a little while, then scabs over, like grease.
Only the obvious, with its odd neck, holds us close,

The endless sky with its endless cargo of cloud parts,
The wind in the woebegone of summer afternoons,
The landscape in its last lurch,
The shadowy overkill
                                        of the evening sun going down.

It seems, somehow, to ignite us into a false love for the physical world.
Our mouths full of ashes, our mouths full of fresh fire,
                                                                        phoenix-like,
Wide wings over wider lives,
We open and close on demand, we open and close.

The woods are thick with sunlight.
Tonight, over the mountain,
                                        the full moon will replenish them
With their own reflected face.

This is the almost hour,
                                        almost darkness, almost light,
Far northern dusk dust sifting over the evergreens,
Chiaroscuro at heaven's walk,
Charcoal and deeper shades where our foot falls and hands hang.

This is the time of mixed masks.
This is the time of sour songs,
                    of love gone wrong, of sixes and sevens,
The almost hour, the zero-zero.
This is the one place we feel at home, this is our zone.

The idea of horses grazes in deep, black grass.
The idea of separation
                    unleashes its luminous line
That holds us at either end.
How happy we are here, how utterly dark our contentment.

Friday, a little perch, a branch, to rest on for a moment.
Yesterday, Thursday,
I rose and fell like a firefly,
                    light off, light back on.
Today, I'm a hummingbird
On Friday's slick branch,
                    my heart like a beat machine, my wings a green itch.

It is impossible to say good-bye to the past.
Whose images are they anyway,
                    whose inability to spell them out?
Such destitution of words.
What hand was seen to wave in the all-absorbing light?

Better to leave it alone.
Better to let it drift there,
                    at the end edge of sight,

Replete with its angel bands and its handsful of golden hair,
Just out of earshot, just out of reach.

But someday that hand will reappear
Out of the awful blear-light.
Someday that hand, white hand in the white light,
                                        will wave again, and not stop.
No reason to look around then, it will be waving to you.

The slit wrists of sundown
                          tincture the western sky wall,
The drained body of daylight trumps the Ecclesiast
In its step down and wide walk,
Whose cloak is our salve and damp cloth,
                                       whose sigh is our medicine . . .

Chipmunk towering like a dinosaur
                                 out of the short grass,
Then up the tamarack, sparrow harrowing, then not,
Grasshopper in its thin, green armor,
Short hop, long bound, short hop and a long bound,
Life and death in the milky sunshine now,
                                       and concealing shade,
Sparrow avenging machine in the crush of inalterable law.

The arching, drought-dried pilot grasses,
                                      earwigged and light-headed,
Nod in the non-wind, directing the small ones nowhere.
Robin lands on the stump root,

Something red and just cut in its beak.
Chipmunk down from the tamarack,
                                        and back on patrol,
In and out of the alleyways and sun spots of his saurian world.

The thread that dangles us
                                between a dark and a darker dark,
Is luminous, sure, but smooth sided.
Don't touch it here, and don't touch it there.
                                        Don't touch it, in fact, anywhere—
Let it dangle and hold us hard, let it flash and swing.

The urge toward form is the urge toward God,
                                                perfection of either
Unhinged, unutterable.
Hot wind in the high country, an east wind, prairie wind.
Unutterable in cathedral or synagogue.
Unhinged, like low wind in high places.
Wind urge and word urge,
                                last form and final thing, the O.

Great mouth. Toothless, untouched.
                                        Into whose night sky we all descend.
Star-like we list there
Restructured, forms within forms.
Meanwhile, the morning's sonogram
                                        reveals us just as we are,
Birds on their bright courses, the dogs at work in the field,
Flies at the windowpanes, and horses knee-deep in their deep sin.

Hard to forget those autumn evenings
driving out to the lake
To catch the sunset,
Harold's wallet already tucked and soft in my coat pocket,
Garda breaking aluminum-like
And curled as the dropping sun sponged out
villas and lemon trees,
Gardone shrinking into its own shadow as Friday night came down
Across the water,
Sirmio glittering like an olive leaf
turned upside down in the west wind,
Riva gone dark under sunset clouds,
The town of Garda itself
Below us with its fistful of lights beginning to come on,
Pulling us down like a centrifuge to the lake's edge,
Where we parked by the plane tree at the Taverna's door . . .
Those were the days, boys, those were the days.

The bulging blue of July
presses us down, and down,
Until the body of the world beneath us slurs to a halt,
Prelapsarian stillness at hand,
Something glistening in the trees,
angel wings starting to stir the dust,
The flatness of afternoon
Exacting, a sleep inside a sleep,
Our tongues like turnip greens,
our dreams a rodeo dog's.

There is a dearth of spirit as weightless as the grave
That weighs and prefigures us.
It's like the smoke of forest fires from hundreds of miles away
That lies low in the mountains
And will not move,
                                        that holds us down with the tiredness of long afternoons,
So weightless the covering, so weightless the spread that spreads it.

There is a desperation for unknown things, a thirst
For endlessness that snakes through our bones
Like a lit fuse looking for Lethe,
                                                            whose waters reward us,
Their blackness a gossamer and grief
Lifted and laid to one side,
Whose mists are like smoke from forest fires that will not move.

Ravens are flying in and out of the summer woods.
Two, I think, no, three, each buzzed,
                                                                  then buzzed again by a blackbird
Up from the tall reeds by the pond's edge.
The ravens bleat and the blackbirds attack and fall back,
Attack again, the ravens
Upstream by now, little dark points, the blackbirds invisible
As yesterday's prayers.
                                              But working hard, Lord, working hard.

Scar Tissue II

Time, for us, is a straight line,
on which we hang our narratives.
For landscape, however, it all is a circling
From season to season, the snake's tail in the snake's mouth,
No line for a story line.
In its vast wheel, in its endless turning,
no lives count, not one.

Hard to imagine that no one counts,
that only things endure.
Unlike the seasons, our shirts don't shed,
Whatever we see does not see us,
however hard we look,
The rain in its silver earrings against the oak trunks,
The rain in its second skin.

Pity the people, Lord, pity their going forth and their coming back,
Pity their sumptuous barricades
against the dark.
Show them the way the dirt works.
Show them its sift, the aftermath and the in-between.
Wet days are their own reward for now,
litter's lapse and the pebble's gleam.

Once in a while, we all succumb
to the merely personal,
Those glass shards and snipped metal

That glitter and disappear and glitter again
                                                                in the edged night light
Of memory's anxious sky.
How could it be otherwise, given our histories?

Like Dante's souls of the blessed,
                                                    they drop from their tiers
Down to our mind's eye
In whichever heaven it happens to be, for a few words,
An inch of adrenaline,
A slipped heartbeat or so,
                                            before they begin to flicker and grain out.

Names, and the names of things, past places,
Lost loves and the love of loss,
The alphabet and geometry of guilt, regret
For things done and things undone,
All of the packaging and misaddresses of our soiled lives—

Ingrid under the archway on Via Giulia,
Quel ramo del Lago di Como,
                                                Mt. Ann and the twice-thwarted tower,
Betsy, the White Rabbit, between the columns at Sweet Briar,
San Zeno sun strobe,
                                    Goldstein and Thorp,
Flashes like bottle glass, no help for it, flashes like foxfire.

Spirit, subjective correlative and correspondent, moves
Like water under the skin of every story line,
Not too deep, but deep enough,
                                                    not too close to the top.

There are no words for these words,
Defining and erasing themselves without a sound
Simultaneously,
                                        larger and smaller, puddle and drift.
In all superstition there lingers a heart of unbelief
For those who walk slip stitch upon the earth
                                                                        and lose their footprints.
One signs one's name wherever it falls.

The wind never blows in the wrong place,
The sunrise is never late,
                                        some Buddhist must certainly have said once.
If not, what a missed sound bite.
The natural world is always in step, and on time,
Absit omen our self-absorption.
Sometimes you eat the bear,
                                        and sometimes the bear eats you.

All morning, out of the sunlight, grainy subtraction,
I've courted the shadow life,
Asleep, or half-asleep,
                                        like a fish in a deep stream.
Dark spot, bright spot, leopard-skin water.
I feel it drifting around me,
                                        my life like a boat
Overhead, floating, unoccupied, back out of sight.

I love to look at the new moon through the bare branches of winter trees.
Always the same moon, the same branches,

Always new entrances
and caustic geographies.
The stars are still visible, like stunned impurities
In the great sea of anthracite that is the night sky.

One never gets used to this—
Immensity and its absolute,
December chill
Like fingernails on the skin—
That something from far away has cracked you,
ever so slightly,
And entered and gone, one never should.

Virginia, Hanover County, December lastlight
Draining into a small hole
Behind the winter wickery
of hardwoods and cedar spires
That bordered three fields of soybean stobs
And uncut sumac runners and dead seed millet stalks.

My son and I and the kind man whose acres these were,
Shotgun and bird whirr,
day, and the drift of day, sun spill,
I've written it all down in footprints in rubbed red clay,
And put it aside, but find
It's no use, you can't keep anything you can't keep your hands on.

A small rain, a feathery, small rain,
has been falling all day

In the neighborhood.
Nothing comes clear, however, nothing is brought to bear.
It snoods our curls, it glosses our lips.
Garbage sacks gleam with a secret light.
                                        Low overhead,
Just north of noon, the grey clouds keep on washing their hands
Obsessively, as though they had something still to prove.
1:51 p.m., and all's well
Elsewhere,
            winter settling over the earth like a parachute
From nowhere, pulled open by no one you'd ever know.

Full moon like a 60-watt bulb across the backyard.
This is the light we live in.
This is the light the mind throws
                                    against the dark, faint as a finger rub
On a rosary.
It doesn't care how old we are, or where our age will take us.
Nor does the darkness, friend,
                                    whose love is a mystery.
Nor does what lies behind it, which isn't.

The outfit was out of town a couple of clicks,
                                            on Via Mantovana,
A chain-link fence, a gravelled car park,
Black Chevys, a deuce-and-a-half and a jeep or two
Under the blue Italian sky,
                                all on the q.t.
The 430th CIC Detachment, your tax dollars at work.

Our job was to spy on our own troops and host country.
Great duty for a twenty-three-year-old, 1959,
The officers all about to retire after twenty years
Of service, the sergeants too,
Leaving the rest of us to put in our time,
two years or four,
Cruising the culture and its sidebars.
On down the road from our light cover,
Just north of Mantova one day after work, Ed DiCenzo and I
Sat in the sunset dripping into the plane trees
and Mincio River
Watching an eel fisherman through the trattoria window,
Both eating roast chicken and *tortellini con le gonne*,
The world in its purity and grace,
at least for a moment,
Giving our hearts a heads-up and a shoulder to lean on. Great duty.

Sunrise, a cold almost deep enough to crack the oaks,
Morning, like strawberry Kool-Aid,
spilling up from the Tidewater.
Middle of January, winter smooth-hipping down the runway.

Hillocks and patches of last week's snow
huddle and desiccate across the backyard,
Still white and vaguely funereal in the sweet light.
Squirrel tails flick like beavers', birds sing.

All day the wind will comb out its hair through the teeth of the evergreens.
All day the sunlight will sun itself
On the back porch of the cottage, out of the weather.

The world has an infinite beauty, but not, always, for us.
The stars will be boutonnieres,
                                        though not necessarily for us.
And the grave is a resting place, but not, however, for one and all.

New skin over old wounds, colorless, numb.
Let the tongue retreat, let the heart be dumb.

Get a Job

Just over sixteen, a cigarette-smoking boy and a bit,
I spent the summer digging ditches,
And carrying heavy things
                                        at Bloomingdale School site.
I learned how a backhoe works, and how to handle a shovel,
And multiple words not found in the dictionary.
Sullivan County, Tennessee, a buck twenty an hour,
1952.
      Worst job of my life, but I stuck it out.

Everyone else supported a family, not me.
I was the high school kid, and went home
Each night to my mother's cooking.
                                        God knows where the others went.
Mostly across the line into Scott County, Virginia, I think,
Appalachian appendix, dead end.
Slackers and multipliers, now in, now out of jail, on whom I depended.
Cold grace for them.
                                        God rest them all road ever they offended,

To rhyme a prominent priest.
Without a ministry, without portfolio,
Each morning I sought them out
For their first instructions, for their laying on of hands.
I wish I could say that summer changed my life,
or changed theirs,
But it didn't. Apparently, nothing ever does.
I did, however, leave a skin there.
A bright one, I'm told, but less bright than its new brother.

Archaeology

The older we get, the deeper we dig into our childhoods,
Hoping to find the radiant cell
That washed us, and caused our lives
to glow in the dark like clock hands
Endlessly turning toward the future,
Tomorrow, day after tomorrow, the day after that,
all golden, all in good time.

Hiwassee Dam, North Carolina.
Still 1942,
Still campfire smoke in both our eyes, my brother and I
Gaze far out at the lake in sunflame,
Expecting our father at any moment, like Charon, to appear
Back out of the light from the other side,
low-gunwaled and loaded down with our slippery dreams.

Other incidents flicker like foxfire in the black
Isolate distance of memory,
cross-eyed, horizon-haired.

Which one, is it one, is it any one that cleans us, clears us,
That relimbs our lives to a shining?

One month without rain, two months,
                                        third month of the new year,
Afternoon breeze-rustle dry in the dry needles of hemlock and pine.
I can't get down deep enough.
Sunlight flaps its enormous wings and lifts off from the backyard,
The wind rattles its raw throat,
                                        but I still can't go deep enough.

In Praise of Franz Kafka

Weather no matter, time no matter,
The immemorially long and windy body of the Hunter Gracchus
Floats again
Through the buoyant dark of the pine forest,
                                        ship-borne and laid out
Like a downed larch on the black, intransitive deckwork.
He passes each year
On the waters that circle above the earth
In his pitiless turn and endless geography.
The wings of the crewmen hang like washing along the railing.
June is his sunlight, and June is his farthering forth,
His world pure circumference.
                                        Follow him if you can.

Vespers

Who wouldn't wish to become
The fiery life of divine substance
blazing above the fields,
Shining above the waters,
The rain like dust through his fingerbones,
All our yearning like flames in his feathery footprints?
Who, indeed?
And still . . .

The world in its rags and ghostly raiment calls to us
With grinding and green gristle
Wherever we turn,
and we are its grist, and we are its groan.
Over the burned lightning strikes of tree shadows
branded across the near meadow,
Over the dusk-dazed heads of the oat grass,
The bullbat's chortle positions us, and holds us firm.

We are the children of the underlife,
at least for a time,
Flannel shirt on a peg, curled
Postcards from years past
thumbtacked along the window frames.
Outside, deer pause on the just-cut grass,
The generator echoes our spirit's humdrum,
and gnats drone high soprano . . .
Not much of a life, but I'll take it.

The Narrow Road to the Distant City

Heap me, Lord, heap me, we're heard to say,
Not really meaning it, but meaning
Gently, my man, ever so gently,
                                        please lay me down,
Allow me all things I've not deserved,
Dandle my heart and tell me I'm still your baby boy.

How could it be otherwise,
                                        our just meat being ash,
Which, don't worry, is set to be served at the next course.
We've said grace in the past tense.
We've said our prayers out of our mouths,
                                        not out of our hearts.
The more we talked, the more our tongues tied.

So pay us some nevermind.
Let us pretend the world's our own dream,
And be unto us as a hard wind
                                        that understands nothing.
In fact, be yourself,
If that is what the nothing that is,
                                        and the nothing that is to come, is called for.

Ghost Days

Labyrinthine, Byzantine,
                                        memory's gold-ground mosaics
Still spill us and drop us short.

Who was the sixth guy in the Fiat 500
With Giancarlo, Pamela, the two drunken Carabinieri and me
That New Year's Eve around 3 a.m.
Circling the Colosseum
                                        and circling the Colosseum?
And what year was it ten inches of snow descended
Like papal grace on Rome, and all the small *macchine*
Crashed on the Tiber's retaining wall?
                                                        What year was that?
The pieces clear and occlude like a retinal bleed.

And where are you now, Giancarlo,
                                                    my first Italian friend,
Mad *marinaio* of the Via Margutta, where are you?
Like a black blot in a troubled eye,
                                                    you fall into place, then fall out
From the eyeball's golden dome.
How high you hung there once in our fast-faltering younger days.
How high we all hung,
                                        artificial objects in artificial skies,
Our little world like a little S. Apollinare in Classe,
Weedy and grass-gripped outside,
                                                    white and glare-gold within,
Our saints with their wings missing,
But shining, nevertheless,
                                        as darkness gathers the darkness, and holds it tight.

The Silent Generation III

These are our voices, active, passive and suppressed,
                                                                and these are our syllables.

We used them to love your daughters, we used them to love your sons.
We travelled, we stayed home, we counted our days out
like prescription pills.
In the end, like everyone, we had too much to say.

We lived by the seat of our pants, we bet on the come
Only to come up short,
and see, as the smoke began to clear,
The life we once thought that boundless canopy of sky,
Was just the sound of an axe, echoing in the woods.

We hadn't the heart for heartlessness,
we hadn't the salt or the wound.
The words welled,
but goodness and mercy declined to follow us.
We carried our wings on our own backs, we ate our dead.
Like loose lightbulbs, we kept our radiance to ourselves.

Not heavy enough to be the hangman's burden,
our noosed names
Are scrawled in the dust discursively, line after line.
Too strange for our contemporaries,
we'll prove to be
Not strange enough for posterity.

O you who come after us,
Read our remains,
                    study the soundless bones and do otherwise.

Time Will Tell

Time was when time was not,
                                    and the world an uncut lawn
Ready for sizing. We looked, and took the job in hand.
Birds burst from our fingers, cities appeared, and small towns
In the interim.
                We loved them all.
In distant countries, tides nibbled our two feet on pebbly shores
With their soft teeth and languorous tongues.
Words formed and flew from our fingers.
                                                We listened and loved them all.

Now finitude looms like antimatter, not this and not that,
And everywhere, like a presence one bumps into,
Oblivious, unwittingly,
                            Excuse me, I beg your pardon.
But time has no pardon to beg, and no excuses.

The wind in the meadow grasses,
                                        the wind through the rocks,
Bends and breaks whatever it touches.
It's never the same wind in the same spot, but it's still the wind,
And blows in its one direction,
                                    northwest to southeast,
An ointment upon the skin, a little saliva,

Time with its murderous gums and pale, windowless throat,
Its mouth pressed to our mouths,
pushing the breath in, pulling it out.

The Woodpecker Pecks, but the Hole Does Not Appear

It's hard to imagine how unremembered we all become,
How quickly all that we've done
Is unremembered and unforgiven,
how quickly
Bog lilies and yellow clover flashlight our footfalls,
How quickly and finally the landscape subsumes us,
And everything that we are becomes what we are not.

This is not new, the orange finch
And the yellow and dun finch
picking the dry clay politely,
The grasses asleep in their green slips
Before the noon can roust them,
The sweet oblivion of the everyday
like a warm waistcoat
Over the cold and endless body of memory.

Cloud-scarce Montana morning.
July, with its blue cheeks puffed out like a *putto* on an ancient map,
Huffing the wind down from the northwest corner of things,
Tweets on the evergreen stumps,
swallows treading the air,
The ravens hawking from tree to tree, *not you, not you,*
Is all that the world allows, and all one could wish for.

Singing Lesson

This is the executioner's hour,
                    deep noon, hard light,
Everything edge and horizon-honed,
Windless and hushed, as though a weight were about to fall,
And shadows begin to slide from beneath things, released
In their cheap suits and eager to spread.

Out in the meadow, nothing breathes,
                    the deer seem to stop
Mid-jump at the fence, the swallows hanging like little hawks in the air.
The landscape loosens a bit, and softens.
                    Like miniature exhalations,
Wind stirs in the weeds, a dog barks, the shadows stretch and seep out.

Therefore, when the Great Mouth with its two tongues of water and ash
Shall say, Suffer the darkness,
Suffer the darkness to come unto you,
                    suffer its singsong,
And you will abide,
Listen to what the words spell, listen and sing the song.

LITTLEFOOT

(2007)

1

It may not be written in any book, but it is written—
You can't go back,
                    you can't repeat the unrepeatable.
No matter how fast you drive, or how hard the slide show
Of memory flicks and releases,
It's always some other place,
                              some other car in the driveway,
Someone unrecognizable about to open the door.

Nevertheless, like clouds in their nebulous patterns,
We tend to recongregate
                         in the exitless blue
And try to relive our absences.
What else have we got to do,
The children reamplified in a foreign country,
The wife retired,
                   the farm like a nesting fowl and far away?

Whatever it was I had to say, I've said it.
Time to pull up the tie stakes.
I remember the way the mimosa tree
                                    buttered the shade
Outside the basement bedroom, soaked in its yellow bristles.
I'll feed on that for a day or two.
I remember the way the hemlock hedge
                                      burned in the side light.

Time to pull up the tie stakes.
Time to repoint the brickwork and leave it all to the weather.
Time to forget the lost eyelids,
                                        the poison machine,
Time to retime the timer.
One's friends lie in nursing homes,
                                        their bones broken, their hearts askew.
Time to retrench and retool.

We're not here a lot longer than we are here, for sure.
Unlike coal, for instance, or star clots.
                                        Or so we think.
And thus it behooves us all to windrow affection, and spare,
And not be negligent.
So that our hearts end up like diamonds, and not roots.
So that our disregard evaporates
                                        as a part of speech.

Cloud wisps, and wisps of clouds,
                                        nine o'clock, a little mare's tail sky
Which night chill sucks up.
Sundown. Pink hoofprints above the Blue Ridge,
                                        soft hoofprints.
If this were the end of it, if this were the end of everything,
How easily one could fold
Into the lapping and overlapping of darkness.
                                        And then the dark after that.

Saturday's hard-boiled, easy to crack.

Sunday is otherwise,

Amorphous and water-plugged.
Sunday's the poem without people, all disappeared
Before the shutter is snapped.
Rainy vistas, wet-windowed boulevards, empty entrances.
Across the bridge, dissolute, one-armed,
Monday stares through the viewfinder,

a black hood over its head.

❧

When the rains blow, and the hurricane flies,

nobody has the right box

To fit the arisen in.
Out of the sopped earth, out of dank bones,
They seep in their watery strings

wherever the water goes.

Who knows when their wings will dry out, who knows their next knot?

❧

In the affinity is the affection,

in the affection everything else

That matters, wind in the trees,
The silence above the wind, cloud-flat October sky,
And the silence above that.

The leaves of the maple tree,

scattered like Post-it notes

Across the lawn with messages we'll never understand,
Burn in their inarticulation,

As we in ours,
red fire, yellow fire.

It's all music, the master said, being much more than half right,
The disappearance of things
Adding the balance,
dark serenity of acceptance
Moving as water moves, inside itself and outside itself.

Compassion and cold comfort—
take one and let the other lie,
Remembering how the currents of the Adige
Shattered in sunlight,
Translucent on the near side,
spun gold on the other.

Which heaven's the higher,
the one down here or the one up there?
Which blue is a bluer blue?
Bereft of meaning, the moon should know,
the silent, gossip-reflecting full moon.
But she doesn't, and no one descends to speak for her.
Time in its two worlds. No choice.

2

I am the sign, I am the letter.
I am the language that cannot be come to terms with.
I will go to my resting place
and will not be born again.

I am what is scattered and cannot be gathered up.
I am small, I am silence,
                                        I am what is not found.

3

Moon like a hard drive
                                        just over the understory
Freckling my neighbor's backyard,
Nightscreen unscrolling along the River of Heaven,
Celestial shorthand
Unasked for and undeletable
In time-lapse upon the early November skybook.

These are our last instructions,
                                        of which we understand nothing.
The road map is there, the password,
                                        neither of which we understand.
They boil on our tongues like waterflies.
They cling to our fingers,
                                        they settle along our still eyelids
As though we would succor them,
As though we could understand their wing-buzz and small teeth.

Wherever I've gone, the Holston River has stayed next to me,
Like a dream escaping
                                        some time-flattened orifice
Once open in childhood, migrating now like a road
I've walked on unknowingly,
                                        pink and oblivious,

Attended by fish and paving stones,
The bottom breaks like mountains it slithers out of, tongued and chilled.

The river is negative time,
                                        always undoing itself,
Always behind where it once had been.
Memory's like that,
Current too deep, current too shallow,
Erasing and reinventing itself while the world
Stands still beside it just so,
                                        not too short, not too tall.

There's no uncertainty about it, negative time,
No numbering.
            Like wind when it stops, like clouds that are here then not here,
It is the pure presence of absence.
November's last leaves fall down to it,
The angels, their wings remodeled beneath their raincoats,
Live in it,
            our lives repeat it, skipped heartbeats, clocks with one hand.

Out of the sallows and slick traces of Southwest Virginia,
From Saltville and Gate City, from Church Hill and New Hope,
The river remainders itself
                                        and rises again
Out of its own depletion.
How little we know it, how little we really remember it.
How like our own blood it powers on,
                                                    out of sight, out of mind.

Outside of the church, no salvation,
St. Cyprian says.
Outside of nature, no transformation, I say,
                                        no hope of return.
Like us, November doesn't know this,
Leaf ends curled up like untanned leather,
                              grass edges bleared back from emerald ease,
Light-loss diaphanous in the bare-backed and blitherless trees.

....

4

Well, the wings of time pass, the black wings,
And the light is not adumbrated,
                                  or dampened down—
Like splendor, there is no end to it
Inside the imagination,
                           then inside of that,
Wind-beat, light of light, and even into the darkness.

....

5

November noon mist, gold coins of leaves
Glittering through it as though refracted by sunlight
Through rain shower,
                          radiant clusters, radiant change,

Mountains rehollowed and blotted out,
Car lights continuous rosary beads
                                    both ways on the Interstate,
Evening already released out over the dark Atlantic.

These are the still days,
stillness being the metaphor
Out of which every grain is revealed
and is identified.
Finger me, Lord, and separate me to what I am.

In nature there is no past or future,
no pronouns, no verbs.
Old knowledge, Slick, old deadlights.
Still, the tongue does not know this, the half-lit and dumb tongue—

Precision of frogs and grasses,
precision of words,
Each singular, each distinct,
The tongue tries to freeze-frame them as they are,
and offer them to us.

Now is precise but undefinable,
now is nonverbal,
No matter how hard we work it out.
Nuthatch or *narwhal*,
like petals, words drift in the air.

Calamities covet us, wild grass will cover our bodies,
We read in the Book of Poverty.
Deliver us, blessed immaculata,
adorn our affections.

Language is luckless and limitless,
as nature is.

But nature is not sincere, nor is it insincere—
The language of landscape is mute and immaculate.

First character of the celestial alphabet, the full moon,
Is a period, and that is that.
No language above to aid us,
                                        no word to the wise.

I leave a blank for what I don't know,
                                        four syllables, ____________________,
And what I will never know.
Thrones, and assisting angels, this is a comforting.

In Kingsport, looking across the valley toward Moccasin Gap
From Chestnut Ridge,
                                the winter-waxed trees
Are twiggy and long-fingery, fretting the woods-wind,

Whose songs, ghost songs, wind-lyrics from sixty years ago,
Float back and exhale—
                                I will twine with my mingles of raven black hair.
Will you miss me when I'm gone?

6

The winter leaves crumble between my hands,
                                                        December leaves.
How is it we can't accept this, that all trees were holy once,
That all light is altar light,

And floods us, day by day, and bids us, the air sheet lightning around us,
To sit still and say nothing,
                    here under the latches of Paradise?

7

Sunset, line like a long tongue-lick above the Blue Ridge,
Mock orange, then tangerine, then blush.
                                        How ordinary, dog,
The rush-hour car lights down Locust Avenue like quartz crystals,
Backlit and foraging forth.
Streetlights gather the darkness to them,
Compassion an afterthought,
                                mercy no thought at all.

Moon down, darkness fixed and unmoving,
Stars bobbing like water lights,
                                three weeks to the winter solstice,
Wind drift and tack from the north,
Night like a distance one could row on,
Whose depths are an afterlife
                                almost, whose sea is remembered
As half-crossed, its wave spray like wind dust.

Good luck bamboo in three shoots in high-glaze south German brown
  vase,
Front yard like a windowpane
Into the anteroom of all things untouchable,
Cycladic ghost mask,
                            little Egyptian and Zuni overseers,

Choctaw and pre-Columbian artifacts arranged
Against the ruinous dark waters
outside the horizon.

Time is your mother in a blue dress.

When was it I first heard of the blank,
The salve of nothingness,
all its engendering attitude?
When was it I felt the liquid of absolution
And all its attendant emptiness
For the first time, and what it might mean?
Not young, I'd have to say,
remembering not one thing about either of them.

How early, however, I learned of their opposites.
Muscadines plump in their plenitude,
Lake waters lowing at night under frog call,
night wind in leaf-locked trees,
Splash of the fishing lure, whisper of paddle blade and canoe,
Clouds like slow-moving cattle
Across the tiny and synchronized tip of the moon.

To walk up the Y-shaped hill
from the commissary
(This was a government town)
In summer under the hardwoods and conifers
Was to know the extension of things,
the deep weight of the endlessness

Of childhood, deep, invisible weight,
Lake-sound and lake-song in high hum, the future in links and chains.

To lie under lake-wind in August,
under mountain laurel
And blue-green North Carolina sky,
Lunch over, campfire smoke-ends
drifting out over water glints,
Was something like nothingness, perhaps, and its caress,
Crusader knights in their white tunics
and red crosses
Like ghosts through the trees, but not enough.

Precious memories, how they linger,
how they ever flood my soul,
In the stillness of the midnight,
precious, sacred scenes unfold.

8

Good luck is a locked door,
but the key's around somewhere.
Meanwhile, half-hidden under the thick staircase of memory,
One hears the footsteps go up and the footsteps go down.

As water mirrors the moon, the earth mirrors heaven,
Where things without shadows have shadows.
A lifetime isn't too much to pay
for such a reflection.

9

Three years, the story goes, it took the great ship to appear
In silhouette from the shadows
hanging above Lake Garda
And dock at the small port of Riva,
The Hunter Gracchus carried upon a bier by two men
In black tunics with silver buttons
Up to a back room in the mayor's office
until it was time to return onboard

And circle the waters of the world.
Unable to set down on land,
unable to leave this world,
The story goes on, because of a wrong turn of the tiller
This side of the other shore,
Some inattention,
The great ship and the great body,
like lost love, languish and lip the earth,

Received sporadically, recognized everywhere,
The ship with its infinitely high masts,
its sails in dark folds,
Cobalt and undulant rocking of lake swells and waves,
Long runners and smooth slatch of the seas,
Creek hiss and pond sway,
Landfall and landrise
like Compostela at land's end.

There is no end to longing.
There is no end to what touch sustains us,
winter woods

Deep in their brown study and torqued limbs,
Fish-scale grey of January sky,
Absence of saints on Sunday morning streets,
                                        the dark ship,
Dead leaves on the water, the muddy Rivanna and its muddy sides.

We all owe everything to those who preceded us,
Who, by the lightness of their footsteps,
Tap-danced our stories out, our techniques,
                                        who allowed us to say
Whatever it was we had to say.
God rest them all in their long robes and vanishing shoes.
God grant that our figures be elegant,
                                        our footwork worthy.

Faith is a thing unfathomable,
Though it lisp at our fingertips,
                              though it wash our hands.
There is no body like the body of light,
                                        but who will attain it?
Not us in our body bags,
Dark over dark, not us,
                    though love move the stars and set them to one side.

Sunlight like I beams through S. Zeno's west-facing doors,
As though one could walk there,
                              and up to the terraces
And gold lawns of the Queen of Heaven.
I remember the lake outside of town where the sun was going down.

I remember the figures on the doors,
                                                            and the nails that held them there.

The needle, though it has clothed many, remains naked,
The proverb goes.
                                    So with the spirit,
Silver as is the air silver, color of sunlight.
And stitches outside the body a garment of mist,
Tensile, invisible, unmovable, unceasing.

....

10

The Holston, past Rotherwood,
                                                      clear white and powder white,
The hills dark jade and light jade,
All of it flowing southwest
                                              against the wind and the wind noise,

Summer enfrescoed in stop-time
                                                      alongside the Cumberlands,
Leo and Virgo slow as a cylinder turn overhead,
Wind in the trees, wind on the water.

....

11

Like clouds, once gone in their long drift,
                                                                  there's no coming back—
And like the wind that moves them, we stop
Wherever we please, or wherever we come to be,

Each one in his proper place,
                                        not too near, not too far
From *That's okay* and *No one was ever interested enough.*

How many years have slipped through our hands?
At least as many as all the constellations we still can identify.
The quarter moon, like a light skiff,
                                        floats out of the mist-remnants
Of last night's hard rain.
It, too, will slip through our fingers
                                        with no ripple, without us in it.

How is it it's taken me almost a lifetime to come to the fact
That heaven and earth have no favorites
                                        in either extreme?
Bits of us set out, at one time or another, in both directions,
Sleeping fitfully, heads on our fists,
Now close together and warm, now cold in the south sky.

Each one arrives in his own fashion,
                                        each one with his birthmark
Beginning to take shape and shine out
And lead forth like a lead lamp.
Look for us in the black spaces, somewhere in the outer dark.
Look for us under the dead grass
                                        in winter, elsewhere, self-satisfied, apart.

A good writer is like a wind over meadow grass.
He bends the words to his will,
But is invisible everywhere.
Lament is strong in the bare places.
Among the winter trees, his words are fixed to music.

Or so we flatter ourselves,
                                        sunset cloud tufts briquettes
Going ash in the ash-going sky.
We never look hard enough.
The grasses go back and forth, up and down, for thousands of miles,
But we don't look hard enough.

✻

Every other building a church,
Each side of the road,
                                    Orebank half a mile long
Under the hill until the last curve
Down to the highway, left to Kingsport, right to Bristol,
East toward the rising sun, west toward home.

"Through the years of dust and sand," Tao-chi lamented,
Meaning his worldly ambitions
                                                —his "single unworthy thought"
That set him adrift on the floating world—
                                                            his old age
Just recompense for what was not found,
Awaiting the great wash, a "final crash of thunder."

For half a lifetime, and more,
                                            his days were the days of an ant,
His life, he thought, no longer than that of an insect
Going north on land,
                                    going south on the raw rivers,
His last painting a single narcissus plant, his thoughts,
He wrote down, still wandering "beyond the boundless shores."

12

Water, apparently, is incomprehensible
At its beginning and at its end,
                                        nothing into nothing,
And in between it's unsizable.
Certainly childhood water's that way,
The rivers coming from nowhere and going nowhere,
The lakes with no stopping place.
The waters of childhood are unimaginable.
The French Broad and Little Pigeon Rivers, the Holston,
Hiwassee and Cherokee Lakes,
                                        Pickwick and Indian Path.
Water's immeasurable.

The heart is immeasurable,
                                        and memory too.
Such little boxes to keep them in.
Like blue herons in heaven's field, they lift their long legs
Silently, and very slow,
In the ponds and back eddies they stalk through and rise from,
Air-colored in the sky-colored air.
How like the two of them to resettle then,
                                        one hunting, one perched above.
Memory is a lonely observer,
                                        the heart has thin legs.
They live in an infinite otherness, on dark snags,
In waters the color that they are,
                                        and air is, the hard, endless air.

Snow, then sleet over snow, then snow again,
                                        the footprints still firm
Into the dark beyond the light's fall.
Whiter inside the darkness to the south than the north.

Whatever has been will be again
                                in the mind, in the world's flow,
Invisible armies outside the windows in rank,
Footprints continuing into the vestibules of the end.

❧

The light that shines forth from the emptiness does not sink,
They'd have you believe.
                          As well as whatever is next to it,
They'd also have you believe.
Philosopher, they are not able, philosopher.
And her begot him, think that.

❧

It's Groundhog Day, and sunlight is everywhere. Thank God.
Winter is such a comforting
                            with its sleet and icy dreams.
Shadows abound, and raw twigs,
The sharp edge of the absolute still snug in its loamy bed,
The template of its wings like shadows across the grass.

What poverty the heat of noon is,
And how we embrace it hard in our dutiful duds.
Short February.
How we will miss you and the actual world,
                                        the singular,
The frozen composition that pentimentos our sorrow.

Still, for the time being, we have the sunlight that eats away
At our joy,
                    and still give thanks for that.
We try to count up the buttons on its golden coat,
But our eyes are unworthy.
We offer both our hands,
                                        but they are unworthy too.

And so we remain transfixed
                                              —the flowers from Delos
Unpurpled and stiff in their tarnished and silver bowl—
By sunlight,
Hoping the darkness will clear things up,
Hoping that what its handkerchief uncovers is what we get.

Just east of midnight,
                                    the north sky scrolls from right to left,
A dark player piano.
No stopping the music, east to west,
                                                  no stopping it.

13

The small lights wander among the vacant trees like ghosts,
Whose roots have no voice in their deep sleep,
These lights that have no warmth in their drugged walk,
                                                              damp flames and feckless.

The stars drift like cold fires through the watery roots of heaven,
These stars that are floating plants.

The small lights are not like that,
but once were, I guess, light as a shadow.

What bodies will gather the lights in,
or the stars in?
What waters will float their anxious rest?
Altar of darkness, altar of light, which tide will take them in?

14

The great mouth of the west hangs open,
mountain incisors beginning to bite
Into the pink flesh of the sundown.
The end of another day
in this floating dream of a life.
Renown is a mouthful, here and there.

Rivers and mountains glide through my blood.
Cold pillow, bittersweet years.
In the near distance, a plane's drone
rattles the windows.
Clear night. Wind like a predator
in the sharp grass of the past.

I find it much simpler now to see
the other side of my own death.
It wasn't always that way,
When the rivers were rivers and mountains were mountains.
Now, when the mouth closes,
the wind goes out of everything.

Fame for a hundred years
                                        is merely an afterlife,
And no friend of ours.
Better to watch the rain fall in the branches of winter trees.
Better to have your mail sent
To someone else in another town,
                                                    where frost is whiter than moonlight.

Horses, black horses:
                                    Midnight, Five Minutes to Midnight.
Rider up, the sparks from their hooves like stars, like spiked stars.
This is a metaphor for failure,
This is the Rest of It, the beautiful horse, black horse.
Midnight. Dark horse, dark rider.

I love the lethargy of the single cloud,
                                                    the stillness of the sky
On winter afternoons, late on winter afternoons,
A little fan of light on the tips of the white pines.

I love the winter light, so thin, so unbuttery,
Transparent as plastic wrap
Clinging so effortlessly
                                        to whatever it skins over.

—The language of nature, we know, is mathematics.
The language of landscape is language,
Metaphor, metaphor, metaphor,
                                                all down the line.

The sweet-breath baby light of a winter afternoon,
Boy-light, half-covered in blue,
                                        almost invisible as breath,
So still in the flower beds, so pale.

Four days till the full moon,
                                    light like a new skin on the dark
Quarter, like light unborrowed, hard,
                                             black hole with its golden floor.

Who knows the happiness of fish,
                                           their wind-raising, ordinary subtleties?
Describing the indescribable,
Image into idea,
                  the transmission of the spirit,
It cannot be done.

The Chinese principle, *breath-resonance-life-motion*,
Engenders, it was believed.
As does the bone method of brushwork,
Creating structure
                  in poems as well as pictures.

Plotting in paint, place in poetry,
Completes composition,
                           the bedrock of spiritual values.
Competent, *marvelous*, and *divine*
Were the three degrees of accomplishment.
                                                   And still, it cannot be done.

Image resists all transmutation.
All art is meta-art, and has its own satisfactions.
But it's not divine,
                    as image is,
Untouchable, untransmutable,
                    wholly magic.

Midnight Special, turn your ever-loving light on me.

15

You still love the ones you loved
                    back when you loved them—books,
Records, and people.
Nothing much changes in the glittering rooms of the heart,
Only the dark spaces half-reclaimed.
                    And then not much,
An image, a line. Sometimes a song.

Car doors slam, and slam again, next door.
Snow nibbles away at the edges of the dark ground.
The sudden memory of fur coats,
                    erotic and pungent,
On college girls in the backseats of cars, at Christmas,
Bourgeois America, the middle 1950s,
                    Appalachia downtown.

And where were we going? Nowhere.
Someone's house, the club, a movie?
                    See the pyramids along the Nile,

WKPT, *I'm itching like a man on a fuzzy tree.*
It didn't matter.
Martin Karant was spinning them out,
                                        and the fur was so soft.

....

16

March is our master, the louche month we cannot control.
It passes like a river over us
—Cold current, warm spot—
                                        whose destination is always downstream,
Out of sight.
White water, easy water,
                                        March is a river over us.

Snow slam and sun burst,
                                        dead grass like peroxided hair
Unkempt among scattershot.
In Knoxville, across the street from James Agee's ex-house,
A small tree in full blossom,
Everything else still underground,
                                        river dark overhead.

I used to live here myself
                                        some sixty-five years ago.
Not here, precisely, but in the town,
Across town,
In a small house off the Kingston Pike,
No blossoming fruit limbs, no stripped, deciduous trees.

Love of the lack of love is still love
                                        wherever you find it,

I once heard an old man say,
In March, when the wind was westerly
and the white clouds white as petals.
In March, in a vacant lot
On Chambliss Avenue, off the Kingston Pike.
And he was right.

I think I'm going to take my time,
life is too short
For immortality and its attendant disregards.
I have enough memories now for any weather,
Either here or there.
I'll take my time.
Tomorrow's not what I'm looking forward to, or the next day.
My home isn't here, but I doubt that it's there either—
Empty and full have the same glass,
though neither shows you the way.

Born again by water into the life of the spirit,
but not into the Life,
Rivers and lakes were my bread and wine,
Creeks were my transubstantiation.
And everything's holy by now,
Vole crawl and raven flyby,
All of the little incidents that sprinkle across the earth.

Easy enough to say,
but hard to live by and palliate.
Camus said that life is the search for the way back

To the few great simple truths
We knew at the beginning.
Out of the water, out to the cold air, that seems about right.

The moon, over Susan's house,
                                        gobba a ponente,
Heading west toward the western reaches.
Snow-strikes streak my hair.
                                        We are all leaves in the current.

17

Leaning on Jesus, leaning on Jesus,
                                        leaning on the everlasting love.
That's a tough lean, Hernando,
When all the hackles of spring are raised,
                                        and its teeth glint
Like flint points in the sunshine,
Bright snarls from the underground.
Not much to lean on wherever you look,
                                        above or below.

I remember my father in the spring,
                                        who leaned on no one
And nothing, inspecting the rose plants
And the crusty, winter-warped mulch beds,
The blue distances over his back, over Cumberland Gap,
Opening like a great eye,
Jesus, he'd always say, Jesus, it's gone and done it again.

In Giorgio Morandi's bedroom and studio, it was always spring.
He would say, "Each time we begin,
we think we have understood,
That we have all the answers.
But it turns out we're just starting over again from the beginning."
Some bottles, a bed, and three tables,
The flowers abounding in little rectangles
all over the walls.

Meanwhile, in New York City,
Branch limbs scrubbed bare by winter;
tiny fuses bumped at each end
Wait for Persephone's match.

Spring freeze, and tulips cover their heads
with iridescent hands;
Robins head for the hedges.
Even the insects back down
And cower inside their hiding holes.
Only the leaves seem cool, the new leaves,
Just butting their arrowed heads into the unforgiving blue.
How many lives these little ones lead.
I wish that one of them were mine.

A recluse should avoid the absolute,
and its hills.
Master of words, Lord of signs, you've left me, where are you?

Down by the muddy waters, feeding the brilliant birds?
Half-returned, half still going away?
Now that you've gone,
                                        I remember we've had an appointment there for years.
Don't move, I'm on my way.

It's quiet, no words, no words.
Is this just a silence, or just the start of the end?
Show yourself, Lord,
                                        Master of What Is About to Be.
Stars turn brown in the river.
We share no happiness here—
Step out of the Out,
                                        uncover your tongue and give me the protocol.

I'm starting to feel like an old man
                                                        alone in a small boat
In a snowfall of blossoms,
Only the south wind for company,
Drifting downriver, the beautiful costumes of spring
Approaching me down the runway
                                                        of all I've ever wished for.

Voices from long ago floating across the water.
How to account for
                                        my single obsession about the past?
How to account for
                                        these blossoms as white as an autumn frost?
Dust of the future baptizing our faithless foreheads.
Alone in a small boat, released in a snowfall of blossoms.

Don't forget me little darling when they lay me down to die.
Just this one wish little darling that I pray.
As you linger there in sadness you are thinking of the past,
Let your teardrops kiss the flowers on my grave.

18

It's been, say, five years since I've been back here at this hour,
Evening starting its light-curling plane
under the clouds,
The east-shrugged, flamingo clouds,
Everything different now, and everything just the same.
Except the leaves and birds,
great-grandchildren, and great-great.

It's not tomorrow I'm looking forward to, it's yesterday,
Or, better yet, the day before that.
The wind keeps gossiping in both my ears for nothing.
I can't go back there,
No matter how juicy the stories are,
no matter how true, or untrue.

We don't know much, really, but we do know some things.
We know the people we learned from,
and know what we learned.
We have to be humble about that—
I know what I got, and I know where I got it from,
Their names inscribed in my Book of Light.

All the while we thought we were writing for the angels,
And find, after all these years,
Our lines were written in black ink on the midnight sky,
Messages for the wind,
                    a flutter of billets-doux
From one dark heart to the next.

Who knew it would take so many years to realize
—Seventy years—that everything's light—
The day in its disappearing, the night sky in its distance, false dawn,
The waters that rise beneath the earth,
Bat wings and shadow pools,
                    that all things come from splendor?

The cardinal in his fiery caul,
The year's first dandelion globe,
                    ash-grey on the ash-green lawn,
Dear tulip leaves, color of carp bellies, wisteria drools
Withered and drained dry—
All light in the gathering darkness,
                    a brilliance itself which is set to come.

The cloud poets of ancient China
Saw what they saw and recorded it,
                    diviners of what wasn't there,
Prestidigitators of nothingness.
                    Let me be one of them.

Sun over plum-colored leaf planes,
                                        shadows at ease in the east-going ivy.
A little wind, like a falling wind,
Tickles the planes, and they rise and fall.
Mid-May in the city garden,
                                    sunlight in designated spaces
Among the buildings, golden for us, dun-dust next door,
The sun like the Green Knight's head,
Rolling in slow motion toward its distant and dark corner,
Bright drops on the bright green hedge,
                                            black on the black borders.

In an opposite corner, splotches of sun and shade,
Like birthmarks all of us have,
Some on our faces, some on our hearts,
                                            all of them afterprints of our ruin,
Through which we step each morning
Gingerly, some of us going east, some of us going west.

19

This is the bird hour, peony blossoms falling bigger than wren hearts
On the cutting border's railroad ties,
Sparrows and other feathery things
Homing from one hedge to the next,
                                          late May, gnat-floating evening.

Is love stronger than unlove?
                                    Only the unloved know.
And the mockingbird, whose heart is cloned and colorless.

And who's this tiny chirper,
lost in the loose leaves of the weeping cherry tree?
His song is not more than three feet off the ground, and singular,
And going nowhere.
Listen. It sounds a lot like you, hermano.
It sounds like me.

20

Don't sew the skins of land and sea animals
into the same garment.
Over each grave, build a wooden house.
Burn children's toys to bring good weather.

And so on, the legends say.
Herons in mid-June stand up to their knees
In creek water, their wings like vinyl siding against their sides.
Next month they'll do the same thing.

Outside the cycle of seasons,
our lives appear meaningless,
No lilacs, no horse in the field, no heart-hurt, no sleeve:
Where time is constant and circular, all ends must meet.

White clouds now dissipating in evening's turnaround,
No sound but the sound of no sound,
late sunlight falling on grass.

A little knowledge of landscape whets isolation.
This is a country of water,
                                        of water and rigid trees
That flank it and fall beneath its weight.
They lie like stricken ministers, grey and unredeemed.
The weight of water's unbearable,
                                                    and passes no judgment.
Side by side they lie, in intricate separation.

This is a country of deep inclemency, of strict
Self-immolation and strict return.
This is the way of the absolute,
                                                dead grass and waste
Of water, clouds where it all begins, clouds where it ends,
Candle-point upshoots on all the upstart evergreens,
Sun behind west ridge,
                                    no moon to sickle and shine through.

Much is unknown up here,
                                        much more still left to be unexplained.
Under the pines there's not much to see,
White clouds and grey clouds,
The shadows they carry inside themselves unto the world's end.
That sort of business. It's hard.

There are fourteen cliff swallow round-mouthed mud nests
                                                                                    under the roof
Of the old barn house.
I stand and watch birds flying frantically after the rain,
Gold-breasted in the suddenly appearing sunlight.
Out of each hole a beak's unlevered.

Wang Wei had something to say about the unknowing:
Unable to throw off my remnant habits
I find the world has come to know me for them
My name and style—these they have right
But this heart of mine they still do not know.

Morning, a small rain on the cabin,
                                        cloud tears like blown fire smoke
Under the slow overcast.
Nothing to do but watch the larch boughs,
Color, almost, of my shirt,
                              flourish their crystal studs.

What is the span of one's life?
How do you measure it
                         before it goes back to formlessness?
This is of some note to the white-haired.
Cubits or years, missed opportunities,
                                        the minor, self-satisfied
Successes that came, as all things must, down to nothing,
The time it took to get there?

There is a resignation in all things deep as dirt,
A knowledge that no one lacks,
A force that finds its way
                          to the tip of every thing.
There is a serenity
Under our layers that rocks like a cradle of calm waters.
There is a freshness that we abide.

Deer huddle like cattle around the salt block,
                                        then burst like flames in the air.
The white clouds slide from the south
Like an edge of ice.
The swallows harangue and arabesque
Over the lawn and lilac rim of the late lilacs,
Then dwindle against the dark green of the evergreens.

Last bird call, sun disappearing
                                        under the right edge of things.
All that I know goes with it,
Isolate, like a body pulled down by weights
                                        into the depths.

21

At seventy, it's always evening,
                                        light diluted,
Breeze like a limp hand
Just stirring the long-haired grasses, then letting them be.
The dark decade, beginning its long descent
                                        out over the blank Atlantic,
Against the wind, inexorable,
The light dissolving like distance in the evergreens.
Even the clouds find a place to rest.

And that's the way it should be,
Swallows swarming like gnats
                                        in the gnat-infested air,

Tree shadows lying like limbed logs across the meadow,
Slowly sinking into the hill's shadow that stalks them.
Deer raise their white flags and leave the field,
The sapsucker leaves her nest
In the barn house wall,
                                        and everything moves toward its self-appointed end.

I keep on thinking,
                                        If I sit here for long enough,
A line, one true line,
Will rise like some miraculous fish to the surface,
Brilliant and lithe in the late sunlight,
And offer itself into my hands.
I keep thinking that as the weeks go by,
                                                            and the waters never change.
I keep thinking that as the sun goes down and the birds fly home.

The sky is cloudless, the meadow seems like a vast plain
Without dust,
                                the Chinese vocabulary of the grasses
Shining like water wherever I dip my dark brush.
I have loved, and been loved in return, by solitude.
Back fifty feet in the pines,
All color relents,
And the quietness there, the stern quietness,
                                                                    is hard as stone.

At my age, memories scatter like rain
                                                        when one sits still, first day of summer,

The noise of the world

over a hundred miles away,

Sun sinking, but not as soon as yesterday, birds flown.

What does one do when you find out your thoughts

are the thoughts of everyone else?

Wait for a monk to come down
From his hill,
Look hard for the people whose lives you cannot explain,
Walk slowly under the shagbark trees?
I can't know, but as one ages

it comes as a matter of some reflection.

There are worse desolations, of course.

Abandoned cities, for one thing,

The thousand miles that stretch out
From one image to the next.
We all hum our own sad songs.
Make yours your favorite, and don't look
At the new grass, at the summer sun

in its dangling descent.

Light falls on the deer and the jump weed,
Light out my west window,

June light, the Sundown Special.

We know where she's headed—

your seat is used, but reserved.

This is the entry of evening light.
Where I am, it seems, it's always just before sunset.
At least nowadays,
Even in memory—
                                        Lake Garda and Mykonos,
Venice, of course, and every place one can stand
                                                                                upon the abiding earth.
Local color still deep in the heart.
O my, as I said one time, I love to see that evening sun go down.

All the little black bugs have left the dandelions,
The robins have gone.
Even the clouds have changed
                                                        to the color of 2% milk.
Out the north window, the grasses stand bright and erect as acolytes.
I remember the way they stood at Desenzano, like that,
Some forty-five years ago,
Though I didn't pay much attention then,
                                                        twenty-three, on my way to anywhere else.

We're always, apparently, on our way to anywhere else,
And miss what we're here for,
                                                        the objects we never realize
Will constitute our desire,
The outtakes and throwaways of the natural world.
The movement of creek water at dusk,
The slippage and slow disappearance of what we love
Into the silence of here-and-now
                                                            that will survive us, and call back.

The barn house is upside down in the motionless pond.
And pine trees.
Two ducks land suddenly
And everything's carried away in blurred, colorful pieces.

22

The summer passing of the black-sailed familiar,
The ghost bier of the Hunter Gracchus,
myth-driven, ill at ease,
Two-masted and low, is now at hand.
A wrong turn, a lack of attention,
a lack, it seems, of love,
Has set its last course.
Like the four seasons, it wheels on the rings of air forever.

When the body is old, the heart becomes older still.

23

One needs no Paradise when the rain falls,
and clouds are not scattered by the wind.
No one's around, the grasses bend at their belt buckles,
Boughs droop and the rain keeps coming down.
There is an edgy serenity in solitude,
when the rain falls and the wind stops,
The perpetual presence of absence, where all things are still.

Rain over everything like sunlight,
out of the clouds.

Shining in strings and beads, a giant hush,
Like tongues in the afterlife.
Clouds like the smoky aftereffect of forest fires,
High-drift and hang.
                                        Out of the stillness, a small splendor.

The line between heaven and earth is a grass blade,
                                                                        a light green and hard to walk.

Bigfoot, the north wind, slaps through the trees
Looking for something that we can't know,
                                                                    or even, perhaps, have heard of,
Pushing the boughs aside,
                                                always gone, just out of sight.
Sunlight fills in his footprints.

After the answer, there's always another question,
Even the last one.
                                        At least we have that to count on.
I am an image picker.
I like the ripe ones,
                                        the ones at the ends of the listing limbs.

To know one's self is the final yes, of course.
                                                                        The no,
However, is right behind it, and just as final.
How easy to lose oneself in the orchard,
                                                                    this tree and that,
Everything shiny, everything slick and close to hand.

❧

The evening prepares for the invisible,
                                        the absence of itself.
Clouds defuse. White cat on the fence pole
Haunched on her throne.
                              Bird feathers glued to the window glass
Where finch attempted his noon flight through the visible.
Better to keep your head down,
                                   asleep in the darkening trees.
Nothing can stop it. One sweep of its cape and it's gone.

❧

The morning is almost silent and cannot declare itself.
Therefore, I say unto it,
                              you are the never-boring miracle
Of sunlight and scrappy cloud,
The absence of rain when rain is absent,
                                          as it is
This morning, green with its wonderment,
Last night's hard frost a wet memory
Scattered in bits and glitzy pieces
                                    deep in the grass.

The ten horses of the field are like
                                    the cities of the plain,
A necessary moment
Of everything that is, and was, and will be again,
Standing in succulence in the brevity of time.
The sunlight grows big,
                              immensity
Of noon approaching, its spurs flashing and its saber on fire.
The green backs off a bit, and mumbles. And so do we.

I have nothing to say. I am a recording machine,
                                        a listening device.
What I hear is what I will tell you.

I am the sluice of dead scrolls and songs,
                                        I am the tongue of what exists,
Whose secrets are whispered and not heard.
Listen to me, listen to what's the nothing I have to say.

The shadows of the floating world
                                        huddle beneath their objects.
Slowly, like hands on a massive clock,
They soon will begin their crawl and creep
                                        to bring us back
Tick-tock in their black sack, tick-tock in their soft black sack.

Lord of the sunlight,
                                        Lord of the leftover, Lord of the yet-to-do,
Handle my heaven-lack, hold my hand.

24

The little birds are honing their beaks on the chopping block stump.
The clouds have gathered for their convention
                                        from deep out in the dark Pacific.
They clear their throats and speak out.

Everything stills and listens,
even the little birds
With their sharp beaks and sharp claws,
clinging inside the tamaracks
Until the storm passes and the cloud bodies adjourn.

That's when the big birds come,
with their sweeping wings and dangling legs,
Their eyes ajar, and the lightning sparks from their keening claws.
The poppies along the near hill glisten like small fires,
Pink and orange and damp red.
Behind the glass window, we hear the swoosh of the giant wings,
And listen hard for the next pass,
but they don't come back.

It's not such a poverty, we think,
to live in a metaphysical world.
Thus we become poor, and spurn the riches of the earth.
Such nonsense.
The crow flies with his beak open,
emitting a raucous cry.
The yearling horses stand in the field,
up to their knees in the new grass.
This is the first world we live in, there is no second.

The mind's the affliction,
asleep for a hundred years,
Nothing to wake it but memory,
The deep blank of memory,
rivers and hills, the morning sun,

Simple things,

the body moving, not much, but moving.

Orpheus walked, the poets say, down to the black river.
Nobody recognized him,
Of course, and the boat came,
the gondola with its singular oarsman,
And the crowd got in, a thousand souls,
So light that the boat drew no water, not even a half inch.
On the other side, the one paved road, and they took it.

Afterward, echoes of the great song webbed in their ears,
They took the same road back to the waiting gondola,
The two of them,
the first to have ever returned to the soot-free shore.
The oarsman's stroke never faltered, and he hummed the song
He had caught the faint edges of
from the distant, marble halls.
It won't work, he thought to himself, it won't work. And it didn't.

Clouds, like the hills of heaven,
Are nowhere in evidence tonight.
Sundown, an empty sky.
Except for the quarter moon, like a sail with no ship,
And no home port to come to.
Its world is without end.

The smallest cloud I've ever seen
floats like a white midge
Over the western ridgeline,
Then vanishes in the wind and the dying sunlight.
How unremarkable,
though no moon comes to shine on its going out.
And nothing arrives to take its place.
Forlorn evening, that makes me want to sit here forever, and then some.
I'll likely meet it again, a thousand years from now,
When it rises up through my bedroom,
buzzing against the windowpane.

We are the generations of the soil,
it is our cloak and put-on.
Somnambulistas of sore intent,
Barefoot or full-shod, it is our destination,
our Compostela.
We rub its rock for luck, and slip inside to get warm,
As though, like our grandfathers before us,
we lie down in our own hearts.

The dogs are barking under the newly planted trees.
When we're transplanted, they'll bark again,
but not for us.

25

I never tire of watching the mists rise
                                        under the mountain
After the rain, like a small detail
On a Chinese screen.
                              The overcast, usually,
Is starting to break, like this evening,
Into its horizontal whites and greys and scrimmed blues.
The mists invisibly come together and dissipate, come
Together and dissipate.
I never get tired of watching this,
As the mists seem to move, then not move.
They don't, of course, but merely disappear.
                                                  Perhaps that's why I like it.
The light is flat and hard and almost nonexistent,
The way our lives appear to us,
                                    then don't, as our inlook shifts.
The horses know nothing of any of this, their heads in the wet grass.
And you know nothing of this, asleep, as you are, in the distant field.
Asleep, as you always will be, in the distant field.

I've always loved, as Auden called them, the chinks in the forest,
(He had the deer peer through them)
Those little slashes and blades
                                    of sunlight cutting streaks
Between the trees, imperceptibly healing over
As sunset pulls back down its high road
And the dark bandages of dusk
                                    are placed on the forest floor.

I love to watch them thrust and retreat,
                                        blazing the trees,
Making a trail so full of light that no one can follow it.

I've looked at this landscape long enough,
                                        time for another book.
One less endless, perhaps, a finitude to count on
And not this enduring verdancy
And chapterless blue.

Sometimes one feels the need of ordinary things,
                                                    flies'
Carcasses along the windowsills, wasps
Resurgent under the eaves,
Dropped feathers, pine chips.
                                    Sometimes you've got to face the dog.

Just after the war (the Second World War), in Kingsport,
I started listening to music,
Local music, east Tennessee and southwest Virginia,
"Rock of Ages," "The Great Speckled Bird," "Life Is Like a Mountain
    Railroad."
Like all children, I just accepted things,
                                        and never puzzled them out.

But "The Great Speckled Bird" was a different lyric.
I never could quite imagine it,
Though the song never failed to move my feet to music.

The great wings shadowed my childhood,
                                        and still do, from time to time,
Darkening some. Then darkening more.

There are songs, we now know, to be sung on the other side of language.
Our tongues are not capable, however,
                                        our eyes can't trill in the dark.

Sometimes I feel I've already told
                                    every story I've ever heard,
Or even once heard about.
God knows, even those are short enough,
And not, in their narratives, deliciously slow and drawn out.
I think, I guess, that immanence isn't a story,
And can't be.
                    In truth, it isn't linguistic at all,
Or metalinguistic either, or any of that.
So stub out your pencil, Pilgrim,
                                    and listen to what the wind repeats
As it starts and erases itself,
Unstoppable storyteller with nothing to say.
I'd like to cry out in its book,
                                especially when it stalls,
On that blank page between one narrative and the next.

In the darkness between the tamaracks,
                                        the light is bundled like little sticks,
Like fatwood for the fire about to start with the evening's match.

26

A word to the wise is a word to the wise,
                                        and isn't sufficient
To anything in this world.
Give me a thing that says nothing.
                                    The wind, for instance,
A wisdom that comes from ten thousand miles to the west.
The trees, for instance, stenographers
Of every sentence it isn't able to utter.
The grass that assembles them all
                                    in its green pages.
The dirt that subtracts each word, syllable after syllable,
Into its dark book, and keeps them there
In ignorance, a blessed ignorance we'll come to know,
A radiant cloud at our mouths,
                                  breath like no other.

Whoever would lay a seed of truth on the table
Had best have his left foot in the stirrup
                                        and both hands
On the saddle, and be good to go.
The wise is without wisdom, and that's as it should be,
So many words, so many.
The truth is another matter, and is, like wisdom,
As speechless as bull clover.
Outside, in the sun, Yugo the dog lies quietly,
His head on his paws.
What he sees he can't say,
                               but he sees what you see and I see.
His look is pure and pitiless and not on the what's-to-come.

The little finches have come and gone
back to their tree.
They lay these words on my eyelids, grains of sleep.
Look for me, witness, look for me.

The one-legged metal-green rooster
Nailed to the wall of the old chicken house
is all that remains
Of Snuffy Bruns, at least in these parts.
A small wooden platform where Beryl, his wife (his sister
As well, it turned out), would feed Marcia,
A pine squirrel she'd almost domesticated,
who would come when called,
Rots on a spruce tree by the outhouse.
He called me Easy Money—I liked that—and made the best knives
You're likely to come across.
Of the two, he died first, and early, much liked by all of us.
And Beryl was taken in downriver
By some family we didn't know well.
They came from Colorado, I think.
I loved his toothless grin and his laid-back ways.
They shipped him there,
Careful truck driver to the end, after the last handshake and air-kiss,
From one big set of mountains to another, in a slow rig.

Tonight the ravens are dominant,
and whoosh the air

With their wings like oars on a black boat.
Who's dead, who's dead, they croak,
                                        going from tree to tree limb,
Five of them, six of them, looking for blood and a place to land.
Not me, I mutter, not me.
Four ducks take off in loose formation like fighter planes.
Not them either, apparently.
                                  So long, ducks, so long,
Ravens resting a moment above the pond,
                                            and then they're gone,
The evening as still and tranquil as the inside of a bone
Till they return. And return they will,
Looking for what's available and warm, and what's not.
We live in their shadow, and under it,
                                        and our days are long.

Don't sit by the side door, waiting for hangnail and radiance,
The past is a yellow dust.

Do what the wind does,
And let your life be heavier: no darkness, no light.

The birds keep flying into the windows.
                                          They see the sky reflected
And keep on breaking their necks.
The birds keep flying into the windows.
                                          They see the reflection of the sky.

27

The level's so low in the short pond,
The snipe seems to walk on water,
ruffling his dagger-drawn wings
As he heads for the next mossed hillock.
Suddenly, under a cloud, the sun's bottom auras the pond's surface,
And snipe is consumed by fire,
still walking, angelic, wings dipped in flame.
It must have been like this on the first retelling, back there on the long water,
Such mystery,
sunlight and surface-shine and something winged on the waves,
Snipe settled now, deep beak in the curls.

The logo is Fra Angelico,
alone in the unfinished rooms
Upstairs in S. Marco, blank windows
He colored with apparitions and visitations,
The outlines already there,
Apparently, waiting to be filled in.
And he filled them, stroke by stroke,
Bringing the outside inside.
He painted, it's been said, the first recognizable landscape.
As for the others,
he gathered the form from the air, and gave it flesh.

The snipe stands on top of himself
on the water beneath him.
When he drinks, he drinks from his own mouth.

What could be luckier, as full of grace and replenishment,
As feeding oneself on one's other self, one's stand-in,
Life's little helper swagged under our feet,
                                                            one's doppelgänger and replica?

Windless, just-August evening.
Only the grasses move, and slightly,
The tall grasses, hearing the whispers of gravity,
And turning their tired necks
                                            as though they'd prefer not to.
Otherwise, not even the stubbed clover moves, nor the snipe,
                                                                                  either of them.

August, blue mother, is calling her children in
                                                            soundlessly
Out of the sun-dried thistles
And out of the morning's dewlessness.
All of the little ones,
                                    the hard-backed and flimsy-winged,
The many-legged and short-of-breath,
She calls them all, and they come.

Listen, this time I think she's calling your name as well.

I wish I remembered the way the stars looked
                                                            up here some thirty-five years ago
When the lights went out.
Pretty much as they do now, I'd guess,

Though I never see them,
given, as now I am, to an early bed.
Original oxymorons, ice on fire, I loved to watch them fall.

And loved them, too, as they stayed in place,
Designs from the afterlife of dreams,
and beyond that,
Connecting the dots of nothingness.
It comforts me to know they're up there,
and that their light
Keeps coming long after my sleep has gone forth, and my sleep's sleep.

We've all led raucous lives,
some of them inside, some of them out.
But only the poem you leave behind is what's important.
Everyone knows this.
The voyage into the interior is all that matters,
Whatever your ride.
Sometimes I can't sit still for all the asininities I read.
Give me the hummingbird, who has to eat sixty times
His own weight a day just to stay alive.
Now that's a life on the edge.

I live here accompanied by clouds
Now that the weather's broken.
They take and release sunlight
like stained glass outside my small window.
A light that sometimes prompts me to want
To leave the world and settle, like some white bird,
on another mountain.

28

What does it profit us to say
The stiff new bristles of the spruce tree
Glisten like bottle brushes after the rain shower?
To what avail is the thunderstorm
Passing just north of us, and south too,
Like a growling and wire-haired dog
still wishing us harm?
Description and metaphor,
The fancy dancing of language,
to what good end, my friend, to what end?
And who will remember us and our enterprise,
Whose fingers will sift our dust?

We'll never know, Horatio, we will never know.

Cold snap, not even mid-August yet,
The little engines of change at work
Unexpectedly in the atmosphere
as well as our lives,
The dragging, black-bellied clouds
That enter our blood from the wrong side of the compass,
The double-clutch of wind-shift
Into off-limits and unappeasable places
Is coming our way soon,
and slow-dropped out of the blue.
One sees it and feels it at the same time,
noiselessly
Pulling toward the meridian, then over the hill.

The evening's homily comes down to this in the end:
Praise for the left-out and left-behind,
Praise for the left-over and over-looked,
                    praise for the left hand
And the horse with one lame leg,
Praise for the going-down,
                    and the farther going-down,
Praise for the half-things, red moon and the smoke-scented sky,
The bling and the left half of the heart,
The half-winded whicker of geldings,
                    light water on top of the dark,
The dispossession of all landscape
As night cuts the music off,
                    and pulls the plug and eases in.

The overheated vocabulary of the sun
Has sunk to just a few syllables,
                    fewer than yesterday.
And fewer still tomorrow, I'd bet.
Slaphappy sidekick, guttering old fool,
                    tongue-tied and toasty,
What are your last ones likely to be, "you"? Or will they be "the"?

Bringing the horses in is like
                    bringing the past of the whole race in.
Sundown, a cloud-flittered sky.
They'd like blood, but hay is what they get,

Ghosts from our former lives,
ghosts who could carry us still.
Breathe lightly into their nostrils, scorgle their muzzles.
They brought us here,
and someday they'll take us far away.

Twenty hours of rain in the middle of August,
No thunder, no lightning strikes.
A gift.
I saw two kingfishers last week outside my window,
Above the creek. I hope they'll come back.
Autumn is under way, already the first gears
notched and turned.

Abandoned squirrel nest under cloud-slide.
Pencil stub.
The dread of what we can see, and the dread of what we can't see,
Crawl in the same manner,
one in back of the other.

Struck by the paucity of my imagination
To winnow the meadow from anything that it is,
I watch the yellow-tail hawk
cruising its edges, the willows
Along the creek's course,
Low down and lethal, then up like a slung lariat
To circle and telescope,

Eventually to noose back down
And crumble,
only to rise, big wings pumping, back to the west.

Beside me, the shadow of the wind chime's bamboo drag
Turns like a fish on a string
Noiselessly in the still waters of morning's sunlight.
A pack train of white and off-white clouds
Works east where the hawk had been.
Almost noon, the meadow
Waiting for someone to change it into an other. Not me.
The horses, Monte and Littlefoot,
Like it the way it is.
And this morning, so do I.

After the end of something, there comes another end,
This one behind you, and far away.
Only a lifetime can get you to it,
and then just barely.

29

The page is dark, and the story line is darker still.
We all have the same book,
identically inscribed.
We open it at the appointed day, and begin to read.

30

There is a kind of depression that empties the soul.
The eyes stay bright,
                    the mind stays clear as Canada on an autumn day
Just after the rain.
But the soul hangs loose as a plastic bag in a tree
When the wind has died.
                    It is that drained.
And overcast. The little jack-weeds
That line its edges exhale,
And everything falls to a still, uneasy remove.
It stirs when the wind shifts,
                    and seasons tumble and stall.
It stirs, but it doesn't disappear.
Though weeds re-up and the clouds relent,
                    it doesn't disappear.

Like a golden Afro, a bunch of eidergrass has blossomed
And paled out
On top of an uprooted pine stump
Across the creek.
                    As the sun goes down,
What small light there is drains off into its spikiness,
And glows like a severed head against the darkness.

Oil lamp lit, outside light a similitude,
                    wet world

From recent downpour,
I think of you back in Massachusetts,
hurting from head to foot heel,
Still summer there, autumn beginning here, no drop of complaint.

Brushstroke, bullrushes in front of pond's mirror,
rain spots
Pimpling diminished mountain.
My seventieth birthday,
such wonderful weather.

Whatever lights there are are ours, or can be,
all things
We see are like that.
And those we can't see gather the light
closely unto themselves,
And look around steadily for us.
How is it we miss their messages?

August the 25th, the snipe gone.
Do they go south?
I suppose they must, but where?
Certainly not to east Tennessee,
Where I held the bag for hours
in Oak Ridge one evening after supper
(There goes the kingfisher, and then the yellow-tail hawk,
One up the creek, the other one down).

I hope they are walking now on a warmer water,
And that their reflections are just as clear,
                                        and the moss as green.
Sixty-two years ago, the year of aluminum pennies,
My hands still burning,
                                the mouth of that croker sack still open.

Lord, when the world is still, how still it is,
                                        contrails and mare's tails
Crisscrossing the sky,
Patterned so lightly on its unmistakable air.
One waits for a presence from the darkening woods,
                                        one large and undiminished,
But only its absence appears, big as all get-out.

Evening arrives so swiftly these days
                                    even the weak-kneed weeds
Don't know which direction to bow in,
The fugitive wind-fingers,
Groping north, groping south,
                                then hanging like unstruck chimes
From their disused and desolate hands.

Out over the sunlit Pacific
Mischief is in the making
                                (Good, there's the kingfisher again,
Then gone in a blue, acetylene flash
Down to the trout horde),
Whose scratches and plum knots
                                    we'll feel in a day or two.

The world's whinny and the world's bit
are two thousand miles away.
How is it I hear its hoofbeats so sharp in my ear?

31

Emptiness happens.
It's like the down-curving dead branch
On the pine tree outside my window
Which ends in nothing, its mossy beard
Moving just slightly, no more than that, in the slight wind.
One hopes, in due time, to be so moved,
in just such a garment.

There's an easy emptiness, and a hard emptiness,
The first one knowable, the second one not,
though some are said to have seen it
And come back to fight the first.
Which is bespoke, and fits like a shirt.
The second one's colorless, and far away,
as love is, or a resurrection.

The bottles my messages are sent in have long disappeared.
Cloudy September jumbles the sky.
The great purity waits for me,
but no one has answered my questions.

These are the night journals,
an almanac of the afterhour,
Icarus having fallen
A long time ago, the sun in its ghostly pursuit
Behind him behind the ridge,
Not enough light to see the page,
not really,
Much less to imagine how it must have been, the pale boy
Scalded by burning wax,
cooled by wind,
The water a sudden oblivion, so nothing, so welcoming,
So many worlds since then, all of them so alike, all of them
Suncatcher, father and son.

The beginning of autumn dark is quick, and it's cold, and long.
My time of life is a preen of feathers, and goes on and on.
If not in me, then in you,
cousin.
I'll look for you in the deep light, on the other side.
The water is wadable,
not too big, not too small.
I'll be the one with white hair, avoiding the mirror.

It's odd how certain combinations
are carved twice in the memory,
Once in the surface riprap and once in the deep seams.
Lake Garda is like that, and Valpolicella wine,

The sun going down above Salò,
The waters, as has been said,
crumpling and smoothing toward Bardolino,
Fish on the grill, the wine like blood in liter carafes,
The dusk a darkish serenity laying its hands
On our shoulders
warmly, with a touch of freshness, but warmly.
When you're twenty-three, you'll live forever, a short time.

One horse up and one horse down.
And Punto S. Vigilio,
Olive trees semaphoring in the wind O love me.
And I did, I did.
I wonder if I will ever see it again?
And Riva, that myth-bag, Gardone,
And all the way over and back to Sirmione?
And Thorpe and Hobart and Schimmel and Schneeman,
will I see them,
And Via Mazzini, La Greppia, Piazza Erbe?
Not as they were and not as I was.
The past is a dark disaster, and no one returns.
Initials are left, and dates.
Sometimes the bodies are still hanging,
and sometimes not.

Hark, hark, the dogs do bark;
The poets are coming to town.
One in rags and one in tags,
And one in a silken gown.

32

Backyard, my old station, the dusk invisible in the trees,
But there in its stylish tint,
Everything etched and precise before the acid bath
—Hemlocks and hedgerows—
Of just about half an hour from now,
Night in its soak and dissolve.
Pipistrello, and gun of motorcycles downhill,
A flirt and a gritty punctuation to the day's demise
And one-starred exhalation,
                    V of geese going south,
My mind in their backwash, going north.

The old gospel song from 1950
                    by Lester Flatt and Earl Scruggs,
"Reunion in Heaven," has a fugitive last verse
I must have heard once
Although it wasn't included when they recorded it.
So I'll list it here,
          that it won't be disremembered.
Just in case.
I am longing to sit by the banks of the river
There's rest for the ones by the evergreen trees
I am longing to look in the face of my Savior
And my loved ones who have gone, they are waiting for me

When what you write about is what you see,
                    what do you write about when it's dark?

Paradise, Pound said, was real to Dante because he saw it.
Nothing invented.
One loves a story like that, whether it's true or not.
Whenever I open my eyes at night, outside,
                                        flames edge at the edge
Of everything, like the sides of a nineteenth-century negative.
If time is a black dog, and it is,
Why do I always see its breath,
                              its orange, rectangular breath
In the dark?
It's what I see, you might say, it's got to be what my eyes see.

So many joys in such a brief stay.
Life is a long walk on a short pier.

If poetry is pentimento,
                         as most of its bones seem to show,
Remember the dead deer on Montana 92,
Lincoln County, last Monday, scrunched in the left-hand ditch.
Raven meat-squawks for two days.
On Thursday, south wind through the rib cage,
Ever-so-slightly a breathing,
                              skull-skink unmoved on the macadam.
Its song was somewhat, somewhat erased.

I'm early, no one in the boat on the dark river.
It drifts across by itself

Below me.

Offended, I turn back up the damp steps.

The dragonflies remain a great mystery to me.
Early October.
At least a dozen of them are swarming
Like swallows over the dying grass
And browned leaves of the backyard,
Each tending to recompose a previous flight path
With minor variations.
So beautiful,
translucent wings against the translucent sky,
The late afternoon like litmus just under our fingertips.

The berries shine like little stigmata in the dogwood trees,
A thousand reminders of the tree's mythology
As the rain keeps polishing them,
as though it could rub it clean.

Such red, and Easter so far away.

33

The song of someone like me
begins on the pennywhistle.
A few notes, just a few, up and down.
The bass line comes in,
then the lead and second guitar.

Brushstrokes on the snares.
And then the singer, Lord, then the singer steps up.
What voice could slip this backdrop?
Only the rise and fall of the newly damned, perhaps,
                                        or the Great Speckled Bird.
Or some sough through the big larch limbs, some sibilance in the pines.
Little lost squawks in the natural world,
                                        lost voices.
I gather them unto me, I become their mouthpiece.

Sordello, with lazy and honest eyes, still waits for us
Beyond the *palude* off Via Mantovana
Just this side of Sabbionetta,
His terraced, invisible mountain
Rising above Lake Garda into the infinite.
Not time for that hike yet, we hoped,
                                        feet hot on the cobblestones
In front of Palazzo Ducale.
Not yet, we hoped, our foreheads already feeling the sword's tip.
And angel wings.
                    You got to carry that weight for a long time,
And pray for the angel's wing
When the time comes, when the time does come.

Moonlight like watery paint
On the yard grass and arborvitae.

Shadows like Franz Kline from the spruce trees.

Circle of neighbor's basketball goal like the entrance to Hell
On stone-spattered, leaf-littered driveway.

October, old ghost month, you outline my *fine del cammin.*

There is a photograph of Stan Hyman and me in our Army dress blues,
2nd Lieutenants, standing in front of a No Parking sign
In Pacific Grove, California, 1958.
There are a hundred million snapshots
Just like it, Stan's wedding day, the 24 August.
Mine means a world to me, a world never to return,
But one never left, if truth be told.
And yours? You have at least one, I know, just like it,
                                        different people, different place,
But the same. What does it mean to you?
Who could imagine it would ever become like this?

All I have left undone, I hope someone will make good
In this life or the next,
                    whichever comes first. Or second.

Moon riseth not, as some Victorian must have said back in the day,
Stars like a motorcycle's exhaust
Through the limp leaves of the maple trees.
                                        Not much excitement here,
Though headlights and taillights go back and
Forth like pine-pitch torches in some Attic procession,
The limbs of Orpheus overhead

At the front,
his blue-tongued and pale head behind on the slow Rivanna,
Bumping from snag to sandbar, but singing, still singing.

The start of things, and the end of things,
Two unmarked graves,
the autumn wind rising west of the mountains.
Goodbye to the promise of What's Left.

The emptiness of nonbeing,
that which endures through all change—
Something to shoot for, for sure,
Something to seek out and walk on,
one footprint after the next.
In any case, after this life of who-knows-how-many-years,
Who's not a shrunken, pitiable sight?

I empty myself with light
Until I become morning.

34

It's dark now, but I remember the five-fingered jaundiced leaves
Seeming to hover above the earth this afternoon
On the tips, the dull tips, of grass blades
under the maple tree,

The dogwood berries on Locust Avenue like scarlet cluster bombs,
Automobiles and ambulance sirens
                                        cutting the sundown, October air,
Thinking, this isn't at all bad, not even one bit,
All the way to the hospital, and all the way back.
And now here's Mars, like a pancake orange,
Northeast in the bleached-star sky,
                                        and that's not at all bad either,
End of October, end of a buffed and edgeless day.

Halloween, All Hallows' Eve.
                                    And what if they came back,
All of them, what would we say?
That the moon looks good through the limbs of the chinaberry tree?
That the night air is as easy as oil on the skin?
That the children parading in their pathetic little costumes
                                                            have it right?
That the give in the natural world
Is as good as the take in the supernatural other?
That the moon looks good and the stars still refuse to shine?
What would we say, Slick, what would we say,
Our hands like skeletal party gloves,
                                        our masks future faces?

I think of the masters of a century ago,
And often wish they'd come and whisper their secrets in my ear,
My right ear, the good one. Not all, perhaps, but a couple.

The fallen leaves
                    litter the lawn and driveway. Autumn.

Indian summer. Nothing ripples.
The other side of the world, they say, is a door
where I'll find my life again.

New moon like a jai alai basket
just over the doctor's rooftop,
Cradling the old moon before her fall.

If angels can see into the ends and beginnings of things,
Why are they still among us
Like widowed birds, circling, circling,
their poor go-betweens at a full stop?

The cold gowns of the masters,
those of a thousand years ago,
Over a thousand, and then some,
Wander the countryside,
brushing like loose crystal against the sumac.
Who here can inhabit them?
Whose arms among us can fill their sleeves,
So clear and transparent, so radiant in the dark?

My neighbor's maple tree shines like a galleon in the dusk,
Kumquat and blood orange,
pomegranate and nectarine.
Within such splendor, everything falls away, even our names,
All trace of our being here, breathed in by the night's lips.
This is as close as we get to them,

Their tinkling crystal folds just ahead of us
how sweet a sound.

Is there an emptiness we all share?
Before the end, I mean.
Heaven and earth depend on this clarity,
heaven and earth.
Under the gold doubloons of the fallen maple leaves,
The underworld burrows in,
sick to death of the light.

35

When death shall close these eyelids,
And this heart shall cease to beat,
And they lay me down to rest
In some flowery-bound retreat.

Will you miss me, will you miss me,
Will you miss me,
Will you miss me when I'm gone?

Perhaps you'll plant a flower
On my poor, unworthy grave,
Come and sit alone beside me
When the roses nod and wave.

Will you miss me, will you miss me,
Will you miss me,
Will you miss me when I'm gone?

One sweet thought my soul shall cherish
When this fleeting life has flown,
This sweet thought will cheer when dying,
Will you miss me when I'm gone?

When these lips shall never more
Press a kiss upon thy brow,
But lie cold and still in death,
Will you love me then as now?

Will you miss me, will you miss me,
Will you miss me,
Will you miss me when I'm gone?

FROM

SESTETS

(2009)

Tomorrow

The metaphysics of the quotidian was what he was after:
A little dew on the sunrise grass,
A drop of blood in the evening trees,
                                        a drop of fire.

If you don't shine you are darkness.
The future is merciless,
                              everyone's name inscribed
On the flyleaf of the Book of Snow.

Future Tense

All things in the end are bittersweet—
An empty gaze, a little way station just beyond silence.

If you can't delight in the everyday,
                                        you have no future here.
And if you can, no future either.

And time, black dog, will sniff you out,
                                        and lick your lean cheeks,
And lie down beside you—warm, real close—and will not move.

Flannery's Angel

Lead us to those we are waiting for,
Those who are waiting for us.
May your wings protect us,
                                        may we not be strangers in the lush province of joy.

Remember us who are weak,
You who are strong in your country which lies beyond the thunder,
Raphael, angel of happy meeting,
                                                        resplendent, hawk of the light.

In Praise of What Is Missing

When a tooth is extracted,
                                        some side of the holy wheel is unnotched,
And twists, unlike Ixion's, in the wind and weather,
And one slips into wanting nothing more
                                                        from the human world,
And leans back, a drifting cloud,
Toward what becomes vacant and is nameless and is blue,
As days once were, and will be again.

By the Waters of Babylon

We live on Orphan Mountain,
                                        each of us, and that's how it is,
Kingfisher still wet
And chattering on his empty branch.

Water remains immortal—
Poems can't defile it,
                                        the heron, immobile on one leg,
Stands in it, snipe stitch it, and heaven pillows its breast.

Hasta la Vista Buckaroo

So many have come and gone, undone
                                                                        like a rhinestone cowboy,
Dazzle and snuff, Lord, dazzle and snuff,
In a two-bit rodeo.

The entrance to hell is just a tiny hole in the ground,
The size of an old pecan, soul-sized, horizon-sized.
Thousands go through it each day before the mist clears
                                                                        thousands one by one you're next.

Born Again II

Take me down to the river,
                                                the ugly, reseasoned river.
Add on me a sin or two,
Then cleanse me, and wash me, O white-shirted Pardoner.

Suerte, old friend.
The caravan's come and gone, the dogs have stopped barking,
And nothing remains but the sound of the water monotonous,
                                                                                        and the wind.

No Entry

It is not possible to imagine and feel the pain of others.
We say we do but we don't.
It is a country we have no passport for,
                                        and no right of entry.

Empathy is emphatic,
                        and sends long lines across the floor.
But it's not the hurt or wound.
It's not the secret of the black raven,
                                        cut out by water into oblivion.

Celestial Waters

May 30th, early evening,
                        one duck on the narrow water, pond
Stocked with clouds,
The world reflected and windless, full of grace, tiny, tiny.

Osiris has shown us the way to cross the coming night sky,
The route, the currents, the necessary magic words.
Stick to your business, boys,
                        and forget the down-below.

Anniversary II

Dun-colored moth past the windowpane.
                                        Now, he's got the right idea,

Fuzzy and herky-jerky,
little Manichaean
Pulled by invisible strings toward light wherever it is.

On the 5th of June, the mother is like a shining,
Blue raindrop the sunlight refracts
on the tip of the spruce tree,
Crack in the bulbous sky the moth is yo-yoed up to.

Sunlight Bets on the Come

The basic pleasures remain unchanged,
and their minor satisfactions—
Chopping wood, building a fire,
Watching the elk herd
splinter and cruise around the outcrop of spruce trees

As the deer haul ass,
their white flags like synchronized swimmers' hands,
Sunlight sealing—stretched like Saran Wrap—
The world as we know it,
keeping it fresh-flamed should tomorrow arrive.

"Well, Get Up, Rounder, Let a Working Man Lay Down"

The kingdom of minutiae,
that tight place where most of us live,
Is the kingdom of the saved,
Those who exist between the cracks,
those just under the details.

When the hand comes down, the wing-white hand,
We are the heads of hair
and finger bones yanked out of their shoes,
We are the Rapture's children.

With Horace, Sitting on the Platform, Waiting for the Robert E. Lee

Seventy years, and what's left?
Or better still, what's gone before?
A couple of lines, a day or two out in the cold?
And all those books, those half-baked books,
sweet yeast for the yellow dust?

What say, Orazio? Like you, I'm sane and live at the edge of things,
Countryside flooded with light,
Sundown,
the chaos of future mornings just over the ridge, but not here yet.

The Evening Is Tranquil, and Dawn Is a Thousand Miles Away

The mares go down for their evening feed
into the meadow grass.
Two pine trees sway the invisible wind—
some sway, some don't sway.
The heart of the world lies open, leached and ticking with sunlight
For just a minute or so.

The mares have their heads on the ground,
the trees have their heads on the blue sky.
Two ravens circle and twist.
On the borders of heaven, the river flows clear a bit longer.

Homage to What's-His-Name

Ah, description, of all the arts the least appreciated.
Well, it's just this and it's just that,
someone will point out.
Exactly. It's just this and it's just that and nothing other.

From landscape to unsuppressed conjunction, it's only itself.
No missteps, no misreading.
And what's more metaphysical than that,
The world in its proper posture, on all fours, drinking the sweet water?

Tutti Frutti

"A-wop-bop-a-loo-lop a-lop-bam-boo,"
Little Richard in full gear—
What could be better than that?
Not much that I know of, at least not in my green time.

It's hard, O, my, it is hard,
To find a sustainable ecstasy, and make it endure.
Detail, detail, detail—God and the Devil
hang side by side between each break.

"This World Is Not My Home, I'm Only Passing Through"

The more you say, the more mistakes you'll make,
so keep it simple.
No one arrives without leaving soon.
This blue-eyed, green-footed world—
hello, Goldie, goodbye.

We won't meet again. So what?
The rust will remain in the trees,
and pine needles stretch their necks,
Their tiny necks, and sunlight will snore in the limp grass.

Stiletto

Why does each evening up here
always, in summer, seem to be
The way—as it does, with the light knifing low from right to left—
It will be on the next-to-last one?

The next-to-last one for me, I mean.
There is no music involved,
so it must be the light, and its bright blade.
The last one, of course, will be dark.
And the knife will be dark too.

"I Shall Be Released"

There is a consolation beyond nomenclature
of what is past
Or is about to pass, though I don't know what it is.
But someone, somewhere, must, and this is addressed to him.

Come on, Long Eyes, crack the book.
Thumb through the pages and stop at the one with the golden script.
Breathe deeply and lay it on me,
that character with the luminous half-life.

Description's the Art of Something or Other

Description is expiation,
and not a place to hunker down in.
It is a virtual world
Unfit for the virtuous.
It is a coming to terms with.

Or coming to terms without.
As though whatever we had to say could keep it real.
As though our words were flies,
and the dead meat kept reappearing.

"It's Sweet to Be Remembered"

No one's remembered much longer than a rock
is remembered beside the road

If he's lucky or
Some tune or harsh word
                                        uttered in childhood or back in the day.

Still how nice to imagine some kid someday
                                        picking that rock up and holding it in his hand
Briefly before he chucks it
Deep in the woods in a sunny spot in the tall grass.

In Memory of the Natural World

Four ducks on the pond tonight, the fifth one MIA.
A fly, a smaller than normal fly,
Is mapping his way through sun-strikes across my window.

Behind him, as though at attention,
                                                  the pine trees hold their breaths.
The fly's real, the trees are real,
And the ducks.
                        But the glass is artificial, and it's on fire.

Yellow Wings

When the sun goes down—and you happen to notice it—
And the sky is clear, there's always a whitish light
                                                            edging the earth's offerings.
This is the lost, impermanent light
The soul is pulled toward, and longs for, deep in its cave,

Little canary.
This is the light its wings dissolve in
if it ever gets out from underground.

Twilight of the Dogs

Death is the mother of nothing.
This is a fact of life,
And exponentially sad.
All these years—a lifetime, really—thinking it might be otherwise.

What are the colors of despair?
Are they calibrated, like vowels?
How will we know them?
Who knows where the light will fall
as the clouds go from west to the east?

Remembering Bergamo Alto

A postapocalyptic poetry
starts with a dog bite
And featherless birds in the ruined trees,
People nowhere to be found.

Mostly it has to do with cities,
and empty boulevards,
Chairs in the public parks with no one to sit in them.
Mostly it's wind in vacant spaces,
and piano chords from a high window.

With Alighieri on Basin Creek

All four of the ducks are gone now.
                                                  Only the mountain remains,
Upside down like Purgatorio
In the pond's reflection,
                                        no tree at the top, and no rivers.

No matter. Above it, in either incarnation,
The heavens, in all their golden numbers, begin to unstack.
Down here, as night comes on, we look for Guido,
                    his once best friend, and Guido's father, and Bertran de Born.

Walking Beside the Diversion Ditch Lake

I love to make the kingfishers fly
                                                  from their bony perches
Above the lake, six or seven, one after the next,
Circling the water and chattering back,
                                                            as I walk along.

Can the fish hear them?
Is their cry like organ chording,
                                                  leading to one vast ultimate stop?
Who was it who first said, "The kingfisher falls through fire"?

The Ghost of Walter Benjamin Walks at Midnight

The world's an untranslatable language
without words or parts of speech.
It's a language of objects
Our tongues can't master,
but which we are the ardent subjects of.

If *tree* is *tree* in English,
and *albero* in Italian,
That's as close as we can come
To divinity, the language that circles the earth
and which we'll never speak.

Bees Are the Terrace Builders of the Stars

It's odd how the objects of our lives
Continue to not define us,
no matter how close we hold them unto us.
Odd how the narrative of those lives is someone else's narrative.

Now the increasing sundown.
The Bible draws the darkness around it,
No footbridge or boat over Lethe,
No staircase or stepping-stone
up into the Into.

When the Horses Gallop Away from Us, It's a Good Thing

I always find it strange—though I shouldn't—how creatures don't care for
us the way we care for them.
Horses, for instance, and chipmunks, and any bird you'd name.
Empathy's only a one-way street.

And that's all right, I've come to believe.
It sets us up for ultimate things,
and penultimate ones as well.
It's a good lesson to have in your pocket when the Call comes to call.

Autumn Is Visionary, Summer's the Same Old Stuff

Half-moon rising, thin as a contact lens.
The sun going down
As effortlessly as a body through deep water,
Both at the same time, simple pleasures
As autumn begins to rustle and rinse,
as autumn begins to prink.

And now the clouds come on,
the same clouds that Turner saw.
Half of the moon sees them, half does not.

Bitter Herbs to Eat, and Dipped in Honey

We lay out our own dark end,
guilt, and the happiness of guilt.

God never enters into it, nor
Do his pale hands and pale wings,
angel of time he has become.

The wind doesn't blow in the soul,
so no boat there for passage.
Half paths of the half-moon, then,
To walk up and down in the forest,
to walk hard in the bright places.

No Angel

In the Kingdom of the Hollow-at-Heart, the insect is king.
In the Kingdom of the Beyond,
all lie where the ground is smooth.
Everything's what it seems to be, and a little less.

In the land of the unutterable,
words float like reflections across the water.
Nobody visits us here.
Like shadows, we spread ourselves until our hands touch,
then disappear in the dark.

Time Is a Graceless Enemy, but Purls as It Comes and Goes

I'm winding down. The daylight is winding down.
Only the night is wound up tight,
And ticking with unpaused breath.
Sweet night, sweet steady, reliable, uncomplicated night.

September moon, two days from full,
slots up from the shouldered hill.
There is no sound as the moon slots up, no thorns in its body.
Invisible, the black gondola floats
through down-lid and drowning stars.

Terrestrial Music

What's up, grand architect of the universe?
The stars are falling,
The moon is failing behind your vaporous laundry,
Planets are losing their names,
and darkness is dropping inches beneath the earth.

Down here, we take it in stride.
The horses go on with their chomp and snatch in the long grasses,
The dogs cringe,
and coyotes sing in the still woods, back out of sight.

Before the Propane Lamps Come On, the World Is a Risk and Wonder

Sundown smoke like a pink snood
over the gathered hair of the mountains,
The sun a garish hatpin
Incongruous in the netting and underfold of the day.

The creek's voice is constant,
and like a shadow embraces many things.

I wish it were my voice, but it's not.
My voice is a human thing, and weak,
and it disappears with the sun.

On the Night of the First Snow, Thinking About Tennessee

It's dark now, the horses have had their half apple,
mist and rain,
Horses down in the meadow, just a few degrees above snow.

I stand in front of the propane stove, warming my legs.

If the door were open, I'd listen to creek water
And think I heard voices from long ago,
distinct, and calling me home.

The past becomes such a mirror—we're in it, and then we're not.

Our Days Are Political, but Birds Are Something Else

Tenth month of the year.
Fallen leaves taste bitter. And grass.
Everything that we've known, and come to count on,
has fled the world.
Their bones crack in the west wind.

Where are the deeds we're taught to cling to?
How I regret having missed them,
and their mirrored pieces of heaven.
Like egrets, they rise in the clear sky,
their shadows like distance on the firred hills.

We Hope That Love Calls Us, but Sometimes We're Not So Sure

No wind-sighs. And rain-splatter heaves up over the mountains,
and dies out.
October humidity
Like a heart-red tower light,
now bright, now not so bright.

Autumn night at the end of the world.
In its innermost corridors,
all damp and all light are gone, and love, too.
Amber does not remember the pine.

Time Is a Dark Clock, but It Still Strikes from Time to Time

Whump-di-ump-whump-whump,
tweedilee tweedilee tweedilidee,
I'm as happy as can be . . .
Pretty nice, but that was then,
when our hearts were meat on the grill.

And who was it, Etta James or Ruth Brown or LaVern Baker?
The past is so dark, you need a flashlight to find your own shoes.
But what shoes! and always half an inch off the floor,
your feet like wind inside them.

Like the New Moon, My Mother Drifts Through the Night Sky

Beyond the boundaries of light and dark,
                                        my mother's gone out and not come back.
Suddenly now, in my backyard, like the slip moon she rises
And rests in my watching eye.

In my dreams she's returned just like this, over a hundred times.
She knows what I'm looking for,
Partially her,
                    partially what she comes back not to tell me.

As the Train Rolls Through, I Remember an Old Poem

Well, here we are again, old friend, Ancient of Days,
Eyeball to eyeball.
I blink, of course,
                    I blink more than ten thousand times.

Dear ghost, I picture you thus, eventually like
St. Francis in his hair shirt,
                                naked, walking the winter woods,
Singing his own song in the tongue of the troubadours.

April Evening

Spring buzz-cut on the privet hedge,
                                        a couple of yellow cups

Downdrafting from the honeysuckle.
One bird in the hapless holly tree,
                giving us liftoff and glide.

It is amazing how beautiful springtime can be,
Bell jar over our ills and endless infirmities,
Transparency into where we know
                the light will never reach us.

The Book

Whose name will be inscribed in the book
                just before mine?
From what country, from what unburiable ever?
Somebody I'll never know, for sure,
Somebody whose fingers will never outline my face.

A splinter of his death will always remain in mine,
However,
        no matter how thick, no matter how thin.

Sundown Blues

There are some things that can't be conveyed—
                description, for instance,
The sundown light on that dog-hair lodgepole pine
                and the dead branches of spruce trees.

They hold its brilliance close against them
For a tick or two
                    before it chameleons away.
No one is able to describe this gold to bronze to charcoal, no one.
So move along, boy, just move along.

"On the Trail of the Lonesome Pine"

The older I become, the more the landscape resembles me.
All morning a misty rain,
All afternoon the sun uncovered and covered by cloud snares.

At night, in the evergreens,
The moonlight slides off the wind-weary branches, and will not stick.
No movement, the dark forest.

No Direction Home

After a certain age, there's no one left to turn to.
You've got to find Eurydice on your own,
                                        you've got
To find the small crack
                    between here and everywhere else all by yourself.

How could it be otherwise?
Everyone's gone away, the houses are all empty,
And overcast starts to fill the sky like soiled insulation.

Hovercraft

Hummingbird stopped as a period, breast embossed
purple-pink-crimson
Outside the northside window,
Wings invisible in their stillness,
unquiet, never faltering.

And then, whoosh, he's gone,
Leaving a little hole in the air, one that the air
doesn't rush in to fill.
Empty pocket.
The world, and the other world, are full of them.

Time Is a Child-Biting Dog

Like rivers, my thoughts flow south,
for no particular reason.
Must be the full moon
That floods the sky, and makes the night wakeful
and full of remorse.

It's not here yet, but give it an hour or so, then we,
Bewildered, who want our poems to be clouds
upholding the sour light of heaven,
Will pass our gray hair through our fingers
and sigh just a little bit.

Nothing Is Written

In a couple of hours, it will start all over again,
The stars will lean down and stare from their faceless spaces,
And the moon will boot up on the black screen of the sky,
                                        humping toward God-knows-what,

And we, with our pinched mouths and pinched eyes, the next morning
Will see its footprint like a slice of snow
                                        torn off over Caribou,
Looking for somewhere else to be born.

Little Ending

Bowls will receive us,
                    and sprinkle black scratch in our eyes.
Later, at the great fork on the untouchable road,
It won't matter where we have become.

Unburdened by prayer, unburdened by any supplication,
Someone will take our hand,
                              someone will give us refuge,
Circling left or circling right.

FROM

CARIBOU

(2014)

Across the Creek Is the Other Side of the River

No darkness steps out of the woods,
                                        no angel appears.
I listen, no word, I look, no thing.
Eternity must be hiding back there, it's done so before.

I can wait, or I can climb,
Like Orpheus, through the slick organs of my body.

I guess I'll wait,
                    at least until tomorrow night, or the day after.
And if the darkness does not appear,
                                        that's a long time.
And if no angel, it's longer still.

Time and the Centipedes of Night

Like time, the meadow narrows
                                    up to its creek-scraped end.
At sundown, trees light-tipped, mountains half-slipped into night.
How easy contentment comes,
Old age at this end, time's double door at the other.
The only way out is the way in.
Now we know which course the drift is,
                                            in this drifting dream of life,

As the Chinese liked to say.
                                        I like to say it too,
The thunderstorm-floating sky, lightening and lumbering gear shifts.
Afterwards, Gainsboroughs to the east and to the south.
How to understand this
Deep sleep,
            deep sleep in the sheared, many-mouth afternoon?

Whatever is written is written
After, not before.
                  Before is blank and pure, and void
Of all our lives depend on.
Prayers rise like smoke, and are answered as smoke is.
Arrange your unutterable alphabet, my man,
                                                  and hold tight.
It's all you've got, a naming of things, and not so beautiful.

If history is any repeat, which it isn't,
The condition of everything tends toward the condition of silence.
When the wind stops, there's silence.
When the waters go down on their knees and touch their heads
To the bottom, there's silence, when the stars appear
                                        face down, O Lord, then what a hush.

Cake Walk

Invisible, inaudible things,
Always something to hanker for,
                              since everything that's written
Hankers alongside with them,
The great blue heron immobile and neck-torqued on the fence post,
A negative pull from the sun-swept upper meadow . . .

Eleven deer in a Mark Morris dance of happiness
Are lighter than light, though heavier
                    if you blink more than once.
There's light, we learn, and there's Light.

To do what you have to do—unrecognized—and for no one.
The language in that is small,
                    sewn just under your skin.
The germs of stars infect us.
The heron pivots, stretches his neck.
He hears what we do not hear,
                    he sees what we're missing.
The deer walk out the last ledge of sunlight, one by one.

Waterfalls

When is it we come to the realization
                    that all things are wandering away?
Is it age, is it lack of adoration, is it
Regret there's no ladder to the clouds?
Whatever, we inhabit the quotidian, as we must,
While somewhere behind our backs,
                    waterfalls tumble and keep on going
Into the deep desire of distance.

The Childhood of St. Thomas

Three-quarters now of waning moon,
                    cold, late summer sky.
Over the broken promises of the day, the nun

Spreads out her wimple and starry cape.
Whose childhood could hold such purity,
                                        such fire-blown eyelids of the dead?

It is a wound that cannot be touched.
Even by either hand of St. Thomas.
                                        Wish him well.
His supper was not holy, his gesture not sinless.
May ours be equal to his,
                                whatever sky we live under.

Everything Passes, but Is It Time?

Sunset same color as maple tree
In my neighbor's yard—
Nature and nature head-butt,
Golden persimmon.
                                And if the stairs to paradise
Are that color, who wouldn't put his old Reeboks down?
Gently, however, O so gently.
The membrane of metaphor is weak,
                                        and has no second step.

"Don't play too long, don't play too loud, and don't play the melody."
Nature's deaf to this beautiful injunction.
                                        And that's okay.
One should live one's life as an acolyte walking into the temple,
Oblivious, the heavens exploding around you,
Your heart conflicted, your footfalls sure.
Time is your enemy,
                                time and its fail-safe disgrace.
Open your arms, boys, take off your shirts.

Homage to Samuel Beckett

There is a heaviness inside the body
that leans down, but does not touch us.
There is a lassitude that licks itself, but brings no relief.
There is a self-destructiveness no memory can repeal.
Such breath in the unstopped ear,
such sweet breath, O, along the tongue.

Cloud swatches brilliance the sky
Over the Alleghenies,
unpatterned as Heaven.
Across the street, Amoret's family picnic has ended.
Memorial Day,
the dead like plastic bags in the blown trees.

In Paradise, springtime never arrives.
The seasons
Are silent, and dumb, and ghost-walk outside our windows.
And so it is down here—
we grovel on our extremities
And rise, rise up, halfway to where the new leaves begin.

And thus, unexpectedly, a small rain commences,
Then backs off.
The sunlight continues its dying fall.
And dying, one hopes to think, will be such a slide, a mild jolt,
Like shifting from formlessness to form.

Crystal Declension

Well, two things are certain—
                                        the sun will rise and the sun will set.
Most everything else is up for grabs.
It's back on its way down now
As a mother moose and her twin calves
Step lightly, lightly
                              across the creek through the understory
And half-lit grasses,
Then disappear in a clutch of willow bushes.
                                                            If one, anyone,
Could walk through his own life as delicately, as sure,
As she did, all wreckage, all deadfall,
Would stay sunlight, and ring like crystal among the trees.

Grace II

It's true, the aspirations of youth burn down to char strips with the years.
Tonight, only memories are my company and my grace.
How nice if they could outlive us.
                                                  But they can't. Or won't.
No Indian summer for us. It's rough and it's growing dark,
The sunset pulling the full moon up by its long fingernails.
It's better this way.
                              The unforgiven are pure, as are the unremembered.

Heaven's Eel

A slight wrinkle on the pond.
Small wind.
                    A small wind and the rumpled clouds' reflection.
Ho-hum . . . What's needed is something under the pond's skin,
Something we can't see that controls all the things that we do see.
Something long and slithery,
                                        something we can't begin to comprehend,
A future we're all engendered for, sharp teeth, Lord, such sharp teeth.
Heaven's eel.
                    Heaven's eel, long and slick,
Full moon gone, with nothing in its place.

A doe is nibbling away at the long stalks of the natural world
Across the creek.
                         It's good to be here.
It's good to be where the world's quiescent, and reminiscent.
No wind blows from the far sky.
Beware of prosperity, friend, and seek affection.
The eel's world is not your world,
                                             but will be soon enough.

"I'm Going to Take a Trip in That Old Gospel Ship"

Did the great ship with the bier of the Hunter Gracchus
Pass by this year? Or is it just late?
Or did it finally find the seam,
                                        the crack between this world and the other,
And slip through, sails furled?

And drifts now, as it was meant to drift,
                    on pure, unpestilent waters,
Still circling the globe, and out of its cage forever?
Hard to know, George, hard to know,
Its left-behinds still vibrant,
                    its wake still ripply in the evening sun.

So difficult to belay the myth,
                    so difficult to hold
Hard to the transmutation of narrative and imagination.
The real world has its hands and feet in the other one,
Though its head's here, and its heart is here.
The clouds, as they always do, present us the option:
Dig down, brother, dig down deep,
                    or keep on walking fast.

Ancient of Days

There is a kind of sunlight, in early autumn, at sundown,
That raises cloud reflections
Inches above the pond water,
                    that sends us packing into the chill evening
To stand like Turner's blobbed figurines
In a landscape we do not understand,
                    whatever and everything
We know about it.
Unworldly and all ours,
                    it glides like the nineteenth century
Over us, up the near hill
And into the glistening mittens of the same clouds
Now long gone from the world's pond.
                    So long.

This is an old man's poetry,
written by someone who's spent his life
Looking for one truth.
Sorry, pal, there isn't one.
Unless, of course, the trees and their blow-down relatives
Are part of it.
Unless the late-evening armada of clouds
Spanished along the horizon are part of it.
Unless the diminishing pinprick of light
stunned in the dark forest
Is part of it.
Unless, O my, whatever the eye makes out,
And sends, on its rough-road trace,
To the heart, is part of it,
then maybe that bright vanishing might be.

Sentences II

Last chapter, last verse—
everything's brown now in the golden field.
The threshing floor of the past is past.
The Overmountain men of the future
lie cusped in their little boxes.
The sun backs down, over the ridgeline, at 5 after 7.

The landscape puts on its black mask
and settles into its sleeplessness.
The fish will transpose it,
half for themselves, half for the water
Ten thousand miles away, at the end of the darkening stream.
To live a pure life, to live a true life,
is to live the life of an insect.

Shadow and Smoke

Live your life as though you were already dead,
                                        Che Guevara declared.
Okay, let's see how that works.
Not much difference, as far as I can see,
                                        the earth the same Paradise
It's always wanted to be,
Heaven as far away as before,
The clouds the same old movable gates since time began.

There is no circle, there is no sentiment to be broken.
There are only the songs of young men,
                                        and the songs of old men,
Hoping for something elsewise.
Disabuse them in their ignorance,
Lord,
    tell them the shadows are already gone, the smoke
Already cleared,
            tell them that light is never a metaphor.

Road Warriors

My traveling clothes light up the noon.
I've been on my way for a long time
                                    back to the past,
That irreconcilable city.
Everyone wants to join me, it seems, and I let them.
Roadside flowers drive me to distraction,
                                        dragonflies
Hover like lapis lazuli, there, just out of reach.

Narrow road, wide road, all of us on it, unhappy,
Unsettled, seven yards short of immortality
And a yard short of *not long to live.*
Better to sit down in the tall grass
                    and watch the clouds,
To lift our faces up to the sky,
Considering—for most of us—our lives have been one constant mistake.

"Just a Closer Walk with Thee"

But not too close, man, just not too close.
Between the divine and the divine
                    lies a lavish shadow.
Do we avoid it or stand in it?
Do we gather the darkness around us,
                    or do we let it slide by?
Better to take it into our hearts,
Better to let us have it.
          Better to let us be what we should be.

Tonight, the sexual energy of the evergreens
                    removes us
From any such attitude.
At least for a momentary intake.
                    And then it's
Back in its natural self,
Between the It and the It.
The fly that won't leave the corpse will end up in the grave.

History Is a Burning Chariot

It is a good-looking evening, stomped and chained.
The clouds sit like majesties in their blue chairs,
as though doing their nails.
The creek, tripartite and unreserved, sniddles along
Under its bald and blown-down bridges.
It is a grace to be a watcher on such a scene.
So balance me with these words—
Have I said them before, I have,
have I said them the same way, I have,
Will I say them again, who knows
what darkness snips at our hearts.

I've done the full moon, I've done the half moon and the quarter moon.
I've even done the Patrick Spens moon
As seen by one of his drowned sailors.
Tonight is the full moon again, and I won't watch it.
These things have a starting place, and they have an ending.
Render the balance, Lord.
Send it back up to the beginning.

"Things Have Ends and Beginnings"

Cloud mountains rise over mountain range.
Silence and quietness,
sky bright as water, sky bright as lake water.
Grace is the instinct for knowing when to stop. And where.

Little Elegy for an Old Friend

Well, there you have it,
                    everything fine and then the heart goes nuts.
Paddles and CPR, slaps and blows.
Jesus, how did it come to this,
                    brain just vacuumed and good to go,
Everyone bending over you, not one you ever knew?

In the light they say you enter,
                    was Via Mantovana a part of it?
Or the ground-floor apartment on Via Duomo 6,
In Verona, 1959?
Or was it all Le Crete,
                    Asciano and S. Giovanni d'Asso?

Sorrow, come pass me from hand to hand.
Time to reset eternity's clock
To the far side of midnight.

Time to remember the unremembered, and the forgotten.
Time to release them, and give them up.
There is no balm, my man,
                    not even in Gilead.

The Last Word

I love to watch the swallows at sundown,
                    swarming after invisible things to eat.
Were we so lucky,

A full gullet, and never having to look at what it is,
Sunshine all over our backs.

There are no words between my fingers
Populating the lost world.
Something, it now seems, has snapped them up
Into its speechlessness,
                    into its thick aphasia.

It's got to be the Unredeemable Bird, come out
From the weight of the unbearable.
It flaps like a torn raincoat,
                    first this side, then that side.
Words are its knot of breath,
                    language is what it lives on.

"I've Been Sitting Here Thinking Back Over My Life . . ."

We are all going into a world of dark.
                    And that's okay,
Given the wing-wrung alternative.
It's okay. That's where the secrets are,
The big ones, the ones too tall to tell.
The way in is twisty and torturous,
                    but easy, they say, easy.
The way out, however, is unavailable, and not to be mimed.

Hard to remember that when the full moon
                    offers its efficacy
Downwind through the winter weeds,
Unpeeling its limitless hope.
                    But not, at least for tonight, for us.

Not for us, bystanders back from the river of light.
So file down your fingertips, boys,
                                        and pull on your skins.
Incandescence is temporary, we know, but it still shines.

And that's it. My life has been spent
                                        trying to leave it.
As though an invisible figure in a Schneeman landscape of Tuscany,
I've always wanted to be elsewhere,
Hair on fire, a radiance
Undeniable,
My shoes golden, my heart tucked away
                                        back under my shirtsleeve.

Not now, not ever, the world in winter.
                                        And this is what comforts us,
Bare trees, bare streets, bare expectations.
Our lives are spent here,
                                our ho-hum and sweet, existential lives,
Stories of cirrus and cumulus.
And why not, this world has been good to us,
                                        the sun goes up and the sun
Goes down, the stars release and disappear,
                                everything *tutta gloria* wherever we turn our faces.

"What Becomes of the Brokenhearted . . ."

Up where the narrow bodies lie, suffused in sundown,
The children of God are stretched out
                                        under the mountain,
Halfway up which the holy city stands, lights darkened.
Above the city, the nimbus of nowhere nods and retracts.

How is it that everyone seems to want
either one or the other?
Down here birds leap like little chipmunks out of the long grasses.
Wind piddles about, and "God knows" is the difficult answer.

The children of Heaven, snug in their tiny pockets,
Asleep, cold,
Under the Purgatorial hill.
Soon they'll awake, and find their allotted track
up to the upside down.

Or not. The gravetree estuaries against the winds of Paradise.
Unutterable names are unpinned from its branches.
A couple
Float down to this pocket, and others float down to that pocket.
Star shadow settles upon them,
the starshine so far away.

"My Old Clinch Mountain Home"

I keep on hoping a theme will bite me,
and leave its two wounds
In my upper arm and in my heart.
A story line of great destiny,
or fate at least.
It's got to be serious, as my poor flesh is serious.
So, dog, show me your teeth and bite me.
Show me some love.

Such little consequence, our desires.
Better to be the last chronicler of twilight, and its aftermath.

Better to let your hair swing loose, and dust up the earth.
I'd like to be a prophet,
                    with animals at my heels.
I'd like to have a staff, and issue out water wherever it fell.

Lord, how time does alter us,
                    it goes without saying.
There is an afterlight that follows us,
                    and fades as clockticks fade.
Eventually we stand on it puddled under our shoes.
The darkness that huddles there
Is like the dew that settles upon the flowers,
                    invisible, cold, and everywhere.

When the wind comes, and the snow repeats us,
                    how like our warped lives it is,
Melting objects, disappearing sounds
Like lichen on gnarled rocks.
For we have lived in the wind, and loosened ourselves like ice melt.
Nothing can hold us, I've come to know.
                    Nothing, I say.

Toadstools

The toadstools are starting to come up,
                    circular and dry.
Nothing will touch them,
Gophers or chipmunks, wasps or swallows.
They glow in the twilight like rooted will-o'-the-wisps.
Nothing will touch them.

As though little roundabouts from the bunched unburiable,
Powers, dominions,
As though orphans rode herd in the short grass,
as though they had heard the call.
They will always be with us,
transcenders of the world.
Someone will try to stick his beak into their otherworldly styrofoam.
Someone may try to taste a taste of forever.
For some it's a refuge, for some a shady place to fall down.
Grief is a floating barge-boat,
who knows where it's going to moor?

Dude

In my mind's eye I always see
The closed door to eternity.
I think I'll take it,
and then I start to think I won't.
As though I had a choice in the matter.
As though the other side of it
was something inexorable, something fluxed.
As though the though would never exist.

The dog gets sick. The dog runs away.
You've got your mind on transubstantiation.
The dog
Runs away. The dog gets sick, the son calls to tell you
That he's been fired.
You've got your mind on transubstantiation.
The world's a mass of cold spaghetti.
The dog runs away, your mind's still on transubstantiation.

The dog's gone missing, the dog comes back.
The same dog, but a different dog,
                                        in different weather.
The droop-bellied dark clouds loom
And suck up their forks of light
                                        and the dog goes missing
A second time, and who can blame him?
If he disappears again, your mind's back on transubstantiation.

We live beyond the metaphysician's fingertips.
It's sad, dude, so sad.
There is no metaphor, there is no simile,
                                        and there is no rhetoric
To nudge us to their caress.
The trees remain the trees, God help us.
And memory, for all its warmth,
                                        is merely the things we forgot to forget.

That's it. The winds over Punto San Vigilio,
Though welcome, are only winds.
In front of us the door tingles.
                                        Behind us, the fingertips tingle.
And here, in the back country,
Junk grass grows down to the creek, the lilacs hang their heads,
And our only world surrounds us like stretched skin,
                                        and beats its drum.

Pack Rats

Up to the upper place to cover the bedstead against the pack rats.
The 10th of August and already they're moving in.
Industrial plastic, waste product from logging companies.

Early winter. It won't work,

they'll burrow in and nest,

Leaving their blood-colored urine and interminable excrement
Coming and going.
They'll leave us something shining, or bright,
In return. Bright and shining.

This gray on blue on white on gray on blue
Montana August skyscape
Has nothing to do with politics, or human relations, or people, in fact.
It has to do with fictions,

and where we place ourselves

Apart from the dread apart.
It has to do with what's unidentifiable,
And where our seat is in it.
It has to do with what the pack rat leaves, what's bright and shining.

Surrounded by half-forests and half-lives,
Surrounded by everything we have failed to do,
It is as though kumquats hung from the lodgepole pine trees.
Everything's doubled—

once it arrives and once it fades.

Angels, God bless them, rebound from the meadow, bruised gain,
I guess, from our stern world.
Back in the pittering dark of the pine trees,

the rats

Are nosing for silver or gold, or whatever glints or shines.

Four Dog Nights

Sunset and dying light,

the robin, dark warrior,

In his green domain.
Beyond West Virginia,
                                        the horses are putting their night shoes on,
Ready to break through.
On the stones of the imagination,
                                                        their sparks are like stars.
This is the stepchild hour,
                                            belonging to neither the light nor dark,
The hour of disappearing things.

I've made my tentative statement
                                                        under the threatening sky,
Honeysuckle in deep distress along the snow-slugged hedgerow.
Eschatology is the underart of the gods,
Patches of bull clover in the high desert landscape,
Installed but never instilled,
The bright, shining mirage our hearts are bedeviled to.
Time, great eraser.

October, Mon Amour

The first dead leaves lie like sea urchins
                                                                browned on the asphalt drive.
It's got to be October,
Slayer of living things, refrigerator of memory.
Next to the wilted lettuce, next to the Simone Weil,
Our lives are shoved in,
                                        barely visible, but still unspoiled.

Our history is the history of the City of God.
What's-to-Come is anybody's guess.
Whatever has given you comfort,

Whatever has rested you,
Whatever untwisted your heart
                                        is what you will leave behind.

—GS

Ducks

Gasoline smell on my hands, perfume
From the generator's toothless mouth,
Opening swallow from the green hose,
Sweet odor from the actual world.

There's an old Buddhist saying I think I read one time:
Before Enlightenment, chop wood and carry water.
After Enlightenment, chop wood and carry water.
The ducks, who neither carry nor chop,

Understand this, as I never will,
Their little feet propelling them, under the water,
Serene and stabilized,
                                from the far side of the pond
Back to the marsh grasses and cattails.

I watch them every night they're there.
Serenitas. I watch them.
Acceptance of what supports you, acceptance of what's
Above your body,
                        invisible carry and chop,

Dark understory of desire
Where we should live,
                                        not in the thrashing, dusk-tipped branches—
Desire is anonymous,
Motoring hard, unswaying in the unseeable.

Lullaby

I've said what I had to say
As melodiously as it was given to me.

I've said what I had to say
As far down as I could go.
                                        I've been everywhere

I've wanted to but Jerusalem,
Which doesn't exist, so I guess it's time to depart,

Time to go,
Time to meet those you've never met,
                                        time to say goodnight.

Grant us silence, grant us no reply,
Grant us shadows and their cohorts
                                        stealth across the sky.

Plain Song

Where is the crack, the small crack
Where the dead come out

Only the dead know that, the speechless and shifting dead.
But it does ooze, half-inch by half-inch,
Under the doorway of dejection,
                                        under the brown, arthritic leaves.

The clock strikes, but the hands don't move.
                                                  The night birds outside
The window are gone away.
The halo around the quarter-moon
Means no good.
Is this the hour of our undoing?
                                        If so, we are perfected.

Whatever Happened to Al Lee?

What happened is what happens to all of us: we walked
On the earth, we threw a couple of handfuls of dirt
Into the air, and when it came down it covered us.

"So Long, It's Been Good to Know You"

Our generation has come to grief, old dears,
                                                  as all generations have to.
Outlaw of physics.
Well, hello stranger, put your loving hand in mine,
                                                        well, hello stranger,
You know me, but you're no pal of mine.
Coming in the front door, coming in the back,
                                                    gonna raise the roof lid

On your daddy's shack.
Speaking in tongues, as we once thought that we were, back then.

Train whistle, bat swoop,
                    twilight papier-mâché in the crimped pine trees,
Cloud deck assembling its puzzle pieces together
One by one.
          It goes like that.
So snarked, so soon, the tenderness that lurks inside us
Massages its knuckles and slips on its dark hoodie.
It's like that,
          it's always been like that.
I wish I was a bird in a tree.

Watch where you're walking,
There's always something bigger behind you,
                              and something bigger ahead.
Twisty the way, and twisty the place you're going to.
A rock here, a rock there, wind in the trees,
                              bright shards of green glass
The bat swoops over, listening for food.
It's starting to rain and I got to go home.
                         Be good,
See that my grave is kept clean.

Detour

It seems to be done,
               the world is not enough with us.
True, the rivers rise to meet us in late spring, the trees,
Conifers mostly, give us their incandescent fingerbones,

And the grasses whelp and propagate,
But it's not enough,
somehow it's never enough to please us.
And so we turn to the other side.

But what an absence—Jordan's a hard road to travel.
The love that we detoured into,
the love that was promised us,
Soon forgotten, Lord, soon forgotten.
Give us our muddy roads, give us our unrequited, forsaken nights,
Give us our barren landscapes,
Give us our desperation,
give us back our disbelief.

Drift Away

At work in the upper field,
hay tops little Buddhas
Calming the meadow and all its attendant tributaries,
Porcupine, Basin Creek, and God's blue hand like a skillet lid
Pressing us down to infinity—
We thought it was up, but it turns out it's down, Jack, down.
Either way we're stuck in the middle,
not a bad place to be.

Later, sun like a struck medallion
Over the west edge of things,
the distance between the woods and water
Immeasurable, tree shadow on water shadow.
I'm here and not here,
above and under it all.

These thoughts begin where words end
Back in the timber, back in the sullen nowhere of everything.

I think I'll take a little time off
And fiddle the underbugs,
Sitting my absence,
                                        dusk growing larger and larger.
This is the story of our lives, a short story, a page or a page and a half.
Eight days after the summer solstice,
Hard frost this morning,
                                        my life just past my fingertips, drifting, drifting.

"Well, Roll On, Buddy, Don't You Roll Too Slow"

Sun out, sun in, cloud gobbets up high, mist candles down below,
Start, and the start of the end of things.
Perhaps. But who knows.
                                        Recluse joys are only skin deep.
If my life were a dream, I'd be warmer and happier.
But I'm on a different road,
                                        mist and sun, and the dust of this world.
Late dusk by now and no birds, what do you know, no birds.

The old have no hiding place.
If it's going to come, you can't outrun it. Depend
On nothing and keep your joy-bag just out of sight.
Two nights till the full moon, a little soft on the lower left,
A ghostly radiance,
                                        almost there and almost not there.
The animals know this and sift away, but we have no clue.

Our lives are in ruins, we think, and they seem to be.
The night will not settle them
Or raise them or cover their spare parts.
Who will discover them
And say what our seasons were?
Who will astound himself one night in the lee of the full moon
In the milky forest, in the scattered and milky forest?

Chinoiserie II

I have tried to devote myself to simplicity
But it isn't that easy.
I trust myself to nothing, not even the star-sprung night sky.

I wish I were able to live in the constant, and wait out
The end, content to live in the come-and-go of things.
But it's hard, boys, it is hard,
a regret and a non-regret.

Li Po was able to detach self from himself, they say, and
Lower and blend his self into the ten thousand things.
Would that detachment were mine, Lord,
O would it were mine.

The summer tumbles me into its shadowy depths.
It's dusk again, enveloping dusk,
No lights to light my way, not here nor there
where I could forget myself.

Chinoiserie IV

All one sees in distance is distance,
                                        clarity of occurrence
Returning to hold us close.
Under the high grass at forest's edge,
                              the voles and mice run back and forth and back.

Their distance is not our distance,
                                        and what they see there
Is not what we don't see. It's something shapeless and strong
And downright unclarified.

I'd like to say it's something I saw once,
But it's not.
          I'd like to say I wrote a poem once on a stone wall,
But I didn't.
          I'd like to say that it's still there, but it's not.

Solo Joe Revisited

Mortality is our mother,
                              mortality is what we hanker for
When the sun goes down.
                              And, boy, let me tell you, the sun goes down.
On Solo Joe Creek, for instance, the ribs of his cabin
Exist still, and the trace of the trail
The horses and mules packed in on,
                                        and the mile-long trench
He diverted water to

To sluice down the rock and gravel shards the gold hid in.
Or did not, it seems, did not.

Distance clarifies the water sounds at 2 p.m.
What are we talking about, man, a dollar and a quarter
A year from these splotched waters?
                                        There's no horizon here,
Only the treetops and half-clouds chasing each other over the blue
   breaks of the sky.
It's all gone.
I'd like to be sad, and say that every one of these outlines
Slices my heart and my memory.
But I have no memory of this,
                                    and my heart is as hard as the lost riprap.

Chinoiserie V

Almost September and the meadow is still green, green.
The widower birds pipe once, or twice, and then are hush.
Nothing comes and nothing goes.
The doors to the mountains remain shut,
Sky still alert, but no moon rising,
                                        grasses alert, but then they're not.

Imagine being a true recluse in straw sandals, wet with the rain,
Never able to settle,
                          going night after night.
Hard times, then, hard times.
Better to watch the light come and the light go through the window.
Better to hear the thunder turn and then return.
                                                  Renown is a half-full glass.

Translations from a Forgotten Tongue

What shall I do with myself?
I'm gone, or I am going,
                    let everyone forgive me.
I tried to make a small hole in my life, something to slip through
To the other side.
               If I get there, don't bother me with your comparisons.
Nobody knew I was going,
                    nobody knew I was coming back.

Under the push of our footprints,
                         the earth is ready for us.
Who knows how long this will go on?
Stand still, young soldier boy,
                         don't move, don't move, young sailor.
Whose night sky is this
With no one under it?
                    Whose darkness has closed our eyes?

Notes

THE SOUTHERN CROSS

"Virginia Reel" is for Mark Strand.

"Landscape with Seated Figure and Olive Trees": Ezra Pound at Sant'Ambrogio.

"Laguna Dantesca": "She" is Picarda Donati, *Paradiso*, III.

"Dog Day Vespers" is for David Young.

"Hawaii Dantesca": Dante and the reed of humility, *Purgatorio*, I.

"Bar Giamaica 1959–60": Ugo Mulas, Italian photographer, 1928–73.

"The Southern Cross" is for Mark Jarman.

THE OTHER SIDE OF THE RIVER

"Driving to Passalacqua, 1960": Caserma Passalacqua, Headquarters SETAF (Southern European Task Force), Verona, Italy.

"Homage to Cesare Pavese": "Verrà la morte e avrà i tuoi occhi," "La terra e la morte," *Il mestiere di vivere.*

"Cryopexy": An operation to repair, by freezing with liquid Freon gas, a tear on the eye's retina.

"T'ang Notebook": *Three Hundred Poems of the T'ang Dynasty*, translator(s) anonymous (Hong Kong, undated).

"Arkansas Traveller": Charles F. Penzel (1840–1906).

"To Giacomo Leopardi in the Sky": *Giacomo Leopardi,* translated by Jean-Pierre Barricelli (Las Americas Publishing Co., 1963): "L'Infinito," "La vita solitaria," "Alla sua donna," "Le ricordanze," "Il passero solitario," "Canto notturno d'un pastore errante nell'Asia," "A se stesso," "Sopra un basso rilievo antico sepolcrale," "Sopra il ritratto di una bella donna," "Il tramonto della luna."

ZONE JOURNALS

"Night Journal": Annie Dillard, *Teaching a Stone to Talk* (Harper & Row, 1982).

"A Journal of the Year of the Ox": *Catullus Tibullus and Pervigilium Veneris* (Harvard University Press, 1976); *The Penguin Book of Italian Verse* (Penguin Books, 1960); Thomas W. Preston, *Historical Sketches of the Holston Valleys* (The Kingsport Press, 1926); Jeff Daniel Marion, "By the Banks of the Holston," *The Iron Mountain Review*, vol. 1, no. 2 (Winter 1984); Ranieri Varese, *Il Palazzo di Schifanoia* (Bologna: Grafici Editoriale s.r.i., 1983); *The Cloud of Unknowing: An English Mystic of the 14th Century* (Burns Oates).

"Light Journal": Salvatore Quasimodo, "Ed è súbito sera."

"A Journal of One Significant Landscape": Giorgio Vasari, *Lives of the Artists*, translated by George Bull (Penguin Books, 1965).

"Night Journal II" is for Stanley Kunitz.

XIONIA

Saint Augustine, *Of True Religion*, translated by J.H.S. Burleigh (Chicago: Henry Regnery Co., 1959).

Language Poetries, edited and introduced by Douglas Messerli (New York: New Directions, 1987).

Georg Trakl, *Poems*, translated by Lucia Getsi (Athens, Ohio: Mundus Artium Press, 1973).

Jonathan Barnes, *Early Greek Philosophy* (London and New York: Penguin Books, 1987).

Grover Zinn, *Richard of St. Victor: The Mystical Ark* (New York: Paulist Press, 1979).

Tian Wen, A Chinese Book of Origins, translated by Stephen Field (New York: New Directions, 1986).

Poesia Cinese, translated by Giacomo Prampolini (Milan: All'insegna del pesce d'oro, 1942).

"Takushanshan": Lakota Sioux.

CHICKAMAUGA

Richard Rorty, *Contingency, Irony and Solidarity* (Cambridge University Press, 1989).

Three Hundred Poems of the T'ang Dynasty, translator(s) anonymous (Hong Kong, undated).

Saint Augustine, *Confessions* (Penguin Books, 1961).

"Pliny's outline"—Pliny said the invention of painting occurred when a Corinthian maiden drew the outline of her lover after he went away to war, so she could remember what he looked like.

Kenneth Rexroth, *One Hundred Poems from the Chinese* (New Directions, 1956).

George Steiner, *Real Presences* (University of Chicago Press, 1989).

Blaise Pascal, *Pensées*, translated by A. J. Krailsheimer (Penguin Books, 1966).

Bruce Chatwin, *The Songlines* (Viking Penguin, 1988).

Wallace Stevens, "The Man on the Dump," in *Collected Poems* (Alfred A. Knopf, 1965).

Franz Kafka, *The Blue Octavo Notebooks* (Exact Change Press, 1990).

Collected Poems: Federico Garcia Lorca, ed. Christopher Maurer (Farrar, Straus & Giroux, 1991).

Vincent Gillespie and Maggie Ross, "The Apophatic Image: The Poetics of Effacement in Julian of Norwich," in *The Medieval Mystical Tradition in England* (unpublished).

The Giubbe Rosse is a *caffè* in Florence, Italy.

The Selected Poems of Tu Fu, translated by David Hinton (New Directions, 1989).

Poems of Paul Celan, translated by Michael Hamburger (Persea Books, 1988).

Giorgio Morandi, *Natura Morta*, c. 1957 (The University of Iowa Museum of Art).

Tu Fu, "Full Feeling IV," in *Bright Moon, Perching Bird*, translated and edited by J. P. Seaton and James Cryer (Wesleyan University Press, 1987).

Piet Mondrian, *Composition in Gray and Red*, 1935 (The Art Institute of Chicago).

Roberto Calasso, *The Marriage of Cadmus and Harmony*, translated by Tim Parks (Alfred A. Knopf, 1993).

BLACK ZODIAC

"Apologia Pro Vita Sua": *The Nag Hammadi Library*, James M. Robinson, general editor (New York: Harper & Row, 1988).

"Lives of the Saints": Walter Raleigh, Gertrude Stein, Wallace Stevens, Dante Alighieri, Adam Gopnik, Bertran de Born, Donald Justice, Robert Graves, Anonymous (early thirteenth century) . . .

"Lives of the Artists": *The Poems of Sappho*, translated by Suzy Q. Groden (New York: Bobbs-Merrill, 1966); *The Nag Hammadi Library*; Giorgio Vasari, *Lives of the Artists*, translated by George Bull (New York: Penguin Books, 1965).

"Thinking of Winter at the Beginning of Summer": Jacques Prévert, "Picasso's Walk."

"Black Zodiac": Roberto Calasso, *The Ruin of Kasch*, translated by William Weaver and Stephen Sartarelli (Cambridge, Mass.: The Belknap Press of Harvard University Press, 1994); Saint Augustine, *The Confessions*, translated by R. S. Pine-Coffin (New York: Penguin Books, 1961); *Poems of Paul Celan*, translated by Michael Hamburger (New York: Persea Books, 1989); Wallace Stevens, "Adagia," in *Opus Posthumous* (New York: Alfred A. Knopf, 1957).

"China Mail": The poems of Tu Fu, various translators . . .

"Disjecta Membra": ("These fragments are the *disjecta membra* of an elusive, coveted, and vaguely scented knowledge." Guido Ceronetti, *The Science of the Body*); *Poems of the Late T'ang*, translated by A. C. Graham (New York: Penguin Books, 1965); Letters of Paul Celan to Nelly Sachs; *The Nag Hammadi Library*; *Poems of Paul Celan*.

APPALACHIA

"Stray Paragraphs in April, Year of the Rat": Simone Weil's notebooks.

"A Bad Memory Makes You a Metaphysician, a Good One Makes You a Saint": The title as well as two lines in the text have been taken and laundered from material in E. M. Cioran's *Tears and Saints*, translated by Ilinca Zarifopol-Johnston, 1995.

"In the Valley of the Magra": Gerard Manley Hopkins, "In the Valley of the Elwy," in *The Poems of Gerard Manley Hopkins*, 4th edition, 1970.

"All Landscape Is Abstract, and Tends to Repeat Itself": Guido Ceronetti, *The Silence of the Body*, translated by Michael Moore, 1993.

"Autumn's Sidereal, November's a Ball and Chain": Wallace Stevens, "Jonga," in *Collected Poems of Wallace Stevens*, 1965.

"Reply to Wang Wei": *Poems of Wang Wei*, translated by G. W. Robinson, 1973.

"Drone and Ostinato": *Ecstatic Confessions* (Meister Eckhart), compiled by Martin Buber, edited by Paul Mendes-Flohr, 1985.

"Half February": Ibid. Thomas Merton/Czeslaw Milosz, *Striving Towards Being*, edited by Robert Faggen, 1997.

"Back Yard Boogie Woogie": Simone Weil, *Waiting for God*, translated by Emma Craufurd, 1973.

"Opus Posthumous II": Ezra Pound, "Canto 90," in *The Cantos*, 1970.

"When You're Lost in Juarez, in the Rain, and It's Eastertime Too" (sic): Bob Dylan; I. M. Pei.

"The Appalachian Book of the Dead IV": Mac Wiseman, "Let's All Go Down to the River" (trad.).

"The Appalachian Book of the Dead V": *The Diaries of Virginia Woolf.*

"After Reading T'ao Ch'ing, I Wander Untethered Through the Short Grass": *The Selected Poems of T'ao Ch'ing*, translated by David Hinton.

NORTH AMERICAN BEAR

"Thinking About the Night Sky, I Remember a Poem by Tu Fu": *Li Po and Tu Fu*, translated by Arthur Cooper (1973).

"North American Bear": *Three Hundred Poems of the T'ang Dynasty*, translator(s) anonymous (undated); Rainer Maria Rilke/Robert Lowell, "Orpheus, Euridyce and Hermes," *Imitations* (1995).

"If You Talk the Talk, You Better Walk the Walk": Li Shang-Yiu, "Written on a Monastery Wall," in *Poems of the Late T'ang*, translated by A. C. Graham (1965).

A SHORT HISTORY OF THE SHADOW

"Looking Around III": Osip Mandelstam, *Selected Poems*, translated by Claren
Brown and W. S. Merwin (1974).

ES

"If My Glasses Were Better, I Could See Where I'm Headed For": Carter Family, "The Pilgrim Slippers" (trad.).

"Is": Annie Dillard, *For the Time Being* (1999).

"Polaroids": Osip Mandelstam, *Selected Poems*; Georg Trakl, *Poems*, translated by Lucia Getsi (1973).

"Relics": Aldo Buzzi, "Notes on Life," *A Weakness for Almost Everything* (1999).

"Nine-Panel Yaak River Screen": Georg Trakl, *Poems*; Osip Mandelstam, *Selected Poems*.

"Body and Soul II": Richard Bernstein, *Ultimate Journey* (2001).

BUFFALO YOGA

"Buffalo Yoga": Georg Trakl, *Poems*, translated by Lucia Getsi (Athens, Ohio: Mundus Artium Press, 1973); Leon Bloy, "L'Ame de Napoléon, 1912," in Jorge Luis Borges, *Selected Non-Fictions*, edited by Eliot Weinberger (New York: Penguin Books, 1999).

Tom Andrews (1961–2001): "Alles Nahe werde fern" (Goethe).

"Rosso Venexiano":

> BERRYMAN: Well, being a poet is a funny kind of jazz. It doesn't get you anything. It doesn't get you any money, or not much, and it doesn't get you any prestige, or not much. It's just something you *do*.
>
> INTERVIEWER: Why?
>
> BERRYMAN: That's a tough question. I'll tell you a real answer. I'm taking your question seriously. This comes from Hamann, quoted by Kierkegaard. There are two voices, and the first voice says, "Write!" and the second voice says, "For whom?" I think that's marvelous; he doesn't question the imperative, you see that. And the first voice says, "For the dead whom thou didst love." Again the second voice doesn't question it; instead it says, "Will they read me?" And the first voice says, "Aye, for they return as posterity." Isn't that good? —John Berryman, *Antæus* #8, Winter 1973

"In Praise of Han Shan": *Mountain Home*.

SCAR TISSUE

"Vespers": Hildegard of Bingen, *Selected Writings*, translated by Mark Atherton (Penguin Books, 2001).

LITTLEFOOT

2. *Nag Hammadi Library*, James M. Robinson, general editor (Harper & Row, 1978).
9. W. G. Sebald, "Dr. K. Takes the Waters at Riva," in *Vertigo* (New Directions, 1999).

ES

10. For Wilma Hammond.

11. *Returning Home, Tao-Chi's Album of Landscapes and Flowers*, introduction and commentaries by Wen Fong (George Braziller, 1976).

17. *Mountain Home*, translated by David Hinton (Counterpoint, 2002).

18. Ryan Fox, Sonny Rollins.

20. Elizabeth Kolbert, *The New Yorker*, June 2005; *Poems of Wang Wei*, translated by G. W. Robinson (Penguin Classics, 1973).

23. *The Collected Poems of Wallace Stevens* (Alfred A. Knopf, 1954).

33. Giuseppe Ungaretti, "Mattino."

34. Bob Dylan, "It Takes a Lot to Laugh, It Takes a Train to Cry."

35. A. P. Carter, "Will You Miss Me When I'm Gone."

SESTETS

"Celestial Waters": Roberto Calasso, *K.*, translated by Geoffrey Brock (Vintage Books, 2005), chapter VI.

"Homage to What's-His-Name" is for Mark Strand.

"Hovercraft": John McIntire, June 27, 1907.

CARIBOU

"Little Elegy for an Old Friend" is for George Schneeman.

"I've Been Sitting Here Thinking Back Over My Life . . .": The line "Stories of cirrus and cumulus" is from "The End" by Mark Strand, found in *The Continuous Life* (New York: Alfred A. Knopf, 1992).

"Plain Song": *Georg Trakl: Poems*, translated by Stephen Tapscott (Oberlin, Ohio: Oberlin College Press, 2011).

"Chinoiserie II," "IV," and "V": These poems are deeply indebted to *Mountain Home: The Wilderness Poetry of Ancient China*, translated by David Hinton (Washington, D.C.: Counterpoint, 2002).

Du Fu: A Life in Poetry, translated by David Young (New York: Alfred A. Knopf, 2008).

"Translations from a Forgotten Tongue": Osip Mandlestam, *Selected Poems*, translated by Clarence Brown and W. S. Merwin (New York: Atheneum, 1973).

Index of Titles and First Lines